To

The Great Mothers

and

The Great Fathers

Author's Note for Second and Third Editions

The first edition of *Danger Close* quietly rolled out in late 1999, making it one of the final books published in a crazy century. As we crossed the threshold of the new millennium, I was slightly concerned that civilization might follow the path of the dinosaurs. After all, it had taken several years to create this book and it would be a shame if the world ended at the moment of fruition. As the clocks marked midnight, I was relieved that life moved forward without a hiccup. I crawled back into bed, fell asleep and woke up to a bright new year. As I watched the sun rise, I realized that the doomsayers had yet again strained credibility, both in predictions for the world, and for *Danger Close*.

Having created this book without soliciting a cash advance from a publisher, I was free to cast aside the stodgy conventions of book writing, to tell my story free form, without some nosy editor peering over my shoulder, making "artistic decisions" knowing the accounting department is peering intently over *his* shoulder.

This would be a grassroots campaign. Word soon got around and bookstores began calling to ask for appearances, and to arrange promoted tours. Yet a larger symphony began to play; journalists read my book, contacted me, and gave wonderful reviews. An increasing volume of e-mails began popping in from Alabama to Australia, from Guam to Denmark to Kosovo. Soldiers, students, doctors, housewives, grandmothers—an astonishing array of people were reading *Danger Close*. They began contacting their local papers and radio stations. This had become more than just *my* book, as others realized that through these pages they too could be heard, and so it became *our* book. Our book had taken on its own life, as if a flower were blooming vibrantly through still soil after a very long, cold winter.

1st Edition October 1999 ISBN 0-9675123-0-1
2nd Edition March 2000 ISBN 0-9675123-1-X
3rd Edition March 2000 ISBN 0-9675123-2-8

©1999 by Mike Yon
ISBN 0-9675123-2-8
Library of Congress Catalog Card Number: 99-91038

Publisher: Apple Pie Publishers, LLC
            PMB 325
            5745 S.W. 75th Street
            Gainesville, FL 32608

            www.applepienow.com

Book design by Andrea Brower and Dawn Grove
Cover design by Buster O'Connor

CONTENTS

26 April 2001

To Tony,
It was a pleasure talking
with you — Since you
were an English Major, I
hope you don't catch any
errors in this book!

DANGER
CLOSE

Remember, Bill Gurley
lives!

Mike Yon

Mike Yon

PROLOGUE AND ACKNOWLEDGEMENTS

I AM SITTING high atop a desolate mountain in the Nevada desert. I scrambled, climbed, and jumped to get to this spot. Despite the desert heat and my thirst, I know that my body is not yet badly dehydrated because of the sweat drop that rolls off my nose and onto my hand. I have come here to consider the path behind and the horizon ahead.

Earlier this morning I ate breakfast with a judge in a Las Vegas resort casino. We were strangers, but he sat at the next table and soon we were engaged in a conversation about gaming and justice. After an hour or so, we said good-bye, and I went to watch the gamblers.

Casinos are created to attract certain personalities. Once inside, people are simultaneously assaulted and coaxed through all of their senses. Against them is arrayed a vast arsenal of scientific research and painstaking preparation. Among other things, casinos are designed to both dull and heighten gamblers' perceptions. No clocks or windows, alcohol by the bucket and beautiful women by the score, paint the cover of this well-oiled machine.

Despite the clever ambush of the casinos, gamblers are not being robbed. They walk through the doors on their own two feet and are free to leave at any time. Some people wager recreationally, as they would go to the movies, and are safe because they will not relinquish their power over their futures on contrived "risks." Some journey here for other reasons, but whatever the case, all are under the same roof, often playing the same games, but for different reasons and by different rules.

Some have systems. One man counts seconds between each quarter he drops. A woman near him says a prayer before releasing her money, and another woman mindlessly goes through the motions as if she were part of the gambling machine—as, in fact, she is. An older man walks by wearing an expensive watch and a shirt that reads, *He who dies with the most toys wins.* I disagree.

Certainly wealth comes with big advantages, but if he believes what he advertises, that poor man has never loved a woman. He should not worry about death; one who has not known the human experience cannot die for he has never lived, and one who measures his life against toys does not know the experience to any meaningful degree.

While gambling for money, those people in casinos who depend on the mercy of the odds do not understand chance, which is understandable; chance is very difficult to grasp. We all have vulnerabilities, such as the tendency to want something for nothing, and casinos are constructed to exploit them. I wonder how many mathematicians, whose training and mindset

1

should provide a degree of immunity, would mortgage their homes to gamble in a casino.

I am a risk taker. A calculated risk taker. I don't know how to play poker and all the money I have spent gambling would not buy a good pizza. We sometimes say "we must play the cards dealt us," or "let the chips fall where they may." I say, chance affects our lives every day, but we do not have to merely accept what comes along.

We humans, even the strongest, have a natural tendency to give up the very power that we can use to guide our lives. Too often we blindly follow the leader, or perhaps we try to eliminate the difficulties inherent in finding a compatible mate by consulting useless astrological signs when we simply need to get to know one another. We often assume that forces beyond our control predestine our futures.

Such are justifications for relinquishing our enormous internal strength, a gift that we *all* have as birthright. It is enticingly easy to simply float down the river on a Little Tour of Life, until finally we drift to the eternity of the sea. If we take the Grand Tour, we must get off the boat and walk into the wilderness, an act which takes immense courage.

I do not advocate taking the hard route or risks just for the experience, but to emphasize that we should meet adversity, especially when in doubt, with resolve that we can only muster by reaching deep inside our souls. We choose the course we take and fortune helps determine what we see. We alter the possible outcomes when we pick our goals. It is true, as Virgil wrote: *"Fortune favors the bold,"* and equally true, as Louis Pasteur observed: *"Fortune favors the prepared mind."* But take caution: fortune punishes the bold who are not prepared, as I have painfully experienced.

The stakes for many of my choices were high. In business, I risked all of my hard-earned college money on one venture. I lost it. I was worse than broke. Nevertheless, that was only money, and I will make more.

Though I do not pretend to be unbiased, which I think would be "impossible"—*impossible being a word I use with extreme reluctance*—this book contains good and bad, so that you may experience the world through another mind.

At first my intentions for writing were entirely personal. I needed to say some things to myself, to get things out and into perspective. I did not plan or consider it. Though I had found success and saw a bright future in my fast growing business, some things are more important than money, even in America. One day, writing called me, and I began.

This is more than a recounting of facts: it is a journey and narration of lessons learned. I am compelled to pass along certain knowledge. For once certain knowledge is achieved—no matter whether ancient or new—it is incomplete when it resides quietly in one's mind. To reach fulfillment, it *must* be passed along.

I embarked on a journey to a new life. I sold my share of the business to a childhood friend. After spending a year of writing that carried me around and outside the country, friends who read the first draft had visceral reactions, and were kind enough to look past the initial form—or lack thereof—and into the depth of the story. I did not study writing in school or dream of becoming a "writer," but when my soul poured onto the paper, they felt it.

They believed so much in the book, they offered me, through their financial support, the opportunity to write undistracted for as long it took to finish. And I took as long as I needed. Two and a half years. Seven days per week. This book never left my mind. There were no electric or phone bills for me to pay, no publisher breathing down my neck to meet a deadline, no distractions whatsoever. I just wrote and wrote and wrote. Words flowed from places deep within and poured out of my fingers into your hands. I wrote more than three thousand pages. When the fat evaporated; these words remained. A writer must toss out the fat, no matter how much he thinks people want and need to hear what he has to say, and enter into a pact never to bore the reader. Not for a single self-indulgent paragraph. Not for a sentence. Merely creating a narrative is relatively easy, but reducing it to the truly essential—*that* is very, very difficult.

One friend who has read the work more than a dozen times tells me that she finds new threads in the fabric with each reading. It is complex, as is life, or it is a simple story, depending on how you decide to approach it. I took extreme care to make it readable, enlightening, and memorable. However, I must warn you that you will not always feel good reading this.

The traveling gave me a lot of time to think. Sometimes I may appear to contradict myself and at times I do. Often the contradictions are conditional. It seems impossible to develop a philosophy of life that is consistent and still capable of withstanding the challenges of life. Therein is a lesson we have heard so many times: *stay flexible*.

We cannot look back at our lives and remember accurately most dialogues and sequences. One can be sure that adrenaline will influence perceptions, and time causes that strange thing called "memory" to become distorted. Where memory or records failed, I took liberties to capture the essence of my story, and this book would properly be called, "creative non-fiction." But, of course, the only real non-fiction books have names like "dictionary" and "phone book."

You will find some areas are without emphasis on the details, though in other places minutiae are important and have been carefully included. Many acquaintances, friends, and experts have assisted with research to keep this book as accurate as is possible, and listing them here seems small thanks for the help they so enthusiastically gave.

First, I would like to thank my mother for standing behind me, and whispering in my ear to keep working, keep trying, and keep up my faith. Without her, none of this would have been possible, and without her, I may not have survived my teenage years.

I would also like to thank my grandmother, my mother's mother, for stepping in at times when I needed her most, and in whose home I completed my final work on this book. And my grandfather, whose soul now rests; I thank him for being a shining light who helped guide me through darkness.

I would like to thank my younger sister, Susan, now a veterinarian (with a heart of gold), for reading the manuscript in its roughest form, and encouraging me so often along the way. I would also like to thank my older brother, Billy, who at first discouraged the project under the presumption that I did not have much to write about.

Billy had asked me, "Who wants to read a book written by a thirty-two-year-old? I mean, what have you done?"

"Well," I answered, "just wait. You don't really know me. You don't know where I have been or what I have seen."

After Billy read the manuscript, he said that he was "shocked."

My former weightlifting coach and mentor, Jim Cuddie, helped elevate my strength to exceptional levels without the use of steroids. With only my mind, body, and diet, Mr. Cuddie, more than any other, helped and prepared me, physically and mentally, to withstand the rigors ahead when I left high school and joined the Army. I am forever grateful to Mr. Cuddie, who is a legend to many.

A retired Special Forces soldier who did three SF tours in Vietnam, and later was one of my Team Sergeants while I was in Special Forces, Glenn Watson, gave valuable feedback, and support from the time that I told him I was writing.

Bob Wallace, an excellent soldier, is a retired Special Forces Team Sergeant, who was the communications specialist on my first A-team when I was twenty. Yosemite Bob read my manuscript and kept me accurate in various areas. He now lives in Ontario, New York, and always could shoot and run better than I, but he could never beat me in a pull-up contest.

While I was in Special Forces I befriended Ted Bookless, who is still on active duty. We roomed together while in college. I call him "Talon" for his incredible grip and monkey-like climbing abilities, and for being the only soldier ever to beat me in a pull-up contest on the torturous "hotwater pipe." I did forty-three, he did forty-five, but that hot pipe blistered his hands, not mine. He calls me a sore loser for that shameless, macho comment, but my hands were not the ones that were sore, though obviously my ego was. Ted was behind me from the moment I told him that I was writing this book, but it would be a year before I allowed him to read my manuscript. To Ted, I am truly grateful.

An excellent former SF teammate while at Fort Devens, Massachusetts, Danny Howe, who now is the executive officer of Assessment and Selection of Special Forces soldiers at Camp Nick Rowe (formerly known as Camp MacKall), helped both by keeping me accurate on this project, and by being very supportive.

Bob Way is an excellent painter. He is also a retired SF veteran and former teammate. Together we have traversed much wilderness, and shared a few snow caves along the way. As are most compelling artists, Bob is a keen observer, and after reading the manuscript, he realized how much more we have in common besides art and Special Forces. Bob's kind words were very encouraging.

Another former teammate, on my second A-team in Bad Toelz, Germany, Danny Cook, gave valuable feedback on the manuscript. Danny, who is an expert climber, has helped me scale innumerable cliffs, and he again threw his weight in to support me with this book.

Former Marine infantryman and current U.S. Army psychologist, Major Jeffrey Stolrow, met and talked with me on numerous occasions, and allowed me to quote his work concerning the psychological aspects involved in the selection of Special Forces soldiers. Thank you Dr. Stolrow.

An Army Ranger platoon leader, Michael Perry, is an excellent athlete who also was trained by the legendary Mr. Jim Cuddie. Mike read my manuscript and gave blunt responses, the kind good Rangers are known for. He was disciplined enough to allow me to travel with him on a meandering two thousand mile cross-country road trip from Atlanta to Tacoma. Mike shared with me many stories about his forward deployed infantry unit on the DMZ in Korea, nicknamed *The Gators*. He will soon be headed to Captain school, then to Special Forces Assessment and Selection. Good luck, and may the Force be with you at SFAS.

Haines City, Florida, employs a valuable police detective. I sometimes listen to his stories of interrogation and how police get suspects to talk when the suspects should be quiet for *their* own good, though many of them need to be locked away for *our* own good. That detective, Richard Ganey, reviewed my manuscript and witness statements, and gave positive feedback from his police perspective.

Detective Bokinsky of the Ocean City, Maryland, police department and former SWAT team sniper, was forthright and helpful with his recollections of the events that led me to being temporarily charged with second degree murder.

My former attorney, now Judge Daniel Long, protected me from the wolves when I was wrongly charged with that crime. I offered him stock in this book as recompense, but his judgeship precludes such favors, and he seems just as satisfied with only a "thank you." *Well, thank you, Your Honor!*

Steve Shaulis, now living in Vero Beach, Florida, whom I befriended during Special Forces training, was with me the night of the incident leading to the false murder charge, and has remained a friend for sixteen years. He is the only ex-SF soldier I know who speaks five languages and who takes the WWF (pro-wrestling) seriously. Steve tells me that in Pakistan, and Afghanistan (where televisions were banned a few years back by the Taliban), there are many avid wrestling fans. Some Afghanis actually rely on Steve for updates on the Undertaker.

A former member of the 7th Special Forces in Panama, Rob Merwin, now living in New Mexico, provided pertinent technical feedback on my manuscript, and at times also helped when my computer malfunctioned. I should have heeded his advice when he told me to "buy a new computer."

My friend of eleven years, Keri Gerke Klein, is a housewife and mother of two beautiful and sweet babies. She read my manuscript and has been like a cheerleader for me from the beginning.

An Arizona businessman, Mark Speck, whom I met in Dayton, Ohio, while I was in my business life, has also been very generous with his positive feedback. However, my advice to Mark in the future would be to bring his wife along to the shooting range so that she can enjoy the fun.

Lana DeSimone is an actress and producer. And though I am usually more inclined to the "Girl Next Door," I read some things about her and she captured my attention. So, on a whim, I contacted her and asked for a date. She turned me down. Flat. Undeterred, I contacted her again and told her more about why she would like me as opposed to the plastic and glitter to which she must have grown accustomed. Somehow, I got my date, and we have become friends. As I got to know her better, I realized that she had been a little girl who came from little means, but who shot for the stars, and reached them. Lana took my book to heart and offered some keen advice relating both to business and art. Thank you, Lana.

At the Colorado State University in Fort Collins, I met Jennifer Dick, my first technical editor, now living in Paris. She gave insightful suggestions, cleaned up my commas, and filled in a slew of grammatical potholes.

My second editor, Dr. Raymond Lott, retired English professor, of Lakeland, Florida, besides syntax surveillance and pronoun policing, also suggested (he insists I say) "the occasional felicitous phrase." Ironically, his chief contribution may be due to his vast, if not total ignorance of military terminology. Because of his stunning incomprehension of Army abbreviations, acronyms, and argot, I had advance warning that the lay reader would be baffled by AFB, sniper magnet, noise and light discipline, etc.

Tena Cox, my former business partner in Poland and later in Ohio, read my manuscript, had faith, and offered encouragement.

I didn't know there were so many ways that I could get sued until Rick

Perry, attorney-at-law in Ocala, Florida, read my manuscript. He had enough faith in my project to invest his money.

Going into the second edition, I hired Julie Decker to scour the manuscript for any typos that may have slipped through our many readings. She told me she had found errors in every book she'd ever read. Since I was by then swamped in author promotions, I passed her myriad suggestions to Dr. Raymond Lott, who taught English at the college level and has been editing for a quarter century. He wrote this:

Of all the copyreaders I have encountered, at all levels of publication, I have never met another as accurate or as exhaustive as Miss Decker. Her attention is unflagging, her memory astonishing (more than once she caught minor variations in form, scores of pages apart), and her mechanical skills excellent. In addition, she has a fine sense of style, and an admirable concern for clarity. Her work is, quite simply, superb.

I asked Julie if she would be interested in working on my next book. To my delight, she accepted.

My biggest debt of gratitude for editing assistance is to another type of artist. An excellent sculptor, and a dear friend and confidante, Audra Morgan. Audra read the manuscript at least a dozen times, and she regretted and squawked that I left out certain stories in the final version. But finally, I said: "Hey, *Audra*, this book has to stop *somewhere!*" I thank her for the times that she read the manuscript aloud to me, and for crinkling her nose when I was unduly graphic in my descriptions, or used language that would cause decent people to recoil and toss the book in the garbage.

Upon Audra's recommendation, in Tampa, Florida, I met Ron Coffman, who was kind enough to proofread my manuscript. A similar thanks to Steve Wade, a Special Forces soldier, for reading through and offering comments.

My best friend of nearly twenty years, John Harrison, is seldom represented in this book, for most of our friendship was after the period depicted herein. Several times throughout our friendship, Big John has been there with me "in stormy seas" when others would have buried themselves below deck. I will never forget the day that John joined the Army; I joined the same day! Thank you, John, for titling this book.

As I started searching for a company to produce this book, I knew that finding the right people for the job would be difficult. It was. Finally, while researching publishing options, I read an article in *Publishers Weekly* magazine about Health Communications, Inc., who are the publishers of the *Chicken Soup for the Soul* series, and more than thirty best selling titles. I contacted HCI's self-publishing division, and there I found Sandy Dolan, who carefully, tactfully, and patiently, led me through the long process of transforming this from a manuscript into a book. The excellent staff at HCI included Andrea Brower, who created ten different cover concepts. After much mixing and matching, we found the right one, with which I am very pleased. Moving past the cover into the book, Andrea did an excellent creative job with the large photo section. Internal book design was created by Dawn Grove, while Larissa Hise coordinated pre-press production and saved me many headaches, as did Joseph Kerman and Anthony Clausi as proofreaders. Thank you at HCI, and get ready for another book!

There are others who helped directly in this work, who for various reasons remain unnamed, to whom I extend my sincere gratitude, but any errors or omissions are mine.

All of the people and events are real, though some names have been changed or omitted in the name of decency, or to protect privacy.

Of course, I invoke the customary pronoun disclaimer in that "he" can be substituted for "she," "his" for "hers," etc. During the process of my telling this story (we all know that the English language discriminates to accommodate the fragile male ego), readers should substitute pronouns as deemed appropriate.

A big thanks to Dr. Richard White, Jr., a childhood friend and major character in this book, now a college professor in Atchison, Kansas, who knows that for every story presented herein, there are many more that likely will never be told—or at least *should* never be told.

This is hard-hitting stuff. For the hardy people who are ready for this journey, it starts here. It's time to step from the boat into the wild.

Maryland

An orange sun is rising over cold Atlantic waters in a place where the journey ended for one man, and nearly for me. No other person is in sight, only gulls hunkering on the beach with fluffed feathers, while waves lick the sand against a biting winter breeze.

DANGER CLOSE

JULY 29 WAS a night of celebration for many people. It was, for instance, peak tourist season and the twenty-third birthday of a man who was about to enter and forever change my life. He had dropped out of high school after a run-in with a teacher, then drifted around the country for five years until our paths crossed on the Atlantic coast.

That night I was with my friend, Steve Shaulis. We had just completed an intensive first year of training for our future jobs and, since we were among the minority that had succeeded this far, we were celebrating.

Steve was from Baltimore and had made the pilgrimage to Ocean City many times, so he knew the hot spots. We were in such a hurry to get there from North Carolina that, when our stomachs grumbled in Virginia, we didn't stop for food, except for some raw corn that we plucked from a field along the way. Finally we arrived, downed some real food, and made our way to a beachside converging point known as the Surf-n-Suds nightclub.

The place was filled with college-types; the drinking age was eighteen, so young blood coursed freely. The post-high school crowd was testing its wings, away from home or the dorm for a summer escapade.

As we toured the bar, a man approached, got uncomfortably close, and snarled his contemptuous opinion of our short haircuts in Steve's face. A brown belt with an Indian head buckle marked the border between his blue pants and beige shirt. He wore a white metal necklace, and on his right arm was a tattoo, which seemed to be a marijuana leaf. I'd experimented a little myself during the waning months of high school. It confused me—but not enough to celebrate with a tattoo. On his left arm he had taken pains to emblazon in red: *Death Before Dishonor*—a clear warning to all of dangerous waters, like a sign that says "No Swimming—*Crocodiles*."

He was nearly half a foot taller than me, heavier and hyped-up as if on some kind of upper. *Coke?* His hand movements were wild and jerky, his head bobbed, and his words revealed that he traded in the currency of intimidation and violence. Steve and I were surprised at the sudden onslaught.

A year later, a newspaper article would quote an eyewitness who had seen the man: "**He seemed crazed.**" A young female acquaintance said that his behavior "**scared me.**" He had cut a swath of fear that day. His scraggly brown hair contrasted with our clean-cuts, maybe reinforcing the idea that we were easy prey. He was there with some friends and his younger brother who, according to later reports, had also felt his unfettered hostility that day, but they were peacefully occupying a table.

His mouth kept talking as if it weren't well connected to his brain. Pressing in on us, he demanded: "**Do you punks want some of this?**" I glanced at Steve, he shrugged his shoulders, and we walked away. But we didn't realize how aggressive the man was, thinking he was just a barroom blowhard. Maybe it egged him on when we didn't take him seriously. Within a few minutes I forgot about him.

Steve had disappeared into the crowd, and music was blaring from the live band *Drawbridge*, when the man suddenly reappeared. He resumed his tough guy routine, pointing angrily in my face. The painfully screeching music blurred his words, but the anger in his gray eyes and violent hand gestures was clear. Some words made it through: "Fuck you! You fucking little punk," he yelled, jabbing his finger at my chest.

I was small, down to maybe 145 pounds after the arduous training, but he couldn't see the muscle fiber through my loose shirt.

"*Please* leave me alone," I asked, frustrated, but suddenly alert. I raised my hands, showing my palms as if to say *Stop*, and said: "I'm not gonna fight you."

I avoided eye contact and was giving him no excuse to attack, which was all he was looking for. When I asked him to leave, he actually went away, but soon returned to badger me, so I went to a bouncer and asked for help. The bouncer spoke to the man, who angrily returned to his friends.

Soon I was chatting with a pretty girl, and Steve was off somewhere doing the same, when the man returned with another blast of profanity, and the smug arrogance of a larger man who knows he is physically in charge, the master of all those who are smaller and weaker.

He must have seen the girl as an opening; if he shamed me in front of her, maybe he thought that he could enrage me. He was ugly and mean, and though the girl had been showing some interest, she wasn't keen on hanging around for a macho display. She left me standing with him.

The night was becoming an ordeal, and when the girl walked away, I felt anger pulse through my body. My hands tingled, there was a wrenching in my stomach.

Enough is enough.

"Let's go outside!" I bellowed above the music.

Excitement flashed over his face.

He headed for the door that opened onto the boardwalk and the beach. I followed closely behind, and for a few moments I had an extreme advantage. One should never pick a fight, then turn his back on the intended victim. My muscles trembled as if under spring-tension, begging for release, for justice. But the world would not be fair tonight.

We made it to the door and he walked out first. *Gotcha!*

This was not the place, and he was not worth it. Once he was outside, I told the bouncers that the man was still harassing me, then wheeled back around to more interesting matters. Inside, I laughed, tickled at my cleverness, but the confrontation left a heat in my body, like that of a lantern after you cut off the gas: the mantle keeps glowing until all the fuel in the pipe is burned.

I searched for the girl to explain, but she was short and had disappeared in the crowd. As I pin-balled through the mob, I ran into Steve and told him what happened. Steve said that if the man caused any more problems, he would ask his friends for help. He knew some bouncers, which was a comforting thought. Steve was very tough, powerfully built and smart. His favorite sport was rugby and his idea of fun included jumping out of airplanes at night. With Steve and his friends, I felt I had a constellation of protection and backup. My body was still tense, but I was doing my best to will it back down. *Relax. Change the subject. Look at all the girls in this place!*

The man returned. Steve took control of the situation, asking him to walk outside where it was quiet, away from people. The man agreed, obviously primed for action, though he was outnumbered two to one. We all three walked outside, where Steve asked a doorman for help.

A bouncer later stated: "I asked what the trouble was, and spoke to [the man] and said, you know, you seem to be having trouble. . . ."

With the bouncers looking on, Steve, who was better with words than I was, explained calmly to the troublemaker that he would be removed if he didn't settle down. It took some time, but Steve's reasoning appeared to have brought peace.

A bouncer observed, "Steve Shaulis and Mr. Yon turned to me and said 'O.K., everything is all right' . . . They shook hands . . . Steve Shaulis put his arm around [the man]. . . ."

I figured it was finally over. We walked inside, and the man actually bought Steve a drink as I headed into the crowd. As they drank, I wandered around the dance area and found the girl, who was by now talking to someone else. I moved in and asked her to dance, but she was put off.

"No thanks," she yelled above the music. My heart sank. She turned away and kept laughing with the handsome vulture that had swooped in. Her words were final. The door slammed in my face, and they were laughing together on the other side, while I stood alone in the crowd. What a night.

I didn't know it yet, but it was only getting started.

I went for a beer and to scope the area for someone else to talk with, but the man apparently had no intention of going away.

Why won't this guy leave me alone?

I did not escape him. Like a nightmare, every time I dropped my guard, he was back. He approached confidently, invading my space.

What a jerk! Where is a cop when you need one?

I went for help, for backup, for a mediator, for whatever it would take to make him leave me alone! I asked for help from the employees and patrons, or just walked away, probably a dozen times.

Finally, after he had stalked me for what seemed like hours, I had the idea of buying him a drink—surely the peace offering would settle him down.

The gesture of buying the beer did not calm him; in fact, he must have felt that the cold, sweating glass in his hand was proof of my submission. I had showed no trace of courage, except for the time I tricked him, and likely he saw that as cowardice. All I wanted was to get away; there were females all over, and I had been training so much over the last year that I had not been on a single date. Yeah, I was girl chasing, but most of all, I wanted to relax and talk with "normal" people. Particularly female people.

In buying him the drink, I accidentally must have led him to believe that if he used intimidation, I would surrender my dignity and my money to make him happy, like a frightened dog rolling over to offer its throat and belly in exchange for "free" passage. But perception is not always reality, and the time had arrived for each of us to pay for our respective blunders.

He said that he was in the Army Reserves. I was not impressed, but attempted conciliation by asking: "Are you a sergeant or something?" My question was not well conceived, nor apparently did he want to lighten the conversation.

His anger-level soared and he replied: "Are you fucking with me?! You know I'm not a sergeant major!"

"No," I answered. "I asked if you are a *sergeant*, not a sergeant major."

You can't win with this guy. No matter what you say he will find something wrong.

If he was in the Reserves, especially with his scraggly hair and the wispy growth on his chin, he must have been a problem soldier. Maybe that's why he zeroed in on our haircuts.

As we leaned over the bar, elbow to elbow—the music was not as loud there—he held the drink that, I now realized, I had misguidedly bought him. The man was to my left, and to his left a patron sat hunched on a stool, elbows on the bar. Earlier, I had asked the man at the bar for help. He saw that the angry drunk was back, and that we were talking. I was unaware that a bouncer had moved closer and was shadowing us.

As the angry man drank, his tone changed. Maybe alcohol made him mean. Maybe life had made him mean. And his tattoo, *Death Before Dishonor*—what did that mean? That he would fight to the death? His death, or mine?

He glared down at me over his right shoulder. Suddenly, he pushed back from the bar and stepped behind me. Defensively, I turned around to face him. He put his hands on the bar so that I was between his arms, his body, and the bar. We were face to face. His alcohol-reeking breath slurred venomous words and spittle into my face. With my back to the bar, my position was bad, so I maneuvered right, pushing through his left arm so that we swapped places. I stayed close, crowding him against the bar.

The spring tension was difficult to restrain. I knew my body would launch into his at the slightest indication of violence.

I figured that the cowboy boots he wore were the type known as "shit-kickers." When you hit the ground, they kick the shit out of you. He wasn't a cowboy, and the Surf-n-Suds was not a country western joint, but he was picking a fight.

He might be armed. *Boot knife?* Some people are walking arsenals, but you can hardly detect concealed weapons. I was unarmed and the only knives I owned were for my job as a soldier.

The most dangerous creature on the planet is the physically developed, yet still immature, human male. In their worst form, young males represent the ultimate killing machines. They are the pinnacle of unpredictability.

The situation was getting too serious. Everything I did provoked him. The act of pushing his arm out of the way upped the ante. It was time to find Steve and go somewhere else, but before I broke contact the man had some final words.

"I'm gonna kill you," he spoke calmly.

I believed him.

Fear—my body shifted gears.

I felt a hard jolt as the evolutionary cocktail of adrenaline and other survival chemicals dumped into my bloodstream.

He had crossed a magical line.

Negotiations were over.

It was time to leave, while it was still a possibility. He said that I would soon be maggot meat, because he would stab me, shoot me, or both. If I had any doubt of his sincerity before—it was gone. He said that if I left, he would kill me outside.

The man is a lunatic! I'm staring at a killer!

Surprisingly, his tone was no longer angry. He seemed calm, like nothing was going on out of the ordinary for him, like this was just your typical Friday night, in your typical nightclub: Anywhere, U.S.A. In my head, alarms screamed: *this is a very dangerous man.*

His body changed somehow. Maybe it was his eyes, or his feet—I don't know. His right hand clenched into a fist, but, probably because he was half-drunk with alcohol and half with hatred, his body showed the obvious signals of attack that are hard to describe but easy to see. I noticed his right fist coming up. I was galvanized by fear.

My left hand landed solidly, striking his right shoulder.

The open-handed blow was forceful and caused him to spin to his right, throwing him off-balance so that his punch was weak. My hand was on his shoulder, my fingers tightly gripping his shirt and flesh.

My right fist slammed into the left side of his face. The blow rattled my bones.

His head snapped back.

There was no turning back. It had begun.

Nothing existed outside of the fight.

If he wanted an excuse, he now had it. His anger-powered response likely would be a bright red, uncontrolled, maniacal rage. By landing the first punch, I gained a momentary advantage, but I could not let up or he might destroy me with his rage and superior size.

I didn't want to die.

I had the power of desperate fear.

I kept him off balance by gripping his shirt and flesh with my left hand, pushing hard while quickly moving in. My shorter reach had become an advantage; so long as I stayed practically on top of him, his longer reach was actually a handicap. He was like a man who brought a rifle to a wrestling match.

As my left hand continued to push on his shoulder, the bar to his rear prevented him from stepping back to punch me.

After the first blow, my right fist followed up reflexively with another. But he was a moving target, and my fist skipped off his face at a bad angle, doing little harm.

He had a chance to react, and for a moment I was completely vulnerable. But he did not respond and was off balance, still recoiling from the first punch. He was still on his feet, or at least gravity had not yet brought him down.

While my left hand pushed his shoulder, the third right-handed punch landed sharply, unopposed on the left side of his face. I threw a fourth punch, but only partially, withholding it for some reason.

He was limp.

It had happened so quickly that few people saw the action. It seemed to me that the fight was over in about two seconds. A witness said four.

I released his body and it flowed silently off the bar, then crumpled into a pile on its right side on the dark, dirty floor at the feet of some patrons. He seemed stunned, or even unconscious. In the rush, I did not search him for weapons.

His friends and his brother were potential threats, and the bouncer was closing in quickly—on *me*. Fear told me to bolt for the nearby door, to escape. But I couldn't leave my friend, so I ran to find Steve in the crowd. Some men began chasing me, but I was quicker at threading through the dancing people who were unaware there had been a fight, and got to Steve first.

A bouncer said later: "He then proceeded back into the bar to Steve

Shaulis . . . 25 or 30 feet away. He said something to Steve. . . ."

"COME ON! WE GOTTA GO!" I yelled in Steve's face.

He replied calmly, yelling above the music, "Wait a minute!"

He didn't believe that we had to leave; he thought we could explain that the fallen man had started it. If Steve wanted to stay, that was his choice, I thought, but to me, the man I'd just issued a black eye and a sore jaw was a lethal threat. When he regained his senses, I knew negotiations were out.

Three or four big men were quickly making their way through the crowd. There was no time to waste.

I grabbed Steve's collar and yelled, **"COME ON!"**

He said, "Just wait!"

I screamed, **"YOU'RE ON YOUR OWN!"** released his collar and sought to escape.

A big man had nearly reached me when I again fled into the crowd. There was an area devoid of people just in front of the back emergency exit. I accelerated and hit the exit in almost full flight. The double doors were chained shut, though earlier they had been open. I crashed into the right door so hard that I recoiled and nearly fell over backwards. My head smashed into the metal. It was a serious impact. I staggered for a few seconds, but shook it off and quickly regained my senses.

A bouncer cornered me. He told a detective later: "I stopped Mike, told him that he was waiting for the police, this boy seemed like he was really hurt and I wanted him to wait. He said to me at that time, 'O.K., I'll wait for the police.'"

I had no intention of waiting for the police.

I raised my hands as in surrender while lowering my head to show my non-threatening intent. I allowed the bouncer to step behind and put me in an arm lock. I would let him escort me to the door, then go for the escape. As we took the first steps toward the front, three men closed in while the man behind me maintained his arm lock. I stayed loose and offered no resistance so that the bouncer would be off-guard.

I was not a karate expert, but the bouncer took the bait, relaxed his guard and did not properly set the lock. I could escape when ready. When the three men were about ten feet away, I moved.

The bouncer said: "At that point . . . he broke through my grasp. . . ."

I popped out of the lock, ducked low to take advantage of my smaller size, and scampered on all fours like a squirrel between two of the approaching men before they could react.

I jumped back to my feet, and threaded my way through the crowd toward the door where another bouncer stood, unaware. Someone yelled to the doorman to stop me. I was flying like a cannonball and would crash through him to unplug the exit if he blocked the way, but with the loud music he didn't hear the alert.

I shot out the door, past the bouncer, the other men in pursuit; dashed down the boardwalk, jumped off into the first dark area, and flew over a fence or some such hurdle, which put an obstacle between us, and that was it.

I got away.
Or so I thought.

I put some distance between us—not much, maybe a quarter mile—and ended up in an area with lots of people. I stopped running, so as not to draw attention, and caught my breath. It was almost midnight, but this being tourist time, some stores were still open.

I ducked inside a shop. To cover my short hair, I quickly picked out a Gilligan hat that I could pull down, almost covering my eyes, and a helium balloon to make me look younger. With the balloon and hat, I probably went from looking fifteen to appearing fourteen. My body trembled and floated with a full dose of adrenaline as I did my best to keep a poker face.

Wearing shorts and a T-shirt, I pulled some cash out of my left sock and walked to the register. I had not bothered to check the price, or how much the cashier rang up; I just handed over a twenty dollar bill and kept watch on the door, being as inconspicuous as possible. The cashier kept talking with another woman and hardly looked at me as she counted back the change in bills and coins, to which I paid no attention. I tore off the price tag, pulled the hat over my head, bent down and stuffed the bills into my sock, said "Goodnight," and walked to the door where I stopped.

I held the coins and price tag in my right hand, the balloon in the left. From the doorway I scanned the sidewalk. It looked clear. I pulled the hat lower over my eyes, stepped out of the shop among the other tourists, began walking down the sidewalk, and dropped the loose change and price tag into the first trashcan I saw.

I had belted him pretty hard. That first contact was for the record books, I thought. The third was solid, too, but my hand didn't seem broken. I would have to wait for the excitement to wear off and for my blood to cool before feeling the damage. After a serious emergency, it is important to examine oneself; the emotional experience can be so intense, that often soldiers and police officers do not realize that they have been shot or wounded until later. I had broken five bones as a kid. I would know in the morning if the number might climb to six or more. But there was no time for that now.

After the troublemaker's cobwebs cleared and he pulled himself off the floor and stood up in his shit kickers, the knots on his head would be a throbbing reminder of my existence. By now, *Death Before Dishonor* and friends must be hunting like rampaging hyenas searching for what they thought was a rabbit. Rabbits aren't supposed to fight back. *Revenge!* They would want my blood and my hide, I was sure.

I didn't know what he and his sidekicks were driving, and if they recognized me first, they could shoot me. Or they might be on foot. If I saw them first, I could probably outrun them, but not their bullets.

The thought of checking in with the police passed through my mind for a moment. A very brief moment. The Army would not be happy about tonight if word got back, so I axed that idea. I was on my own.

But there was another problem: Steve had stayed behind in the bar. We needed to link up and get out before the police got involved. We had not rented a hotel room. Steve was supposed to meet a friend, who would put us up, but I didn't know the friend's last name, and this was my first trip to Maryland. Linkup would be dangerous.

It would be crazy to walk inside the Surf-n-Suds to try to find Steve. So I crept back in the shadows and watched his truck from a distance, sitting down, crunching up like a cannonball, letting the balloon bob overhead in a way that said, "I'm not the one; I'm just a kid."

Surely Steve realized that I would get in position to watch his truck, but he didn't come out.

The police and an ambulance arrived.

Uh oh—an ambulance. Two ambulances. I hit him pretty hard. Must have shattered his jaw. Son of a bitch deserved it.

What about Steve? Oh my God. Nothing I can add now with the police and ambulances there.

Steve might be injured, or worse, which worried me immensely, but if that were so we would link up at the hospital—I hoped. It was senseless to get arrested for nothing, and to create serious problems for both of us if Steve was okay.

My universe was focused on self-preservation.

The past year's military training kicked in: *gather information.*

I boarded a local bus and, as the driver wrestled the big steering wheel, pulling away from the curb, I sat up front to hear the radio. A scattered handful of passengers were on board, but none were talking. Soon the speaker crackled with an inaccurate description of me, suggesting I was much larger. The distant voice added that I was with Special Forces, a "Green Beret."

They had correctly identified me. That meant that Steve was still around, or someone who knew him, maybe one of the bouncers. The voice said that the man had been hurt, which explained one ambulance. I figured it was probably a broken jaw.

Well, it looked like I needed to settle the dispute. After all, there were witnesses galore to support me, and the police knew my name so there were no good options. Better to settle it quickly, to contain it, because if the Special Warfare Center at Fort Bragg caught wind about a "barroom fight," the

Maryland police might be the least of my concerns. I had a secret clearance to protect, and if they couldn't trust me to avoid fights, my brief stay in Special Operations was over.

I figured that I would file a complaint against the man and, with all the witnesses and some luck, he would get the broken jaw *and* the charges. *Ha!* The ambulance and the radio report meant that he was out of action and not looking for me. It was doubtful that his friends were searching without him leading the pack, especially now that the police were involved.

I would have to deal with the Special Warfare Center, but that was for later. For now, I was shaking but starting to feel better, much better, even euphoric. I wanted to laugh loudly and sing a happy song of victory for whipping his ass after all that he had said and done. He had followed me around the club, scared off that nice girl, and threatened me.

The euphoria transformed everything that had been so frightening into something extremely funny.

He'll think twice before pulling on his boots to go downtown!

Ha ha, those men chasing me looked like a Chinese fire drill. Whoa! That was close. They almost clobbered me.

The closer the horn, the sweeter the pass. *Toro!* I was never an adrenaline junky, but I could see how people get addicted to the stuff.

I had cracked my head against the back door of the Surf-n-Suds, but no teeth were raining out, and I didn't have a headache or even a scratch, so far as I could tell. I floated in the clouds, high on the survival chemicals in my blood, and feeling that justice had been served. A lesson had been taught to a very dangerous man, a menace to innocent people, *after* I had done every-thing possible to avoid trouble. My mind replayed the scene.

I even bought him a drink. Boy, that was dumb. But he didn't get to enjoy it. I bet they'll pump his stomach at the hospital before they fix his jaw.

Sweet victory and justice all at once. I only needed to find Steve and fig-ure out how to approach the police.

As I considered my next move, an update burst through the airwaves and into the bus with a tense statement that the "victim" had died. I was wanted for a possible homicide. The voice continued, and, as it repeated my descrip-tion, I froze.

Homicide!

He died?

Oh my God.

I sat motionless.

Adrenaline flooded my veins.

The world went silent.

I was alone.

The only person alive.

Standing in a silent wasteland.

Whamm!
A blood red fear exploded throughout my body.
I was back in the world.
Not alone.
They were after me. I was the enemy.
An All-Points Bulletin was issued and off-duty officers were called in. They were throwing all their forces at me. The warning was reissued every fifteen minutes.
Homicide?
I'm no murderer.
The bus driver sat only a few feet away and said, "I sure hope that I don't run into that guy tonight."
This was just too weird to fathom. For an interval of distorted time his remark hung in the air, then seemed hilarious.
I responded with, "Me, too! There are a lot of crazies out there," and I laughed.
What am I laughing about! Suddenly I felt sick, and nothing was funny. There was no humor left in the world.
"Where are you from?" asked the bus driver.
"Alabama," I answered, covering for my Southern accent; "I'm looking for my girlfriend." Changing the subject, I said: "We came here with my parents, and she wandered off with them."
He pulled the bus over to a stop where a couple waited to be picked up.
I stood and, as the doors opened, said "Goodnight," keeping my head down as I passed him.
He said "Goodnight" to my back and I stepped down and passed the couple standing on the sidewalk. They boarded as I walked away.
Outside, tourists were everywhere. A steady stream of traffic sprinkled with police cars flowed up and down the road. I wore a T-shirt, shorts, running shoes and my Gilligan hat, holding the balloon that bobbed and tugged on the end of its string, pulling to be set free.
It was after midnight, and everything under the moon was fatally serious. I walked down the sidewalk and slipped into a dark area where I sat down to bring things into focus. I needed a break to sort things out. From my hiding place, the voices of passersby sounded like trains.
I had completed some "field craft" training a few weeks earlier. It was brief and they warned us that we were not spies, that it was only an introduction to guerrilla warfare concepts, but I was doing my best to make what

we had learned fit the situation.

My mind was churning every available piece of information. Meantime another part of my mind was defending me.

But . . . I'm innocent. He attacked me.
Oh my God. He died?
I'm nineteen and he's dead.
What will Granny think? What will my friends think?
But there are so many witnesses.
*They **know** I'm innocent.*

I was in mortal danger and being hunted. They would label me a "Green Beret" and assume I was a martial arts expert, crazy, specially picked because I could kill efficiently. Without feeling. The fact that I ended up in Special Forces as a teenager instead of college was as unlikely as killing someone in a fist fight. It was just a bizarre chain of events. I felt like I was in the Twilight Zone.

When people say, "He is a Green Beret" at times they are probably dehumanizing the person in question, and saying he is a Rambo. I was young but experienced enough to know that they would not treat me like a fellow human.

We were warned in Special Forces training that soldiers returning from behind enemy lines are often killed not by the enemy, but, ironically, by the friendly troops with whom they try to re-establish contact. They are mistaken for the enemy and killed at the last moment by their own. Death by "friendly" fire—fratricide.

I wanted to turn myself over to the police but there was an important difference; they would not treat me as one of their own, but as a criminal. They were already labeling me the *assailant* in their written reports. The real attacker was being called the victim. After all, I had fled the scene, which could only be interpreted as a sign of guilt, *right?* I was the "Green Beret," *right?*

The police may shoot me.
Maybe I should wait a couple of days before turning myself in.
Maybe I should go to another town where the tensions are not so high.
I think this is an island.
They will watch the bridges. I may have to swim. I need a map.
I can go to a base and turn myself over to the military police.
Where is the nearest base?
But if I get spotted they might shoot me.
Oh shit.
Maybe I should go to Mexico.
Maybe go live in the woods. Steal a boat.

He's dead. I can't believe this.
They might shoot without giving me a chance to surrender.
And my "other mind" chimed in, *Why didn't I just leave when I'd had the*
chance?
No time for that now.
Pay attention.
Size up the situation.

The idea that I was presumed guilty and in danger of being shot turned out to be correct. If I wanted to run, it was better to go for it immediately, before they got organized. Normally the safest bet during evasion is to get far away, fast. If I could make it to the mainland, I would have the advantage of terrain—North America is a big place to hide in—and it would be dark for what, six more hours?

I would not make the mistake of taking a bus or hitching a ride. I would swim away. After I got to the mainland I would stick to the woods. Even if they had a clue, they would need bloodhounds and a lot of luck to catch me. On foot, I could easily make a hundred miles a week and find food along the way. It was summer. Cold was not a problem. Water was everywhere. I could stick to the woods as much as possible and be in Mexico before winter. *I'll have to learn Spanish.*

The human desire to live told me to evade. Run away. My upbringing told me to face up to it. My gut told me that they would see my innocence; it also said that they might kill me.

To run away meant that I could never call my family again. I decided to have another look before making a decision. Even if I chose to run, I could always turn myself in later when it was calm. I left the relative safety of my hiding place and moved in closer to the scene to watch Steve's white Datsun pickup. To approach the truck still seemed dangerous so I observed from a distance—luckily—since a closer approach would have taken me into a police ambush. (I later learned that police officers, too, were hidden, watching the truck.)

Police swarmed as if their hive had been kicked. Some wore plainclothes. They were easy to spot because they were searching, not just wandering about like the throngs of tourists. Besides which, they had antennas. I walked by them with my hat and balloon.

I decided to face it. To face the police. When they heard the facts, they would know that his death was an accident. I was not a criminal. I would turn myself in to face justice.

Earlier in the month, I had parachuted as a member of a twelve-man team under moonless sky into the black wilderness for a two-week-long guerrilla warfare test. We had just been airlifted out by helicopter earlier in the week, after successfully linking up with the "guerrillas" and hitting our guarded "targets." That was nothing in comparison. This was not an exercise. This was live fire.

A witness later said, **"He didn't look scared."** He was wrong.

I can't believe this. They're looking for me.

More than twenty officers from the Ocean City Police Department were at the immediate scene, and who knows how many were searching elsewhere. The ones I saw looked jumpy. Danger hung thick in the air. I felt like every breath might be my last.

Two big policemen stood asking questions by the door of the Surf-n-Suds. Somehow I concluded they were less likely to hurt me when they were together, so I ditched the hat in a trashcan and released the balloon. I stood and watched it float into the void of blackness and wished I could go with it.

I approached the two uniformed men and said, "Hello, I think you would like to talk to me."

They were holding notepads and had been taking the names of everyone who left the bar, and the police had been photographing the crowd. Another area outside was cordoned off with crime scene tape. The two police stood talking to a bouncer and to Steve, who surreptitiously signaled me to leave. The police didn't notice the signal or pay attention to me. I motioned to Steve that I knew what had happened.

Earlier, when Steve learned that the man was hurt, he tried to help him. A police report said that Steve had found a pulse, and that he performed first-aid by treating him for shock. No wonder, with a man dying, Steve missed the linkup.

Now, standing next to the police, I silently mouthed the words *"I know"* so that only Steve saw. He strongly reiterated his signal for me to leave while acting as though he didn't know me. He was afraid that I would be hurt and silently screamed with his actions *"Go away!"*

The closest policeman dismissed me with the wave of a hand—*shoo fly!*—as if I were a pesky adolescent who should be at home. At that moment I wished I were.

They are called "police" or "law enforcement" or "officers," but at times, as with soldiers, they are merely people with guns, and all that stops them from misusing deadly force is self-discipline and training. Wispy laws written in a distant world cannot keep a frightened or angry human from pulling the trigger if the mind tells the hand to shoot.

The men with guns turned away and kept talking, as I stood alone, trembling, within arm's reach. Walkie-talkies for calling other people with guns hung on their left hips. They each wore pistols on their right hips. These men were right-handed.

I focused on the policeman closest to me. To regain his attention, I reached out with my left hand and with my pointer finger, flipped the black rubberized antenna of the walkie-talkie hanging on his police belt. I was afraid to touch him for some reason. Both policemen looked at me with obvious irritation, causing something inside me to bark: *Leave!*

Walk away!

My feet took me away.

The ocean was only a rock's throw beyond, so I stepped off the boardwalk and trudged through the soft sand until I was on the harder sand next to the water. Waves licked the beach from dark waters, and there was the smell of salty air carried by a warm summer breeze. I thought about swimming out into the dark ocean, but kept walking slowly, going nowhere. Certainly not running away.

My grandmother kept intruding on my thoughts. It was bad enough that I had been in a bar. *What if I die tonight? It could kill her.* And her final memory would be of me fighting in a dimly lit bar. I was drinking beer for Christ's sake! Drinking, fighting, shot dead on the beach. My little sister looked up to me and was so proud of me, and now this. Some last memory.

I've got to turn myself in before something happens.

While walking, I watched numerous police patrolling up and down the brightly-lighted boardwalk—the police supervisor had called everybody and they were hunting intently, though I was in clear sight.

I walked slowly on the beach. Sounds murmured from the mouth of the ocean as black water collected in waves and collapsed on the shore. The ocean to my left meant that I was walking south. By now the police must have called Fort Bragg. *They definitely know that I am with Special Forces. Maybe they know that I am trained as a weapons specialist?* My job title, along with the dog tags that hung around my neck, was a heavy burden in light of my being hunted for murder.

To them, I was a *Green Beret*, a title unlikely to evoke mercy from a man with a gun.

It had been more than two hours since the fight. I was within their grasp and watching them for much of that time as they pressed their manhunt.

A witness described the encounter with the two policemen who had dismissed me with the wave of a hand: "[Mike Yon] just walked up . . . and then he started to walk away and I said to the policeman, that looks like the guy and they said he's . . . too short . . . [The suspect is] five eleven and [that guy is] five nine or something and I said, Well, you should stop him I should think."

Finally, the police realized who I was. They were on the boardwalk trying to look inconspicuous, which was difficult to do, since they formed what amounted to a skirmish line. It was obvious that the people carrying guns were afraid and prepared to use deadly force. Judging by the way they were forming up and taking their time, they were respectful of their quarry and their movements suggested they were approaching a cornered lion.

Any false move on my part and I would be dead. I could do everything right and *still* be dead. My pace slowed to a shuffle as I estimated the center of the line of police and veered from the ocean darkness toward the light. I wanted them to see me clearly, to know that they were in complete control.

My hands clearly empty.

No need for violence.

My heart raced.

This was it.

More survival chemicals poured into my veins and I felt the jolt. If they shot me I would feel no pain. I would simply feel the thuds and die. I was helpless, utterly at their mercy. My life was theirs to take, or to leave.

Don't trip or stumble.

They say that before you die, your life passes before your eyes.

THIRTEEN YEARS AFTER that night, I felt that I had to tell this story:

Every story has a beginning and an end. Let's start at the beginning with eight paragraphs leading up to my birth.

. . . a life passing before your eyes

"Yon, where did the name come from?" My blood is the confluence of many lines from many places, and we are all related back there, somewhere, once you get to the root. Though Yon is a Korean name, there are no Koreans in my family. It is also a French name; maybe I am French, but only fractionally. Some drops of Native American blood run through my veins from my mother's side, but our predominant line is some kind of hardy European stock. I know it's hardy, because most of my family members have lived long and relatively healthy lives—real money makers for the insurance companies. Other branches in the tree include names like Carter, Eason, Rothwell, Vincent, Sconyers and Tillman. Maybe I am English, or German. Whatever. I am an American, a mixed-breed.

During the Great Depression, my maternal great-grandfather—my mother's mother's father—was a choir director in Oklahoma when he answered a newspaper ad for a position at a small church. He won the job and moved to a little town in Florida with his young family that included my grandmother, then a child.

My maternal grandfather was born on a farm in South Georgia. He was nineteen with a sixth grade education when he escaped the poverty of the farm by hitchhiking south to look for work. Winter Haven, Florida, was the center of the universe for the citrus industry; jobs were plentiful, so he picked fruit. He stood on wooden ladders picking oranges and grapefruit in the unrelenting sun and stifling humidity. The work was mind-numbingly exhausting. Granddad seemed unfazed by the kind of work that causes heatstroke.

He found his way to the church where he spotted a pretty, well-mannered girl. Romance and marriage quickly ensued. She was sixteen and he was twenty-one. He was devoted to his wife, sometimes writing love poems in the morning darkness while sitting in the cab of his Velda Farms milk truck, waiting for the first store to open. He had switched from picking oranges to delivering milk, and remained at this work for about forty of the more than fifty years they were married.

As a boy, he smoked cigarettes because that's what farm boys did. Cigarettes weren't considered bad for a fella back then, so there was nothing wrong with it. They grew tobacco and it didn't cost much to roll your own, so even poor people like him could smoke. He stopped cold turkey the day he learned that his young bride was expecting their first baby saying no child of his would see him smoke. They had a boy, and almost four years later, a beautiful baby girl, Callie, my mother.

My paternal grandparents grew up on farms in Alabama and North Florida. They met, married, and farmed in North Florida where my father, William Yon, was born. Eventually they lost the farm and moved to Central Florida so Granddad could pick fruit.

There was a significant difference between my father's and mother's families. My mother's relatives were mostly hard working, churchgoing, respectable people. My father's side was sprinkled with hell-raisers, and religious fanatics.

But my father was determined to climb out of that life, and he met with some success. He had a promising start as a bank officer and seemed destined for a better life in Winter Haven, which in addition to citrus was thriving as a tourist destination. He met and married my mother when she was just nineteen. They had a son, Billy, then a year and a half later, another, Michael Phillip Yon (me).

And so my life began. A yellowed newspaper clipping in a family photo-album reads:

If your child is born today, he or she will be one of those persons who seems to do best under pressure or when an emergency arises. Be sure that much exercise and sports are enjoyed in early youth to increase this fine ability and education should be slanted toward trouble-shooting professionally. Teach not to monopolize a conversation, but to listen carefully to others as well.

I don't give credence to such predictions, but that was eerily correct.

The time and location of my birth were nearly the same as for one of my best friends, Richard White. As far as we could figure, we were in the hospital nursery together, and years later we joked that we were switched at birth. We officially entered society in the Winter Haven Hospital as healthy baby boys, each with a great family to introduce us to the world. Fortune was with us at our most critical moments. But it would be a long time before Richard and I could formally meet and shake hands. First we had to learn the basics. Besides our parents, we had other teachers. Richard had an older sister and I had Billy.

My earliest memory is of my mother washing me in the sink and changing my diaper. The next memory to which a date can be assigned reaches back

27

to when I was twenty-one months old at Christmas in the first house I lived in. My mother was frying something in the kitchen and told me to stay back but I scurried up to her anyway. *POP!* Grease burned my arm! My thin skin was unaccustomed to the slightest discomfort, so I screamed—and ran to my mother instead of away. She was my only chance to make it better and she did. She instantly healed my injury with a kiss and a hug. I ran out to Daddy who was sitting in the living room by the Christmas tree. I remember little else about the house except riding home from Sunday School, pulling in the driveway and jumping out as fast as I could to ride my red tricycle on a cold day. Life was fun!

We vacationed annually in a park called Cataloochee in the rugged mountains of western North Carolina. Once, Billy, Daddy and I were outside a nearby town called Waynesville when we encountered a large black bear. My father was brave, as fathers are. The bear was brave, too, as bears are. Dad knelt beside me and was snapping a series of photos when the bear suddenly charged. I froze. Daddy screamed and waved his arms: the bear ran away.

Face to face with a bear—*that* was scary. I have several pictures of the bear taken just before it charged. According to the date scribbled on the back of one, it was a month before my sister, Susan, was born.

Our family was upwardly mobile, and we moved to a brand new two-story house with a pool. I had to be two and a half when the new baby arrived, which in retrospect was the cause of our move to a bigger house. I remember reaching into her crib and touching her. Suddenly, I had a little sister. She was fantastic!

While Susan slept in her crib, I was growing. By the time I was three or four I had explored the great outdoors in a neighborhood of big houses. Living things were all around and I liked to touch. As I played near the garden, I hit a wasps' nest and got stung on the cheek, and when I found a green caterpillar and touched it—it stung me! I ran to Mommy crying. She told me not to hit wasps' nests or touch caterpillars anymore. She was magic and knew everything, but I figured out some things myself. I loved to feel the ground on my bare feet, so once I found myself limping home with a roofing-nail (with shingle) sticking in my foot, crying as if caught in a beartrap. She soaked my feet in hot water and Epsom salt more times than I can remember. Finally I stopped taking off my shoes. Injury made me think.

There was adventure, and sometimes danger, around every corner. My grandmother says I was about four when the accident occurred. Our mother was driving, Billy in the front, and I in the backseat on the right. I'm told we were going about thirty miles per hour. The traffic was busy. My door flew open. I didn't scream, so my mother didn't realize I had fallen out. It was a big car, the kind with a strap on the door. I had grabbed the strap. My survival depended on my ability to continue holding that strap.

Somehow I knew that to let go would be fatal. My feet were dragging on the road, which quickly took the skin away. It stung. I held on. Getting tired. I held on. I was too afraid to cry or even scream. My grip was slipping away with my life.

A man saw me dangling and flagged my mother down. She stopped in the middle of the busy road in front of a McDonald's. And though my feet were skinned on the road, everything turned out okay. My mother held me and cried like it was the end of the world. That was the first time that a stranger saved my life. It would not be the last.

Billy remembers that day. He remembers people yelling from the side of the road, and a man driving up next to us beeping his horn and pointing. Then he remembers Mom at home, collapsed over the table sobbing with her face buried in her arms. Billy touched her arm and said, "Mommy, why are you crying? He's okay."

Kids like me are the reason for safety locks, child seats, tamper-proof bottles, and all those ridiculous instructions that are printed on everything we buy. My apologies.

When I was young, there was a law that swimming pools must have safety fences. Our pool had a fence—in fact it had two. Luckily, my mother taught me to swim at the same time she taught me to walk, and later we had some terrific water fights. As time marched on, little Susan learned to crawl. We were at the pool and I suppose it was time for her swimming lessons. Susan crawled well enough to get close and then fall into the pool where she immediately sank like a rock, though I now know that babies float like a cork—usually.

I was a confident tadpole, so I dove in to save my baby sister who was very important to my mother for some reason. *Zoom!* Mommy shot past like a dolphin and whisked her baby back to the surface. Little Susan was fine.

Mommy congratulated me on trying so hard and gave me a big hug and a kiss. Being a little rescuer carries its own rewards! A little boy never forgets when his mother calls him a hero and tells him how proud she is, even when he knows that he got in the way.

My being so small made the world one big challenge. I couldn't open the back door into the house. The doorknob was too high or too hard to turn. I would yell for Biwy (I couldn't say Billy) to open the door, or Mommy would hear me and meet me with her big smile. One day I did it! Biwy tried to teach me to say his name but my little mouth just wouldn't do it. But I could hear it and knew I wasn't saying it right, so I would try and try and try. One day I did it! Whenever I passed another milestone, I got a kiss and a hug—and sometimes ice cream!

When I was about four, Granddaddy taught me to throw rocks. There was a Stop sign near the house. Rocks, cars, Stop sign—what luck! When the cars stopped, I was hidden behind a hedge and rained rocks on them.

It went well. At first. Unfortunately my little arm, though capable and sure, did not possess the range-capability that my little legs needed to outrun an angry driver.

A car came to a slow halt at the Stop sign, and as the unsuspecting driver checked both ways, a rock arced through the air—my heart raced as I had just committed the childhood equivalent of bank robbery—and pat pat pattered across her hood. Her head jerked to the left. *She sees me!!!*

Her door flew open and the chase was on.

I made a run for it. I was going to run all the way to the other side of the world.

She crashed through the hedge.

"**STOP!**" she commanded, and for a moment my legs stopped.

Then started again, going as fast as they could.

Her footsteps pounded behind me. I looked over my shoulder. *A Giant Woman is chasing me!* **Godzilla!** *She's gonna kill me!* My legs pumped furiously.

Suddenly my right arm was jerked into the sky and I was on my toes. The chase was over. I was caught. My car-pelting career was cut short. Abruptly.

It was fun while it lasted, but I needed a safer pastime and baby birds were more fun than angry, fast-running drivers. Billy and I were playing with a baby bird when it hopped into the street. A woman driving slowly up to the Stop sign was going to run over the bird, so we screamed and jumped up and down to make her stop. Finally she did, though she seemed confused and must have been thinking, *Why are those kids screaming at me?* She inched forward, looking at us. We screamed and jumped and pointed at the little bird that she could not see.

She stopped so we started out into the street to rescue the bird, which was crying for its mother. Her car lurched forward and crushed it. I was gasping and crying and when the woman stepped out and looked, she started crying too. It was smashed flat. I felt like I was the one crushed under the tire. I ran to Mommy. "A baby bird got smashed. What can we do?" She explained that after something dies it is gone forever and never comes back, ever.

She told us not to play with baby birds because if we did, the mother would smell our hands on her baby. The mother would let the baby die because she was afraid of the smell. *Wow. . . .What if Mommy is afraid of me because I smell?* (It didn't matter that most birds can't smell. We thought they could.)

So much for baby birds, wasps, caterpillars, hanging out car doors and angry drivers. But there was always something new. A back yard is a very big place for a tadpole. It turned cold, which is a relative condition in Florida. Anyway, the neighbors across the street ran their water sprinklers through a freezing night. In the morning a big tree in their yard that was close to the Stop sign had gigantic icicles hanging off the branches. *Wow!* The grass was all covered in ice. It was lots of fun rolling around on the crunchy grass, and the tree sounded like bells when I threw rocks into the icicles.

The neighbors provided endless recreation. I tried to sell them some rubber bands that were in a drawer in our house. Nobody at home knew that I was a door-to-door rubber band sales-boy. I just thought it up and did it; probably imitating somebody that came through selling vacuum cleaners. Family lore says that the neighbors started calling each other and my mother, warning of my approach. The asking price was five bucks each, but one neighbor somehow negotiated me down to a nickel. Still a good deal for a pre-kindergartner with no formal sales training.

Animals surrounded us. Our biggest pet was a German Shepherd, Duchess. We rode her like a horse. She was so big that I regarded her more as an adult than a pet. The big, majestic oak trees in the neighborhood provided a daily circus of squirrel activity, and the local grey squirrel community was large and well-fed. Each morning when it was cool, they raced around the trunks and branches chasing each other in a high-speed drama of jumps and hide-and-seek. Rodents of unusual agility. I sure wished I could climb like that. *Don't they get scared? Naw, squirrels don't fall.*

Under a big oak tree, Billy and I found a baby squirrel that had fallen from its nest. We wouldn't touch it because we didn't want to leave our smell on it, but it was bleeding and making baby squirrel noises. We had to do *something*. I ran home to Mommy, who was the mother of all babies, even squirrels.

As always, she knew what to do to make the squirrel stop crying. She brought a box and we took him home. He was now in our family. He was a boy because we were boys and we never considered that he might be a girl. When Daddy came home from the bank, he was very proud that we had done the right thing. *Rescuers!* We named him Chipper.

Chipper grew and made himself at home. He taunted the cats with a strange chirping noise from a perch, usually a curtain rod out of the cats' perceived range of action. Maybe Chipper didn't realize the gravity of his situation. The cats never fully accepted him the way we did, and I was afraid that they would catch him like a mouse. When he was old enough, Mommy let Chipper go. It was a sad day because I loved him, but she said he had to be free.

"But why? Isn't he happy with us?"

She said he needed to find a mate.

"What's a mate?"

Often, when I see a squirrel, I think of him. I wonder now what really happened to Chipper—did the cats finally get him and make him pay for his chirping, or did my mother really let him go?

I liked to play with living creatures, but Billy liked to play with "things," like matches. It was his style of adventure. Well, Billy was a living creature, so together we lit lots of matches. It was great fun up to the point when Mommy yelled for us to come home. By her voice we knew something was wrong. As we hurried home, Billy warned me not to tell that we were lighting matches. *Why would I want to lie to her? I never get in trouble like you. You are the troublemaker—I am the angel.* That's how I had it figured.

Soon we were standing next to her and I was holding her leg. She pointed to a big fire on the horizon. Being so young, I had difficulty judging distances and the fire was in the direction where we had been playing.

I couldn't lie to her; she always knew what I was thinking. She knew when I was hungry, sleepy or sick—she *always* knew. The fire was so big—*maybe I started it.* But no, it was too far away—but it was the same direction . . . confusion. I couldn't figure out if I had started it, but I was sure that it was too far away.

"Mommy, Mommy, I didn't do it!" (Turns out it was about three miles away. It was a monster of a fire that burned down a citrus packinghouse.)

I was growing up and it was time for preschool. A milestone. Lots and lots of other kids to play with. The world got bigger and more fun. I was at my Aunt Shirley's preschool when I decided to climb on the windowsill. Knowing that the world was a dangerous place, I considered the possibility of falling, and decided to tie myself to the cord that went to the Venetian blinds. I wrapped the cord around my neck and started to walk on the sill. I fell.

I was hanging by my neck fighting for life. I could not breathe or cry for help. I was alone in a separate room—it was just me against the cord. I was kicking my feet, clawing at the cord, swinging in circles. I don't know how long I hung, but I think that it was only some seconds, when my Aunt Shirley walked in and saved me.

So I learned that I should not tie cords around my neck for safety. There were some intense moments and I knew that I had nearly died. By then I was well aware that everything can go from fun and games to life and death in a single breath.

We went to church. That's probably why when I was around four I decided to go ahead and kill the Devil and get it over with. I was digging him up when Billy asked me what I was doing.

"I'm going to kill the Devil. *Jesus* is on my side!"

Billy was game so he started digging beside me. I imagined that there would be a metal roof. I would have to find a way to get in. I was afraid because I knew how bad the Devil was. *What if I can't kill him and he gets out into the world?* I kept digging.

Up to my armpit, dirt under my fingernails and all over me, my fingers found something. I told Billy and ran to Mommy. She would know what it was. She washed it off in the kitchen sink—it was a shark's tooth!

Even for a four-year-old, especially for a four-year-old, it raises the question, *How did a shark lose a tooth in our backyard? Why did it bury its tooth?* She explained that the ocean used to cover Florida and if something sits still long enough it can get buried. *Wow. Why? What if I sit still too long?*

Then I discovered the best living creatures of all. I started kindergarten at the First Presbyterian Church nearby and met the prettiest, sweetest, bestest girl I ever knew. Her name was Pam. I never told her that I loved her. Instead, I played near her—she was fun to watch. I wanted to hold her hand or kiss her but I was too polite and shy. She was different from the other girls. I was going to marry her. We would have our own playground. When I looked at her I felt good and warm. I didn't know what to say. *Can I hold your hand? I love you!*

Every day after kindergarten, my mother would walk to the big church and get me; it was only a few blocks from the house, or she would pick me up in the car and we would go somewhere, like Granny and Granddad's house. They were fun and always loved me and played with me. Granddad had a special smell, like something mysterious. I didn't know what he did when he left the house, but he always came back sweating and smelling different than everybody else. It was the smell of hard work.

One afternoon, I stood outside the kindergarten, wondering what adventure Mommy would take me on that day. *Swimming? McDonald's? Walking?* Maybe we would go to Granny's house! The kindergarten teacher said my mother would be a few minutes late. Mommy walked me to kindergarten every morning, so I knew the way. When the teacher was not looking, I sneaked out and walked home.

When I got there the door was unlocked. I walked in and looked, but she was not there. I looked everywhere, checked every hiding place. . . . I was alone . . . paralyzed . . . screaming like a wounded baby squirrel. I stood there and cried for what seemed like hours and finally she walked in and picked me up.

Whew! I almost had a heart attack. She knew *everything*—including where I was. Maybe God told her because she knew God. *Does Mommy's mother know what she is thinking?*

We did everything together. She played with me constantly. One day she was upstairs and I wanted to play.

"Mommy! Come down and play with me!"

"Just a minute, I'll be right down."

I knew how long a minute was because she taught me, so I started counting the seconds: "56, 57, 58, 59, 60! Come on! You said a minute!"

She walked downstairs and we went off to play. She used to scratch the bottoms of my feet until I fell asleep, and I don't even know if it felt good, but I liked her to touch me. As long as we were together, everything was okay.

I felt safe at home. Billy and I slept in the same bed, and we got tucked in every night. When we heard her coming up the stairs—that was our signal to stop any pillow fights or jumping on the bed, which was against the law for some reason. It had something to do with a monkey that jumped on the bed and banged his head, and went to the doctor.

When Mommy walked in, it was like magic. She didn't need to say a word—we opened our mouths like baby birds waiting to be fed, only she was checking to see if we had brushed our teeth. Somehow she could tell if you didn't brush your teeth, and it was better to do it because she said if you forgot, your teeth would fall out. Which didn't seem so bad to me. When Billy's teeth fell out he got quarters under his pillow. You swap quarters for candy, and candy made your teeth fall out.

She would lift up my lips like I was a dog, and peer inside. It was silly to skip brushing. There was no way around it. She would know. And she checked my mouth for chewing gum, which in the mornings always ended up in my hair—or, worse yet, Billy's hair! I tried to hide the gum in my mouth, but she always found it because she knew where to look, even when I hid it in different places.

After the sticky formalities, she knelt with us beside the bed and we put our hands together to say our prayers. For some reason God can only hear while you are kneeling by your bed with your hands together and eyes closed. If you open your eyes, God can't hear you. *And now I lay me down to sleep, I pray the Lord my soul to keep. . . .* Sometimes she said prayers with us, or we said them alone while she listened. After all, there was no need to say prayers if Mommy couldn't hear them.

After prayers came the fun part! I knew that I was going to get tucked in and get a kiss and there was no way I could sleep without getting tucked in and a kiss. Then Daddy would come in and say goodnight. I loved him, too. Then Mommy sang or read a story—and I woke up to another day.

Being five is fun!

We went to the circus! Just Mommy and me. I was sitting to her right and we were about halfway up. There were few people around. Maybe it was morning. My leg started to burn. It burned some more and I scratched. I didn't say anything. The burning marched up until it felt like fire from the waist down. She must have thought that I was excited about the show. I was scratching and clawing with both hands, but I didn't want to bother her. She saw what I was doing and stripped off my pants in front of everybody. I was covered with fire ants from the waist down. We went home. She told me that if I was hurting, it was okay to tell her.

On the other hand, being afraid was easy to communicate. Central Florida has frequent and tremendous lightning storms like almost nowhere else in the world. Lightning was exciting, loud, and scary. Mommy warned us to come inside when it was lightning. I was not going to stand outside and get struck—it would flatten me.

We were driving together when I saw lightning hit a telephone pole only a hundred yards away. I must have panicked. It scared me much more than Godzilla breathing fire. If Godzilla came, I could crawl under my bed, but the lightning came from nowhere and could easily kill Godzilla *and* King-Kong. The blinding flash and earsplitting, body rocking **WHAM!** stopped everything. I jumped onto her like a baby chimpanzee fleeing a lion. I would not let go, but she said it was okay. Finally she convinced me to let go.

Daddy was not as believable. My fifth year was exciting, even historical. Our family was in our boat anchored on the Banana River next to Cape Canaveral when I asked Mommy what the rocket blast-off would sound like. She said that it would be very loud, rumbling like thunder, and my father said it would make a "crackling noise."

Billy, waiting for the launch . . .

10
9
8

Everybody holding their breath
6
5
4
3
Smoke's coming out!!!
1
BLAST OFF

Crackling noise? Mommy was right, Daddy was wrong. It felt like Apollo 11 nearly blasted me out of the boat. *Wow!* Amid gigantic clouds of smoke and bright fire, the rocket, which was longer than a football field, punched a hole through the sky and was gone. Nothing left but a smoke trail and a rumbling like thunder, thunder, and more thunder. Lightning *never* thundered *that* long.

"Mommy, Mommy, I want to be an astronaut!"

Apollo 11 was the first mission to land people on the moon. I was afraid the astronauts would meet monsters that were hiding behind the gray rocks. I asked Daddy how many guns the astronauts had. He said astronauts didn't need guns and there were no monsters on the moon.

"There are *so* monsters on the moon. There are monsters on all the planets because I saw it on TV."

"Don't pay attention to what you see on TV." Then he said that the moon was not a planet and tried to explain why, but I didn't understand.

I saw it like this: it's in space, it's round, and you need a rocket to get there—it's a planet. There are monsters on planets. How could he say that the moon wasn't a planet?

Astronauts flew in airplanes and so did we. Daddy was learning to fly, and his friends let me steer the airplane when we were up high. Sometimes we flew over our house and waved the wings at Mommy—I was definitely going to be an astronaut! I could wave at Mommy from the moon!

More rockets flew into space with more astronauts. My mother and father along with some grown-ups were huddled around the TV. They were worried that some astronauts might not come home—ever. They were saying how brave the astronauts were. But I didn't understand. The astronauts were like supermen; everybody loved them. They were brave and talked nice. They were like the preacher. They were going to the moon for America, whatever that was. They were going to the moon for me! Daddy said so.

This rocket was called Apollo 13, and they were about to die. But they were so brave, and the grown-ups loved them because they were brave, and I loved them and I wanted to be brave like them. The grown-ups were sitting around talking about the astronauts and praying. I was praying. They made it back! *It pays to pray and to be brave.*

Daddy said that brave boys don't act like girls. Billy and I were taking a bubble bath with Mr. Bubble in the pink box when he came in and said, "Boys don't take bubble baths. Girls take bubble baths."

I'm not a girl and I like bubble baths. What do you mean, boys don't take bubble baths?

He was kooky and always said stuff like that. No monsters in space. Astronauts don't need guns. The moon is not a planet. Rockets make "crackling" noises when they really rumble so loud that they shake my body. Now he says that boys don't take bubble baths!

Daddy and the other grown-ups were not always right. Except Mommy, but she was more than a grown-up. She knew more than they did. When the phone rang and I ran to answer, people always asked for her. They called to ask questions. I asked what was wrong with Daddy. Why did he get mad and say that boys don't take bubble baths? She said that I could take as many bubble baths as I wanted and she would talk to Daddy. Mommy is *King!*

Another year passed along with my sixth birthday. Birthdays were big events with lots of friends, cake, ice cream, piñatas, clowns and presents. Billy's birthdays were extra special since he was born on Halloween, so all the kids wore costumes to his parties.

That year we moved to another home, and Mommy said that I would get to start first grade. But it seemed like forever until I would get to go. A week felt like a month, and years, well, that was just too much time to even think about.

Like magic, the months finally passed and Mommy took me to the first day of first grade at Elbert Elementary. This was it, the Big Time. I was no longer in kindergarten; I was in School! *School!* I would have *homework* just like Billy!

I was excited and happy, but feeling all alone and afraid when she left. Although it was a lot like kindergarten, the kids were different from the ones I'd known. In kindergarten they had all been white, acted normal, and were clean. At school, some didn't know how to talk or act right, and a few needed to take baths.

On the first day of first grade, my mother said she would be there to pick me up after school. She did, like always—she was always there when she said she would be. But I started to feel a need to do things myself, so I bugged her to let me ride my little red bike to school. Finally, she said okay, but told me to lock it up or it might get stolen. *No-way. People don't steal stuff.* She was starting to say crazy stuff like Daddy. I didn't lock it up and one day someone stole it. *But who? People don't steal.* I got mad like a little twister and searched day after day until I found it only one road away next to the school in somebody's yard. Mommy was right again, like always, so I started locking it up.

In first grade reading class the kids were sitting in a circle taking turns stumbling through the words.

One boy was reading, *"Tha* dog ran fast. . . . "

A little girl waved her hands in front of her as if to say **stop the music!** and said, "It's not *tha* dog it's *theeee* dog."

"Nah uh," he said.

"Uh huh," she said, "and you can't count either."

"Teacher," the boy whined, "Please tell her it's *tha* dog!"

The teacher said, "Tha or thee, it's all tha same. Either way is okay."

The boy smiled. The girl crossed her arms and put her chin on her chest. She was prettier than an angel. I smiled at her and whispered, "It's *thee."*

She smiled back. Almost like Pam. I think I loved her.

I didn't notice until they made it clear, but I was smaller than the other boys. One day after reading, a couple of them pounced on me like jackals. Maybe they didn't like it when I could say the words better and read faster. My mother read with me all the time. *Don't they read with their mothers?*

I didn't understand what was going on. I'd never been in a fight and had no idea what to do because we didn't fight at my house. I learned that not fighting was the way to get beat-up. I had to fight back.

At home I started to have the same problems with the neighborhood kids, who were all bigger and older than I was. In that neighborhood there were no kids my age, and the others had mini-bikes and go-carts—big toys. They liked to pick on me. I didn't understand why they liked to fight all the time—and especially why they liked to fight *me*. I would run home crying and watch cartoons and play or read with my mother while Billy was out. I was, by all accounts, a momma's boy.

Billy sometimes ran into the house with his friends where I was reading or watching cartoons, and they asked why I stayed inside. "Are you a sissy?" they would ask.

Once, one of the bigger kids at Cub Scouts punched me for no good reason. The poor kid was a bully, but not as big or as tough as the kids at school or my neighbors. I beat him up and threw him in the swimming pool. I already knew that there was a difference between being a sissy and not wanting to fight. I was afraid, but I would fight. I was no sissy.

My mother was an adventurous woman who was a scuba diver, and planned to take up skydiving, among other things. She was active in the community in various programs like the March of Dimes and was given to helping people. But when I was in first grade, she started having some sort of health problems of her own, and elected to have some "routine surgery."

Before going to the doctor, she waited for me to get home so she could tell me that she would be back soon. I wanted to go with her. She said that I had to stay home. She asked me for a hug and a kiss but I was upset. I had had a bad day at school with the bullies and now I couldn't go with her to the doctor. I was mad and did not want to hug or kiss her, so she said, "Goodbye. I love you. I'll be back soon."

As she drove away, I felt guilty that I didn't go to her for a kiss.

She waved and smiled as I stood at the front door of the brand-new house that we had recently moved into at 826 Lake Elbert Court N.E. A neighborhood of respectable people. The maid was inside.

A couple of days must have passed and people were sending her "get well" cards. One card said,

Dear Callie -

Just heard about your operation from Betty Blouth yesterday. Hope you get along fine & I'll see you when you get home—Susan and Michael went by my house yesterday. Michael went on but Susan stopped to chat with me & tell me all about her Mom. "She's going to be gone a long, long, long time. Maybe a week."

As ever your neighbor

Dot Johnson

By the postmark, April 15, I wonder if she ever got to read it. It was addressed to Room 418 in the Winter Haven Hospital.

The next night after the card was mailed I stayed over at a friend's house, but his parents took me home unexpectedly in the morning. Something was up, some sort of surprise. When I got home there were lots of people at my house, like a party. *She must be home from the doctor!*

I walked in and the preacher and a strange woman took me upstairs to my bedroom. They sat down beside me on my bed; the woman was on my left and the preacher was on my right. The woman was holding me, which I thought was weird.

The preacher told me that my mother got sick and had passed away.

"What is passed-away?"

He said she'd died.

I didn't believe him.

"You're joking! Where is she hiding?"

I jumped up from my bed to check the closet. She wasn't there. *I know this game!* I checked everywhere and everywhere, under the bed, in the other rooms, the bathrooms, everywhere.

Finally convinced, I ran off, unwilling to cry in front of the others. I found a private spot and almost died with sorrow. I was in the garage. I could not breathe.

I felt like I was standing alone in the world forever.

I knew that I would never ever see her again and I loved her so much. I wanted to go with her. I never gave her a last kiss and hug. I felt so guilty and horrible. She had just wanted to give me a hug and I'd said *no*. I had been mad at the bullies but had taken it out on her. I knew that she could not come back and I wanted to die and be with her. I remember this vividly. And then nothing.

I am told that there was a search and that my Aunt Shirley finally found me alone after I'd disappeared. I remember none of that.

I remember nothing more until I saw her in her casket at the church where I spent my Sundays. She looked asleep. I could only see her for a few seconds and then they took me away. I was numb.

The next thing I remember was that my father made me go to school. I could not go to the funeral where she was buried under an oak tree.

We moved out of that house and to a different part of town because my father said that he didn't want to live there anymore, but I don't remember moving or any of that. I only remember we ended up in a new house a few miles away.

I have many vivid memories up to the age of seven, and most of those were with my mother. Yet I don't remember anything for a long time after she left. I don't know how long it lasted. There is a big blank-spot.

My first life ended with hers.

I was alone.

Through the years I have been told that my mother's funeral was unparalleled in the town. Though she was only twenty-eight years old, she was highly respected for her helpfulness and generosity. The doctor who performed the surgery was the same doctor who delivered Billy. Later, my father explained that the doctor had been in debt, so he took on a large caseload to make money. After the operation on my mother, he prescribed drugs, possibly an overdose of two drugs, which might have been what caused her to slip into a coma.

The doctors put her on a life-support system. The next morning they removed the life-support and she passed away. Though I have investigated further, I still don't know why she died. I will probably never know. It is possible that the doctor was not at fault.

I do know there are a million smiles we never shared, and that I miss her still, every day. I know she never saw what happened to me, and would have prevented it at any cost if she had. I know that she would have been proud of me, of how hard I tried, of how I kept the faith. If I could tell her only one thing, it would be that those seven years she gave to me were the most important, and the best of my life. She was a great mother. She never really died. A mother lives on in her children.

as the years unfolded . . .

Dad had three kids to raise; Susan was four, I seven, Billy was eight. At first he hired maids and nannies but nobody can replace a mother. For about a year after our mother passed away, we had a caretaker we called "Nana." During the writing of this book my sister and brother pointed out that I never mentioned Nana. And Nana herself, now living in a Jacksonville nursing home, told Billy that she was upset that I was "the only one in her family that forgot about her." But it wasn't that I forgot. I simply do not remember that period. I only vaguely remember Nana—that she was a good woman, that she was good to me. But my recollections of that blank period would not be enough to fill the rest of this page.

Billy was much larger than I was, and took out his frustrations on me. Fighting became part of my normal day. I lived in constant awareness that I might have to defend myself with little notice. Dad thought that boys should not cry and that they should always fend for themselves. He said that if I ever started a fight I would get a whipping, and if I got into a fight that I should finish it—or I would get a whipping. That's what his father had said to him, and now the law was laid down to me. I was trapped. The options were simple. Either I could take a beating by a bully then another by my dad, or I could win. That was straightforward enough.

The more I defended myself against the bullies at school and from my brother, the better I learned how to fight. It was a new world of sink or swim. There was nobody to run to. No leg to hold when I was afraid. There was only my pillow to cry into. And I did. All the time.

Dad came from the old school. Spare the rod, spoil the child. Not that he went to church, or that the saying is even in the Bible. Many Americans believe that there is nothing wrong with flogging their children—though some cultures find it abhorrent. Some of us think that it is a divine *right*—a necessity—like polio vaccinations or vitamins and minerals. Some think that parents who don't occasionally beat their children are simply creating problems for the world.

Beating the smallest and most impressionable people in society is more of a tradition than a necessity. Even the teachers at school would grab our hands and wrench our fingers back, smacking our palms with rulers. I certainly didn't need it, but I got my traditional dose anyway. Dad gave terrible belt whippings and I was afraid of those more than anything else—*"Go pick out a belt"* he would yell. Now, I'm not sure what adults *think* they are teaching children when they use violence to correct them, but I know that they are teaching that violence is an acceptable way to solve even simple problems.

Dad didn't beat us arbitrarily. He made sure there was probable cause. Justice, whatever that is, is central to the human species. But his punitive whippings only made me fear his wrath. On the other hand, I defend my father's actions in that he only punished me one time when I was completely undeserving. It was a case of mistaken identity, but when he hit me, I kicked him as hard as I could in the shin. Children's sense of justice is strong. (But kicking him was a bad mistake. I got more of the belt.)

My life was not a total shambles; there were friends at school. I got along with just about everyone, but had a special affinity for the "pocket-protector" crowd and became friends with a kid named Louis, who seemed like a genius in the sense of brain-power. We stayed over at each other's houses, and he taught me how to tell military time. One morning, as we were walking down the sidewalk at school I said the "military time" and Louis said, *"Shh!* It's a secret!"

We talked about science. He liked science fiction and science fact. I only liked fact. My world was wild enough without the addition of fiction. Most of my friends then were "junior geeks," just like me.

Chess is a pocket-protector-type game, and Billy taught me how to play. Soon, I could beat him and realized I could watch his eyes and see where he was thinking of moving, or what he thought about my moves. I watched his body and face and knew whether he was feeling good or bad about what was happening. Sometimes I let him win so he would feel better, or I sacrificed pieces to make the games harder on me. Eventually the games got boring, so I told him about the trick. After that we had to shade our eyes with our hands to play. Stealth chess. It was inconvenient, but the games became harder so it was more fun.

I loved dogs and found some free puppies in a cage at the locally famous Doty's Feed Store. Doty's perpetually kept a cage of giveaway puppies out front, and I pedaled my bike miles to play with them. But this litter was terribly infested with fleas and I felt sick to see them suffering. The poor puppies had no mother and I understood how they felt. Who would take mangy little puppies like that? They were simply abandoned to the world. If I brought all of them home one by one, they all would have to go back, so I decided to try to save one.

I clapped my hands and one in particular seemed alert and attentive and happy to see me. So, puppy under arm, I biked home and soon she was in the bathtub. The red-tinged water was so full of the bloodsucking fleas that it looked like a peppershaker had been emptied on top. Having mostly rid her of her pestilence, I named the yapping fur-ball "Snoopy." I told every-one that I got her because she was so smart, but I really took her because she grabbed my heart. But I was not always as lucky as Snoopy was.

WELCOME TO THE JUNGLE

AFTER A SHORT courtship, Dad married a woman named Della. Maybe he married her out of loneliness, I don't know. I do know that if you are hungry enough, you will roast a vulture and call it turkey.

Della learned French in school and it sounded really neat. I asked her to teach me and got excited when she agreed. I wondered, *What would it be like to speak in a foreign language? What would it feel like to think in a foreign language?* Then it occurred that my friends only spoke English, so, I thought, *who cares?*

She brought two kids to the family: Rose and Joseph. Rose was a nice girl about Susan's age and Joseph was about three. They were a result of Della's first marriage, and it soon became apparent that little Joseph was "baggage" for Della.

After some time passed, Della changed temperament and was not so nice. A notable revelation occurred in the kitchen. As I resealed a loaf of bread, twisting the twister-thing, I wondered if the extra air in the bag would make the bread stale faster. So I asked.

Della said, "That's ridiculous," and tore into me for all my "stupid" questions.

Dad defended me and said it was a good question. He admitted that he didn't know the answer, but guessed that it would stale faster. Unfortunately, the question lit the fuse to a keg of mental gunpowder. Like many of their exchanges, the tiny spark sputtered down the fuse until it got to the *Bang!*

Della called arguments "pissing contests," and it took me some time to figure out what she meant by that. But when I did figure it out, I knew that if she were a boy, she could shoot pretty far. Far enough to reach violence.

She treated Rose like a little goddess and Joseph like a demon, and did things to him that should have landed her in prison. Joseph had problems with potty training, so she rubbed his feces all over his face. She beat him mercilessly while tears streamed down his excrement-smeared cheeks. She would forcefully seat him on his potty and scream horrible things down at him. He must have felt worthless.

Joseph cried, *"Mommy, please. Please."*

There was no rescue for little Joseph. No divine intervention. No cops breaking down the door to take her away from him so that a decent woman could take over and show him that he was allowed to live, that it was okay to be an imperfect child, that he was still worth loving.

It must have been the cruelest of tortures to have his own feces smeared across his face by the most powerful being on Earth, his own mother; proof of his unworthiness to join the rest of the family. She kept him in daycare because she did not like to have him around, I suppose, and daycare does not teach or love a child like a good mother. When Joseph was at home, his potty was often his "babysitter." He would sit alone sobbing in the bathroom and nobody was allowed to talk to him. He was denied the basic dignity of controlling his own bowel movements. Joseph was forced to defecate on command in a bucket, and when he did not perform, the magical door jerked open and he was beaten. Sometimes Della would blow in like an angry tornado and jerk him up by his arm, his skinny naked body dangling on tiptoes, screaming like he was being killed. This would go on for hours.

There were people around who could help, but they simply turned away. I was too afraid to help. What could I do?

With a military POW there is always a chance of escape or release. There is often training to help one to survive. There is the knowledge that the treatment is cruel and "not normal" that can provide at least a tiny finger-hold on sanity.

Prison and torture is all the abused children know. That is their world. It's happening all around us now. Those children will grow up and they will live around us. They already do.

The turmoil was difficult for Susan, Rose, Billy and me, not to mention little Joseph. Della wanted me to call her 'mom' or 'mommy' or something. *No way,* I thought. One day she threw out the china set that belonged to our mother, perhaps trying to erase any memory of her. Luckily, Billy had the presence of mind to call our grandmother who came over and salvaged from the garbage what wasn't broken. (Today it's mine.)

I would rather go live in a hole with an alligator than call Della my mother. My mother was a great woman. She loved kids and she loved me.

I was respectful, but was not Della's son, and she was not getting into my heart. It was odd, because Della actually seemed to like me and she was not always mean. We talked a lot. She told me that I was a good kid, usually. I did not shun her for not being my mother, but because she was a terrible monster to Joseph.

After some time she grew comfortable in her new home. Then she began to go after Susan and me. Not so hurtfully at first, "just" some verbal abuse. Maybe she was testing the waters to see what she could get away with. Dad put an end to that immediately, so she shifted her attack to him. He prevented anyone from attacking us physically or verbally. He protected us. But Della seemed to need an audience of children to prove how big she was, and she was not one to lose a pissing contest.

Adults are not supposed to argue in front of children; even we kids knew that. Normally, Dad would try not to argue in front of us by trying to defuse situations or taking them somewhere else, but Della would not allow it. She anchored herself, usually wherever we were, and went crazy with anger, throwing her hands up in the air, a mean scowl on her face, screaming about things that even we could see were not worth argument. When we tried to leave, she often yelled at us to stay where we were. She wanted everyone to see her win.

Dad was trapped, but as an active participant. After it started, *he* wanted everyone to see *him* win. If the kids were to argue and fight like that in front of the adults, it would have been grounds for a good belt whipping followed by a lecture.

There was no love in that relationship, no sharing or trust or respect. It was an "us and them" place, and I saw violence nearly every day, either directed at me from bullies, or from Della to little Joseph. Sadly, the worst of this violence was caused not by children, but adults who should have had the maturity to work their way through the inevitable tensions. Yet it was not all Della's fault—Dad had married her.

During one argument that turned violent, a wild look seized her face. It was a crazy look that always sent me running for cover, or left me watching in dismay, the way people watch a house fire. That time, when the wildness seized her, she was holding an ink pen. She ripped off the top and ran at my father.

She hacked down with the pen into his neck. Dad, caught unprepared, panicked; his ineffectual defense resembled the flailing of a frantic octopus. As usual, it happened very fast, so my perception of the action was foggy. It seems that she ended up on the floor screaming as if she were burning alive and her only hope was to embrace someone to burn with her.

Blood. She hacked straight for his artery. I believe that she tried to kill him. I ran to the neighbors, who were good friends during the daylight, but they would not get involved. After all, Dad was a businessman in the community. So one of us kids called the police.

Police. Police again, and again. Why didn't they stop it? I thought the police were supermen. Dad had taught us that police and firemen were there to protect us, but they never stopped it. *Somebody—just stop it—**Please.***

The police walked around inside the house and talked into their radios and their radios talked back in strange codes. They came in pairs, and when they left, the storm raged again. The kids were warned not to call the police, but the neighbors heard it all. The neighbors were gutless, and Della and my dad seemed to have lost all sense of dignity. It was very embarrassing to face the gutless neighbors in the daylight, knowing that they knew all about my shameless family.

I had known Della for maybe a year when I realized she wore a wig. I walked in the house and she had her curly brown hair in her hand! On her head she had straight blonde hair. She changed colors like the lizards that were everywhere in the grass and trees around the house. Lizard, alien woman. Talks nice and sweet, but really is cold and mean.

By the time I was nine, I had run away several times, but had returned when I got hungry. Nobody noticed and I never told them. I felt terribly alone in a crowd of people who were doing crazy, mean things. I didn't *want* to run away. But the bullies and the fighting and the cruelty blasted into my daily life with the regularity of clockwork, or like Central Florida's daily summer thunderstorms.

I was not supposed to say how I felt because I was supposed to be a "little man." But I was not a little man—I was a little boy—alone, without his mother, helpless among the hyenas. I seemed passive and that invited more problems, because kids thought I was weak. Actually, I only *appeared* passive because I would not fight over many of the things that other people, including adults, thought worthy of dispute. I was often too slow to anger. As the years unfolded, I learned to show anger sometimes, even when I didn't feel it. They say some people keep anger bottled up and then explode. I never have, and I don't feel any explosion building.

As a child I felt overwhelmed. Always problems, never peace. Always fighting and arguing over stupid things. I hated to see adults arguing and bickering and being so childish. I was confused and did not know what was happening and felt like no one loved me. I missed my mother so much that it physically hurt and I wanted to be with her. I would go off into the woods alone and cry until there were no more tears. I wanted life to be the way it was when she was alive. But there was no way to bring her back, though I thought a lot about it.

I was about nine when I was walking in a field of scraggly bushes and knee-high grasses. Suddenly there was a sharp pain in my ankle. I jumped— it burned badly. I was wearing shorts and looked down and saw the two fang marks. A rattlesnake had bitten me. I looked for the snake but couldn't find it. My brother loved to catch snakes and I had been bitten several times while helping him, but never by a poisonous snake. I didn't want to go to Della or my father about the bite. It hurt. I missed my mother. I felt it was time to die.

I waited for the poison to kill me. I was so confused and hated every day on Earth; home was hell. I wanted to get sick and die. I waited, and waited.

Nothing happened. Maybe it was only wasps that had stung twice.

I went home to the kitchen. I was not wearing a shirt. I knew where my heart was. I found the right knife, skinny and long, put it under my sternum and pointed up. I pressed the blade against my skin until it was ready to break through. I knew that I could do it. Suicide. I could be with my mother.

What would my grandparents think? *To quit or to fight?* What if there is no Heaven? What if I go to Hell? I pulled the knife against my hot skin, deciding whether to jerk the blade into my heart. Dad always said never to be a quitter. A quitter is far worse than one who fights and loses.

47

I screamed cuss words as I threw down the knife and ran out the door.

I knew that I was good and that I was different from them. If I were going to die, it would be fighting. I missed my mother, but I had to let her go. It was only me and it was up to me.

On that day I became independent. I realized who I was, and that I would never quit. I knew that no matter what happened around me that was bad, it didn't mean that I was part of it. My puppy, Snoopy, was a mutt but a fighter, too. We were a team. The others could do whatever they wanted, but they could not drag us down with them.

In retrospect, I see that I had to look over the edge just to see me. I grew much stronger, realizing that if life didn't get any better, I simply would have to make it better myself. My life was up to me. I consider that realization to have been one of the best things that ever happened to me, though I never told a soul about it.

That night Dad came home and found me reading out in the rain under a piece of plastic. There was lightning all around, with blinding flashes and booms shaking the house. He screamed at me to come inside. *"Have you lost your mind! You could get killed sitting out there. Get inside, Sport!"*

I was reading about how a tribe of primitive jungle-people lived a long time and how some scientists guessed that the charged air caused by frequent rains may have caused it. I was going to live long like the natives, and was going to have fun.

I was going to be a doctor, a scientist, and an astronaut.

PEOPLE IN FIBERGLASS HOUSES

AFTER OUR MOTHER died, Dad quit his banking job and bought a small factory that manufactured products from fiberglass, which was great for me—lots of chemicals to mix. Billy and I labored at the factory over the summer cleaning and mowing. It was an uncomfortable place to work. The fiberglass made me itch like a dog with vicious fleas.

Dad said the best way to stop the itch was to take a cold shower, but a hot bath would cause my pores to open and the fiberglass would slip inside and make it worse. I hated the cold showers, but itching was worse, so I did what I was told. Every day it was itch, itch, itch, then cold shower.

Dad had a mildly innovative spirit, but he knew that kids often come up with the best ideas. He came home and asked for any ideas on new products that could be made out of fiberglass. *Hmm . . .* I thought and thought. A man who wanted peace should never set a boy like me on such a quest. I took it to heart, like I was chosen for a mission from God. By the time I was finished I imagined an entire world made of fiberglass.

I liked to go to the factory, those times when I didn't get itchy. There were untold treasures of mischief to get into, and a river of novelties to quench my thirst for knowledge and adventure. I learned that if you pulled the pin on a fire extinguisher and squeezed the trigger, the white stuff went everywhere and Dad got mad, though he laughed it off and told me never to do it again unless there was a real fire.

I liked to go to the plant with Dad. One night, when I volunteered to go with him, I discovered the fire. As we approached I asked, "Dad, why is there smoke coming from the roof?"

He stepped on the pedal and screeched into a nearby gas station and called the fire department. Soon we heard the screams of fire trucks in the distance. They were fast. I had seen plenty of fire trucks but had never stood at their convergence. They rumbled out of the darkness, red lights spinning, earsplitting sirens blaring so loud that I stuck my fingers in my ears and squinted.

Maybe it was every young fireman's dream. A burning factory with nobody inside, but with nearby houses to be saved! Just brave firemen battling one of mankind's greatest friends/enemies, with the other great friend/enemy, water.

People in uniforms were running around like fire ants, and the firemen and police began evacuating nearby residents because of the explosive, poisonous nature of the chemicals inside. *My chemicals!*

Clouds of smoke billowed into the darkness and mingled with the nighttime clouds, creating a noxious stew. Employees began driving up. They parked their cars just off the road in the grass, and walked around in the darkness watching the inferno. They clumped into little groups and nervously talked about adult things like jobs, kids, money, and house payments.

I recognized some of the workers. They spoke with heavy Southern accents and their tension was as thick as the smoke rising away into the darkness. The fire lit up the surrounding area, turning night into day. The heat and excitement were tremendous.

The firemen battled the flames well into the night, but the monster was insatiable and kept eating and eating. It roared and crackled as it ate further through the place. It was like a blast furnace, and got so hot that later I found a melted fire extinguisher in the rubble.

A wife of one of the workers punctuated the tension as she sobbed uncontrollably in the darkness against the backdrop of fire, noise, smoke, and firemen. I searched for my dad and found him talking to some firemen, and told him about the lady. He tried to console her saying he would rebuild the business. *See! It's not so bad,* I thought.

The factory did not burn all the way to the ground. The firemen stopped the fire's assault, but the damage was severe. Dad set about rebuilding, but in the meantime the customer-base eroded, and that was that. The business failed, and we were on the road to poverty.

Dad tried to recover and raise us kids, but he didn't do well at either. He was on a personal downward spiral and we were along for the ride.

Life went from fresh milk to powdered milk.

But at least Della moved away.

THE LIGHTNING BOLT THAT NEVER STRUCK

GRANNY AND GRANDDAD would come to pick us up for church while Dad stayed home. When I was about ten, in Sunday School class, the subject of rabies popped up. I told the teacher that the scientific name for rabies was hydrophobia. She "corrected" me by dissecting the word and said, "*Hydro* means water and *phobia* means fear, so the word means fear of water."

I knew that.

"Rabies makes it very painful to drink," I explained, only trying to justify myself. But the teacher was not receptive and became defensive. It was one-way communication. If a teacher asked a kid a question there was only one answer: the teacher's answer.

It was like training parrots. Dad had a tape recorder that was installed inside a fake parrot. The contraption was called "Pete the Parrot." Pete was rainbow-colored like a real parrot and large, about the size of a small eagle, and when it talked its eyes lit up. Its beak opened and closed like it was talking while its wings flapped half-heartedly. The dogs hated it and wanted to kill it.

Pete was decidedly the easiest bird in the world to teach. But it had no mind of its own and only repeated what you told it, precisely the way you told it. In Sunday school, some of the other kids seemed to be like Pete the Parrot. I felt like I was sitting among parrots.

The teacher went out of her way to stifle and embarrass me—to make me a parrot. She was not there to teach, but to dominate and enforce her beliefs on our malleable minds. *Click* . . . I developed an ability to tune out closed minds and bad influences. I would just "click" them out. I watched the parrot-people and tried to figure out what they were thinking—and not thinking. On the other hand, non-parrot-people had open minds and got my complete and utter attention because I wanted to know what they thought, too.

For some reason, the teacher continued to push the rabies issue, and I became more defensive. I quickly passed through embarrassment and became angry. *Hydrophobia means rabies no matter what the teacher thinks and no matter how much the parrot-people believe her.*

The hydrophobia incident was important. I learned that people in power positions should not beat down their underlings. And that when I knew I was right, it was irrelevant if the class thought something else. I chose my own path.

If her mind was so closed on one subject, it likely was closed on others, and how was I to know which ones? Therefore, the safest thing for me to do was to be skeptical about whatever she said because her mind obviously was not open to all sides. One should not underestimate children; most are innately curious and have a refreshing willingness to learn, until that willingness is suffocated by social forms. They lack only experience (the lack of which is sometimes a good thing).

My appetite for learning was unquenchable and I was constantly thinking, wondering and asking. *Do others think like me? Do we see the same colors? Are the colors green and blue the same for other people? Maybe what looks green for me seems red to someone else?* I knew that there had to be some difference; my right eye sees hues differently than my left. Since colors looked different through each eye, I wondered if my eyes were different, or if my mind perceived the message from each eye differently. Was the message different, or only the interpretation? These are the kind of questions I asked. Constantly. Dad called me, "My little Philosopher."

In Sunday School they taught about all the bad things that would happen if we did not behave. Eventually, my questions must have driven the poor Sunday School teachers nuts. I was not asking to be a troublemaker who did not believe what they were teaching, but because kids naturally ask, ask and ask. Often my questions were met with a rebuke. So, *Click.* It was around that time that I changed my mind about becoming a preacher, which somehow had made it to the list of "Things to Become." Why be around Sunday School teachers who won't answer your questions without getting mad? I was going to be a doctor, a scientist, and, of course, an astronaut.

I wanted to see my mother. The teachers said that we would meet again in Heaven, and that she was waiting for me. Others said that there were no such things as Heaven and Hell.

I decided to find out.

On Sunday mornings, Granny gave me a quarter for the collection. I knew that God knew what I was thinking. So, around came the offering-plate and the teacher watched the children make their obligatory "offering." I was about to take the biggest chance of my life—I have never risked more than on that Sunday morning. If I were wrong, a bolt of lightning would blow me to pieces. *Would I go to Heaven, or Hell?*

Whatever the case, I would be dead just the same, if that's what God wanted. The worst consequences were a bolt of lightning, then Hell. Lightning was scary; Hell was worse. As the offering-plate came around, I held my breath and squinted (just in case) and refused to tithe. The teacher became irate and tried to embarrass me again and force me to give up my quarter. "I'll tell your grandfather," she threatened.

I could explain it to Granddad and he would listen without getting mad. Coercion never worked with me and I had no respect for hollow threats, even at that age. I'd faced death several times, including the times when I'd fallen out of the car and when I almost hanged myself. A Sunday School teacher just didn't seem scary. So I held my ground and was waiting for God's lightning to blow me out of my seat.

Nothing happened.

I knew it! *(Whew!)*

The teacher was angry and confused about why I was so happy. She probably thought I was mocking her, but the joke was between God and me, and God was letting me smile and be excited.

From a logical point of view, I thought I had narrowed things down. Based on what I had been taught, I figured I proved that either there was no God—and I did not like that because I wanted him to exist—or that he existed and was good. At the very least, he didn't kill me over my quarter.

I hoped that he existed because if there was no God, then there was no Heaven. No Heaven meant I would never see my mother again. I wanted to believe that God exists and is good, and that my mother was watching over me from Heaven.

At home I said my prayers every night: *"for Thine is the kingdom and the power and the glory. . . ."* I had a personal connection with God, though it felt like I lived in Hell. But the TV showed kids who were starving or had bombs dropping on their houses, so I figured that I was lucky. It's all relative.

My life had made some twists and turns, but I kept my sense of humor. Of hundreds of childhood pictures, it is difficult to find one where I am not smiling, even so far back that I was bare-bottomed and probably three months old—in my core there was happiness. Things would get better. The world was getting rougher and rougher, but because of my positive outlook—tomorrow will be better—I adapted to each new situation and learned to meet challenges and be an active participant in my life, not a leaf carried by the wind. I couldn't change the wind, but I could learn to fly. I refused to be a hapless leaf when I could be an eagle.

Other neighborhood kids thought they had it rough because their mothers made them come home at a certain time for supper. Some kids even talked back to their mothers. I thought, *If they only knew how lucky they are.*

The only thing that matched my bad luck was all my good fortune. When I was about eleven, I won a trip to the Bahamas on a radio contest and gave it to my grandparents because they had never left the country. It was great fun listening to them talk about their trip, eating big conchs and strange stuff—*octopus!* I was not so interested in hearing about the Bahamas; I didn't care about foreign places, but because it made them so happy, it made me happy to hear about it.

I was most fortunate that Ethel and Phillip Eason were my grandparents.

We kids never told them how tough it was at home. All they saw from me were smiles. And when Granddad talked about God, I listened. He was not a parrot tamer.

Grandparents are very important people.

LIFE IN ANOTHER WORLD

THERE WAS A fun side to life, and there were dinosaurs! Sometimes Dad took us out to the phosphate mines near Mulberry in Central Florida. There were big mounds of dirt created by the gigantic machines that dug up the earth twenty-four hours a day, every day. The machines reminded me of rockets. They looked like launch pads that did work. Dad said that there were fossils in the mounds, and true enough, I found lots of fossilized bone fragments and sharks' teeth.

My interest in dinosaurs grew as big as a T-rex, but my favorite dinosaur was the Brontosaurus. I went to the Winter Haven public library and collected about a dozen dinosaur books. The librarian actually allowed me to check them all out, but they were so heavy that I couldn't haul them all at once.

Dinosaurs were fascinating. I knew them by heart: what they allegedly ate, how much they supposedly weighed, and where they might have lived. Where they lived seemed rather obvious at first, because that's where they died, but then the scientists threw me another curve by saying that the continents had drifted. Of course, you could look at a globe and see how some of the pieces must have fit together. Some things seemed obvious.

In church they would say that evolution never happened, that the scientists were atheists, and that dinosaurs never existed. Sometimes they would present the evidence of a friendly scientist or doctor who supported their views. This was all so weird to me, because they were adults and had cars and kids and stuff. How could they just overlook all those mountains of evidence? Look at the globe! Those pieces really do fit.

They could never convince a kid like me by overlooking all those signs, but I kept quiet because I didn't want to get stoned or something. I liked most of the people at church, but I simply disagreed. I almost put one of my fossils in the offering-plate, but I was too chicken; besides, I didn't want them to think that I was making fun, and I didn't want to lose my fossil.

But it seemed like God came to my rescue time after time. I was staying over at Louis' house when his sister suggested we play strip poker, or maybe it was strip Go-fish.

"What! You mean every time you lose you have to take something off? No way. Not Me."

After much persistence and hounding they corralled me into playing this most risky of games. Soon I was losing badly. Maybe Louis' sister was a genius like him.

Judging by observation, I suspected that girls were smarter anyway, and she was proving it by beating the pants off me. Finally, predictably, came the moment of truth. I was down to my underwear, sweating bullets, and facing all these moral dilemmas. Though I was pushed, I had of my own free will entered this game. I had to fulfill my end. They were waiting and she was smiling and telling me to do it. I was gathering my courage, which was in short supply, when their mother walked in and caught us with a deck of cards and a pile of clothes.

Thank you God. I would have done it. (I think.)

I had lots of friends and we busied ourselves with lots of mischief. My best pal during childhood was Matt Laird. We met in a fistfight after his younger brother, who was my size, tried to beat me up. I whipped both of them in my normal brawling fashion. They were chumps compared to Billy. Matt thought he was tough and said he knew someone who was away in Vietnam. I knew about the war because it was on the news and people were getting hurt. As far as I knew, nobody in my family had been in the military so I didn't think much about it. All that Army stuff sounded crazy, but Dad said good things about the military people. He liked them, and really hated the hippies for some reason. The hippies didn't seem so bad to me, but they did wear funny clothes, and most of them needed a bath and a haircut. But this was a military neighborhood. Matt taught me about the Army and we did "missions" around the neighborhood.

Mission

We found a dog in the neighborhood that didn't get enough to eat and its ribs were showing. It was hostage to a rich man who liked to hunt. My dad said that the man was a millionaire. Millionaires are mysterious people, and this one mysteriously didn't take care of his dog. Even *hippies* fed their dogs.

He kept the hound in a small cage and it constantly wore a shock-collar that had two little prongs that stuck into its throat. We figured that when the poor dog barked . . . *Zap!* like when I touched a battery to my tongue.

Well, that just wouldn't do. Some of our best friends were dogs. Over popsicles (Matt liked cherry, I liked orange), we planned the mission.

We slipped over the brick wall and made our way to the cage beside the house. (This was pretty risky; people in the house could see us through the windows.) I went into the pen and took the radio collar, while Matt dropped off its food resupply. We took the expensive collar to a nearby house that was under construction. One of the cinder block walls was not finished, so we dropped the collar inside the wall. It's still there, now part of the house.

Mission complete—no casualties.

We played all kinds of pranks. Billy put one of his snakes in a neighbor's mailbox. The lady walked out to check the mail while we played football nearby. She opened the box, reached in, and **screamed,** so loud that it seemed her hair would blow out.

No more snakes in the mailbox.

I asked Dad about pranks and wanted to know what he did when he was a kid. Maybe he had some good ideas. Dad said that he and some friends stood on the side of the road and acted like they saw something exciting up in the sky and they jumped and pointed excitedly. Cars would stop and people would get out to see what was going on. Of course, nothing was going on and the boys would simply run away laughing. Sounded like a lot of fun.

Matt and I picked a fast and dangerous road to try it on. It worked great! So great that we were lucky that nobody got hurt.

Then we got a better idea. We took a white sheet and spread some medicine on it: a red liquid antiseptic. It looked like blood and thanks to all the scrapes and scratches I came home with, the stinging stuff and I were well acquainted, if not old friends. Matt and I went to the same road and I would lie down on its side with the sheet over me like I had been hit by a speeding car. I was just a limp figure under a red stained sheet. Matt would wave crazy-like, and the first car would screech to a stop. Matt would yell *"LET'S GO!"* But he never needed to yell because I could hear the sudden braking, sometimes followed by screeching and skidding. It was a hearty, fulfilling sound. We ran through the orange trees, from which we sometimes picked oranges to throw at cars, to a hiding place.

In order for any angry drivers to find us, they had to drive a half-mile around a loop to get to the entrance of our private neighborhood. But by the time they drove around we were in our tree fort hunkered down to watch them looking for us. Peeking out the window from the tree was the other half of the fun. The angrier the driver, the more fun it was. As an adult I see how nasty it was to take advantage of people's good will, but as a kid, it didn't cross my mind—because *it was just a joke, man!*

The tree fort was in a wooded area next to the home of the wealthiest family in the neighborhood, who, in retrospect, must have been "worth" many millions of dollars. The kids in the neighborhood were the children of well-off people, mostly business people, doctors, pharmacists, the normal amalgam of the upper-middle class. These kids had access to a wide range of resources and we built a nice tree fort, complete with carpet. That's where we kept the dirty books that the boys had taken from their fathers. Wow. I had a crush on one of my teachers and now I knew why.

Didn't their fathers have wives? Why did they have these books? Did their wives look at the magazines, too? No, this stuff is secret, only men know about these books, I thought.

Back at home one afternoon, the mail arrived when the next-door mother and father were both out in the yard. I was close by, climbing high in a tree, and could see everything. The woman went to the box and was sorting through a pile of mail when she said: "Honey, your *Playboy* is here."

My God! I nearly fell out of the tree.

Playboy magazines come though the mail and women know about it— mothers know about it! How do they get women to take off all their clothes? What if their kids see them? What will happen then? What if their grandkids see them some day? Nobody seemed to know.

Cigarettes also made it to the tree fort. Some of the kids from a poorer neighborhood were already learning to smoke. They thought it was cool. I knew, somehow, that they were just following the leader, like parrots. They would jump off a cliff if it were fashionable. That's what my Granny said, and I believed her.

Dad smoked Benson and Hedges. I lectured him on "secondhand" smoke, and would tell him that he was hurting me, though this was possibly before the first secondhand smoke experiment was done. I was a window opener and this was an often argued issue. Dad and his smoking friends took the opposite position, so we debated. Dad was a stubborn arguer, and sometimes when I was cornering him he would pull the "There's my little philosopher" line on me.

The smokers usually said that I was wrong, but I knew that they knew I was right. If they admitted to everyone, including themselves, that their smoke was hurting others, they would have had to puff outside or stop, or continue being social misfits who care nothing about other people.

I told them that they were denying the facts so that they didn't have to face them. They just said that I was wrong and argued that there was no proof that it hurt other people. They talked about their "rights," which any idiot could see were trampling on other people's rights.

I was rather direct. Once I said something like, "Only a kookoo-bird would think that the smoke hurt the person who lit the cigarette but nobody else. How is the smoke supposed to know who to hurt?"

That turned the adult heads. Time to shut up. Some adults said that I should be a lawyer. No way was I going to be a lawyer; I heard that they steal and cheat everyone and nobody liked them; that's what the grown-ups said. Besides, I thought, the laws are not "real"; they are just made up and always changing. I was going to be a doctor, a scientist, an astronaut.

Probably should have studied law.

IRAN

THE YEARS PASSED by and I acquired what amounted to a small physics library, but my education was all home grown. I never took a physics class in school and my home life was so abysmal that I didn't care about grades.

I liked school because of my friends, but the classes were intensely boring. On October 19, 1979, during my sophomore year, I jumped at the opportunity to skip a few classes by agreeing to take the ASVAB (Armed Services Vocational Aptitude Battery), a written psychometric test administered to people prior to their entering military service. My plans did not include the military, though I had the common childhood fantasy of being an "Army Man."

Two weeks later—04 November 1979—I was sitting in front of the TV screen when the news flashed that Americans had been taken hostage at the U.S. Embassy in Teheran, Iran. Scary. Unknown to me at the time, I was watching my own history, or rather my future, unfold.

Hours later at Fort Bragg, North Carolina

Delta Force is our country's premier counterterrorism unit. It consists of a small group of soldiers meticulously selected, like racehorses, then rigorously trained in a manner similar to that of professional athletes. They were alerted.

Soon, intelligence sources realized that some hostages were not being held in the Embassy but in a different building. An undercover section of the 10th Special Forces Group in West Germany, whose missions also included counterterrorism, was to hit the second building. A similar building suitable for the practicing of the rescue mission was found in West Germany. For security reasons, so as not to attract attention, the Special Forces team remained in Germany to rehearse their assault at night, while Delta rehearsed in the United States.

In April of 1980, four spies infiltrated Teheran to gather intelligence before the rescue. The first was a young Air Force sergeant with no commando or espionage experience but who spoke the native language of Iran, Farsi. He was just a sergeant like any other when because of his language capability, he was asked to infiltrate a hostile foreign nation along with three "Green Berets." He must have felt like he was in the Twilight Zone. He was a brave man, but nobody knew it when he answered the call. The other three spies were ex-Special Forces soldiers; two spoke German—not much help in Iran.

Seizing an Embassy is an act of war. The Iranians had our people. Our men were entering a hostile country as spies, and if they were captured, they could expect to be tortured and possibly executed. The Air Force sergeant had to hope that his new friends knew their business.

On April 24, 1980, as the sun retreated, the first MC-130 Combat Talon airplane rumbled away from a staging point toward Iran. Soon the four-engine, propeller-driven aircraft was flying low to the earth, making hard turns, frequently changing altitude and course to hug the terrain, avoiding enemy fire-control radar.

This was Operation Eagle Claw. Army Rangers would provide security while Delta Force and Special Forces would conduct the actual assault. Also, there were Air Force, Marines, and Navy service members taking care of critical support aspects of the operation.

An unexpected sandstorm caused problems while the rescue force was deep in the "desolate" Iranian desert at a location code-named "Desert One," staging for the next phase of the mission. Unfortunately for some unlucky Iranians, the spot turned out to be not-so-desolate, and the Rangers did their jobs.

Among other aircraft, the rescue force started with eight helicopters—they needed six to continue the mission. Unexpected mechanical failures reduced them to five helicopters and the mission was aborted at Desert One.

While the rescue force prepared to return to base and the aircraft carrier *Nimitz*, the pilots of the fixed-wing aircraft on the ground at Desert One started gunning their engines for departure. The propellers were kicking up too much dust and it was too gusty. A large helicopter lifted-off and . . . careened into an aircraft on the ground filled with rescue team members.

The flames and exploding ammunition shattered the hopes of a rescue. The four spies in Teheran were to have departed with the rescue team after the assault. Dangerous business. They were left behind.

It had been more than five months since the news flashed on the television that Americans had been taken hostage, and now this. I sat again in front of the television, motionless, as a mixture of feelings swept through me.

I felt weak, a weakness that others must have shared. It looked as if my country could not defend me. We were supposed to be a powerful nation that could put people on the moon, yet. . . . And I wanted to kill the Iranians. I didn't understand why they had taken our people and were dancing around burning our flag. No matter how justified they felt, I wanted bombs to flatten their cities. Our dead were on TV. Our best were dead. By our own hand.

The bodies of five Airmen and three Marines lay abandoned in the desert. I watched the Iranians make fun of our people, and saw the televised image of a burned corpse. I didn't know anybody in the military, but I felt sick that day. Then the press talked about incompetence. Due to its level of difficulty and seemingly unavoidable inter-service rivalry, it was an overly complex mission, and was justifiably very controversial.

But I became infuriated with the press. Not because they reported the facts; that is their job, but I felt that some among them were mocking our dead heroes. Weren't these reporters Americans too? If I were a hostage, it would be comforting to know that someone would risk his own life to save me. It gives meaning to the words, *If you ever need me, I'll be there.*

It must have been very demoralizing to have been on active duty and see that happen, to spill blood, and to have the Iranians, then your own people, rub it in your face. At least our military people had the guts to try, I thought. I wondered if I could be so brave as to fly into an enemy country and risk my life to rescue people that I didn't even know. Would I save a journalist who would mock me?

Probably the world thought that the United States had lost its resolve after the accident. But, quietly, Delta Force and the Special Forces unit in West Germany geared-up for another go, which never flew.

That event had a profound impact on my life. After Vietnam, Special Operations Forces had been allowed to wither away, but the misfortune in the desert showed what happens when we don't maintain a strong Special Operations capability. The burning aircraft in the desert was a harbinger of President Carter's failed bid for reelection, but it was also a step toward the rebuilding of our Special Operations Forces.

In large part, because of that failure in the desert, Jimmy Carter went back to Georgia, while the voters ushered Ronald Reagan into the White House. The Iranians were wise enough to release the hostages when Mr. Reagan's shadow loomed over the globe.

President Reagan's position concerning the "Evil Empire" was clear. Soon, the Special Operations Forces were flush with money and breathing room, experiencing a rebirth after Vietnam, a rebirth of which I was a part. On the GT (General Technical) portion of the ASVAB test, I scored a 125. The Army recruiter said that I needed at least a 110 and the equivalent of two years of college to go to Officer Candidate School, and that I had the highest score that he had ever seen for a fifteen-year-old.

(A note concerning the ASVAB: the test has changed and no direct comparison can be made between previous and current scores.)

I didn't bother to tell them that their ASVAB test had to be messed up. I scored the highest of any fifteen-year-old he had ever seen? *Get real!* I had had a hard time passing my English classes. I didn't even know when to use a comma in writing a sentence—literally.

On the other hand, I did read whatever was available, ranging from books to cereal boxes, and spent a good portion of my less than abundant money at bookstores. My default mode was reading and sports. It was an escape from, and adaptation to, a harsh reality. Of course I wanted the ASVAB to be legit; it would validate the grand ideas I so often had.

In my junior year the recruiters began making occasional calls. Some of my high school friends had taken the plunge and joined, but I wanted to go to college. However, due to the unfortunate chain of recent events, my parental support was gone, and, with my grades, there was no chance for an academic scholarship. Sports scholarships were not available for weightlifting, in which I excelled. As an athlete, my accomplishments—a result of defending myself against bullies—were well beyond my years, but that wouldn't finance an education.

So I listened to the recruiters and considered using the service as a stepping stone. Besides, the military would provide a quick ride away from home. I needed time to think and sort things out after all that had happened in the last decade.

As for the military, I was not much interested in combat units *per se,* but I couldn't become an officer without college, and I needed to become an officer to become a pilot. So I looked at other possibilities. The recruiters pushed the technical fields for which there was difficulty finding qualified recruits. They offered big money bonuses, but the lures they dangled didn't attract me. If I were going into the military, it would be to become the best of the best.

Though I worked very hard to develop myself, remarkable coincidences and a fluke of history have greatly shaped my life. One of those coincidences was that President Reagan funneled massive amounts of money into Special Operations units such as the Navy SEALS, Army Rangers and Special Forces just at the time I was coming of age.

I looked hard at those units and at the Marine Corps, which was my first choice. But the Marines didn't offer what I could get in the Navy or the Army. The Air Force was out because I couldn't become a pilot without a degree. In the Navy I could try out for SEALS, and in the Army I could try out for Rangers or Special Forces.

I did a great deal of homework, and liked the idea of the toughness required in SEALS and Rangers, but I figured that most of the SEALS and Rangers were younger men. Their jobs seemed to revolve around high intensity missions of short duration, and it seemed that they didn't get to use their minds as individuals. Right or wrong, that was my youthful estimation.

On the other hand, Special Forces also conducts high intensity direct actions such as strike missions and counterterrorism, but their main mission is unconventional warfare, which is multi-faceted and includes guerrilla warfare. After doing my homework, I concluded that Special Forces required not just toughness but lots of smarts. Not genius type thinking, but "get the job done" abilities. Also, many Special Forces soldiers learned foreign languages, which sounded like the right stuff for me. I figured that as an athlete I had a solid shot at the physical part, and I loved to learn. So I was ready, I hoped, both ways.

Another historical fluke strongly affecting my future was that for a short period the Army allowed kids straight out of their initial military training to try out for Special Forces (nicknamed the "Green Berets"). They had done the same thing during Vietnam. Afterward, it was generally concluded that it was a bad policy to let young people jump straight into big league soldier-land simply because they could pass the course. However, old-timers later admitted that some of the best came straight from the civilian world and, precisely because they were lacking years of military experience, had less to unlearn.

Homework done, I opted for the deal offered by the Army: $5,000 cash bonus and about $20,000 for college. I chose Special Forces for the opportunity to see the world, and learn a foreign language.

School friends said the Army rejects candidates with flat feet, and therefore I was not the right stuff. No flatter feet have trod dry land. I have absolutely zero arch, a deficiency which seemed likely to be the first hurdle.

I took a half-day long bus ride to the Jacksonville processing station, sitting up front so that I could see where we were going. Sometimes the driver talked into the radio, and it talked back, but mostly I just watched lines passing on the road.

In Jacksonville, they checked me from head to toe, looked in my ears, eyes, took some blood and examined other, more private places. I tried to hide my flat feet by arching them a little bit, but since I was standing naked in front of the doctor, it must have seemed rather obvious. "Do those feet hurt you, son?" he asked.

"No sir, not in the least," I answered.

"What do you want to do in the Army, son?"

"Clerk typist," I answered proudly.

He turned and kept walking down the line of naked teenagers.

Except for the feet, I was in perfect condition. One hurdle was now behind, but there would be a thousand more, and another was straight ahead.

After the physical, I dressed and waited to meet with the "career counselor," a sergeant who checked the computer for my job so that he could reserve a training slot. The recruiter in my hometown had already "reserved" it, so this was just a formality, I thought. The job title was **Special Forces Light Weapons Specialist** (read: *Green Beret Gun Slinger*). Sounds like the title of a real tiger, doesn't it? Sounded good to me.

Well, the counselor glibly noted that no SF slots were available, and automatically started reading down a list of other jobs with names like, "missile systems repair specialist" which sounded to me like "electronic repair boy who eats donuts all day." He pretended that the particular job that I chose was not so important; it was just a formality to get me in the Army. As he tried to go down the list of alternative jobs, I said, "No, no, no. I came here for *Special Forces.*"

"None are available," he cut me off, "sorry." He didn't even glance away from the screen.

The sergeant probably sold used cars on the weekends as a hobby. He was a good salesman, explaining that I should go ahead, join up now, and submit my paperwork for Special Forces later. I smelled a rat. And a trap.

I had invested three days, two of them largely cooped up on a stinking bus ride to Jacksonville and back, and one to get picked over by a nosy doctor only to have some scumbucket try to send me down the wrong road in the wrong car. To him it was just a quota, but to me it meant years of my life.

"Goodbye," I said and walked out.

Other teenagers were sitting with counselors in front of their screens and heard our exchange. They watched me walk out. Some kids simply didn't care much what job they got so long as they were "allowed to join." It's like walking up to the personnel office of a company and saying, "Please give me a job. I'll take anything you have, and you can set the pay and hold all the cards." And the recruiters would say that it's an "honor" to serve in the military. What kind of bullshit, reverse logic is that? "Sure," I thought, "it's our *duty* and it's *honorable* to protect our country and our people, but it's not an *honor.*" I wonder how many people felt honored to be drafted for Vietnam?

Many recruits just take what they are offered because of test scores or physical limitations, but I wasn't joining the Army merely to run away or get a job. That was only part of it, and the college money was only part of it. I had demons to slay. Big, mean demons that haunted and chased me. I was going to kill them.

I pushed out the front door and sat down on the curb to wait for the bus. I was disgusted with the Army. *Goodbye.* The Navy recruiter in Winter Haven knew my face from all the times I had dropped by. With his help, I was ready to plunge headfirst into the SEALS. Excitement filled me as I imagined all the swimming and scuba diving, and slipping into harbors at night to fix explosives to the bottoms of enemy ships. Who needs Special Forces when you can go SEALS!

Just then, the used car salesman came out waving a computer printout. He said, "A slot just came open," and explained that I could report for active duty on 22 July for Basic Training, then Infantry School, then Airborne Training, then Special Forces Selection.

I was very happy at having stared down the counselor. The ultimate negotiating position is being able to walk away, and mean it. However, the trickster sergeant was doing Special Forces, and those recruits who weren't ready, a big favor, even if it was by accident. Later, I heard other soldiers compare similar experiences with counselors who tried to steer them astray, and many of them were railroaded. But if they were that easily tricked, they didn't belong in Special Forces anyway, so it balanced in the end, I suppose. Selection starts before one even joins the Army.

I took the oath that day, but there would be a half-year delay before Basic Training. First I had to graduate from twelfth grade. My friends at school were in an uproar over it. Some girls concluded, via committee, that the Army would "ruin my sweetness." And the boys weren't helping things when they heaped it on that Green Berets were the ultimate assassins, baby killers, and snake eaters. One guy said that part of the Selection process included biting the head off a live chicken and sucking out its blood.

A classmate wrote in my yearbook:

Sgt. Rock,
One day you will be a tough roach-eating, baby-killer for real. Too bad we never had war games. Hope that we will always be friends.
Sam Y.

The stories got worse and worse, and students stopped me in the halls to ask about it.

Between classes one afternoon, I felt a friendly tap on the shoulder, the kind of light caressing touch that only a female hand has. I felt her energy enter my body through her fingers and got all excited inside.

She asked, "You're not really gonna bite the head off a live chicken, are you?" tilting her head to the side.

"Uh, of course not," I said, wondering if I really would do it, and wondering what it would be like to kiss her on the mouth right now in this hallway. *She drives me crazy! I wonder what she would do if I asked her? Do it, do it, do it! Ask her! Ask her, you Green Beret wannabe!*

My imagination didn't stop there. Suddenly we were on the shore next to a lake. She looked at me again with that smile and I. . . .

"Well, we better get to class before the bell rings," I said.

Another micro-fantasy bites the dust. Time for class.

Coward! Coward! Maybe I don't have what it takes?

A different girl, who was an absolute knockout, wrote in my yearbook:

Mike,
All I can say is that you are a great friend and foxy as hell! Don't be

good but keep in touch. I'll never forget you. Good luck in all you do.
Forever, I'll love ya,
Kim

When this beautiful girl, Kim, smiled and handed back my yearbook, and I saw what she wrote, the yearbook practically exploded in flames in my hands. *What!*

I was clueless. I had no idea she liked me like that. The girls kept writing similar stuff in my yearbook. I was about to *die* when I read their messages. Another Kim said: . . . Remember when we first met in 7th grade in Coach Frazier's PE class? I always had a crush on you since then, but that's a different story. . . .

That's *two* Kims! Both very nice and very pretty and very interested. Holy lost opportunities Batman! The second Kim had a crush on me for six years and never took the chance by asking me out! What in the *hell* was wrong with that Kim! I would have said "yes" in a heartbeat. I had a crush on her, too. Why didn't I ask *her* (them) out? They never seemed interested. I was simply blind.

Probably, the most common word that girls used in my yearbook was "sweet."

Sweet!

Me?

Get real!

It was further concluded by my high school friends and acquaintances that the "Green Berets" would change my personality and make me mean, and that I would learn secret ways to kill people with my hands, and that during the training I would get beaten up a lot. Mostly with rubber hoses. You get locked in a smothering metal box, they said, and they leave you in the hot sun for days without food. They splash cold water on your legs to taunt you while they beat the coffin—*yeah*, it was a metal *coffin*—constantly with a pipe so that you can't sleep. That's how they break you and make you mean and not afraid to die, because you have already died, or at least death would be a relief.

They make you parachute alone into the Amazon jungle without food and with only a knife. That's when you learn how to kill *everything*, and that's when you go crazy and become a killer. You just don't care after that. You will do anything and you have to fight through a hundred miles of jungle to get out. There are leeches and snakes and crocodiles.

Only three men out of a hundred make it to the end. That's what the song said, anyway. And if you do make it, the missions would be so secret that if you got caught, it would be your duty to bite into the cyanide capsule disguised as a wart on your shoulder. It's on your shoulder in case you get strung up, like on a cross, being tortured. That way you can always get to it, and laugh at the enemy as you die.

Well, I didn't believe the cyanide part, but I couldn't sleep at night because I was so worried that I wouldn't make it. I had caught gators and hunted lots of small game, but had never seen a jungle. And sometimes I felt so thirsty just at football practice that water seemed more precious than gold. Of course, when you need it, it is.

So I trained very hard by running, running, and more running, as well as keeping up my lifting. For the past several years I had been written up in the papers for bodybuilding and lifting. One article shows a picture of me holding 225 pounds overhead, and the caption says that I was a sophomore competing in the 132 pound class. (Meaning I weighed less than 132 pounds.) As a senior I bench pressed 300 pounds while weighing less than 150. During high school I trained in the "best Gym within fifty miles." It wasn't a fluffy gym. A fluffy gym is where people go to meet, socialize, and rarely break a sweat. Nor was it a money-making gym, though the customers did pay $20 per month to keep the lights on. By the time I was sixteen, I was running the place, keeping the books, paying the bills and all the rest.

The doctors and lawyers who trained at The Gym filled my head with doctor and lawyer stories. They said that women really go for professionals, and that I should go to college. I agreed on both counts. And they talked about the stock market. I started reading the *Wall Street Journal* but couldn't understand the damn thing. The Merrill Lynch office was a block away, and, since I was making more money than I spent on food and clothes, I decided to invest in the market. Since I was only sixteen, they wouldn't let me buy stocks without the consent of a parent or guardian.

I talked an ex-Marine who trained at The Gym, Carmine Cardillo, into signing for me as if he were my guardian, and I bought stock in *Telefonas de Mexico*, and a gold mine in Africa named *Vaal Reef*. Every day I went to check the stock prices on the computer in the Merrill Lynch office, and wrote them in my log. Tuesday: + $1/4$. Wednesday: + $1/16$. Thursday: + $1\frac{1}{2}$. Alright! Getting rich is easy! Friday: -$2\frac{1}{4}$. Bummer. Ah, but it's not so bad, the gold mine is doing a little better.

Finally, the stockbroker said, "Mike, you come in here and check that computer every day. Don't sweat it. If you can't afford to lose it, don't gamble it, and when you invest in the market, you must have patience. Nerves of steel!"

Back at the Gym, Carmine told me how much women went for Marines, a reaction which, according to the men, seemed to be the ultimate measure of a profession. (Though, of course, they never said so in mixed company.)

Carmine said there was only one choice of respectable service, and that was the Marines.

The Gym, aptly named, was sacred ground. One man had moved to town from "Up North" just to train with the owner, Jim Cuddie. Mr. Cuddie was a superb lifter and a tough coach, who himself could hoist more than four hundred pounds from the floor to arms locked-out overhead. His speed and explosive power were actually frightening when I first saw him lifting. He was not fat like some lifters, but very muscular. And his muscles weren't the kind that are big and showy but not strong; he was more like a gorilla. As an Olympic lifter, he was a serious "technician" who achieved much of his success by honing his lifting technique, rather than, as often happens, relying on pure power.

Small talk was taboo in The Gym. This place was for serious lifters. There were other clubs where chatting was part of the "workout," and Mr. Cuddie made it clear that members were welcome to leave The Gym and join one of those. He enforced his rules with vehemence and utter clarity.

Once, two men stood talking by the dumbbells—appropriately—when Mr. Cuddie walked up to them and screamed in front of the whole Gym: "If you're not here to train, **get the f— out!**" He was a cussing man, and as I said, The Gym was sacred ground. This was the atmosphere of seriousness of purpose in which my strength was developed, and achievements were recognized by people that I looked up to.

Mr. Cuddie's paying job was as a Systems Analyst at Martin Marietta. He told me Air Force stories about Vietnam, and said that he had flown with some Green Berets. "Crazy f—ers," he said, "Don't join the Army. Go Air Force, they treat you better."

A couple of years earlier, he had noticed how hard I trained, and took me under his wing. I won competition after competition, and he attended many of the meets. He figured that I would become a world class lifter, and told me so all the time.

Unlike so many people, even students, who pushed and used steroids, I was drug free. Drug use was rampant, and I knew more athletes who were using them than who were not. Mr. Cuddie said that I didn't need steroids, and that I was too young for them, anyway. I believed him, and was beating steroid users left and right in competition.

It comes down to diet and motivation, he said. Besides the natural talent—and he was convinced that the majority of people have vastly more potential than they think—desire is 99% of what is needed.

The bullies had provided me with the incentive to get stronger. I had been reduced to a bloody, fighting mess as a kid, had become very strong, and now wanted to learn how to fight like a professional soldier so that I would never have to worry about another bully. My brother, Billy, said that I would never make it in Special Forces; that I wasn't tough enough. I probably should have thanked him for providing even more incentive.

With so many people warning me and filling my head with the stories they had heard (and exaggerated), my imagination made the Special Forces training out to be a long torture-fest. Civilians normally don't call the unit by its proper name, "Special Forces," but by its scary name, "Green Berets." And I was scared down to the core.

It was risky business. I had signed a contract with the Army promising four years of my life in exchange for what I wanted. If I failed the course, I would be in default on my end of the deal. Our "contract" would be invalidated and they could reassign me to any field they wanted, in which case I would squander four years doing something for the Army when I could have been working my way through college.

But I am a risk taker, which, unknown to me at the time, was typically part of the psychological profile of the successful Special Forces soldier. However, if you are going to take on a lion, perhaps more important than being a risk taker is something I wrote large in my senior high school yearbook: NEVER GIVE UP.

ONE MONTH AFTER HIGH SCHOOL GRADUATION,
FORT JACKSON, SOUTH CAROLINA.

MY ARMY JOURNEY began at a bus stop only blocks from the kinder-garten where I had encountered my first love, but been too afraid to tell her, and the Stop sign where I had ambushed cars, and been chased down by the Giant Woman.

Once on the bus, I sat up front, as usual, and watched Florida disappear behind me, one line on the road at a time. It was the beginning of a very long journey that started when the Greyhound dumped me at the in-processing station at Fort Jackson. I felt like a specially bred and trained fighting bull bursting from the pen after a long haul to the contest, but also like a lost kid being thrown into the arena, the world. *Let's see if you can break me, Mr. Army; bring it on. Hit me with your best shot.* I was psyched, physically pre-pared, and motivated, but apprehensive that I wouldn't measure up.

Some of the raw recruits stayed at Fort Jackson for Basic. The rest stayed a few days, then were hauled to various bases, depending on their future spe-cialty. Everything is a specialty—driving, cooking, clerking—everything. A sergeant, dressed in camouflage and combat boots, herded my group of sev-eral dozen recruits into the barracks, yelling at us to get squared-away and that he would return in one hour for first formation.

Alright! Army words!

There were beds and lockers, as in *Gomer Pyle,* but the building was nice and air-conditioned.

What! Air-conditioned? I thought the Army was tough! What a disappointment.

As the sergeant walked out the door I started unpacking, but most of the other recruits were just hanging around yapping with no direction. They told stories about their brothers, uncles, and dads who had been in the Army, Navy, Air Force or Marines, in World War II, Korea, Vietnam, or places I'd never heard of and didn't care about. Zeroes telling stories of heroes in their bloodlines as evidence of their own worthiness, I thought. Blah, blah, blah. *Didn't they hear what the sergeant just said?*

"C'mon, unpack your stuff and get squared away!" I shouted, "hit the restroom." My hopeful imagination propelled more words from my mouth: "The sergeant might come back in fifteen minutes and we could be digging ten-foot-deep holes through concrete with toothbrushes."

That got their attention.

"Are you serious?" asked a wide-eyed Southern boy.

Within a few minutes I was the nucleus. The recruits gathered around and were asking what to do and what came next. *How should I know? I haven't*

71

been in the Army long enough to eat chow. I was picking up those Army words, though, and awkwardly using them at every opportunity. The restroom was now the "latrine," food was now "chow," and chow was at "eighteen-hundred hours."

"What time is 1800 hours?" asked one recruit.

Military time is not mysterious, but many people have not been exposed to it, so I briefly explained. Instead of two 12-hour periods, the hours are numbered 1 through 24. In the morning, 8 is 0800 (zero eight hundred). Noon is 1200 (twelve hundred), 1:30 P.M. is 1330 (thirteen thirty) . . . 11:59 P.M. is 2359. I loved it! More important things happened at 1300 than at 1 P.M.

In the barracks, shamefully air-conditioned as they were, I gave the best advice I could, and when a sergeant rumbled in he put me in charge. After a few hours in the Army, I was loosely responsible for several dozen other recruits, but I was more like a go-between, or a shepherd dog, than a leader.

Next day, wake-up was at zero five hundred. We ate the morning chow that normal people call breakfast and the lessons kept coming. Folks from Up North, also known as Yankees, weren't used to eating grits the way we did Down South. Many didn't even know what grits were!

"What's this white mushy stuff?" A Yankee piped up.

A Southern drawl answered, "What d'ya mean?"

"This, man, what's this stuff?"

"Grits!?" The Southerner couldn't fathom that a person didn't know about grits, which were as normal to him as milk or eggs.

"Never heard of it," said the Yankee, "but it looks like Cream of Wheat."

To which the Southerner replied, "What's Cream of Wheat?"

A sergeant screamed from across the room, "Shut up! This ain't no social club!" His eyes narrowed with accusation delivered in the form of a question, "You tryin' to get a date? Is he your new sweetheart?"

All the recruits had stopped chewing, and I was trying my best not to burst out in laughter, knowing that drawing attention would spell trouble. Normally, the best thing to do during initial training is avoid being noticed.

The sergeant thundered: "For those of you who don't know about grits, grits is grits. Now stuff 'em down your hole and get out of my mess-hall!"

Alright! Abuse! Things started looking up.

They said that the hardest Basic was at Fort Benning, and that the toughest there was the MOS 11 Bravo: infantryman. My first Military Occupational Specialty (MOS) training was to be 11B, which in Army-talk was also known as Bullet Stoppers, Trigger Pullers, Grunts, Ground Pounders, Cannon Fodder, or whatever. My training was to begin with a combined thirteen weeks of Basic and AIT (Advanced Individual Training, 11B for me), followed by three weeks of Airborne Training—military parachuting.

The Army was having difficulty finding recruits for infantry, which is probably the toughest and least glamorous job imaginable—and that's why they paid me the $5,000 enlistment bonus. But . . . infantry and parachute training were, among other prerequisites, necessary for admittance into the weapons portion of the Special Forces Qualification Course at Fort Bragg. So, for something I was going to do anyway, the Army was to pay me $5,000 extra, which would be a great boost to my college fund.

I was still in processing and hadn't even gotten my two arms-full of shots yet. But the sergeants said that I was in for a wake-up and would change my mind about Special Forces before I got to Fort Bragg, or shortly after I arrived. Later I learned that few people in the military have even a clue about Special Forces, though many think they do.

The second night at Fort Jackson we were sitting around the barracks, waiting to be shipped out, and the recruits were comparing future jobs. It was like college freshmen comparing majors. "Oh, you are *pre-med*?" As if you already had breezed through all the years of hard training, made it, and were a renowned pediatric cardiologist, valiantly saving young lives.

When someone asked me, I said I had enlisted for Special Forces. There was silence. All eyes rested on me. Then someone asked the inevitable question: "What's Special Forces?" A teenaged expert, seasoned by books, movies, and war stories, chipped in with the wrong answer, which I ignored.

By then I knew that some people, upon hearing "Special Forces," were awestruck. The mere words evoked fear or respect in some hearts. From the other end of the spectrum came derisive comments, and yet others invariably told me why I was not Special Forces material. I didn't care to hear anybody's opinion about my chances unless they met two prerequisites: 1) They had made it into Special Forces themselves; 2) they knew my capabilities.

That person didn't exist, though many thought themselves worthy of passing judgment. I figured that anybody who put me down had either washed out, had never been there, or was too chicken to try—and in any case was not my career advisor.

Fort Jackson was easy going and I was terribly disappointed that we didn't dig holes with our toothbrushes, or stand on our heads in the rain while eating grits, but the sergeants did say a few derogatory things that amused me.

"SPECIAL FORCES!?" The nameless, faceless sergeant laughed. "You look fourteen years old! You look like a Cub Scout! No, you look more like a Brownie. Brownie Forces. You got on the wrong bus. Here's a quarter, go call your momma and tell her to come pick you up."

I sure hoped Fort Benning would be worse than Fort Jackson.

BASIC TRAINING

THE SERGEANTS LOADED us on a touring bus in Fort Jackson. I sat up front and watched the old driver wrestle the giant steering wheel through South Carolina to South Georgia. During most of the trip, the fresh meat was laughing and acting like teenagers, talking about girls, cars, guns, fishing, or talking tough.

The closer we got to Fort Benning, the less the boys talked. The festive atmosphere of adventure was replaced with an air of impending doom. As we drove onto Fort Benning, nobody said a word. Outside the windows were soldiers wearing camouflage; some carried automatic weapons, and they all looked like they had a purpose in life. I wasn't exactly sure what that purpose was.

I wondered if there was a secret war going on somewhere, kept out of the public eye. Then I thought, *Oh, that's silly.* I wasn't the type who thought that the government was always busying itself with conspiracies and secret wars. (Actually, there were several secret conflicts being waged, but I hadn't heard that—and probably wouldn't have believed it if I had.)

The air brakes made their ***psssshh!*** and the old bus driver chuckled knowingly while he opened the door. Eight or ten drill sergeants descended upon us with screams and orders. Many of the kids were nervous or even afraid as we piled out onto the field and ran the gauntlet of screams, then lined up on four lines that had been painted especially for us.

The air-conditioned bus was replaced with the stifling July heat, and we began to sweat while the sergeants paced up and down the lines yelling so hard in our young faces they must have been risking aneurysms. There was a caravan of buses. The sergeants opened one can of recruits at a time, so they could all converge and concentrate on each load. Surprise and concentration of fire are basic infantry concepts, and they were using them to good effect. There were plenty of insults and pushups to go around, and the sergeants made sure that we each got our share.

As we stood at attention, a recruit had his mouth open, as if in surprise. A sergeant was on the lookout for that defect and seized on him with a canned remark, "Why is your mouth open! Are you comin' on to me! Am I your type?! Drop and give me twenty!" They often made insinuations and accusations about our manhood.

Standing at attention, you could practically hear the suction-breaking *smoop!* as sergeants ripped boys away from their mothers.

Then came the important lesson on how to do pushups, how to count pushups, and how to address drill sergeants.

"One drill sergeant, two drill sergeant . . . twenty drill sergeant."

The unsuspecting recruit, having done his twenty, jumped to his feet and stepped back in line.

"Maggot! Did I tell you to recover?"

"No, Sergeant!"

"Do you think I'm stupid!"

"No, Sergeant!"

"Then why are you telling me what I already know! Drop and give me twenty! Check out the nametag. You're in my Army now, maggot!"

"One drill sergeant, two drill sergeant . . . twenty drill sergeant."

"Do you think I'm being fair, maggot?"

"Yes, Sergeant!"

"One thing I can't stand is a maggot who won't stand up for himself! I'm gonna ask you again. Do you think I'm being fair, maggot?"

"No, Sergeant!"

"You *don't?*" The sergeant stooped down nose to nose and screamed, "You don't think I'm fair! *I'll* tell you what's fair and what's not! You've got guard duty tonight! Do you think that's fair?"

The sergeants are masters at creating situations that you can't win.

Then more lessons, and the recruit suffered through each until he fell exhausted on his chest in the dry Georgia dust. The sergeant bellowed until the prostrate maggot managed to do some more pushups. The rest of us learned the lessons free of charge—that time.

They taught some things the first day. For instance, don't stand at attention with your knees locked or you will pass out, and maybe smack your teeth on the concrete. Any high school band member knows what happens, but it was new for me. They warned us repeatedly, yet over time I saw and heard many bodies hit the ground for that very reason. Humans make a special sound when they hit the ground: *Karuumph!*

Some people simply didn't do as they were told, and I learned why it is so important to follow instructions and listen to experience, or risk getting your parts scattered over a large area. Later, while we were learning to shoot M-16 rifles, a drill sergeant told us that female recruits tend to shoot better than males. He said that males tend to have more past experience with firearms. The females, he explained, learn to shoot as they are told, so do better.

But we had just arrived, and were still by the buses being yelled at for any and no reason. If there was no reason to scream, the sergeants manufactured one. There is no such thing as a quiet or reasonable drill sergeant.

We had been issued uniforms at Fort Jackson, and our duffel bags were in the bellies of the buses. While the sergeants rampaged, the smiling old bus driver opened the cargo doors and we lined up to take the first two duffel bags we could grab. It didn't matter which; our names were stenciled in black on the green canvas, and we would sort them out later.

The smell of new uniforms mixed with the smell of sweat and South Georgia pine as Army trucks drove by, big airplanes flew over, helicopters whopp'd around and *real* soldiers were everywhere. I caught a glimpse of a soldier wearing a black beret. A Ranger. To me, it was like a Bigfoot sighting. This was it. *Yeah.* Four months of hard training here and I would be ready for Special Forces training. I hoped. *Maybe I can go to Ranger school!* I had already forgotten all about the college money.

A recruit needed to hit the latrine and was innocent enough to say, "With all due respect, Sergeant. . . ."

"With all due respect" is good for the movies, but should never be uttered at Basic Training. "With all due respect" is just a flowery appeal that a few young recruits mistakenly think they can use to charm a sergeant, as they would their mothers. But there is a big difference: A mother always forgives her baby for talking back or making a mistake—a sergeant wants men who take responsibility for their own bodies. This was the Army. A man would have known to hit the latrine on the bus. If you want to make men out of boys, you treat them like men, and clarify that they are *expected* to be men. If they still want to be boys they can step out of line and call their mothers to pick them up. As for those who go forward, from now on, they pay for their own mistakes and are likewise rewarded by their *own* hand. A man never looks back and says, "the world did not give me what was due." Boys are to be taught that *regret* originates from hard lessons learned after the fact.

The maggot didn't get the sentence out of his mouth. The sergeants were ready, waiting for the first boy in every class who would venture to say it. "With all due respect" he did pushups and guard duty for days. Those words were never uttered in our platoon again.

I was feeling more confident, and couldn't get enough of the sergeants' endless store of canned insults, though sometimes they were clearly ad-libbing as they found personal defects in people and tried their best to make a mountain out of a mole, or a pimple.

My selected defect was a baby face.

"Where's your pacifier! I don't want cryin' from any little babies in my platoon. Maggot, when you feel like cryin' and you don't have a pacifier, you better stick that little baby thumb in your mouth and keep it shut! Do you hear me!"

"Yes Sergeant!" Fun!

The first day rolled into the second into the third. They shaved our heads and stripped us of the superficial indicators of our identity. They were unmasking us to make the first level of our deeper identities apparent. In daily life we make observations and immediately begin to classify people by how they speak, walk and so on, and by what surrounds them—their cars, jewelry, money, or whatever. Those things are useful indicators, but they are also tools used by the clever to fabricate façades, such as the tinman with no heart, and the one dressed as a lion, but with no courage. We all wear masks; it's a necessity in society. But when people cross the magical line and start believing that perception is reality, they are handicapped.

After one witnesses the surfaces stripped away from many people, the witness of the unmasking matures in a certain way, and quickly. Later, Special Forces training was even more effective at ripping away the façades.

Dark and early we were in formation outside under floodlights. Some recruits were like newborn kittens whose eyes had not yet opened. It was a sight: all those bald, shaven heads. There were about 240 hairless basket-balls, and at least 230 were made ugly by various deformities, knobs, pro-trusions, and strange shapes along the scalp. This meant about ten non-ugly heads, of which about five were neutral, leaving only five sufficiently free from deformity to be considered good-looking. Of these, mine was the most good-looking, or at least that's how I had it figured. It's hard to see the knots on your own head.

I first had my head shaved as a small child, because it was fashionable and anti-hippie, so my father saw that it was done. The next time it was shaved was as a senior at Winter Haven High School, as a member of the **Blue Devils**, when the football players all buzzed their heads. That time, I had been at the barbershop with a few football buddies. There stood the same barber who had cut my hair when I was a boy. And there was the same chair, like the dentist's chair, but without the light in your face and the hands in your mouth.

A couple of my buddies got buzz cuts while I waited, so I had a few min-utes to think, and several possibilities were competing in my head. My friends smiled and rubbed their bristling heads as I eased into the same old barber chair that I was used to climbing into, and announced that I wanted a Mohawk. They looked as if I had announced an intention to streak around while waving a red, Commie flag over my head.

The barber protested that it would upset my Granny, and that he thought it was a silly idea. My buddies encouraged me. After much discussion, the barber refused.

"*Jeeeeez* . . . It's just a haircut," I said, and I went to the mall and got a woman in a beauty salon to do it.

Sometimes I worked late at night as manager of The Gym, so I didn't get home until after my grandparents were asleep. They didn't see the Mohawk that first night. They didn't see it the next morning, either—I had a key to

The Gym and trained before school, so I was gone before dawn. But I was looking forward to seeing Granny's reaction that afternoon.

At school the Mohawk was an instant hit.

However, the first sign that the Mohawk affected people adversely came at the grocery store. An old lady was in the checkout line in front of me. I was always nice to old ladies, but she took one look at my Mohawk, tensed like a startled cat, and promptly wheeled her cart out and went to another line. She was frightened, as if I had a sign written in blood on my forehead that said "Needlepoint Naked!" or "Do Drugs with Satan!"

I wanted to say, "*Stop*, I made the football team, that's all." But I said nothing, paid for my peanut butter and walked out. I didn't like it when little old ladies were afraid of me. It would have felt better had she just slapped me across the face, but I learned a bigger lesson when I got home.

I walked in the front door and found Granny smiling in the living room. She always smiled when I came home. I proudly displayed my Mohawk— and she burst into tears! She thought I'd gone punk rock, or maybe had taken drugs and gone crazy.

Granny's reaction was sudden, worse than the supermarket lady's. She hid her eyes with her hands and turned away because any glimpse of the Mohawk resulted in a torrent of tears. I figured she would get over it in a couple of days after I explained it was just a football-thing, but she didn't. Each time I came home, she retreated to her bedroom and cried.

I had to do *something* to make her feel better, so I first treated the symptom by wearing a hat, then the cause by cutting off the offending crest with shaving cream and a razor blade. Then I promised to let it grow. That's when I discovered that I had a pretty head, because the girls at school actually liked it shaved, and they liked to touch it. A girl asked if she could draw a picture on it, but that's where I drew the line. Finally, my head got sunburned and I have never had a Mr. Clean (or Mohawk) cut since.

But this was Basic Training and there were no girls, unless you listened to the sergeants, in which case there were no men. There were just maggots and shitbirds. Of course, they were not supposed to cuss (that's "curse" in Yankee talk) or hit anyone; we were in the midst of the "transition to the new Army," a perpetual condition. The sergeants completely disregarded the prohibition of profanity, unless officers were around, but were more careful about the hitting part. They wore those Smokey the Bear brown hats and there was one sergeant who would get in recruits' faces and peck them in the crook of the nose between the eyes with the edge of his hat, like a woodpecker. Coincidentally, his name was Sergeant Wood.

The Army has a seemingly inexhaustible supply of strange names for its components: divisions, brigades, battalions, companies, and so on. I was in

1st Platoon, B Company, 7th Battalion, 1st Infantry Training Brigade, or 7B1. We were the *War Eagles*! A sergeant yelled, "You shitbirds landed in the best damn training company at Fort Benning!"

Before people started washing out, the "company" consisted of four platoons of about sixty recruits each, for a total of around two hundred forty. Of course, our drill sergeants said that we had landed in the best damn platoon in the company. And 1st Platoon was dubbed "The Blackhawks!" So we were actually *War Eagles*! and *Blackhawks*!

Platoons were further sub-divided into squads and teams. During the first few days, the sergeants selected eight team leaders, four squad leaders, and a platoon leader for each platoon, meaning there were thirteen leaders at various levels for each sixty-man platoon. Platoon leader was top dog.

There was the Army leadership structure to learn about. They don't have managers and vice-presidents of marketing, but there are officers, warrant officers, and enlisted ranks. I had memorized all the ranks before leaving Winter Haven.

Each platoon had two drill sergeants and a drill corporal. They wanted badly for their platoon to do well; it reflected in their performance reports. Basic Training is an important time for molding recruits into the mind-set that the military needs. Basic is somewhat like infancy or early childhood. It's the first time that many recruits have ventured more than an hour's drive from home. For some, it was stressful not having their mothers to wash their clothes and make their beds. Many had never even had a job.

The sergeants spent considerable time and effort getting the right recruits into the leadership positions. It was important that the recruit-leaders do well, because that made the sergeants' jobs easier and made them look good. The sergeants initially chose the leaders by their records and ages. Some recruits had college behind them and were older, so they were picked to fill leadership positions at first. As for me, I was just a basic shitbird perched on the bottom rung of the lowliest ladder in the "lowliest service," the Army. I was barely in charge of my own socks. I say barely because the socks had to be rolled a special way and kept in a prescribed place.

SERGEANT

Though I was not initially in a leadership position, within about a week a sergeant replaced my team leader with me, so I became a team leader in the best damn platoon of the best damn company, in the best damn Army on the best planet in the solar system. Possibly the universe. The sergeants

STAFF SERGEANT

79

presented me with fake sergeant stripes, just as they had done with the other team leaders. I was a "Buck Sergeant." Three stripes. It's funny how the act of putting on those little stripes actually puts a lot of pressure on you to measure up to the title. If they don't feel heavy, you don't deserve to wear them.

I went about squaring away my little seven-man team to make it "the best damn team." Also, I started cussing more. It's bad manners to cuss all the time but, well, I was in the Army! Soon I grew out of team leader and was promoted to squad leader, which added yet another stripe, actually a rocker—which is the little crescent-shaped thing that hangs below the stripes—and made me a "Staff Sergeant." The little rocker was twice as heavy as the first three stripes, and there were suddenly twice as many subordinates. So I squared away my squad of about fourteen other maggots and shitbirds.

Once, a sergeant found that a member of my squad left his locker unsecured while we ate morning chow. I had failed to check up on my men. He said nothing to my squad member, but put me on KP—kitchen police. I was placed in the kitchen, literally peeling potatoes, and when I returned after peeling and cleaning all day, he made it crystal clear that I was responsible for my subordinates, period. In the military, there is no exoneration to be gained by claiming: "I told him but he failed to do it." I was taught that *results*, especially bad results, fall heaviest on the shoulders of the leaders. If two squad members were sleeping on guard duty and because I failed to check up on them, the platoon was overrun, it would be my fault. I would not get the opportunity to ruminate over my shortcomings while peeling potatoes if we were all killed in combat. Lesson: *Leave excuses at home. Get Results.*

Soon we went through basic NBC (Nuclear, Biological, and Chemical) training. We learned to react to a nuclear blast, how to conduct individual decontamination, and to self-administer atropine injections if there were signs or symptoms of certain types of chemical exposure.

A chemical attack may not announce itself as clearly as bullets zipping by. Bullets loudly demand attention, while chemicals are the quiet death. Even trace amounts of some toxins can ravage your body for life, so you must be alert to their presence. There are fancy machines for detecting chemicals, but you can't count on machines. If the enemy drops bombs that don't rock your body with massive shock-waves, or if you find dead animals, dead birds and such that are not mutilated as is normal in violent death, and if you find dead insects, well—*Suit up!!! And get out of the area.*

One improvised alarm for chemical attack is to bang metal against metal. If you are around American soldiers, and you see one wearing chemical gear who is furiously clanging pieces of metal together—*Suit up!!! Or get out of the area.*

Part of the training for chemical exposure consisted of going through a chamber filled with concentrated tear gas. We entered one squad at a time. As the leaders, we always went last or first depending on which was the more difficult. Similarly, good leaders wait until their men have gotten their food before getting theirs. Leading by example is the stated foundation of U.S. military leadership—*Follow Me*. So, I was last in line with my squad, meaning that I would be in the burning tear gas the longest.

In the chamber each recruit was required to take off his mask and say his name, rank, and serial number, which is his Social Security number. The Georgia heat kept our pores wide open, and the gas burned our skin, eyes, noses, and throats. Inside the foggy chamber, some of the squad members were having difficulty continuing, so I encouraged them, though I too was in pain. It truly burned but it wasn't *that* bad. We knew that it was only tear gas and would soon be over. It wasn't something serious like a blister, blood, or nerve agent. Nevertheless, when I finally was permitted to leave I couldn't see well and was a slobbering, burning mess.

As a squad leader, I wanted to set an example for the recruits who were struggling, so I ran straight to a group of sergeants who were standing together. Upon reaching them I dropped to the ground and began doing pushups in the dust, and through the burning tears requested permission to re-enter the gas chamber with the next squad. I didn't really want to go back into that den of burning, choking gas that was scientifically made to cause disorienting, unnerving pain. I just wanted to be a good leader and show that a man could take a dose, and go back for more if he had to.

The sergeants were caught off-guard—and sent me back.

Stupid jerk! What have I done?

My squad was watching—the whole platoon was watching—and the other three platoons were there, making over two hundred recruits for my audience.

Stupid, stupid, stupid.

With all those tear-gassed eyes watching, I had to do *something*. I was a squad leader wearing the stripes of a staff sergeant. A Leader. So I thanked the sergeants through tears and slobber and ran back into the chamber without my mask.

The sergeant inside wore full chemical gear. He yelled through his mask something that had to be profane, and kicked me out. *Thank You, God.* It felt like I was on fire! I was choking, but made it back to my squad and started checking on my men to show that you could take two doses, and still keep going.

To shed tear gas, just face into the wind (you hope there will be wind) and let it blow away while

SERGEANT FIRST CLASS

81

resisting the temptation to rub your eyes. Above all, resist the temptation to touch certain areas when nature calls.

The gas was painful, but it wasn't as if I were shot or wounded. A leader really earns his or her pay when things are bad, and this could not even remotely compare with the danger or difficulty our people faced in Vietnam. Some recruits thought I was a lunatic, but I figured it was my job, so. . . .

I became the new platoon leader, and was given one more rocker, making me a "Sergeant First Class," the "same" as the senior drill sergeant who had been to Vietnam. Talk about heavy. That one little rocker suddenly meant that I had four times more subordinates than a squad leader, and eight times more than a team leader. I was the only recruit who could walk up and talk to the drill sergeants without asking permission.

It had not been my intention. The promotion was due to discipline and motivation and simply helping those around me, not out of a desire for power. At eighteen and with no leadership training, I had nearly five dozen subordinates, some of whom had even been to college. There was a lot of responsibility and I needed to figure out how to steer the ship—quickly.

I started writing letters home. Over the course of the next year, I wrote my friend, Richard White, approximately one hundred pages.

> By the way, don't write those funny return addresses, the sergeant smashed my fingers for that. One of my sergeants went to Vietnam the other was soldier of the year at Fort Benning. They aren't supposed to hit you, but one . . . is very good about keeping people straight!
>
> I am Platoon Leader. They kept giving me promotions, first from team leader . . . to squad leader . . . to Platoon Leader . . . as high as a soldier can get. It sounds easy, but a lot [of these guys] went to college (average education 12.6 years). The man that I replaced had 3 years [of college].
>
> It's great! Out of 218 men in Bravo company [twenty-two had washed out], 16 men were set as honor soldiers for [excellence on] the physical readiness test. I'm getting a medal.
>
> No way of explaining what's been happening . . . all I can say is ALL THE WAY!
>
> Tomorrow we qualify with our M-16's . . . have fired hundreds of rounds so far. Tuesday we fire grenade launchers (live). Wednesday we fire LAW rockets (Light Anti-tank Weapon). We were ambushed by some sergeants with

concentrated tear gas (3 times). I survived all the attacks, but some people (about half) panicked and got messed up. . . .

Company commander knows me . . . they have given my platoon special privileges . . .

EXCUSE THAT INTERRUPTION. We just had a fire drill and it was plenty wild.

Being Platoon Leader I have little time to write . . . give me a phone number.

Gotta go trouble is starting.

Richard and I, along with my friend John Harrison and others, lived some of the most mischievous teenage years on record, if such records were kept. Richard was off to college and John had joined the Army.

The following week's letter to Richard:

I love the Army . . . Sometimes late at night when it's raining or the woods are real quiet Jimmy Buffet still rings in my head or I think about all the things we did . . . those times will come once more . . . So study those books, and I'll study war . . . Gotta go, a Platoon Leader's job is never done!
ALL THE WAY

There were recruits who didn't like taking orders from little me. I looked like I hadn't reached puberty, and shaving was as alien to me as to an eleven-year-old. So there was yet another battery of bullies to negotiate, and I received some threats. When the sergeants were around, the troublemakers minded well, but when I was left alone, things changed.

At first, I tried to bring the troublemakers around by reasoning with them, but that only made matters worse. By paying attention to them, I was feeding the fire. Yet, to ignore them was also a mistake. They made trouble for the sake of trouble. There was nothing that I could do—they thought.

I took a different view. I recruited spies by giving special favors and silently set about rooting out all those who were causing problems. In the end, the troublemakers made themselves apparent, so the spies didn't root out anybody, but were helpful figuring out what the malcontents were up to. Many people would take issue with my tactics, but at night I was afraid to sleep, and a successful leader needs his rest. For various reasons, a few recruits had already been thrashed by others. In its potential for sudden violence, Basic resembled jail. Also like jail, there was no easy escape from Basic.

Whereas everyone else slept in a big bay, I had—believe it or not—my own room. Anybody who wanted to get me could do it easily because my room connected to the bay. In such situations, it's healthy to wonder if you are being paranoid, but as it happened, I was merely being prudent. I set up noisemakers by the two doors to my room. After lights-out I also quietly placed around the room various devices that could be used as weapons. I even slept with my e-tool (entrenching tool—a folding shovel that makes an excellent, even lethal, weapon).

I had hardcore allies; most in the platoon were at least supportive, some were indifferent, and there were only a handful of troublemakers. Luckily, the most hardcore supporters were also the best recruits, and the trouble-makers tended to do the minimum necessary to get by—which is good, because it's better to have a lazy detractor than an industrious enemy.

Four rows of fifteen single beds ran lengthwise down the rectangular bay, each row representing one squad. The sergeants allowed me some auton-omy, so I rearranged the bunk order, putting the troublemakers away from my room, at the end of the bay. I put my spies in the beds next to them. Closer to my doors were the hardcore allies, including the four squad lead-ers. Thus we held the handful of dissidents in check.

I was running, by any measure, a military regime within a military regime. But it was a matter of survival, so I make no apologies. Perhaps because of these precautions, I was never attacked at night. One day out in the woods, however, while we were alone for only a minute, a dissident swung at me with his M-16 because of something insignificant. He almost got me. For some reason I didn't have my rifle or any means of defense, so I ran away.

He was about twenty-five, a little taller, twenty pounds heavier than me, and very immature. He was always whining about something, or complain-ing that his boots were too tight, though I knew that they were not. One thing the Army doesn't play with is your boots. No feet, no soldier. They make sure that you have the right sized boots in Basic. If you ask.

The attack created an awkward situation. In my eighteen-year-old opin-ion, telling a sergeant would have been like running to Daddy, which had never worked for me anyway. So I found another solution.

We were on bivouac (camping) at a shooting range that week, so when nature tapped a recruit on the shoulder, he took his e-tool into the woods to dig a hole. I instructed one of my spies to watch my assailant after evening chow, and when the dissident went into the woods the spy was to quickly find me and give the special signal. Then the spy was to find the troublemaker's squad leader, whom I had briefed, and we would take it from there.

The time came, the signal was given, and soon we crept through the woods, camouflaged, stalking our prey. On our bellies, peering through the bushes, we watched him dig his hole. He dropped his camouflaged trousers around his boots and soon was squatting as we moved in.

He saw me at the last second. His eyes went wide and he almost got out a scream when I slammed him full-force with a resounding tackle. The impact was solid and it knocked most of the fight out of him, but he struggled for a few seconds.

His pants were around his ankles and boots, so his legs were effectively shackled. It was easy for the squad leader and me to completely subdue him on the ground with his head stuck in the fork of a tree that fortuitously grew there. We didn't punch or hurt him, but he understood the serious consequences if there were any more problems. We weren't in a playground or a sandbox. There would be no more warnings.

After that, he was a perfect angel, and I treated him like nothing had happened. I held no grudge. Quoting an old Southern man: *Carrying a grudge is the least useful form of exercise I know.*

There were still some odd surprises at training. For example, some black people had told me earlier that the infantry was mostly black. They said the white leaders of the country didn't want their kids killed in combat. That's a safe bet, and history shows other disadvantaged groups, such as poor whites, fared as badly. But those who said that the infantry was mostly black were wrong. From the comments of blacks I knew in Winter Haven, I expected to be one of the only whites in the infantry. In reality, there were only 27 blacks—give or take a couple depending on where you draw the line—in our company of 192 recruits who remained of the original 240 when our "yearbook" pictures where taken.

I think that the various disadvantaged groups, which included all types of poor people, had been so disproportionately disregarded, degraded, and generally abused during our military history that the latest generation wasn't keen on the idea of getting into combat units, and now there was no draft; it was all volunteer. So, though combat units tend to be racially mixed with Hispanics, blacks, Asians, whites, Native Americans and who knows what, my experience was that most in such roles were white, and seemed to come predominantly from lower middle-class families.

People said that the infantry, unlike some other specialties which often required more education, consisted of dunderheads. I was again surprised at the educational level of many recruits. They weren't Ph.D.'s, but all had at least high school diplomas. There was no longer a choice between jail and service, nor did the military accept people who qualified by being able to tie their own boots and take orders. Which may not be a good thing, actually, because many a veteran will vouch that lots of the best fighters come from the basement of a peacetime society.

Outcasts in peace; heroes in war. If they survive war, soldiers often return to being outcasts in peacetime. Their military duty and loyalty are not seen as evidence of how well they adapted when challenged, or as evidence of their loyalty, but as further proof that they are dangerous. Too often when they step out of line or are innocently involved in an event that can be interpreted as questionable, they are sent to prison and branded "veterans." Of course, some veterans truly are criminals, as are some business people, lawyers, and presidents, but it's a shame when a person's service record is used against him. The tactic is no different than using a person's race or religion as evidence against him. But I hadn't learned that yet.

There was a young recruit who chose to have one of the most negative attitudes that I have witnessed. I tried to bring him around. He had a healthy body like the others, and had passed the physical readiness test, and survived the tear gas and many other contrived inconveniences. Yet, every day he said, "I can't." I can't do this, I can't do that.

From his actions and words I wondered how many times he was told in his life "*you* can't do that because *you* are not *big* enough, *smart* enough, *old* enough. . . ."

He was driving me crazy with his relentless negativism. I wanted to scream to God, to appeal to a higher authority, to give this boy the spirit to be a man. Men don't walk around counting the things that they *can't* do.

This went on until the day I found him crying, sitting by the front door of the barracks with his head buried between his knees.

"Get with it, you can make it," I encouraged him.

"I can't."

"You can."

"I can't!" sobbing, "You don't understand. I *caann'tt*."

I took his "cant's" as a personal affront to my leadership ability. If I can't motivate him, then something must be wrong with me.

"You've got a lot of guts to join the Army," I told him, "You should be proud of that. And *infantry* of all things! That took real guts."

"I didn't want to join the Army," he answered, "My parents made me do it."

"Well," I countered, sidestepping the losing argument, "You chose *infantry*, man! That takes real guts, even if you have a hard time making it. Especially if you have a hard time!"

He whimpered and mumbled, always refusing to make eye contact, "My recruiter said that infantry was not that hard."

I could have choked on my tongue. He must have some mean parents, and what a joker that recruiter! The recruiter needed a boot in the ribs. You don't send "Cant's" to the infantry. That's irresponsible to the "Can't," and to the Army.

I started to think that I couldn't bring him around. I just couldn't do it. I had tried everything. I was ready to quit. *Arrrgh!* He was rubbing off on me. His "can't" was trying to enter my body and become "can't" in me.

I don't like silly motivational speeches and hollow words but the way you speak really is important. Of course people do have limits: I can't pole-vault over the Empire State Building, but I can swoop over it in a helicopter.

He refused to fight. If he had only said "I can" one time, his hands would have been free. He looked up with his puffy red eyes, wet and sobbing, and said, *"I can't,"* one time too many. If he couldn't help himself, I couldn't help him.

A textbook example of a self-fulfilling prophecy.

Some say that the object of Basic Training is to break your spirit and then build you back up the way they want you. I can only say this about Army Basic Training during my class: If that training broke anybody's spirit (and I don't mean that it wasn't challenging at times), that person has no business in the military even as a potato-peeler. The military is deadly serious business. People are killed on a regular basis even during training, despite its being a time when they are burdened by seemingly endless safety rules. Combat units are not places where personal trials and tribulations should be considered. Weakness-means-losing-means-death.

Lay all equal opportunity thoughts and liberal rationalizations aside for a moment: we were training for the ultimate trespass, the ultimate insult to other humans. We were training to go into the final arena together. Our lives would depend on each other. It's not just somebody else's business if he gets killed. It's my business!

The military is not college, where one's performance is unrelated to others. In college, those who do well can tout it on their résumés and be fully satisfied that they learned their lessons. In contrast, in combat units you regularly depend on others for your life, even in peacetime, and they depend on you. Some of the weapon systems and training activities are enormously dangerous. This is about War. War is why we have a military. It's not there only to provide jobs, though some people seem to think that it is.

The military is not a place for nurturing the weak so that they can function in society; it is about killing, or *dying*—as a team. In sports, winning or losing is determined almost exclusively during practice. The official competition is at times merely a formality. I figured it was the same with war.

As I write this I see that to some extent it is unfortunate that Coalition Forces had such an easy time in the Gulf War against Iraqi forces. Since then, people have asserted (more times than I care to remember) that war is now a video game of smart bombs and cruise missiles. Many civilians, and a significant number within the military, believe that rigorous military training is no longer needed, and all future wars will be won by the button pushers. They are wrong.

It has been said that sending unprepared troops into combat is murder. Poorly trained troops also means poorly disciplined troops who commit more atrocities in war and in peace. The same holds for the behavior of police forces.

Most young soldiers who try to get into combat units *want* the training to be tough. The good recruits want to overcome great challenges. Ask a young infantryman why he chose the Marines, or the infantry in the Army, when he could have chosen an easier path. If he picked the Marines, it is likely because Marines have the reputation of being Men. Tough men. *Real* Men. The Marine on the TV commercial wearing his uniform makes the only sales pitch many boys need to hear. We are looking for a *few good Men*.

I am not one who believes in clinging to old, worn out traditions, but throughout history, virtually all cultures have had rites of passage. And, of course, I'm not referring to the fabricated, one-size-fits-all view that says when people turn eighteen they are "adults." Outside the tunnel-visioned technicalities of law, down in the trenches of reality, there are fifteen-year-old adults, and forty-year-old adolescents. Many of the adolescents are males who have not crossed a magical borderline to become men.

The magical borderline from boyhood to manhood does not have to be in the armed services and is obviously available elsewhere, but the military offers a traditional rite of passage. When the training is truly difficult—and that means that some will not make it—for those who succeed, it does wonders for their self-esteem and for unit *esprit de corps,* not to mention helping to keep more of them alive and the rest of us safer. And men are created from boys.

A function of the military, unofficial and unspoken as it may be, is to take boys away from their mothers and bring them in with the men. Many young servicemen take strong issue with training that leaves them feeling untested and thus unproven.

There are twenty-one-year-old, baby-faced Marines, airmen, sailors and soldiers out there who are fully mature, reliable and strong under pressure, who are confident and capable of leading other men into combat, while there are middle-aged, restless males, who never became men. Publicly, of course, some may rail against this idea, and say that war is silly—but a rite of passage has nothing to do with war. They might say that they are lovers—not fighters; that military service is a waste of time. This doesn't change the fact that boys, to feel complete, need a rite of passage, or they will remain restless and insecure overgrown boys.

And while the initiation rites are conducted, the boys are taught what is expected of them as men in their nation, the United States of America. We are a warring nation. As a whole, we have a martial mentality. That is a fact. In addition to other things, as future warriors, we were required to learn the six Articles of the *Code of Conduct* by heart.

Article I

I am an American fighting man. I serve in the forces which defend my country and our way of life. I am prepared to give my life in their defense.

You can't ask boys to adhere to that level of commitment.

As for "Can't," he had no spirit that he was willing to summon. Some may say, "Maybe the Army was not for him." I agree.

The only thing that mattered was that he was too weak to hack it. I'm not saying he's not human and that he does not have his place, or that he was a bad person, only that his place was not in the United States military, and especially not in a combat unit. Playtime was over.

"If you think you can or you think you can't, you will always be right."

—Henry Ford.

"Can't" left the Army.

For those of us who kept going, there was a pull-up bar outside the mess hall, and we paid for admission by cranking out as many pull-ups as we could before every meal. As a leader, always standing last in the chow line meant that I didn't have enough time to eat. I wanted to show the sergeants that I could be a good soldier and a good leader by doing my best to max every test. After all, it's hard for a slouch to demand performance from others and be taken seriously, but when you blaze a trail and lead the way, they will follow and even try to outdo you. And that's what you want. You want them to fight to outdo you. Not just because you are in charge, but because you are *damn good*, and in charge. You want them to try harder.

When it came to my weapon, the M-16 assault rifle, I practiced almost every spare moment: disassembly and assembly, immediate actions drills and fast magazine changes. After much practice, I could assemble my weapon with my eyes closed, clear a jam or change magazines without thinking.

We practiced trigger squeeze by putting a dime near the end of the barrel, just behind the flash suppressor, and controlled our breathing, stock weld and trigger squeeze, so that we could dry fire the weapon without the dime falling off. I must have done hundreds of dry fires before launching the first bullet down range.

To my amazement, a few of the recruits quietly decided to shoot their own way, rather than the Army's. Maybe it was the way their daddies had taught them. It seemed arrogant, or naive, that someone off the street thought he knew more about marksmanship with an M-16 than a U.S. military marksmanship instructor. When the drill sergeants caught somebody holding the weapon contrary to their instructions, there was hell to pay.

At the range, the pop-up targets were man-like silhouettes. We were not shooting at bullseyes or plinking tin cans. We were being desensitized to firing assault rifles at human-like targets. When the dark green target popped up, you engaged quickly before it popped back down. If you hit it, it fell down.

The sergeants were tense each time we fired weapons. After all, the recruits whom they constantly harassed now had loaded automatic assault rifles in their hands. Sergeant Wood said that if a recruit tried to shoot anybody, he kept a thirty-round magazine of tracers in his pocket, and he would grab an M-16 and kill him by dumping all thirty burning tracers on full-auto into his body.

Well, I thought, *if anybody is planning on killing anyone, Sergeant Wood will be the first to go.* For some reason the thought of tracers scares people more than regular bullets, but with tracers you can see where they came from and where they are going.

At that time, to qualify as "expert" you needed to successfully engage thirty-six out of forty targets ranging in distance from very close to several hundred yards. Surprisingly, one of the targets people miss the most is the closest. It's so easy that shooters just point quickly and launch the bullet, which promptly hits in front of the target, the likeness of an enemy soldier lying down, and the bullet ricochets over its head. *Zinnggg!* The grass was blown away where so many thousands of bullets impacted and tossed sand at the silhouette.

Some recruits did not learn to shoot well, and had a hard time just qualifying with a minimum score because they did not listen. Others did as they were told and practiced dry firing, and therefore often qualified as sharpshooters or experts. I shot at the expert level at every qualification while on active duty simply because I did as I was told, and practiced. *Lesson: Listen to experience, then practice, practice, practice.*

At Basic, a few soldiers shot better than me, and they loved to rub it in. Good. That's what you want. But they have to practice hard for their ego boosters or no egos will be boosted. No freebies. You have to set the standards as high as you can. Reach deep in your guts and try very hard. The drill sergeants taught me these things, and behind closed doors, the sergeants told me they were ecstatic that a competitive atmosphere had emerged.

We were practicing to kill people. That's what the military is for. To kill, or threaten to kill. Sure, we call it the Department of Defense, but it is truly the Department of *War*. At bayonet practice—*slash! parry! **thrust!***—we learned the spirit of the bayonet. Every time a sergeant screamed, "What is the spirit of the bayonet!?" there was only one answer. It was screamed so hard that you got a headache, ***KILL! KILL! KILL!*** And we practiced, practiced, practiced, if only for a few days. While running the bayonet course, we practiced stabbing man-like targets so we would become desensitized and not hesitate in combat. Of course they don't tell you that you are intentionally being desensitized.

The drill sergeants often took me aside and spent extra time with me. Sometimes we sat in the office and Sergeant Christian, the Senior drill sergeant and a Vietnam veteran, a grizzled and serious man, drank his coffee and told me what I was doing wrong, or right. He didn't smile much, but when he did, he meant it.

He asked questions and expected direct answers, man to man, not Private to Sergeant. I was the subordinate, but he didn't want a limp washrag leading his platoon; if I couldn't look him in the eyes and deliver the good and the bad, he did not want me around. That's what he said. I knew he was in charge, and he knew he was in charge. Man to man does not mean talking back. He constantly reiterated that the most powerful leadership is done from the front and by example. *Follow me!*

He taught the importance of a working chain of command. A member of the platoon was always welcome to talk to me, but when they had problems they were first to go through their team leader, and if he couldn't help, the squad leader, and finally me. Otherwise, you end up flooded with petty issues that could have been solved if people just put their heads together. The boss cannot allow subordinates to waste his time with trivia that adults should be able to handle themselves. Likewise, I was to solve problems that I could handle and insulate drill sergeants from below.

In return for their time, the drill sergeants expected incredible effort. They were direct, and feedback was instant, which greatly speeds the learning curve.

There was a way for sergeants to physically beat unmotivated recruits and troublemakers without going to jail. Most of the sergeants in the company were good and serious men, but I saw that one in particular managed to beat recruits by proxy. He would never say it directly, because by doing so, he would risk serious consequences, but he somehow induced punitive beatings, and there was "wall to wall counseling" at times. It was easy to have someone thrashed. The most divisive tool that all the sergeants wielded was smoking privileges.

We were competing for Honor Platoon, and a single member of our platoon who was not performing up to standards could cause us to lose, even if everyone else did well. If a recruit was doing poorly, the entire platoon's smoking privileges might be suspended. I didn't smoke, so it didn't matter to me. However, certain members of the platoon, who were otherwise good people, became very edgy when their nicotine supply was threatened. They tended to patch the problem by "motivating" the problem-recruits to higher levels of performance. Under-achievers were ambushing the nicotine train and in effect, were calling for air strikes on their own positions, and a few were roughed up.

To make sure that everyone understood the problem *exactly,* a sergeant would get in front of the platoon and call Private Snuffy to the front where he would stand at attention. The sergeant would bellow, "Due to Private Snuffy's unwillingness to stay awake during the M-21 anti-tank mine class, smoking privileges are suspended until further notice. You shitbirds can thank Private Snuffy for helping you kick the habit." Soon the mere mention of smoking privileges caused the unmotivated to perk up, and the sergeants used the tool with unfailing success.

Many young men who set a course for Special Forces thought they were tough and mean, though mostly they were overly optimistic. Some wanted to be transformed from whatever they were into *Killers.* They wanted to know the black arts, to be ninja, rattlesnakes, and lady-tamers all at the same time. They figured that once they became respected and feared "Green Berets," the world would lay gifts at their feet.

There was one man that I will call Lizard. He was about five-nine, medium build, and beady eyed. He constantly bragged about how well he would do in this or that training. When he didn't do well, he complained and made excuses. When he looked at you, it was like he was sizing you up, perhaps plotting to do evil. When recruits collapsed during marches he often laughed at them. He gave me the creeps.

Fights were common. One day I walked into the latrine and found Lizard beating the hell out of one of my squad leaders. Lizard was on the floor kneeing him in the ribs, so I pulled him off and it was over, but there was often something going on, and Lizard was often involved.

At the opposite extreme was another fellow headed for Special Forces. He was a superior athlete and a nice person, but he seemed entirely at the mercy of his girlfriend's letters. Practically every time a letter came from her, he cried. He cried as if she wrote on onion paper, so I called them onion letters.

A bad onion was like a tear-gas grenade; he was worthless for the rest of the day. Good onions transformed him into a superman. The worst days were when nothing came, allowing his imagination to run amok.

We earned phone privileges, but there were far too many recruits for the number of pay phones, so an anxious line of camouflaged soldiers formed. The limit was five minutes, not a second more. If the first people took too much time, those at the end would lose the chance to call and might not get another opportunity for days. If nobody was home or the line was busy, Tough Luck. A recruit who wants to talk with his girl or his mother but can't reach her can get irritable.

Inevitably, Private Onion would nearly incite his own lynching as he spent more than his allotted time while shedding layers of tears. Talk about a volatile situation, this was it. The scene was always the same. With the receiver pressed hard against his ear, his hand on the wall and his head bowed, within scant minutes he was standing in a puddle of tears.

His pain was awful, so dreadful and complete that others pretended not to notice, looking down at their boots, or turning around to look away while nervously eyeing their watches, knowing that the Onion would again push the time envelope.

There was the distinct impression that his girlfriend enjoyed peeling away his layers and flicking them with red fingernails into a fire. Why else did she answer the phone only to torture his soul? And why did he allow her to commit such crimes?

"Stop calling her," I advised.

"She doesn't understand," he cried.

And neither did I, at that point in my life. Later I did. Love seems to make no sense; it can be absolutely wonderful, or the most horrible, sickening feeling imaginable when it brings on despair, hate, jealousy and who knows what else. When it grows sour, it really stinks and can make you physically ill. To those looking down with an eagle's-eye view, the Onion was growing his love in the wrong field, but love-sickness makes perfectly healthy people go blind.

When he refused to leave the phone, recruits ganged up and chased him away, or complained to me. I hated dealing with the Onion while he was in the throes of his love pain. He was irrational, volatile, and seemed not to care whether he lived or died. Any night I expected him to slip out of the barracks and go AWOL. His uniform was often sloppy, for which he was constantly doing pushups and extra duty; he was slow at cleaning his weapon, and he moaned and wept in the barracks at night.

He got the idea of "buying" phone time so he could talk longer. He paid so much by doing guard duty for others, that soon he had created a market. Others got in on the action. He practically never slept, which was poor management on my part. I should not have allowed it, but it seemed harmless at the time.

Maybe sleep deprivation was the final push for the Onion. I think he finally became suicidal, or maybe it was homicidal. In the barracks one night, a recruit tipped me off that Onion had stolen some ammo from the range, which is a serious crime.

I found Onion perched on his bed, staring at the shining waxed floor with elbows on his knees, wringing his hands. We had already cleaned and turned our weapons in to the Arms Room. He was still in uniform when he should have been showering, then shining his boots, and squaring away his gear for the next day.

I whispered to him so that others would not hear, *"I heard you got some ammo."* It didn't matter if he confessed or not, so I didn't ask. I was going to find every bullet.

"I'm gonna search your gear," I said.

He did not appear concerned, and acknowledged my presence only with a grunt.

I rifled his gear and his locker, searched his laundry bag, and from boots to helmet. There it was, in an ammo pouch of all places, a thirty round magazine of M-16 ammo. Thirty rounds of high velocity assault rifle ammunition specifically designed for hunting humans. I kept searching, but that was all I found.

If I took it to a sergeant, the Onion would rot in prison. That's what they said. Cause and effect, no fancy excuses will help you.

Steal ammo = go to prison.

The Onion must have realized the folly, and the magnitude, of his act. I told him to follow me outside where we could talk in private.

Outside the barracks, under the lights, I asked: "Why did you steal the ammo? You know that you can go to prison, right?" He would not see his girl in prison. Fear gripped him.

Suddenly he was deeply concerned; the implications of his crime must finally have dawned on him. He began gushing apologies and promises not to do it again.

"What are you going to do?" he asked.

"Nothing, if you get your act together."

It was a mistake on my part, a giant mistake, but I took the ammo and stuck it in the amnesty box, and told the Onion to pull it together and get squared-away. No questions were asked for anything that showed up in the amnesty box. I believe in second chances, but it was a horrible lapse of judgment on my part to risk the lives of others so that Onion would not go to prison.

Nevertheless, he did not make it to Special Forces Selection, nor did he ever snap a magazine into his rifle and chop down the platoon for running him away from the phone. In fact, I seem to recall that he did not finish Basic and AIT. The Army sent him home where he belonged. During the first months of training, the Army sent lots of people packing who did not adapt.

I watched a drill sergeant as he unlocked the amnesty box the next day and found the ammo. No questions were asked, but we got the big prison lecture again. Steal a bullet, go to prison. Steal a weapon—well, that would not be advisable.

When a sergeant heard about recruits swapping phone time for guard duty, it may as well have been Watergate. They fired me on the spot as platoon leader. I was again on the lowest rung of the proverbial ladder, and was terribly upset that I had disappointed the sergeants after they had entrusted me with so much authority. I had not tried to hide the practice, but was so busy with other matters that I hadn't thought through the implications of people not getting their sleep. During training, we were constantly being tested on what we learned. Lower test scores by sleepy recruits reflected on the sergeants' ability to train the troops.

The bright side of getting fired was that I had less responsibility and got more time to eat and sleep. My demotion was like a vacation, but it didn't last long. A week or so later, I was again promoted to platoon leader.

The border between Basic and AIT (Advanced Individual Training: for our class, infantry training) was about as big as this sentence. One morning at formation SFC Christian said to us, "Congratulations. You graduated Basic and are now in AIT. We are now going to celebrate. Drop and give me one hundred."

Around this time in our training, we began using MILES (multiple integrated laser engagement system) equipment. Our weapons were outfitted with lasers and we wore sensors so when we got "hit," a loud beeper sounded off. That was it, "dead soldier." For near misses, there was a quick "beep."

There is no way to simulate true life and death fear. MILES is a good training aid, but as for fear, even BB guns are more frightening, because in facing one, you could find your eye splattered out onto your cheek.

One of the first days that we used the MILES system, the drill sergeants gave us a tiny, tiny idea of how frustrating it must have been in Vietnam. As we walked through the woods, "Bam," a single shot rang out: **BEEEEEP.** . . . Somebody was hit. It takes a special key to turn off the beeper, which prevents soldiers from cheating by turning it off and pretending they were not hit. And we couldn't tell where the shot had originated. Over a period of several days, it became obvious that the enemy could pick us off one by one by simply firing a single, well-aimed shot, and calling it a day.

A couple of months into training we were "attacking" a fixed position that was defended by a different unit. We were having a hard time getting in. Beepers were going off around me, and it seemed that just about every time I moved I heard a quick *beep!* from my system as someone tried to shoot me. The sergeants taught that we should advance in three to five second rushes; if you ran for longer than that, the enemy was much more likely to get you. But it's hard to keep getting up only to sprint a few seconds and then hit the ground again, so some soldiers tried their luck and went for long dashes. *BEEEEEP!*

As we attacked the position, the heat attacked us. South Georgia summers are so hot that watermelons and soldiers alike can shrivel like big raisins. Though the Army safeguards against soldiers dying of heatstroke, by now I had seen many heat casualties, mostly heat cramps and heat exhaustion. Whenever you felt that chill come across your body, you knew that you were pushing the red line. It was the middle of summer, humid, and the sergeants were walking around in T-shirts. They also had sticks in their hands pointing things out while we attacked the position.

I got an idea. I took off my camouflaged shirt along with my combat gear and left it with a member of the platoon. I picked up a stick to look like a drill corporal and walked through the unknowing "enemy perimeter." The drill corporals were younger men who helped the sergeants, so I didn't look out of place while barking orders and pointing with my stick as if I knew what I was doing, "Keep that head down troop!" *beep! beep! BEEEEEP!* our guys were shooting in and getting some hits. I walked right up to the enemy positions, got a good look around, walked back and put my gear on and kept "fighting." I was having a blast. Lesson: Audacity is a virtue. (If it doesn't get you killed.)

Later we were conducting a "bait and ambush." The sergeants were letting me tactically lead the platoon for short times, rather like letting your teenager take the car for a spin around town. For someone who had joined largely to earn money for college, I figured that I had found my niche. I was going to college alright, then coming back to become an officer. Later, I learned that the backbone of the Army is made up of the NCO's, but I still planned to become an officer.

During high school I had checked out going to one of the military academies such as West Point, but didn't have the grades to compete with other applicants. So, I looked for other ways to get in. I talked with a lieutenant in Alabama who helped to recruit officers. He mailed me a two page handwritten letter along with lots of information on how to get into the academy. First, he suggested that I demonstrate my potential to become a stellar soldier:

Dear Mike,

Army Regulations enclosed, about West Point appointments. Read them carefully. . . .

The most important thing I can tell you going into the

service is don't follow the crowd. Be a leader among your peers. Never lose sight of what you are trying to do. If you want a college education then get one. But you are your best friend and you have to take care of yourself and don't depend on anyone else to get it done for you but you. (I'll help all I can, but up there [Fort Bragg] it'll be tough.)

. . . One other thing. You are about to go through some of the most degrading and mentally stressing times you can imagine [Ha! This was like a beach vacation in comparison to my last ten years growing up.], just play the game. They want to see how bad you want it. So show that you do set yourself apart. Play the Game and Play it Better than them . . . Once you get to Bragg, I'm going to [call] a friend . . . that has a platoon up there and can help . . . He's a very squared away guy.

Yours truly,
2Lt. George V. -

I liked his attitude, and he seemed like a squared-away man himself.

And there I was, as advised, taking charge. I instructed two soldiers on LP/OP (listening post/observation post) that when they saw the OPFOR (opposing forces/enemy) move to a certain position, one of the two soldiers should fire a thirty round magazine on full automatic and quickly reload. After firing, they both should "retreat" to our ambush position while trying to get the OPFOR to follow, as we had been taught. It was important that the LP/OP's take the correct route back because we were trying to lure the OPFOR into an easy avenue of approach to our position, a "deathtrap" for the enemy. We were waiting.

The instructions were *extremely* explicit. Our men's route back would be more difficult, but safe. "Whatever you do, do *not* come up that draw!" We had lots of rifles waiting for the OPFOR and I was in position to initiate the ambush at the right moment. This was incredibly fun.

Pop-pop-pop-pop. . . . A couple of hundred yards away one of our men cut loose with blanks. Then some enemy fire. Soon came the first enemy, the point man. *Wait a minute . . .* I thought, *he looks like one of our men. And, he got here awful fast. But he looks like our man. He's getting too close.* When he was close enough that I could see the whites of his eyes behind his camouflaged face, I hesitated pulling the trigger, then—*Pop-pop-pop* . . . I fired a three round burst of blanks into his chest. ***BEEEEEP!*** I shot at the second man, but he dodged for cover and came up the way he was supposed to. In combat I would have done the same. Accidents like that are called "the friction of war," "fratricide," or a "friendly fire accident." But dead is dead.

Now we had another problem. The unit that we were to ambush was much larger, and our chief advantage was to have been surprise. In reality, we should have pulled out and avoided further contact, leaving a small delaying force behind and other delaying forces at pre-selected spots. But we had not learned all that yet, so the sergeants made us stay and fight.

Soon, beepers were going off all around me. Eventually we were overrun and all "killed," but I had learned how to reduce the chances of being shot when shooting from a hole. In that situation, it's important not to keep coming up from the same position to shoot, or the enemy will merely put his sights on your position, and when you pop up—lights out. Even in a hole, you can be slightly unpredictable, but it's tough when the enemy is closing in from multiple angles and keeping your head down with suppressing fire while others are moving in to get you with a grenade.

As they closed in, someone yelled for me to surrender!

My "dead platoon" was all around; the sergeants had already turned off their beepers and they were rooting for me.

"Come out of that hole. Surrender," yelled the voice again.

"Yon ain't gonna surrender to you shitbirds!" yelled SFC Christian. And he was right. "Kill those sons of bitches, Yon! Kill all of 'em!" He sounded like a father rooting for his son at a football game. "Take better shots, Yon! You are shooting high when you pop up! Just take an extra second to get a quick aim, shoot, and keep moving like you are."

The *Code of Conduct* provides a terse summation of what is expected from a warrior.

Article II
I will never surrender of my own free will. If in command I will never surrender my men while they still have the means to resist.

That says it clearly enough. If you have any means to resist, and there are no orders to the contrary, you are to fight. Implied is that you are to fight to the death.

I screamed at the "enemy" from my hole that was almost as deep as a grave. "Come and get it!"

And they did. They were closing in. I popped up with my rifle and shot a green faced recruit who had taken cover behind a pine tree that wasn't big enough to protect half his face. *BEEEEEP!*

"Good kill, Yon! That's how you do it!" The sergeant then turned his attention to the "dead" soldier: "And you, you shitbag, what were you thinking taking cover behind a tree that ain't big enough to make a box of toothpicks? Yon could have killed you with a rock!"

And there were the beeps! as they nearly got me.

My platoon was frenzied. The sergeants were rooting for me, and a sergeant actually brought me more ammo that he had taken from a "dead soldier." Americans love the underdog who fights. After all, we came from the underdogs, and we love a good fight. We are a warring nation. We believe in violence more than we believe in peace, though we claim the contrary. My first combat training came when I learned to play cowboys and Indians. I killed a lot of Indians. I loved killing Indians. Usually you just yelled, *"Bang! You're dead!"* and when they were playing fairly, they just fell down and died without much fuss or blood. They never screamed or anything like that. And it was fun; you weren't killing *people*, you were killing *Indians*. After you killed them, they got up and you were the Indian. I loved killing cowboys, too. We call it play, but it is training. Our new batch of killers, the latest generation of man-children now in kindergarten, is being desensitized and trained to wage killing more clinically with video games and violent movies. Killing seems to be in our genes—and we reinforce it zealously.

And now I was being trained to join the official U.S. Killing Team. It's sort of like the Olympic downhill ski team, but more serious. As we practiced killing each other, there were only two of the enemy left, and they seemed timid as we swapped shots. I was running out of ammo. If I stayed there, I would almost surely die. There comes a time to call it quits. I popped up and fired my last magazine on full-auto to put their heads down, then bolted from the hole and was making a run for it when I heard the shots from behind. ***BEEEEEP!***

But, as I later learned in Special Forces training, the mentality that leads one to fight from a losing position, against an overwhelming force, is not just foolish, but least likely to achieve victory. In Special Forces, the saying is "Run, run, run away: live to fight another day." *Never become decisively engaged with an overwhelming force.*

The military can be an incredible learning experience.

Despite myriad safety rules, a few people were getting hurt while we trained. We learned to drive Armored Personnel Carriers (APC's) which is an overly optimistic name, since the armor is unable to withstand direct fire from even medium sized machine guns, or small anti-armor weapons.

American kids are used to watching tanks plow over trees in the movies, and APC's resemble boxy-shaped tanks, so it followed that teenagers driving APC's would try to knock down trees. The drill sergeants warned that smashing into trees would result in our knocking out our front teeth. Cosmic justice, I guess. The trees weren't hurting anyone.

Well, maybe those who smashed into trees did it accidentally, or only said it was accidental, but that was hardly relevant to their dentists. When you drive an APC with the hatch open, your eyes peer out, but your teeth are at the level of hard metal. And when you hit the tree, which is easy to accidentally do, if the tree is big enough, the metal bites your front teeth. Despite the warnings, the lumber gods claimed some smiles.

We were no longer in high school. This was the Land of No Second Chances. As we began to figure things out, we became more like a unit and less like a bunch of recruits just heaped in together. I certainly would not say that we were *cohesive*, which is a big word when you describe a military unit, but we did learn how to work together on a small scale for our mutual benefit. We were achieving the transformation from civilians to soldiers, barely passable soldiers, but soldiers nonetheless.

That was my world. Simultaneously, in a different unit was another platoon leader named Steve Shaulis. Steve was in college when he heard about the opportunity to go directly into Special Forces, so he took a chance. He was having similar challenges with his platoon, in a parallel military universe. It would be a few more months before we met, then only half a year after that I would be charged with murder in Ocean City while out on the town with Steve.

Meanwhile, I befriended a squad leader in another platoon, Rob, who had enlisted for Special Forces. Rob was a quiet, likable character. He looked like any other bald-headed recruit, and had a good sense of humor, but he already took the Army seriously. Sometimes, while the others were turning in for the night, we ran laps around the barracks, running for miles in the moonlight because we thought we weren't getting enough exercise to prepare us for SF Selection. We were right.

We knew graduation was close when we did a twelve-mile march. It was hot and people were falling out. Some just quit, others actually collapsed: *Karuumph!* We carried maybe twenty pounds of gear in a small pack, an M-16, and wore helmets—not a lot, but the Georgia heat and humidity were savage. I hustled up and down the ranks, talking to the platoon, helping those who looked weak, so I ended up doing a lot more work than they, and my uniform was drenched with sweat. But the encouragement helped to motivate some, so it was worth it. Problem was, at the end of the march my legs were exhausted—"smoked" is the Army word.

Almost at the end, with only few hundred yards to go, both of my legs suddenly cramped. Frozen from the waist down. I dropped my M-16, fell forward and caught myself in a pushup position. *Where did that come from!* My legs were completely frozen in a wave of cramping muscles.

It caught me so off-guard that I nearly screamed in agony. Had I been alone, likely I would have screamed, but somehow I managed to swallow it back. A couple of recruits helped me to my feet. My muscles started working again, though not very well. I tried to squat and stretch, but they cramped again and I fell over.

That time I managed to get up by myself. There was a truck for those who "couldn't" go on, but there was no way I would willingly board that truck. That was like suicide. The option is always there if you want to quit when it hurts, but to hell with that option! Somebody handed back my weapon and I made it to the end.

Most of the recruits handled Basic and AIT well. Others cried their eyes out because they missed their families and sweethearts, or the accumulated stress got to them. At first I thought, *This isn't hard! Two-a-day football practices were much tougher than this.*

But it wasn't the training that got to some recruits; it was the separation. I missed my grandparents and wanted to show how much I loved them. I spent what amounted to more than a month's pay to buy them some ceiling fans and a microwave. I realized just how lucky I had been to have my grandparents—the luckiest kid on Earth after they gave me shelter from my father's home.

Loneliness must have been a big problem, because the sergeants warned that after AIT ended, some recruits would marry women they had only known for a few days or weeks. They warned us, pointing out that it was almost always a mistake. I thought, *Yeah right, ain't nobody gonna get married to a girl they just met.* Getting married was a big, gigantic, galaxy-shaking decision. On the other hand, the sergeants' outlandish predictions about human behavior had so far proven infallible. . . .

I felt like I had done my best during Basic and AIT, and that I had accomplished something worthwhile, but also knew that this was the easiest part of my Army experience. The sergeants who at first said that I was nuts to go to Special Forces, now encouraged me and told me what they knew, which was not much. SF was a hush-hush world.

They also asked me to stay to help with the next class. I would be "promoted" from private to drill corporal.

I wrote to Richard White:

> The first Sergeant called me in last night . . . offered Drill Corporal position for next cycle . . . I'm not sure . . .

We had an open house and civilians were allowed to attend.

... after the civilians left on Saturday we went to a foot-
ball game . . . 4 people with parachutes fell in the stadium
. . . things got back to normal . . . won the last 4 out of 5
inspections losing one by 2 stinking points (out of a 100).
Write back with college reply [about your adventures].

Graduation: My grandparents and Richard White came to the ceremony.
Our platoon graduated number one in the company out of four platoons. As
platoon leader, I graduated number one in my platoon, got my $5,000 bonus,
and immediately invested it for college.

Just as the sergeants had warned, after graduation, while some of the new
soldiers were in Airborne Training, they married women they had known for
less than a week. The record was three days, I think. (I don't know how
quickly they actually captivated their partners-for-life, but the proposal was
delivered and accepted in about seventy-two hours.) Two people had to actu-
ally bump into each other, start a conversation and decide that quickly to get
married. I was stunned—and learning a lot. *Never go grocery shopping
when you are hungry. . . .*

The sergeants asked me to stay as a drill corporal because they wanted
volunteers. The best people to do difficult work are volunteers. The promo-
tion to corporal would not be real; the stripes would be only for show when
the next class arrived. I was honored but declined because I wanted to go to
jump school. I already had orders, in this case, a sheet of paper covered with
stilted Army writing.

The sergeants upped the ante by saying that I had a lot to learn about lead-
ership, and they would teach me if I stayed. They could get the orders
delayed. I didn't refuse that offer, and stayed back while the others went to
Airborne Training. The sergeants delivered on their promise.

During the next class, a sergeant told me to go take the test for my

CORPORAL

Military Driver's License. I needed to pass that test to
drive a "deuce and a half," the Army name for a big,
2½ ton truck. I said that I didn't know how to drive a
stick shift, except on a riding-lawnmower, and that I
wasn't a good driver even with cars—much less big
trucks.

"Ah, you'll do just fine. Now get down there and
take that test."

Okay—I was behind the wheel of a deuce and a
half, and sitting beside me was a fidgeting sergeant who was evaluating my
driving. Somehow I got the big truck out of the parking lot and was trying

to make a right-hand turn at a Stop sign. I was nervous and not exactly in control of the truck, but I could loosely influence its behavior. I turned the wheel to the right but drifted into the other lane and suddenly a car was coming straight at us. He blew his horn and ran off the road, and I ran off the road, then managed to steer back up, but into the wrong lane. By this time the sergeant was screaming at me to *"pull this thing over!"* though his choice of words was considerably more colorful.

He drove us back to the parking lot and I had to walk back to my unit. I had graduated number one in Basic and AIT, but couldn't drive a truck. When I got back, the sergeants—after they stopped laughing—taught me to drive, and I got the license about a week later. But after that, when I said that I didn't know how to do something, they *listened.*

Unfortunately, a week or two later I ran off the road in another deuce and a half. We needed a tow truck to pull it out. After *that*, the sergeants usually wouldn't let me drive.

Rob had also been asked to stay back as a drill corporal and I noticed something familiar about him: He read and studied constantly. Unlike many of the other recruits who enlisted for Special Forces, Rob had done his homework both mentally and physically. We often did PT (physical training) together and he normally brought a book to read while we ran. That's right, we would run for miles at a good pace while Rob held his book out front and read. When he got tired, he switched hands. I wondered how many people like Rob would be at Selection? *Spooky.*

I was running alone in a training area when I found a dead fox on the road. It had been hit by a car, but was still fresh and warm, complete with fleas. Foxes sometimes carry rabies, but this one looked perfectly healthy (except that it was dead), so I slung it over my shoulder and started running home.

People drove by and saw the fox flopping, and as I passed other runners there were some strange looks. Soon I was sitting out near the telephones where Private Onion had once stood, tacking the pelt to a wooden pallet preparing to salt it when a couple of sergeants walked by and saw the fur-less-creature in the grass.

The first drill sergeant gasped, *"Oh my God!* Yon skinned a dog!"

SFC Christian bellowed, "**YON!** Have you lost your mind! What the *hell* are you doing!"

What the hell does it look like I'm doing?

"I just skinned a fox, sergeant," and I displayed the beautiful pelt as if I were a spokes-model on *The Price Is Right.* I don't like the idea of clubbing baby seals, but fur is fur, and it would be shameful to let such a fox fur rot away after a car had done the hunting.

SFC Christian barked in his command voice, "You can't go around here killing animals. This is a military base."

After I gave them a short explanation, SFC Christian smiled and said, "You really are like those SF nutcases I have known." And they walked away shaking their heads.

Letter to Richard White:

> Most of the stuff we do is military, so I'll just give you a brief outline of what is in the news this week . . . ran 8.6 miles Sunday, 2 miles Monday, 2 miles yesterday, 5 tomorrow, 7 Friday . . . learned to take apart 3 Soviet weapons (They assemble the same way. If you can do one, you can do the others) . . .
>
> Give me a college run down.

Although Richard and I were born in the Winter Haven Hospital only days apart, our next meeting would not occur until we were in high school. At the beginning of our sophomore year, before we formally met, there were student body elections. (Our high school was tenth through twelfth.)

Richard had a friend named Bill Gurley who had political aspirations. Most sophomores were nervous because it was our first year at the big high school that had close to two thousand students, and Bill wanted to run for sophomore representative, but being just a tenth grader, he was timid. Good leaders are not usually meek, but Richard decided to help Bill anyway.

Together, they plastered campaign signs all around the school:

Vote!
Bill Gurley
Sophomore Representative

As a prerequisite to run, in addition to rallying voter support, Bill needed fifty signatures from students and three from teachers saying that he was a good man for the job. Candidates also needed a certain grade average from their previous schools, so the front office had to sign-off, showing that they had checked the records. In this way, the school ensured that it maintained a puppet government "representing student interests."

As the elections drew closer, Bill-the-timid was out sick, so Richard-the-lion-hearted went around and collected the signatures from the students and teachers, then got permission from the principal's office.

Most people couldn't remember Bill Gurley, so Richard reminded them what he looked like and who he was. Richard said things like, "You remember Bill. He's the guy with curly hair, about 5'10", always nice and funny. Real smart. He knows you and hopes you will vote for him. He said you were in civics class together in eighth grade and that he really likes you."

The teachers, students, and front office all endorsed Bill. They wanted him to win because they all knew that he was such a good guy, and that Bill knew them even though they only vaguely remembered him. He put a lot of work into those election signs, so obviously he was a serious character, and his name was well known. Everyone liked him.

When it came time for the speeches, Bill was still out sick, but Richard was gracious enough to get in front of the entire sophomore class assembled in the gymnasium and deliver a moving speech. Richard easily evoked sympathy for Bill-the-bedridden, and during his illness Bill Gurley was elected by a landslide.

Every morning before classes we put our right hands over our hearts and began the day with the Pledge of Allegiance . . . WITH LIBERTY AND JUSTICE FOR ALL. Then we listened to the morning announcements crackle over the intercom. There was the football news, Chess Club news, . . . the threat that smoking was (still) not permitted in the restrooms and that smokers would be caught and punished by death or worse, and then there was the list of which buses were late. Finally, each day at the end of the announcements, there was a little request, *"And will Bill Gurley please report to the main office."*

Monday: *"And will Bill Gurley please report . . . "*
Tuesday: *"And will Bill Gurley please report . . . "*
Wednesday: *"And will Bill Gurley please report . . . "*
Thursday: *"And will Bill Gurley please report . . . "*
Friday: *"And will Bill Gurley . . . "*

People started asking questions: *Where is the Sophomore Representative? Why doesn't he report to the office so they will stop asking? Why don't they just go to his homeroom class and get him? Is he that afraid? Who voted for him?*

The Student Council was having meetings, but Bill never attended. He was totally remiss in his duties. The principal was miffed.

This went on for weeks. People asked Richard about Bill, and Richard simply said, *"Ask Bill,"* which was not easy because nobody could find him, and apparently nobody even had his home telephone number.

He was elusive. An enigma. The school was buzzing. Most people remembered Bill and most sophomores had voted for him, but nobody could find him. Bill Gurley would not show his face and he had a very good reason. He did not exist.

A non-existent person was swept into office as our student body representative, which was simultaneously very funny, and more than slightly alarming. Richard planned and pulled off the shenanigan all by himself. His idea was brilliant; his execution was beautiful. There was no reason why his plan would work, and every reason why it would flop, but sometimes pure genius is nothing more than a good idea rumbling forward under the steam of utter audacity. Richard was fifteen years old.

He'd thought up the idea during PE, he told me later. Richard was by no means athletic, but he played a mean game of ping-pong, and a tougher game of chess. He resented having to dress out for the PE class, so he'd sought revenge while sitting on the wooden bleachers in the gym.

Finally, to add insult to injury, Richard had "Bill Gurley" T-shirts made, and Bill Gurley became something of a cult figure, retaining his "popularity" for almost three years, until we graduated. You could find his name scribbled on desks or on bathroom walls, **"Bill Gurley was here."** Richard even had one of his friends insert a "Gurley, William A." student file at the front office. Bill Gurley was the name of a real person that he had never met, but Richard thought the name sounded good for a funny prank.

Someone checked out a library book under the Gurley name and apparently didn't bring it back, so the principal called Richard down to the office and accused him.

Richard denied it. The principal accused him again and again, but Richard held his ground. Finally, the principal was livid and screaming at Richard, and commanded him to sign his name on a piece of paper. The principal said that he was going to take the signature down to the police station and have them analyze the handwriting to prove that Richard did it. The principal gave him "one last chance to fess-up," but Richard admitted nothing. Richard, who is now a college professor in Kansas, still denies it.

Richard-the-Audacious was my kind of guy. To the principal, Richard was a marked little man. So far as Richard was concerned, the principal, too, was a marked man. Later, he was replaced with another principal, but the Bill Gurley story was passed on to the next tyrant with a paddle—and he really was a tyrant-principal in my opinion, worse than the one he replaced. We fought back, and caused the school faculty considerable heartache during our senior year.

Richard and I must have known that we were destined to team up for adventure. Before we met, we had "gun battles" in halls between classes. We didn't even know each other's names, but when we spotted each other, we approached like cowboys ready for a shootout, and when we drew, one or both of us always dropped and wiggled and died bravely on the floor scattered among our books as the students changed classes and laughed. This was not something we did once or twice, but countless times, and our classmates seemed to enjoy our duels as much as we did.

We met formally in a drama class and quickly became friends. Soon, we had debates. Richard and I were on opposing teams and clashed head-on. There were nasty arguments as we each led our debate teams, and some members of our panels lost their tempers and sank into name calling. We didn't agree on everything, but I learned to respect his well-thought-out positions. Richard was not one to be trifled with. He played chess the same way, and his defense was in the attack. He came prepared, was aggressive, and, when in doubt, simply lunged for the prize!

Publicly we debated, but privately we compared notes. We found that we both had tried bomb-making, which is the type of fun that turns many boys into hamburger. Since we had arrived at our pastime independently, our "technologies" were radically different, so we learned a lot from each other.

We had graduated from the minor leagues of mailbox-sized devices long ago, and stuffing firecrackers down toad throats was never our modus operandi, but we could make devices that would destroy an average house. We were high-tech and, as it happened, our improvised devices would have made a soldier proud.

We set out to see who could build the biggest bomb, but remained very safety conscious. Bomb-making is not a game, and is fraught with hidden dangers. Unfortunately, one of our cohorts also tried his hand, but his technique was not so well-thought-out. A bomb detonated in his face. But that is a story for later.

As for now, I was helping in Basic Training as a drill corporal.

Richard's sister was about to marry an Army helicopter pilot, so he wrote asking for advice on pranks to pull at the wedding. Obviously, he was a master prankster himself, but most of the fun is in the planning and mulling over the details with your friends, so I offered some advice.

> So college life is pretty wild, eh? With your acting talents, I'm sure it's more exciting than the faculty intends.
>
> [In] response to your most urgent request . . . How about putting some kind of plastic creature inside the wedding cake? It may take some work, but the screams you get from the old ladies would be worth it . . . I'm convinced with your sneaky ideas and talents you could successfully camouflage a plastic roach . . .
>
> . . . Drive on . . . Drive on . . .

But that kind of thinking was small time for the likes of Richard White. I got the weekend off as a drill corporal. Winter Haven was only a half-day car ride from Fort Benning, so I hitched a ride, and attended the wedding, which was held at the church where I went to kindergarten with Pam. Richard allowed the wedding ceremony to go undisturbed, but showed his colors at the reception that was held next to a lake, a location which increased his options.

During the reception, Richard's sister, the bride, went crazy when he skied behind a fast boat, close to the shore—wearing his tuxedo. The guests loved it and were howling. He was a very good skier, and could have pulled it off without getting too wet, but things didn't go exactly as planned when the driver of the boat, also a teenager, did some fancy maneuvers that left Richard drenched. Richard returned the rented tuxedo, soaking wet, in a plastic bag.

I hitched a ride back to Fort Benning. As drill corporal, I found it interesting to watch when the new recruits were first issued weapons. Some of them admired the weapons, others bragged that they had shot similar rifles, and all seemed to be enchanted with the idea of flicking the selector to full-auto and squirting out a thirty round magazine of tracers. Shooting full-auto—and tracers at that—pings the teenaged male fun meter pretty near the top.

Decades ago, research on combat wounds showed that most times when an enemy was hit by small arms fire, the shot was not carefully aimed. Simply putting rounds downrange in the vicinity of the enemy results in hits. For instance, at nighttime, the enemy may be impossible to see, so soldiers simply shoot into the dark. It was determined that if a soldier could carry more bullets, he could hurt more enemies.

But one of the biggest enemies of a soldier is weight, and big bullets weigh more. Therefore the M-16 was designed to fire a smaller bullet so that more ammo could be carried. The problem with a smaller bullet is that it won't penetrate foliage and other impediments as well, and it loses its killing power more quickly even from air resistance. So, there was the trade-off. More bullets downrange, but smaller.

In order for M-16 bullets to pack sufficient killing power, the smaller bullet had to travel very fast. In fact, the muzzle velocity of an M-16 bullet, which is the speed of the bullet the instant it leaves the barrel, is about Mach 3. The round is designed to kill by inducing shock. When it strikes a living body, this supersonic round causes hydrostatic shock, resulting in enormous tissue damage. These weapons were made by scientists and engineers at great expense for the sole purpose of killing human beings. (However, the M-16 is more apt to wound than to kill.)

In the new class, a few recruits stroked the rifles as if they were fondling cherished parts of their anatomies. The M-16 was their Power, and power begs to be used. I feel safer with professional soldiers who are trained and understand that Power than I do with many individuals that I meet on the street who may have that Power in their trunk, but little self-discipline.

If you have never seen the destructive capability of an assault weapon up close, or felt it rumble through your body as it spits those deadly supersonic bullets downrange, the sheer violence of the experience is hard to imagine. Just the sound of a bullet passing your ear will cause it to ring. **Snap!** *rinnggg.* . . .

Taking a few steps back from the picture to gain a broader perspective, the young soldiers themselves are viewed by many political and military leaders as just a part of the weapon system. Soldiers wielding weapons are the leaders' Power. In a warring nation, that Power begs to be used.

Being a drill corporal, I was in a unique position to lead the new class. After all, I wasn't a sergeant, I was eighteen years old like most of the new recruits, so I had respect but not the usual separation in age or rank. I spent time with the recruits like a platoon leader, but got to leave post at night when I wanted. Mostly I stayed on base, training for SF Selection.

I lasted a couple of months as a drill corporal, but was eager to go to jump school and get to Fort Bragg. I was spinning my wheels at Fort Benning. I asked the sergeants to release me, and so . . . off to Airborne.

Jump school was three weeks long and was hyped as being rigorous, vigorous, tough, dangerous, and other little words that mean big things. In reality, the majority of the people from combat MOS's found it easy, refreshing, fun . . . (except for the annoying fear of dying).

Letter to Richard White:

> Write your adventure stories so I can use them for enter-
> tainment. (If I start to miss lines its because I have very little
> light. In jump school they seem to <u>attempt</u> to put you under
> pressure . . . I shouldn't be writing now . . . writing in the
> dark.)
> AIRBORNE!
> [I am] thinking about going to college . . . do they have
> ROTC and physics at your college? . . .
> My vocabulary is dwindling. All I can say is: "Get up!" "Get
> down!" and "Maggot!"
> Tell me what's happening in the outside world . . .

Some were at jump school to test their limits, and I respected their purpose. Others were there simply to get jump wings, a badge. I did not respect badge-hunting for its own sake. Others were passing through because it was a prerequisite to getting into units such as the 82nd Airborne Division, which has a richly deserved reputation for being tough and serious—and I liked people who didn't run from a challenge, but sought it out for whatever personal reasons.

Unfortunately, like many military specialty schools, jump school is no longer as challenging as it allegedly used to be, and old timers like to rub it in by saying things like, "Back in my class in '68, it was *tough*. Really tough. Half the guys didn't make it. Today they are letting practically anybody into airborne units."

It bruises the morale of young soldiers when they hear old-timers say: "Today's military is no longer what it used to be. Back in my day, they made a *man* out of you." To that I'd like to say, "Shut up! And my generation could kick your generation's ass any day."

Teenagers do not set national military policy. Teenagers are not the ones who lack the political guts to give the new generation of warrior-types what it wants and craves: Rites of passage into manhood, and hellfire-grueling military training that they deserve and can be proud of having survived, and that they can brag about.

What better could the responsible citizens do for our country than raise the next batch of boys into a breed of men with honor, who will protect us like lions, while we simultaneously give them the rites they want? Eventually they will leave military service fully confident in their manhood. That's what *they* want. That's what we need. The next generation of boys is ready.

Of course there will be those who don't make it, who don't measure up. So what? Some people don't make it through medical school either. We don't want just anybody treating cancer, or defending our lives. That is the nature of hardball playing fields.

On the other hand, the old-timers do have a point that the training could be tougher. There should be two jump schools, I thought. One hot, and one mild. The mild one would be for the mild people, who are just as mild today as they ever were, and the hot course would be reserved for the fire-breathing dragons who are just as ready today as they ever were, if not more so. The athletes of yesteryear, for instance, for the most part, could not hold a candle to modern athletes. The latest generations have not suddenly gone soft the way many old-timers seem to like to think.

As for me, I had no desire to jump out of airplanes other than for fun and curiosity, and because it was a prerequisite for attending Special Forces training. I figured that was where my mettle would be tested.

At Jump School, there are three 250-foot-tall towers used for parachute training. The towers have winches with cables that hoist up the "jumpers," who are wearing parachutes that are held open mechanically. When the "jumper" is released, the chute is already deployed; he or she just floats down and practices landing.

From 250 feet, it takes less than 15 seconds to reach the ground, but that's plenty of time to hurt yourself if you forget your training. It's important after release to immediately steer your parachute away from the tower, and to land facing *into* the wind. Unfortunately, many people fail to follow instructions, or get scared, frazzle out, and don't control the parachute, leading to bad accidents. If you don't steer the parachute, it will automatically track the wrong way, *with* the wind.

Letter to Richard White:

> After receiving your letter I have a renewed sense of motivation towards the Army and doing something crazy (they don't mix.) . . .
>
> Yesterday we trained on the 250' towers . . . only two exciting mishaps. The first was the most common mistake. The soldier (an enlisted man) failed to land properly thus causing damage to his body. I'm not sure what happened to his body, but the landing was indeed spectacular. An ambulance took him away and that's the last I heard of him.
>
>
>
> The second accident involved a 2nd Lt. (The officers have been making a considerable number of mistakes . . . and other accidents . . . [they] don't seem to listen as well as they should.)
>
> While floating down from the 250' tower, he ran into it. He could have died. The parachute tangled in the tower at the 100' mark (lucky for him) and he proceeded to get beat by
>
> PARACHUTE TOWER
>
> the tower until he grasped a beam at the 75' mark . . . 3 instructors went up and got him . . . It was <u>real</u> drama.
>
> . . . Another day of training is over and it's getting

to some people . . . [they] lose their tempers very quickly . . .

Richard suggested that we ride over Niagara Falls in barrels, and when I declined, due to the risk, he insulted me. So I wrote back: [Returning] to the main issue, I personally have had no training in the art of riding over large waterfalls . . . We are taught: Improper Training + High Risk = Upset Insurance Company . . .

We never made it over the Falls—not Niagara, anyway—but three weeks, five jumps, and one minor mid-air collision later I was "airborne."

Richard, now I can say from experience that jumping out of large airplanes and jets is definitely for you! That is, of course, if you aren't scared!

On your first jump you probably won't be that scared. I was more scared on my 4th and 5th . . . my first jump was all a joke. I laughed and yelled all the way out the door until I landed . . . almost totally without fear. However, on my 4th and 5th I was shaking . . . One guy literally pissed his pants before he made his 5th . . . Before you put your knees in the breeze make sure you know and understand what is going on around you. Remember, it's the guy sitting next to you that will kill you . . . Also remember: Upset Insurance Company = Fun times and Good Memories.

I had been in the Army for almost half a year of non-stop adventures, and was having a great time shooting machine guns, assault rifles, blasting off some hand grenades and claymore mines, LAW rockets, learning how to plant landmines, jumping out of big jets and airplanes, and doing pushups. Doesn't that sound like fun?

Yet, despite my big talk, deep inside I was just a kid playing Army. Despite my youth, deep inside was a soldier pecking at the inside of his shell.

Playing Army was over.

SPECIAL FORCES SELECTION—THE "Q COURSE"
John F. Kennedy
Special Warfare Center and School
Fort Bragg, North Carolina

Richard,

[We] arrived at Fort Bragg yesterday . . . tomorrow excitement is going to start . . . training is going to be . . . much harder than what I've done so far . . . physical factors are . . . large part of the high attrition rate . . . have to keep your nose in the books, too . . . some things taught will be precise and dangerous . . . As long as I hang in here, you can make a 3.5 GPA or better . . . should be considered a challenge.
Good night
Good luck
Drive on
Carry on
Airborne!

Welcome to Show Me country. The barracks were not air-conditioned, but since the weather was chilly, it didn't much matter. However, the lack of A/C (artificial comfort) proved an accurate predictor of what was to come.

Special Forces Selection has a reputation of being grueling, and if you make it, your job will be harder, more dangerous than normal duty, and often without much recognition, if any. In fact, the Selection has become increasingly sophisticated due to the investment involved. According to the Special Warfare Center, it costs somewhere between $80,000 and $100,000, not including previous or future training, to get a soldier basically qualified (through this course) to operate on a Special Forces team.

Of those who think that they have what it takes, who have successfully completed prerequisite MOS training, are medically approved, are airborne qualified, who have passed a background check and met a few more prerequisites, some will get a chance to attend Selection. Contrary to popular lore, the goal of such a stringent Selection process is not to boost the egos of those in the group by guaranteeing a high failure rate. Rather, because mistakes are monetarily costly and waste precious slots for chronically under-manned positions, the Army's intention is to pre-select candidates with a high potential for success.

Historically, it has been difficult to keep manpower and quality levels up

Thinking About Special Forces?

Answers to your most
often-asked questions

Special Forces: "The Quiet Professionals"

to par in Special Forces, and at times the standards have been lowered for the sake of having more bodies. To meet those directives, non-Special Forces material were allowed into the unit. This was an incredible mistake and was damaging to morale and effectiveness. In fact, it is so difficult to find the right type of man for this environment that, on average, only about one new "Green Beret" is created per day. Special Forces actually must *advertise* for volunteers because so few qualify.

As for my generation, the standards were not lowered, though some *prerequisites* were. We still had to pass the course without compromise. But there actually was a compromise as to age; I was so young that I would not be an asset to the unit for years, even if I succeeded. After Selection it takes much seasoning, studying, and training before a soldier is ready for some of the sophisticated missions such as guerrilla warfare.

The Army seems to continuously rename its organizations, and names have changed since my class. At the time, it was called the Special Forces Qualification Course, or simply the Q course. However, to set the proper tone and to simplify, I will call the entire process "Selection."

Finally, it should be noted that (sorry ladies) this is one of the last true boys' clubs. For, although women do have the opportunity to crawl into the cockpit and become fighter pilots, they can't go through this course. This is a final frontier. You are getting a tour of one of the last male-only clubs in the United States.

Major Jeff Stolrow was a Marine infantryman for eight years as an enlisted man. He then became an Army psychologist who acquired extensive experience in various aspects of Special Operations. As part of this extensive experience, he wrote <u>The Assessment and Selection of Special Forces Qualification Candidates with the MMPI</u>, for his Ph.D. dissertation at the California School of Professional Psychology in Los Angeles.

In his dissertation, Dr. Stolrow states that in 1981 the calculated attrition rate for the Q Course was 65 percent. Dr. Stolrow told me that among the greatest potential indicators of failure in the Q-course are high levels of rebelliousness, impulsivity, and self-centeredness.[1] His work cites many

---

[1] Dr. Stolrow's opinions do not necessarily reflect those of the Army.

characteristics that are important indicators of success, for instance, "the investigators suggested that the successful Q Course candidate was intelligent, persevering, calm, enterprising, and had a good background in basic military skills prior to attending the Q Course."

He also observed that:

> . . . effective personnel demonstrated more maturity, positive response to authority, and viewed their jobs as less demanding and exciting. They also showed a willingness to assume more responsibility and prefer physically demanding work. Additional research with veteran Special Forces personnel suggested that successful personnel exhibited team playership, perseverance, dependability, moral courage, adaptability, autonomy and initiative . . . relatively better emotional development in comparison to unsuccessful candidates . . . Successful candidates also appear to report lower overall levels of stress throughout the training in comparison to nonsuccessful candidates, which suggests better coping resources. . . .

In short, his work suggests that interpersonal ability, motivation, and character are important for effectiveness in SF.

Dr. Stolrow also talked about "moral courage," meaning the ability to make and follow through on difficult ethical decisions in the face of danger or hardship. He suggests that demanding, realistic training accentuates the strengths and vulnerabilities of character that are already present in the candidate. In his work he states:

> If one looks beyond the Q Course to performance in Special Forces operational detachments, these results also have significant implications for leadership and effective performance in real-world missions . . . a comprehensive review of Special Forces history, roles, and missions indicated that Special Forces personnel operate in small, cohesive Groups in foreign countries with minimal daily guidance from higher military authority . . . perform a broad array of missions, especially as key leaders for indigenous populations of military or guerrilla personnel. Missions may vary dramatically and change quickly. For example, an

engineer sergeant has the capability of training foreign personnel to construct buildings and bridges in peace, but he may also be ordered to demolish these structures during war. In fact, the history of Special Forces suggests that personnel must have innovative, aggressive, and energetic personality traits to perform both peaceful and hostile missions. However, they must also be compassionate and tactful to successfully "win the minds and hearts" of the indigenous populations with whom they work. . . .

As indicated above, persons who would "Kill 'em all and let God sort 'em out" are unwelcome in Special Forces.

Finding men who possess the right qualities is not easy and, adding to the list of desired traits, the soldiers must be able to both lead and follow. Dr. Stolrow wrote:

. . . the personality of a soldier, especially a leader, is a key factor which determines the success or failure of military units. If this is true for conventional units, it is even more relevant for Special Forces soldiers, who are all leaders operating with great independence to execute highly sensitive missions. Therefore, the assessment and selection of Special Forces personnel . . . is a key aspect of attempting to ensure that only the right individuals are given this special responsibility.

Another particularly important characteristic for SF members is a propensity for action. Soldiers are needed who will undertake risky missions, but who do not seek risk as a way of life. Special Forces, as Dr. Stolrow indicated, is not a good place for thrill seekers or would-be heroes. However, these types do come knocking, and such undesirables sometimes filter in.

The various Special Operations Forces (SOF) units, such as Rangers, SEALS, Delta Force, Task Force 160, Special Forces, etc., each need a different type of person. Someone who excels in a Special Forces environment may not make it in Delta Force, and vice versa. Many Special Forces soldiers would flop in the Ranger world, and many Rangers would not pass Special Forces Selection. But there is a lot of cross mixing, and some soldiers seem able to do well wherever they go. Success depends largely on the person involved, and most especially on his level of motivation toward what he is doing.

A shared characteristic of all SOF units, however, is that they require people who will willingly seek out and close with the enemy, not simply because they are ordered to or are pushed from behind, but by nature. Yet, people who will fight anybody for any reason are unwelcome, and SOF units seek to eliminate those immature males who choose not to control their tempers, or those who might misuse their training.

During some parts of training, candidates are not told how well they are doing. Consequently, a candidate may have already failed, and might be pushing, suffering, and doing his best for no reason. As for me, I didn't know any of this at the time of my own training; I just figured I had to make it.

The course was designed for more mature and experienced soldiers, so we younger men were disadvantaged. The air was getting thinner and the company was getting tougher and smarter, and it was all volunteer. Of those from Basic and AIT who had enlisted for SF, Lizard was the only one still around besides Rob and me. But there were young men from other places. Some had been waiting for a class and others had been injured and "recycled." They were sources of information about what awaited us around the next corner; people who *quit* were immediately removed, so I didn't get to talk to them.

Many candidates got jostled around for months before getting a class assignment, but I got lucky and was assigned to Charlie Company for the next class, the third class in 1983. Our motto: **"Flash or Crash, 3-83."** (If we made it through Selection, we would be awarded a "flash" to wear on our berets, signifying that we were Special Forces qualified.)

Selection consisted of four parts, if one counts Pre-Phase, which was meant to prepare candidates for Phase One. In fact, Pre-Phase itself abruptly wiped out a good portion of the class. Of those who endured Pre-Phase, about one in three would succeed through Phases One, Two, and Three to graduate.

At times Pre-Phase was very demanding, but it was still *kind* of fun. I played a secret game that I called "energy eating." When a man quit who I knew could have pushed on, I got all his leftover energy. He sacrificed his leftover spirit to mine. As for people who got hurt, or who simply didn't have the right stuff, I didn't get their energy; they took all of it with them.

During some of the runs and marches, I felt like I was going to meltdown and die. I learned a lot about people's tolerance for stress and discomfort, how they act, how they get medevac'd. I became accustomed to the sounds of human bodies hitting the ground as they collapsed. It was a familiar song I heard many times over the next five months: *karattle* (first the M-16), *karuumph* (then the body). *Karattle karuumph. Karattle karuumph.* I didn't need to look, and I didn't like that sound.

In stressful situations, some people rise to the occasion, while others

117

crawl inside themselves or run away. It was more apparent than in Basic and AIT that teamwork was critical, and those who didn't work and play well with others were not welcome and wouldn't last long.

I met Steve Shaulis in Pre-Phase. He was a year older, but still a relative youngster given our environment. His father was an attorney in Maryland, his mother a court stenographer who hung a picture of JFK on her living room wall. We had the same attitude and I liked being around people who believe that "impossible" is a sacred word to be used sparingly.

Many of the TACs (Tactical Advisor and Counselor—evaluators/instructors) and students were combat veterans and some had been in other elite units such as Rangers or Delta Force. Sergeant First Class Sibley was the senior TAC and was easy-going, tough-to-rile, often joking and hardcore. Another TAC was Staff Sergeant Jenkins. He was no-nonsense: his morning motto: *Today is a great day to excel.* And for the rest of the day: *Pain Builds Character.* When he saw someone coming to grips with his character, he'd shout: *"Pain is only weakness leaving the body!"* There was a lot of weakness leaving my body at times. It seemed that Jenkins was a man driven by duty, honor, country—but mostly by SF. It was strange and corny at first, but I respected him because he was without pretense. What you saw was what you got.

Staff Sergeant James Gritz (pronounced "Grites") was on the TAC-team. At about 5'2", he was vertically challenged, and people called him the Bridge Troll, but not to his face. If they did, he'd whip their ass. I saw him do it, later, but not over a Bridge Troll comment. A soldier was sleeping against a tree when Gritz walked up and took his rifle. No big deal. Gritz gave it back and said, "Secure that weapon soldier," and started to walk away. The soldier, who had been sleeping, jumped up, all six-plus feet of him. "You could never take my weapon now," he mouthed off.

"Oh, yeah?" Gritz said.

"Yeah." The exchange was like that of two schoolyard boys.

In a flash, the big soldier swung the butt of his rifle at Gritz's head. The bigger man swung with such force that, had the rifle landed, it might have killed Gritz. But Gritz was quick as a timber rattler. He ducked and stepped aside as if he were in a choreographed "fight" in a karate flick. The big soldier swung again, but with less force because he was off-balance, and Gritz stepped into the swing.

It all happened so fast that I am not sure what happened, but basically Gritz blocked the rifle with his left arm, which had to have hurt, and simultaneously kicked the soldier in the stomach—***thump!***

The man dropped to his knees and Gritz somehow ended up with the rifle. "Secure that weapon, troop," he repeated his earlier instruction. The soldier got back to his feet with a shocked and pained look on his face, and Gritz handed back the rifle and walked away.

I was incredibly impressed and more than ever wanted to get into Special Forces. I secured my weapon.

James Gritz's father was retired Colonel Bo Gritz. He spoke to us during Pre-Phase about his recent attempts to locate POWs in Vietnam, during the last of which he ended up in a Thai jail. The event had been all over the news, and though Bo Gritz was unquestionably a war hero, he fell from the graces of many in the wake of the operation which was said to have been funded in part by Clint Eastwood.

On to other matters. Shortly before the Americans were taken hostage in the Iranian Embassy, two of Ross Perot's employees had also been taken hostage in Iran. They were held in a large prison and our government felt powerless to help. Mr. Perot turned to "Bull" Simons, a retired Special Forces commander then living peacefully in Florida. Simons had led the famous Son Tay raid in North Vietnam, and Mr. Perot secretly asked him to lead a rescue of his employees.

Colonel Simons, along with a volunteer crew of Mr. Perot's employees that included some veterans, slipped into Iran, rallied a mob in Teheran that raided the prison, and broke the hostages out, along with about 11,000 other prisoners. Simons led the Americans to escape with a 450-mile overland journey to Turkey. The only pay he was said to have accepted was the good feeling he got from rescuing our people. He died shortly thereafter. A movie was made about this private operation, called *On Wings of Eagles*.

These people possess a character trait that I hold in the highest regard: *They stand by their people—even if it means putting not just their money on the line, but their lives.* And though I disagree with some of their political views, I very much respect their loyalty.

At Pre-Phase, each morning and afternoon formation there were soldiers who had had enough, and quit. In the mornings, afternoons, and at night the TACs often played a Queen song from a boom box:

> *Ain't no sound but the sound of his feet,*
> *machine guns ready to go*
> *Are you ready, Are you ready for this*
> *Are you hanging on the edge of your seat*
> *Out of the doorway the bullets rip*
> *To the sound of the beat. dum dum dum*
> *Another one bites the dust. . . .*

I loved it when they played that song! While some cringed, I was often choking back a laugh, when not in too much pain. People who didn't take setbacks and irritations too seriously did better, I felt. Laughing was one of my ways of coping.

Update to Richard White:

> [Your] letter came at a very good time [I] was exhausted, hungry, soaking wet, filthy from three days (maybe two, maybe four)without a shower, very cold, people were quitting (get the picture) . . . out of the blue some jerk started handing out mail. He was dry and clean, I wanted to hurt him . . . the cold was moving in and we were moving out. Richard, it's not easy. I got lost in the swamp that day. So did a lot of other people. We had individual missions to accomplish. I triumphed . . . more than a few people were lost for over a day. Working alone is something you and I are naturally good at . . . proud to say that I did not get scared while I was lost . . . Jimmy Buffet is talking about islands now. Brings back some of our craziest adventures. Remember the tent blowing in the river?. . . we don't carry any type of shelter . . . If you want shelter, you make it. I don't make any shelter. It's a waste of valuable energy. I'd rather be sleeping. Looking at the stars, freezing, driving on . . .
>
> We live in a great country . . . Yes, the good old U.S. of A. Enjoy it . . . a chopper just flew overhead only 150' with rotors smackin' the air. . . .
>
> It's 2400 hours.
> Mike

I was really tired when I wrote that sappy letter.

Always the philosopher. Unfortunately, my idealistic view of the United States and its people made it even more painful when I was later charged with murder and many automatically assumed I was guilty without listening to my side. They assumed the feared "Green Beret" was their enemy.

A strange thing happens when your people accuse you of a crime when you are innocent. Objectively, you know you are innocent, but you *feel* guilty and begin to question and defend yourself—which makes you *seem* guilty. Very strange. But that was in the future. I was still in Pre-Phase and very idealistic, like SSG Jenkins.

Training involved constant movement, especially learning how to move in the boonies undetected. Also, we learned to react to various threats, how to move to contact (combat), how to avoid contact, etc. One chilly night I didn't have a sleeping bag, only a sleeping pad, poncho, and poncho liner. (Usually, SF only use tents in extremely bad, usually intensely cold, weather.) I fell asleep at 0200 and woke up a couple of hours later, cold, shivering in the darkness. I couldn't feel my feet or wiggle my toes. I thought, *My feet are frozen solid! My toes or feet will be amputated and I will wash out of the course. My friends were right; I washed out before I even got started. Plus I'm gonna have wooden feet. Who will marry me with wooden feet?!* The stupidest things ran through my head.

I started punching my left instep trying to regain some feeling. There was none, so off came the left boot. My foot was not frozen, just cold and completely numb. After some massaging and doing some exercises to warm up, I got the feeling back. Then I tried to go to sleep again, unsuccessfully.

Later, I was sitting under a tree eating a freeze-dried LRRP ration (Long Range Reconnaissance Patrol) when a Blackhawk helicopter landed about 50 meters away—I didn't talk in yards and miles anymore. I talked in meters and klicks (kilometers). A soldier ran out carrying a sack and the Blackhawk roared away.

"Mail call!"

I got a letter from my grandmother: *Happy nineteenth birthday.* I didn't even remember my own birthday.

Two days later.

> Richard,
>
> So you're gonna be a lawyer, eh? That's great! . . . it will be to our advantage to have a lawyer in our never ending drama skits . . . I was only doing a skit when I joined the Army! Great skit, huh? Are you too? These are the most realistic we have ever done!
>
> Your letter was right on time . . . just got in from the woods and swamps . . . been doing some real life Green Beret training . . . very exciting, stimulating, entertaining and makes a lot of people quit . . . difference between here and jump school is that they have good reason . . . and more people quit . . .
>
> I will tell you honestly, we are not supposed to tell anybody what we do, how many of us are doing it, or how many

of us quit . . . So I won't tell you. It's not that I don't trust you, but the Army doesn't and they do trust me (I think) so that's the breaks . . . as long as I hang in here you get a 3.5 GPA or better. Deal? . . .

Richard, ever the optimist, calculated the odds of my being killed in Special Forces.

As for my 15% chance of getting zapped, we did some pretty crazy things as high school students, remember? That % hasn't changed much.

Some of our training is awesome . . . can only be explained by experiencing . . . Some can't be explained because we are not authorized . . . spend a substantial amount of time flying around getting dropped off by choppers . . . classes involving helicopters to include their fire power and vulnerabilities . . . fly at tree top level a lot.

Richard was having some troubles with his roommate so I offered a little advice.

[I suggest you] overcome your good nature for the time required for you to complete your mission.

Remember: **MISSION COMES FIRST.**

MISSION COMES FIRST.

MISSION COMES FIRST.

MISSION COMES FIRST.

MISSION COMES FIRST.

MISSION COMES FIRST.

MISSION COMES FIRST.

MISSION COMES FIRST.

Do you understand? Let me say it again: **MISSION COMES FIRST.**

In SF or SEAL teams you may have to die to complete a mission. In college you may have to run 3 miles and stay up all night. Don't whine and cry about inconveniences until the mission is complete . . .

Make some brownies or chocolate cake with Ex-Lax chocolate in them. Don't be stingy with it . . . Go overboard. Lay it out so that he will eat some. . . . Don't assume the defense. Always be on the offense. Make him miserable.

Remember, just because I'm not there doesn't mean you
should stop doing ridiculous things.
DRIVE ON
GIVE 'em HELL
MISSION COMES FIRST
AIRBORNE
RANGER
SPECIAL FORCES

That was some letter.

Lizard was still around from Basic and he had a certain ruggedness, but he was used to bluffing and bullying his way through life, and one simply can't bluff and bully SF instructors. This is Show Me country.

In Basic, Lizard had boasted that he would shoot expert, but had only qualified marksman or sharpshooter. He had a big mouth, but not much behind it, except in fighting, and he was cruel when he fought. In Basic, when he beat up the squad leader, he was not just trying to win. He was trying to hurt another person beyond what was necessary to win. There's a big difference between winning and being cruel. Lizard was cold as ice. But Selection, too, was cold as ice, and soon his ruthlessness was replaced by the whiney look on his face. He was reaching the end of his rope, a beaten man on the verge of quitting.

But Lizard had ego. He faked an injury. Shin splints. I saw the deception in his eyes and heard it in his voice. Because of my sports background, and what I had just experienced at Basic, AIT, and as a drill corporal, I could often tell when a person was feigning injury.

Repeatedly, life has shown that cold and vicious people do not tend to be fierce or tough. They tend to be vulnerable. They are vicious and mean because they are weak, but want to appear strong. They know they are weak and being mean is their way of coping. Anyway, that's how I saw it through the young eyes of Dr. Sigmund Yon, master of amateur psychology.

In Selection the weak didn't do well. Also, mean types are not good team-players and so have two strikes against them. Outsiders are often surprised to learn that an important trait of effective SF soldiers is their compassion. A person with little compassion will tend to be an outcast even if he makes it through Selection. After all, SF operates mostly in small teams, so working and playing well with others is essential. So, out with the mean and vicious. Lizard quit.

Some of the young soldiers wanted to "get blooded" (kill someone). I have known more killers than I can remember. Many have killed, most have not actually taken a human life, but they were killers just the same. There is a killer in every human soul. Except for the few among us who are afflicted with some mental illness—who are carefully weeded out of Special Operations units—I think it is not possible to take another's life without some effect on oneself. Few people can easily take human life; that is precisely why we take great pains to dehumanize our enemies: so we can kill them without remorse. But inevitably, when we dehumanize others we also dehumanize ourselves. Deep down we know our enemies are still people, and that ultimately we are killing our own kind. Nevertheless, the *reason* for killing makes a big difference.

Later, while I was still on active duty, I met a man who carried a heavy burden. He revealed to me the details of a killing—a murder, actually.

He was a good man. As I recall, he was drafted at about seventeen or eighteen. They gave him his few months of perfunctory training, and, like so many other innocents, he was then thrown in the ring with the Viet Cong— an incredible guerrilla opponent. It must have been nauseatingly frightening and overwhelming for him. He was an infantry soldier, as I recall, and after the war he came to Special Forces. His regular unit was constantly harassed by the vastly more experienced Viet Cong who were not merely skilled fighters, but fighting for a cause. Most of the American kids in his unit only wanted to survive and come home. They were growing up too fast, were taking casualties, and not killing many VC. They must have been very frustrated, especially knowing that no hero's welcome would greet them at home. Instead, there would be insults and jeers, though many had been drafted and were only doing what was expected of them—whatever that was. In effect, they were just kids who were trapped in a conflict of other people's making. No matter which way they turned, they faced an enemy.

One day he was driving a military truck in Vietnam when he saw an old man on the roadside. The kid, who by the time he told me this story was a veteran around forty years old, pulled the steering wheel a bit to the right and killed the man. He didn't stop, but he was sure that it was a death blow. He said that he had never told anyone that story before, but he wanted to tell me, and he finally felt better for doing it. More importantly, he said, it bothered him every day of his life. He had been so angry at the Viet Cong and the Vietnamese people, he just wanted to lash out to even the score. But he did not even the score. He made it worse. Each time he sees a dead animal on the road it reminds him of that sound and that day, and he regrets that he ever did it.

Military people should take heed. Many young men think there is something macho about "getting one under the belt." They are wrong. If they kill under the wrong circumstances, if they misdirect their force, they may carry crushing emotional baggage for many years. Maybe even a lifetime. *It's not worth it.*

People have confided to me extraordinary experiences, shown me scars on their souls. There always was an underlying theme with these good people who did bad things: *It's not worth it.*

SPECIAL FORCES SELECTION, PHASE-1

ON 30 DECEMBER, 1968, I was four, ambushing cars at the Stop sign, digging to find the Devil, or trying to catch the moving shadow cast on the grass by my mother, who was jumping around and laughing, playing with me, encouraging me to try harder. As I jumped for her shadow, she jumped around or ducked and tried everything to keep me from catching it. I was running, tripping, diving, but above all, laughing.

We were able to have that fun because of people like Robert Howard.

Sergeant First Class Howard was on a Special Forces mission in enemy controlled territory in the Republic of Vietnam (some say Laos) to rescue a missing American soldier. His platoon was a mixture of Americans and Vietnamese. They came under intense enemy attack, at the beginning of which his weapon was destroyed and he was seriously wounded by a grenade blast. His platoon leader was badly wounded and exposed to enemy fire, and the platoon was far outnumbered. Howard was unable to walk due to his wounds, but he crawled through enemy fire to help the platoon leader. He made it to the fallen officer and started to administer first aid as a bullet smashed into an ammunition pouch carried by the officer, causing some of the ammunition to explode. Howard retreated, then came back yet again, and dragged the wounded man to relative safety.

SFC Howard was now a lieutenant, thanks to a battlefield promotion he would later receive, though he was still on the battlefield, and the new leader of a platoon that was disorganized and battered by enemy attack. He began to rally the defenders by crawling from position to position to administer first aid, giving encouragement and directing fire on the encircling enemy. Despite terrible injuries, Howard continued to lead his troops. Finally his platoon was in sufficient control to permit rescue helicopters to land. In the U.S. military the wounded are the first to be evacuated, but Lieutenant Howard refused to board the helicopters with the wounded until he had personally supervised the complete evacuation of all his troops.

For his courage and extreme devotion to his men, Robert Howard was awarded our nation's deepest gesture of respect: the Medal of Honor.

Fifteen years and four months later, Robert Howard, now Major Howard, was standing directly in front of our formation. He was said to be the most decorated U.S. soldier, put in for the Medal of Honor three times, and awarded it once. He was wounded on numerous occasions but continued to return to battle.

He was the commander of Phase-1, my commander for the next month. I was inspired, more than ever, to do well around those men with Major Howard leading the way. The company intimidated some candidates, but for

125

others, like me, it had the opposite effect; quitting was not an option. Serious soldiers, men of consequence, were all around. It was the TACs' and Major Howard's duty to pick through the volunteers and identify Special Forces material. I was worried that they wouldn't trust me enough to take me with them in combat.

But if they thought we were made of the right stuff, it was their duty to take as much of their military and combat experience as possible and cram it into our heads. To teach us how to defend the United States, and our people.

Letter to Richard White:

> If you don't receive a letter from me by May 10th, write my Grandmother. If your letters are returned with the word "DECEASED" (Ha Ha) stamped on them, discontinue writing!
> Enclosed are a few pictures . . . airmobile operations . . . the green faced guy (me)is just before an assault. We were preparing to move out . . . don't know why we were smiling!
> Got to pack
> Got to jump
> Got to go
> DRIVE ON

18 April 1983, Beirut, Lebanon. A truck containing approximately 2,000 pounds of explosives detonated at the U.S. Embassy, killing 17 Americans, reportedly including CIA personnel, and Army trainers.

Often when it is reported that "Army trainers" were involved, the designation is a euphemism for Special Forces. When that bomb exploded, I was in Phase-1, dodging grenade and artillery simulators. We had conducted Pre-Phase on Fort Bragg, but Phase-1 was away at a secluded Special Forces training site known as Camp MacKall.

Letter to Richard White:

> [Our] training has been very demanding these last 11 days . . . 8 people [failed Selection] yesterday. One guy was from Lake Wales [neighboring our hometown] . . . getting to be friends with him but he didn't make it.
> It takes quite a bit of thinking here. More than I expected

. . . it takes a 110 GT to qualify to be a pilot. The avg. GT score for this Special Warfare class is 119 . . . These are our kind of people . . . smart, crazy and fun (ha ha).

[I] got plenty of sleep last night and I feel like a million dollars, except my body hurts.

I'm hanging in there Richard. They can't make me quit. I refuse to fail. When the going gets rough I think of some of the times we have yet to come . . . I've been thinking a whole lot!

[I] got a letter from you . . . My Grandmother wrote me also. Boy was I happy . . . did a lot of pushups for those two letters . . .

As for my adventures here, well, just leave them to your imagination . . . excellent place to learn about foreign cultures . . . training with many foreign officers. . . .

Some of the TACs (now called "Assessors") played a private game called "Stud or Dud." The rules were simple. When a batch of new soldiers showed up, each member of the cadre secretly looked through the group and picked one Stud and one Dud. It's remarkable that even soldiers with twenty years of Special Forces experience just as often mix up the Studs with the Duds. I have never known a person who could reliably gauge men by appearance, even after talking with them.

And obviously the psychologists, to this day, haven't figured out infallible screening indicators, or the fail rate would not continue to be so high even with throngs of scientists out there picking and prodding, and the vast accumulation of psychological knowledge available. On the other hand, with their current system, the scientists are saving a tremendous amount of money by screening out approximately fifty percent of the applicants before they are allowed to attend actual Special Forces training. Together, this still leaves an attrition rate of roughly seventy percent, which is approximately the same as SEAL training. But no direct correlations can be made, since each unit requires a different type of character, and selects for greater or lesser degrees of different attributes.

In SF, the ideal soldier is basically a good athlete, is very smart, is comfortable outdoors, is mature and can work alone, and likes unstructured, challenging environments. On the contrary, a Ranger unit is *highly* structured and rigid with regard to traditions and uniforms. Rangers tend to love uniforms and structure; SF tend to shun rigid structure and tradition, although, of course, there are always exceptions.

Some men are great athletes, but can't take being alone in the dark, or need a coach who will constantly tell them what to do. Others get frustrated and flustered when the pressure is on, or are not good team players. Some are very smart, but emotionally weak. Some are emotionally strong but slow at learning new skills.

The ideal man for the Special Forces environment sees opportunity when others see impossible odds and danger, and he takes initiative to identify things that need to be done, then does them. When others are saying "impossible," he may be saying, "I've been looking for this kind of challenge."

Even at the close of the twentieth century it is still true that the only way to reliably select the right people for the right job is to test them, stress them, and watch.

Every class is different, and another soldier, even in my class, will have had different experiences. This is Phase-1 through my eyes.

We spent time in the wilderness practicing various skills, staying "tactical" a lot, meaning that we trained as though it were real combat: complete camouflage, exercising "noise and light discipline"—which meant not coughing loudly, sneezing, or smoking a cigarette in plain view at night. I found that I could smell men after my nose adjusted to the wilderness. Hot, sweating, American men begin to reek of ammonia and are easy to smell. (Different nationalities tend to smell differently due to varying diets.) They are "loud" to your nose. If they wash their bodies or uniforms with soap, you can easily smell them after your nose has adjusted. If they wear cologne or use aftershave, it is the olfactory equivalent of shooting a flare or singing aloud while they sneak through the woods.

For those who have not spent enough time in the wilderness for their senses to adjust, it may be difficult to understand just how much of an advantage one has who has been in the wilderness for an extended period, as opposed to a person who is just entering it from civilization. Any part of your body that is not camouflaged—especially if you are Caucasian—stands out like a beacon to someone who has adjusted to the natural environment. Even the whites of your eyes or your white little fingertips, sticking out of the holes that you cut in your gloves, can give you away. And if your skin is dark, don't assume that you are camouflaged. Your skin shines and will give you away, as will your teeth and eyes, especially if the enemy is close.

When we loaded our gear to go out, we did a "jump test" by jumping up and down to see if anything rattled, pinged, banged, sloshed, or made any unnecessary noise. When we drank from a canteen, we drank it dry to prevent it from sloshing, so our canteens were either empty or full. Each time we crossed a water source we slugged down a canteen and refilled it, plopping in one or two iodine pills, depending on turbidity, to kill the parasites. After refilling the canteens, we were taught when in enemy territory to urinate in the stream, which carries the scent away. It's good to do this in the right order. (However, in training it is absolutely forbidden to defecate near water sources, which can have deadly consequences for those using the water.)

When we changed socks we took off only one boot at a time, then dried, and sometimes powdered that foot. The rule was: Don't take off more than one boot at a time, and always keep your weapon within arm's reach. While in the field, we slept in our boots and kept all combat gear within reach, and everything that was not being used was always packed to go without notice.

Any kid who grew up hunting knows that a cough or a sneeze can be heard a surprising distance. You have to be quiet in the woods. But when you are hunting people with other people, sometimes you need to talk. There is a way to whisper that makes it much quieter: let out most of your air before whispering. The tricks and techniques of operating in the boonies could fill many books, and could take a lifetime to master. We were getting a basic introduction.

When in camp, our morning physical training normally included some basic hand-to-hand combat. It wasn't super karate stuff and had nothing to do with fighting fairly. It was mostly about killing or getting away. It was basic, and if you were not a good hand-to-hand fighter when you arrived, you knew just enough to get your butt stomped when you left. We did, however, practice two techniques enough that I became proficient in them, especially with additional practice on my own. The first was using a garrote, which amounts to slipping up from behind and wrapping a wire around the enemy's throat and killing him quickly and silently. The reason that you can become relatively good at the garrote without years of practice is that it is simple to do and requires more resolve than athletic talent. The other move that I have employed many times, and actually successfully used against opponents in training, is the "sleeper."

There are various ways to do the sleeper, but it amounts to a choke hold around the throat. It only takes four to five seconds to knock someone out, and it is completely painless. Through the years I've seen it done at least a hundred times. I have done it myself, and have had it done to me many times and never saw an injury or fatality. It works not by cutting off the air supply, but by blocking the blood supply to the brain. The person simply falls unconscious. A few seconds after the hold is released, the victim's body begins to quake as in seizure. When they wake up some seconds later, they often ask, "what happened?" But if you hold it too long they urinate, defecate, then die.

That, and little more, was the extent of my "Green Beret" hand-to-hand

129

training. Hardly enough to make me a lethal weapon with secret punches. Speaking of which, there is no such thing as a secret punch. When given even the briefest consideration, the notion is actually rather ridiculous.

Here is a thirty-second-thought that can clear up the all-too-prevalent fallacy that elite soldiers learn secret ways to kill people. *Premise:* Man has been fighting for thousands of years. The only thing that is truly secret is new weaponry, and methods for using that weaponry. Some of today's most deadly devices, nuclear weapons, are no longer a secret. We could not, with all of our resources, keep the ideas and methods for the production of weapons of mass destruction secret forever. The oldest weapon system conceivable (to me, anyway) is the human mind and body. It follows that any "secret punches," which surely would have been discovered thousands of years ago, would no longer be secret shortly after the first tribe began using them in combat.

What you see is what you get.

Sleep was at a premium in Phase-1, and, with so much training, at times it was difficult to stay awake. Self-discipline could remedy the problem. Often it was necessary for us to "ration sleep" just as a unit may have to ration food or ammo. Sleep rationing may be necessary when a small unit, say twelve men, is so active that they don't get enough rest over an extended period. Inadequate food and intense physical activity exacerbate the problem of sleep deprivation.

Unfortunately, no matter how tired the men may be, guard duty is a necessity. Being killed by the enemy negates the need for sleep, but at an unacceptable cost. There are ways to reduce the number of people on guard duty for a small unit, one of which is to slip into a thickly vegetated area, such as a swamp, where it would be hard for an enemy to sneak in without making a lot of noise. But letting everyone sleep at once borders on insanity for many reasons. For instance, when men sleep, some snore and must be stifled. Part of the patrol should always be awake, and we usually had guard shifts of one hour each, and staying awake for a mere hour while lying on one's belly totally exhausted can be difficult, especially for the inexperienced, which I was.

A soldier woke me up. It was my turn for guard duty, 0300, one of the worst shifts, and therefore one of the best times for the enemy to catch you off-guard. I was exhausted, but it was just a matter of exercising my mind. The shift would be over in an hour.

I woke up just before it was time for me to rouse the next man. *I fell asleep!* I knew better than that! I would do in combat as I trained in peace, and I could have gotten us all killed—and been the cause of a mission failure. During wartime, falling asleep on guard duty can be punishable by dishonorable discharge, and court martial. The military court can hand down a death sentence; this means napping at the wrong time is potentially a death penalty offense during time of war.

Nobody knew that I fell asleep, but if I had been caught, I figured that Selection would have been over for me. I felt terrible because I prided myself on doing what was right, especially when nobody was looking. I didn't want to be just another good soldier, but the best of the best. Falling asleep on guard duty was the worst of the worst. I could never do that again, period.

If a TAC, like Gritz, who had been the honor grad of his Ranger class, caught you asleep, he would steal your weapon and shoot you in the head. (With a blank, of course.) In fact, the TACs would try to steal your weapon even when you were not on guard duty. On one occasion, I was asleep when a TAC slowly lifted my weapon away in the darkness. He thought he had it, but I had tied the weapon to my body with parachute cord. When I felt the tug, I was in his face so fast that it scared him.

"Good job, soldier," he whispered, and disappeared into the darkness.

A Ranger taught me that trick.

As for guard duty, the TACs checked the perimeter often to see if we were awake. On the few occasions that they found someone sleeping, after they "killed" him, they would do one of two things. If the TACs were feeling generous, they would only make his team dig a hole and ceremonially dump his body in it. He was not allowed to help because he was "dead" and lying on the ground. Otherwise, they would "call in" an "air or artillery strike," as they so often did anyway, using the very loud simulators they carried. The strike would force the team to evacuate to an alternate patrol base far away. The team would have to carry the "dead" body and equipment, then "bury" him at the next base. This caused a considerable degree of peer pressure.

I thought about what happened when I fell asleep, and concluded that self-discipline can be short-circuited. I had been so tired at times that I'd fallen asleep while standing and leaning against a tree, and one time I thought that I would fall asleep while walking if I didn't somehow keep myself alert.

This is how I figured self-discipline was bypassed: I was not really awake to begin with, and it took maybe thirty seconds of lying on my belly looking over the barrel into the darkness, unable to get up due to noise discipline, to doze off. After I dozed off, discipline was not a factor. Having identified the problem, I looked for solutions.

I asked the experienced soldiers, especially the ex-Rangers, what they did to stay awake. Most of the Rangers chewed tobacco but I tried that and got sick every time—too wimpy they said. We were in a little patrol base, everybody struggling to stay awake, when an ex-Ranger said in his Southern drawl, *"Shee-it.* I'm outta chew."

He asked another Ranger if he had any chew, and the reply came in the form of another Southern drawl, "Naw. This is my last wad, but it's fresh. I jest started on it 'bout five minutes ago."

Without a second thought, the Ranger with the oversized wad pulled it out of his mouth. It was a brown, gooey, slobbery mess of nastiness, and he tore the wad apart with his dirty fingers and gave half to the Ranger who was out. Each Ranger plopped the gooey wad in his mouth. "Thanks man."

And that was that.

The Ranger who shared the wad of tobacco saw me staring at him (in disbelief) and pulled the wad from his mouth and again divided it in half. He held out the dripping brown goo to me with eyes wide open in an offer of friendship. I didn't mean to be rude but I could think of a couple of reasons why I didn't want that chew, so I said something like, "You know that crap makes me puke, but thanks anyway. What else can I do to help me stay awake?"

"Drink coffee. That's what it's for."

But often we couldn't make coffee while being tactical. So I made "Ranger coffee" by ripping open the packet of Army super-charged freeze-dry that came with every ration and dumped it into my mouth. I liked cream in my coffee, so I ripped open the creamer packet and did the same. Then I found it tasted better if you emptied the creamer packet in your mouth first, followed by the coffee, and chased with a slug of water from a canteen. It tasted bad and I made faces like a baby drinking sour milk, but it worked. For insurance, I sharpened a stick enough so that the point would poke me, and put it under my chin—I never fell asleep at the wrong time again. It is true that one will do as one trains—that is why you train—so you will figure out what to do, correct yourself, and get better.

Phase-1 was a revelation, but not like Pre-Phase; now I was used to people collapsing, so it was mostly fun again. Nobody could hide behind money, a cool car, good looks, fancy clothes, or wittiness. Sink or swim, survival of the fittest, no excuses. It was just mind, body, and especially heart. The TACs gave no special treatment to the combat vets or anyone else. Well, actually they did give special attention to the younger men who were there—they were *harder* on us—we didn't belong in SF and they knew it. But the president wanted more Special Operations people so that's what he was getting, even if it meant lowering the age and experience standards and letting people in who were too young to buy a pistol or drink whiskey in most states.

In the Army, a backpack is called a rucksack and that gets shortened to "ruck." Marching with a ruck is called "rucking" or "humping." We had lots of fun with those words. I maxed my PT (physical training) tests but was not a great runner. I was carrying too much muscle to be an outstanding runner. Being unusually strong is not particularly useful in Special Forces and the muscle that comes with exceptional strength is not worth it. It's like carrying fifteen canteens of water in conditions where you rarely need more than four. Those extra canteens just weigh you down, and you can almost never use them.

Most big musclemen didn't last long, and I suffered for my extra muscle on the runs and the fast rucks. While the weight hurt me on speed events, on endurance events, like long rucks, in which I excelled, it seemed to have little effect one way or the other.

But there was another aspect of my earlier sports training and experience. As a kid, one of my sports heroes was Arnold Schwarzenegger. I watched the movie *Pumping Iron* more times than I can remember, and every month I was down at Charlie's Newsstand, around the corner from The Gym, waiting for the next issue of *Muscle and Fitness* to hit the racks. I devoured everything there was to read about the top bodybuilders. Their common denominator was a serious and positive mental outlook. The more I read about them, the better my outlook became. Bodybuilding itself is a very tough sport. The training is grueling and so is the diet regimen—if you want to be really successful. I directly attribute much of my later success to the discipline I learned while lifting and bodybuilding, and listening to the top athletes in those fields. So, while my extra weight had its drawbacks in certain activities, the associated psychological advantages, such as increased self-confidence and self-esteem, were enormous, and I was reaping these benefits at Camp MacKall.

Normally the TACs wouldn't tell us what to expect or how far we would run or ruck; that would take all the fun out of it. During the first week of Phase-1, we went on a blazing run—about four miles. My body felt like it was on fire, like my lungs would explode and I would burst into flames leaving only a pile of ashes and a set of dog tags between a pair of charred running shoes.

Lots of "tough people" say that it's wimpy to run in shoes while in combat training. They say boots should be required, but that's just BS that flows from inexperienced or non-athletic minds. There is no need to destroy your skeleton during cardiovascular training, and we didn't lack experience with running in boots in the wilderness, where it counts.

Back to the course: We had done very hard runs in Pre-Phase, but this time was different. We ran in through the front gate of the compound. I was happy just to finish without having a heart attack. Sometimes I could literally taste what seemed like blood or raw meat in my mouth, the pain was so severe. As we came through the gate, a TAC yelled, *"Mind Fuck!"*

We did the whole run again. They started fast and people dropped like . . . people. A few days later, at the end of a seemingly endless run: *"Mind Fuck!"* People dropped like . . . quitters . . . lots and lots of quitters. We ran out the back gate and went just a short distance at a blazing pace, where we were stopped and marched back to the compound. By now the quitters were assembled in a formation and . . . *goodbye, thanks for the energy points* . . . back to Fort Bragg. And so it went, sometimes the "MFs!" were real and sometimes not. Either way, they usually netted quitters and I always hated to hear those words.

One of the best times for the TACs to thin out the ranks was not during or after a difficult day, but before. Especially at about four or five in the morning when bodies are aching and stiff, eyelids seem to weigh about five pounds each, the air is chilly and we were shivering. Everybody knows that another long day is being born that may not end in sleep; it may smoothly fade into the next day without pause, an "MF" or two along the way. Could be the day to get dusted-off—via medevac helicopter—a ride to the roof of some distant hospital. Feet sore with raw meaty spots, several toenails had fallen off the day before, ankles weakened, stomach growling, back raw from abrasion, M-16 in hand.

Then the TACs would come out ever so nice, like kindly grandfathers, and gently announce that a truck was headed back to Fort Bragg in about thirty minutes. The TACs would calmly explain how we could sleep on the truck and have great chow in the mess hall. In addition, they said, you can have a few days off while your orders come down for a new assignment. After all, they would explain, Special Forces *is* crazy, and normal people *don't* belong here. It's better, if you have even the slightest doubts, to just jump on that truck and head back to Bragg. It's honorable to be courageous enough to leave. The Army needs you somewhere else just as badly. Do you remember who went home yesterday? Did you think they were quitters? Of course not, and I doubt you even remember who they were. You can sleep with your girlfriend or wife tonight. She will see your feet and be proud of you for having done your best only to have the medics send you home. Nobody knows what happens out here but us, so no matter how well you do nobody will ever know. You could be killed in combat and they might say you died in an accident. There is no glory here. You may never be recognized, earn no medals.

When someone quit, the TACs often called it, "deciding this is not for you." To take away the stigma of giving up, quitting is now called a "voluntary withdrawal," or "VW." No need to be a quitter when you can be a VW. But then, if you change the oil, VW's never quit. When men made that decision, as they did at most morning formations and at various times throughout the days, the TACs treated them like old buddies because "they had the courage to do what they knew was right."

The TACs' goals seemed inconsistent. They wanted as many people as possible to pass, but were inducing as many as possible to quit. They administered stress like doctors. "Coffee and donuts if you quit now! Blue light special! We will keep doing this until somebody quits! Make it easy on yourself—do it now! You know you're thinking about it. If you are thinking about it now, wait 'til it gets tough. What's wrong with you? You're making everybody else suffer. Just get up and go get yourself some good, hot chow. It's okay. There's no shame in deciding that this is not for you. Do you want to die?"

Often if they could get one person to quit, someone else would follow. When the TACs saw someone cracking up, they only needed to concentrate on the one, knowing they would likely get more. Leadership goes both ways.

I had figured that the slightest mistake got you kicked out, but that wasn't true. They gave a lot of people second and third chances if they kept trying. Even people who occasionally fell out of runs were not always kicked out, though that was a giant step toward the door. Contrary to what it may seem, based on most of this description, they wanted as many people as possible to pass because, again, the training was expensive and slots were difficult to fill. Nevertheless, I figured out their mind games and thought the TACs were super cool action heroes.

Surprisingly, there was no peer pressure to stay. In fact, when candidates saw another showing signs of mental weakness, apathy, or, worst of all, not being a team player, he became an outcast. Team players who were mentally tough didn't have to be physical supermen. People watched out for those who were team players. I figured I was doing okay because I never considered quitting and I relished teamwork. I could work as an individual but I was *alive* in a team.

We ran the obstacle course at Phase-1. The event is a mile long with thirty obstacles. The time limit is forty-five minutes, and the course leaves even super-soldiers super-exhausted. It is not a baby course with safety ropes and nets; many people actually get hurt, occasionally seriously, and it doubles as a confidence course.

A confidence course is specifically designed to scare you in various ways, ranging from claustrophobia, to fear of falling, to fear of being smashed in the groin. One obstacle is a metal ladder about ten feet off the ground, that is horizontal instead of vertical. You have to walk across the rungs in your boots. If you slip, you can break bones, or perhaps get smashed in the groin as you fall through the rungs. During a recent class, I was told, one soldier broke a rib on this obstacle, and another smashed his groin. When the other soldiers see something like that happen, and hear the screams that sometimes accompany the injury, they often decide that Special Forces is not for them.

Most of the injuries are minor. For instance, you may be so tired by the time you reach a rope obstacle that you lose your grip and plummet to earth. The rope immediately burns the skin off your palms. This is bad; raw palms are not a ticket for sympathy. You don't get the rest of the day off, and you still must complete the course.

Even if you don't make the forty-five-minute time limit, it is not grounds for immediate removal. Nobody excels at everything, though in this environment it is important to excel at most things. The TACs grade the "whole man." For instance, a soldier may be an excellent athlete and smart, but if he doesn't get along with the other candidates, the soldier can be "peered-out." This means that the other students can remove the soldier by voting. In virtually every class there are men who possess poor social skills, so—*good-bye*. One of the obstacles is simply getting along with other people—being a positive force—during stressful situations.

The confidence obstacles are designed so that you must confront, and overcome, some of the mental obstacles in your head, but if you fall . . . *Karuumph!* . . . it's real. One of the obstacles was an abandoned sewer. It consisted of long concrete pipes underground. There were a couple of tiny "rooms" to negotiate to get in the right pipe and to the end. There was, of course, a story about someone getting lost by going down the wrong pipe, and that there was a cave-in.

We could not carry lights, and had to crawl and think small in the pipes. We did all this while men were in front and to the rear of us, so we had to be careful not to get kicked in the face, or to kick someone behind us in the face.

If a soldier is claustrophobic, he should decide this is not for him *before* crawling into the dark, narrow pipes. As with some of the labyrinthine caves that I later traversed, and at one time even got briefly stuck in, I felt as though I would be chewed and eaten. The darkness was not at all the same that you experience in the woods or jungles at night. In the wilderness you can just sit down on the knee of a tree and eventually the sun will rise. Some soldiers felt unable to return to the confinement and helplessness of the dark, in this case man-made, even for a brief visit, so they ate donuts and drank coffee in the morning mist. When we emerged, by climbing a rope back to the daylight, there were fewer among us and we continued on to our next passage.

The pipes weren't particularly scary to me, but some of the climbing obstacles on other parts of the course gave me a good jolt, and for good reason.

My buddy fell and landed on his back. There was a nasty *karcrackumph* sound when he hit. I was beside him on my knees gasping for breath, and I knew he was hurt. At first he couldn't catch his breath, then he coughed and choked a little and got his breath back. He was a tough-as-hell black sergeant, and gutted it out.

He slowly pulled himself off the ground, first to his knees, then to his feet, and I brushed some of the dirt off his back—for what that was worth. He would not quit, so I helped him through the rest of the course when I could, thinking maybe he was only bruised and would get better.

Over the days I looked into his eyes and saw such pain that I wondered if I was that rugged. He was mentally prepared, I knew, but had suffered an unlucky slip.

Finally, after my buddy had been in intense pain for several days, a medic noticed that he was hurt. He was caught. He was a team player, inspiring. But it was good that the medic caught him before his fighting-spirit worsened his injury. There is a point in training when enough is enough. His rib was broken. I don't remember his name or what he looked like, but I remember his spirit.

Goodbye . . . And the next one—*goodbye, goodbye, goodbye . . . .*

Lots of good people bit the dust because of something as simple as a twisted ankle—bad luck. If they were good soldiers up to that point, they could get recycled to a later class when their injuries healed.

Though I hated to see good men fail due to injury, I was having a great time so far, and was learning more about people and about myself than about combat.

We were doing a blazing ruck march, burning, gasping, drenched in sweat. When we marched, we hauled full combat equipment and weapons. You could not sling your weapon, but had to keep it in your hands, ready for action. Often Major Howard came with us, and on this day he eased up next to me and started talking to me while we half-ran, half-walked. He carried the same weight we did, forty-five or fifty pounds. He was forty-three years old.

I wonder what he was thinking when he looked at me. Was he thinking, *What's this kid doing here?* Or maybe, *That's fighting material.*

He asked me, "How are you doing, soldier?"

About to catch on fire! How is he keeping up with us?

"Great sir, can't we speed this up a little more?"

Robert Howard was said to be more decorated than Audie Murphy, by which I do not mean to suggest that men can be judged fairly, accurately, by the awards they have garnered—but to suggest that he is one of our country's most accomplished soldiers. Yet few people outside of Special Forces have heard of Robert Howard, who did five tours in Vietnam. Had Major Howard, the Southern boy from Alabama, served in World War II instead of Vietnam, you probably could go to Blockbuster and rent movies about him.

He was a living legend, but one that few people had heard about. Major Howard was not a mere human to me. He was something bigger—he was pure inspiration. Though the word "warrior" is worn out by overuse, true warriors really do exist. They are not mythological, but rare, and Robert Howard was at the top of the hill. It's not often that a person has the honor to train under the leadership of a man of the caliber and experience of Robert Howard, but when you do, you never forget.

We were surrounded by strong character examples, and they were filled with "inspirational" sayings. Some were a little corny like:

"'I Can' is part of being Amer *I can*."

And every morning when I woke up, I said "I can."

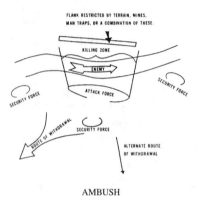

AMBUSH

We learned more infantry-tactics, including basic introductions to things like: near-side ambush, far-side ambush, hasty and deliberate ambushes, demolition ambush, and L, T, V and Z ambushes—so named for their respective shapes. There were closed triangle, open triangle, rise from the ground, point and area ambushes, harassing and destruction ambushes, and reaction to various types of ambushes to learn about.

Ambush, Ambush, Ambush. I couldn't believe all there was to know about something so apparently simple as bushwhacking people. I was lying in ambush quietly chewing on a twig, thinking of my grandfather. He took good care of his teeth by using twigs for toothpicks and as a toothbrush. You can nibble certain types of twigs until the end is reduced to fibers and *presto*—toothbrush! (It's actually more like a tooth broom.) With nine kids, his family was so poor that store-bought toothpaste was out of the question. Yet, when he was seventy-eight he still had all his original teeth except one. When I was older I read in a scientific journal that wood has natural antibiotics and that wooden cutting-boards can kill bacteria, and might be safer to use than plastic cutting-boards. *Hmm.* . . . Makes a fella wonder if there is more to wooden toothpicks than just picking and, if the wood itself actually is part of the process, which types of wood might be best suited for the manufacturing of toothpicks to help prevent tooth decay. I often busied myself with such thoughts to pass the time.

During one ambush we made our assault through the kill zone and returned to search the "dead and wounded." My buddy was searching one of the wounded. I was on my belly covering him, my M-16 pointed at the wounded man's temple. I told him not to move or I would shoot. He moved his hand suddenly toward his body. ***Bam!***

He was angry that I pulled the trigger and jumped up, dusting himself off.

He shouldn't have been angry, I thought, it was just a blank. He could have learned a lesson. When a person with an assault rifle pointed at your head says: "don't move or I will shoot," that's probably what he means. You will do as you train.

There are many ways to cross a river. For instance, you can wrap two ponchos around your ninety-pound rucksack in a certain way and it will float. You just swim across while pushing it in front. If the weather is freezing, you might not want to swim, and there are other crossing methods. They drilled into your head that when you see an apparently impossible obstacle, you sit down and think. Think like Tarzan. Tarzan would know what to do. Figure it out.

Always, there was noise, light and odor discipline: helmets make it difficult to hear and are heavy, so in Special Forces they are only worn for parachuting and certain specific applications such as during a counterterrorism assault when the likelihood of being shot or fragged is high. ("Fragged" means getting hit with primary projectiles, such as hand grenade fragments, or secondary projectiles, like flying glass or rocks kicked up by an explosion. "Fragged" also picked up another meaning during Vietnam, when soldiers sometimes murdered their own officers, for instance by rolling a hand grenade next to them when they were sleeping, or shooting them during a firefight.)

We learned departure and re-entry into friendly areas—challenge and password—and that it's as dangerous to approach friendly positions as those of the enemy. Phase-1 training could easily make a book. In fact, many books cover the material taught.

But for me it was like Disney World, and though I wanted to get through to graduate, I wished that it would never end. Since many of the skills taught in Phase-1 took time to develop, we were merely learning the basics; it would take years to become proficient in such a broad range of subjects.

STAY OFF THE BEATEN PATH!

PRECISE LAND-NAVIGATION (orienteering) is as basic to military operations as reading is to writing. The land-nav course was said to be the most challenging in the military at that time, and the grading was the same. Many good, even combat-experienced soldiers spent their final days in Selection trying to negotiate this course.

The main object was to get from point A to point B, tactically. The points were little metal fence posts that were difficult to see in daytime, and virtually invisible at night. To prove that we found our points, we used a little "pin-stamp" that dangled on a chain from each stake. We used them to punch a signature set of holes in the grading cards that we carried.

The first thing we learned was our pace count, which is important for estimating distance on the ground. Pace count is generally defined as the number of steps it takes for a person to walk one hundred meters. My pace count was 63. In other words, for every 63 steps with my left foot, I traveled about 100 meters—depending on weather, terrain, fatigue, light conditions, weight-load, speed, vegetation, and so on. It is more sensible to count 63 left or right steps, than 126 right *and* left.

As taught, I tied a length of parachute cord to my equipment and if there were, say, 800 meters to travel to the next remarkable feature, like a stream, I tied 8 overhand knots in the cord. After about 63 steps, or I figured that I had traveled 100 meters, my left hand untied one of the knots. On the eighth knot, I should have traveled the 800 meters and arrived at the stream. There are other methods for keeping distance, but the point is that keeping distance accurately is critical to good land-navigation and thus staying alive to destroy the enemy.

We learned about navigation in remote areas: For instance, why people get lost and tend to travel in circles. Some of the reasons are fascinating and have both physical and psychological roots. If we are swimming in open water with no visual references, most of us veer to the left and so will circle to the left. Lack of visual references can occur because we are far from land or because it is dark, foggy, snowing, or whatever. Wind direction can help if you pay attention, as well as other clues such as waves, sounds, etc.

We also tend to circle left when rowing a boat. As with swimming, this is because about 90% of us are right-handed. The dominant side tends to pull harder. But seldom do most of us find ourselves traveling on open water.

Usually, we are walking on land where the psychological as well as physical factors are important.

There is a lot to learn about going in circles, and I discovered that it pertains to non-military aspects of life as well.

One physical reason for circling while walking is that people's legs are unequal in length. Unlike our travels on water, on land the direction in which we tend to circle does not seem to be strongly related to whether we are right- or left-handed. The distribution of people who circle right or left is said to be about equal. It tends to be leg-length related, or related to other physical factors, such as injury. Other "psycho-physical" reasons for circling can be sunlight, strong winds, or any other irritation. This means that if we are walking in steep terrain we will tend to deviate by drifting downhill. We tend to avoid what irritates us, so if a cold breeze is howling or we are being sand-blasted, we deviate toward comfort—as in life generally.

The natural circling rate varies from person to person. Again, surrounding conditions are a factor. The faster we are moving the more pronounced the drift. It is said that people normally will complete a circle in a half-hour to six hours. It's easy to see how much you naturally deviate by blindfolding yourself and walking in an open area to see how much you drift. You should do this in such a way that you don't have other clues like the warmth from the sun on your skin, wind direction, sounds, elevation change, etc.

You can eliminate many of these influences by trying it in a hallway or in a big gymnasium, but you may want to wear a football helmet or have a friend watch so that you don't end up with a head wound. I drift right. Even big groups of people without a compass tend to circle. Another physical reason is that we each have a dominant eye, which has a visual influence on our direction. Also, anything that throws us off-balance can cause deviation. Simply carrying something in your hand can pull you off.

But the interesting part of circling that applies more to daily life, beyond land-navigation, is its psychological aspect. When we approach obstacles, we have a tendency to negotiate the obstacle the same way each time. If a fallen tree is in the way, we tend to consistently go either right or left around the obstacle. Most people tend to go right deliberately, if unconsciously, rather than merely "drifting" in circles. In most countries we drive on the right side. When there are two doors at the entrance of a building, we tend to enter the building through the right door. There are many examples and reasons, but the tendency is clear: The majority of us have a psychological preference to go right.

In the woods, all those tiny deviations to the left or right around obstacles add up. Even when a person has a compass or is using the stars to navigate, he can still get lost because he keeps going the proper direction, say north, but drifts off laterally. In some terrain, for instance, a jungle, obstacles are so numerous that the deviation can quickly become extreme. A method to compensate for this is to alternate between right and left. Every other obstacle you negotiate to the right, and on the others, go left, so that your tendency to directional deviation mostly cancels out. In the end, like many things taken to extremes, land-navigation begins as science, and drifts into art.

This tendency of people to go right has other interesting applications. Since most people are right-handed, they will tend to fire around the right side of their cover. If all else is equal and an enemy is behind a big tree, he will usually expose his head, shoulder, and weapon around the right to shoot. A soldier might want to aim his sights to the left side of the obstacle, and wait—or often the shoulder comes out first—*Bam!*

Even without a compass, there are many clues for telling directions, including the ways that dwellings are constructed, the growth patterns of plants and trees, wind, sun, stars, and lots of other indicators. In a northern climate, the paint on the south side of many fences or houses might be peeling. The list of potential clues goes on and on.

A skilled person can "read the power lines." A couple of years after the initial SF training, I sat through seemingly endless classes on reading power and railway lines. The direction they run tells an obvious story, but they have other characteristics that tell other stories. As for TV antennae on houses, in many foreign countries the antennae point toward the center of the closest big city, or to a hill, which is where the station's transmitting antenna is usually located. But you must know something about the country to use those kinds of signs. The country might have more than one television station, which could be confusing.

If a person is merely lost and looking for any civilization, he can follow a river or creek downstream, or track a power line, which will eventually run into people.

The Phase-1 land-navigation course consisted of daytime and nighttime portions. The buddy-system days were over. We navigated alone to multiple points and at each point used the special stamp to mark our grade cards. The time limit was strict and the points, the metal stakes, were small. If a soldier's navigation was just a tad off, he had the type of problem that often ended a brief visit in Special Forces. There was little time for recovering from errors at land-nav.

Small Special Forces teams move at night much more than in daylight. So, after the daytime portion, during which we lost some people, it was time for the more difficult night navigation. We had heard about the large number of people who got eliminated here. Not only would it test our ability to navigate, but, as with the rest of the course, the material would come quickly and test our ability to learn and rapidly adapt to new challenges. It was time for the long night movements as individuals.

Though it was strictly forbidden to team up, some people lacked self-confidence and broke the rules. New lesson: *I did not get lost when I was alone, and fewer people got lost when they operated alone, as opposed to operating as a group.* Those who had the confidence to think for themselves and make their own way, tended to know what they were doing and checked and re-checked everything.

A committee of incompetent people merely creates mass incompetence. Such a committee is more like a support group than a decision-making group. At land-nav, the incompetent committees arranged secret rally points far out in the woods. They were good enough to navigate to the secret rally points alone, but there they would usually team up in groups of two to four people to complete the course. They figured several heads were better than one, besides which, they gained company.

A law enforcement officer has mentioned to me that when there are two or more officers working together, they often make mistakes leading to injury or death, that a single officer would have avoided, because each assumed that the other was taking care of things. Doctors and veterinarians have their own stories. Many a "female" cat has had its belly opened on the table to be spayed, when the vet suddenly realized it was male. Vets are warned during training that this mistake happens as follows: The cat owner walks into the clinic with a supposedly female cat, paperwork is filled out, the receptionist receives the cat, the syringes are filled, surgical tools are laid out with care, and the routine operation begins. With the cat anesthetized, the vet picks up the scalpel, cuts open the cat, looks inside and finds no ovaries. The vet lifts up the cat's tail—she's a male.

Flocking together like sheep, and assuming that others know what they are doing, or have checked things out, is a natural human behavior and permeates much of what we do.

At land-nav, I saw what happened next on numerous occasions. Often, they *all* got lost. Others got busted in "honor code" ambushes and kicked out. If one was caught paralleling the roads from a distance or talking with another student, it was "Goodbye. Thanks for the energy points." The honor code was serious business. We were warned and had signed a document saying that we understood that there were no second chances with the honor code. The TACs didn't care how many medals a soldier had—it would not save him in an honor code violation.

A TAC stood before our formation wearing his camouflaged uniform and that funny-looking green beret. It really did look kind of silly for such a man to be wearing a hat like a French painter. His body, words, and tone screamed: *"Don't test me!"* He warned about the tribe of Indians who lived in the area, and that talking with them was also an honor code violation.

Indians? I thought, *on a military reservation?*

143

"The name of the tribe," explained the TAC forebodingly, "is the 'Fuk-ah-wees.'" He continued, "The Fuk-ah-wees will try to talk with you. Do not talk to them." He began stressing the name in disgust: "If you run across a *Fuk-ah-wee* in the swamp and he asks for help, *ignore* him," stressing the word *ignore*. "Just walk away. It doesn't matter if he is lost. *Leave* him. Do *not* let him follow you. *Fuk-ah-wees* are followers who will lead you to trouble. They will cause you to be removed from this course. Their mission is to make your life miserable, and if you adopt a Fuk-ah-wee, he may *kill* you someday and there will be only *you* to blame. We lose good students every class to the Fuk-ah-wees, and I assure you that we will lose some this class, starting tonight. You can be one of them if you like, or you can pass this course. The choice is yours."

Great. Now, not only do I have to worry about snakes, swamp monsters, breaking my leg and getting lost, I thought, but there is a tribe of Indians out there who will harass me. What if a Fuk-ah-wee is really in trouble? What then? Leave him? We were duly warned.

The TAC said, "The Fuk-ah-wee Indians dress just like you, and carry the same equipment. They are masters of disguise. Their greatest deception is to pretend to be Special Forces soldiers." He continued, "For all of their clever tricks, you can readily identify a ***Fuk-ah-wee*** by his call." The TAC cleared his throat and switched to a nasal, urban accent and said, *"Hey*, where the *fuck ah we?"* The formation erupted in laughter.

When soldiers get lost, that is the first thing they ask. Problem was, the TACs would wait in ambush at night, and would ask you for directions as if they were Fuk-ah-wees. If you helped, *goodbye*. An Indian who can't find his way through the woods was not welcome in Special Forces, and any candidate who would help lost souls slither through training and infiltrate Special Forces was equally unwelcome. After all, incompetence is an enemy. Would you want someone who cheated through medical school performing surgery on you?

I liked to see the cheaters flunk, not because I was jealous, but because they were not learning the skills that were required. This job was dangerous enough already; incompetence could get me killed on an ordinary day of training. Some thought that the name of the game was to "get the job done at all costs." They had confused the need to be devious in guerrilla warfare, with being devious to get through the training. It's one thing to be resourceful; it's another thing to sell out one's fellow soldiers by not learning the job.

Since land-nav included many long, timed movements performed while we were humping gear through somewhat rough terrain, it was exhausting. We always carried our M-16 rifles. It was difficult to hold a map, compass, and rifle while moving as quickly as possible through dense underbrush, sometimes swamps, and similarly difficult terrain. To make it easier, some soldiers disassembled their weapons and packed them in their rucksacks. Strictly forbidden, for obvious reasons. If they got caught—*goodbye*. But if they got lost or were late, it was goodbye, too, so some took their chances.

During night training we were not allowed to use flashlights no matter how dark it was. To read a map you had a red filter on your flashlight, which makes seeing you more difficult for the enemy, and preserves your night vision. If you didn't have a red filter, you could improvise by sticking a green leaf behind the lens, or think up something else. (Red light is the best, though, both for your vision, and because military maps are specially printed so that they can be read with red light.)

By throwing a poncho over your head you can contain even the red light, a measure not required in land-nav. For those who smoked, in tactical situations they had to do so under a poncho; an enemy with night vision equipment can see a cigarette from a great distance (hence the military slang "sniper magnet," for a lit cigarette)—and when the sniper sees it get brighter, he knows that the smoker is inhaling with the cigarette at his lips. He will know if the smoker is facing sideways or head-on by the way the cigarette moves. The sniper will put the cross hairs on the cigarette, or slightly off to the proper side, and when it gets brighter, **Bam!** Imagine a warning label on the pack: The Surgeon General has determined that smoking can get your head blown off.

White light, the kind most often encountered in ordinary illumination, burns up the visual purple, which is a substance in the eyes that aids night vision. It takes about thirty minutes to restore visual purple (depending on certain factors such as the viewer's fatigue and general health). There are methods that one can use to see much better at night using ambient light, but nothing beats direct light. Walking in the woods on nights so dark that you cannot see your hand in front of your face is as scary to many people as jumping from an airplane. Rightly so, because you keep running into things, and in more dangerous terrain, soldiers sometimes walk off cliffs.

A TAC told a story about an earlier class in which a soldier on the night course came running back to camp without his equipment. His weapon was smashed and broken. He managed to keep half of it, but the other half was missing. The soldier told a bizarre tale about being attacked by a hairy creature in the night. A tremendous fight ensued. During the course of the struggle, the soldier smashed his weapon over the hairy creature—he must have been very afraid to be able to break it—then ran screaming into the night after having jettisoned his equipment. When the TACs went out to investigate this wild tale, they found the equipment, the other parts of the broken weapon, and a deer that had been bludgeoned to death. It was remarkable that a man stumbled upon a deer, but the assumption was that it was sick or injured before it was attacked.

145

Some soldiers find that moving alone in the darkness is unsettling. Some decide that the constant crashes with trees and the branches that search and rip for their eyes are more than they can endure. They decide that Special Forces is not for them. And it's easy to quit and not look like a quitter. Simply don't find all the points and they will kick you out, or lose your map and join the Fuk-ah-wees.

It was about midnight in a downpour so heavy it felt like an entire cloud was falling out of the sky. I was on the night course, exhausted and cold, moving through the wilderness at a rapid rate to find one of my points. It was just me, my unloaded weapon, compass, map, and more than fifty pounds on my back, though the rain made the equipment heavier. I could barely see my dim green luminescent compass.

On nights when lightning flashed, the compass would get slightly brighter for about thirty seconds, but it was so dark in the driving rain that I had to bring the compass closer to my face to check the azimuth. The only light around was the eerie glow of the compass. At intervals, I stuck the Army-issue flashlight onto the compass face to recharge its radioactive tritium, glowing parts. The compass face was the same size as the face of the flashlight for that purpose.

That night in North Carolina there was no enemy hazard, other than the Christian Militia that the TACs repeatedly warned about. Some said "Christian Militia" was a euphemism for the KKK, and that they were out to steal our automatic weapons, which they knew would be unloaded. I'm sure their weapons would be loaded. It would be a perfect night for them to ambush and steal a weapon. The noise from the rain would dampen any noise they made. They could simply hide near one of the points, or anywhere around, and wait for somebody to come along. Me, for instance. That was not a comforting thought.

It was so dark I simply closed my eyes and made my way through the wilderness by feel. After all, I couldn't see my hand in front of my face anyway, so why take a chance on getting a branch in the eye? I figured, optimistically, that the KKK would not get me that night, so I closed my eyes and made my way. I was walking at a good rate, only opening my eyes to check the compass several times a minute, crashing through the wet woods like a bulldozer. The rain was so loud that I could not hear my own breathing.

Occasionally, I might catch the white glint of a flashlight. If it was white light, and not the dim red of someone checking a map, it was a Fuk-ah-wee who was looking for a road to get the heck out of the woods and back to Fort Bragg. It was safer at Bragg, the people were nicer, and they would give you directions. Constantly.

I heard one guy's mutter from a few days back, "I can't believe I volunteered for this *shit*! This ain't worth it just so I can be around a bunch of you assholes," as he headed for the TAC shack for his complimentary coffee and donuts. Often when people quit, they found reasons why it just wasn't worth it, while others realized that they had just been humbled.

I was drenched to the bone. Just a black figure groping to find his way in darkness. My uniform hung limp. The brim of my camouflage hat was like a tiny waterfall, so I couldn't possibly see.

I stepped into a big hole—maybe an old foxhole—it was filled with water—and went completely under, head and all. I was weighted down with equipment. Choking, I clawed my way out on my hands and knees in the deafening rain. I popped the quick releases on my rucksack and burped up some water. I caught my breath as the rain pounded my back. My hat was gone and I had lost my M-16. I crawled back in the hole to search for my weapon underwater. The compass and map (w/waterproof case) were attached to me by parachute cord so I didn't lose them. The water was maybe chest deep, so I held my breath and groped in the mud in the total darkness and quickly recovered the weapon. I searched a little longer and somehow found my limp hat.

Though I had been moving, the rain was taking the heat from me faster than I could make it, and, thanks to my unscheduled swim, I started shivering. I fumbled for my rucksack and strapped it on. I felt the sores on my shoulders, back and hips, worn raw and stinging. As I tightened down my ruck and readjusted the straps, I started to sing. I sang as I trotted with my gear, crashing through the wilderness in blackness and rain, my feet bleeding and raw, branches ripping and grabbing at me. My hands were covered with scratches.

It felt like there were at least three species of parasites in my crotch, all fighting for food. It felt like they were digging foxholes in my skin and napalming each other, searing me. I was hungry, cold, and alone.

I thought, *If I break my leg because I am going too fast, they'll find me in a day or so.* I was laughing. I was miserable. It was finally pushing me and that's why I was there. So I found all my points and made it back to base camp, which consisted of a tent with a lantern burning inside. Since I had been moving so fast, there was lots of time to spare. The TACs graded my work on the spot and land-nav was behind me. I had passed.

I quickly set up a poncho-hooch out in the woods, and shivered my way into my sleeping bag. A hooch is just an improvised shelter. The rain kept coming and life was good. I couldn't sleep because I was still so cold and clammy, but soon started to warm up, and my body started shutting down for sleep when I heard a voice in the darkness, "Where is Yon? Have you seen Yon?"

Uh oh. What did I do? Did I go to a wrong point? No-way, I knew what I was doing.

"Over here."

Somebody stumbled through the darkness searching with a red flashlight. I guided him in with my voice until he was kneeling in the rain beside me. It was one of the students, in his early twenties.

His voice quivered from cold and exhaustion. He said, "I lost my bolt." To save time and make the course easier, he had disassembled his weapon and put it into his rucksack. The bolt fell out. It had happened to others.

"What should I do?" he asked.

If he didn't find the M-16 bolt, Selection was over for him, even though he wasn't a Fuk-ah-we; he had found all his points. I was warm in my sleeping bag, knowing I would only get a few hours of sleep even if I stayed put. My uniform was drenched and cold and lying outside my sleeping bag, and the rain kept coming. I thought for a minute that since he had cheated, I shouldn't waste my time helping him. Then I figured that he had learned a lesson.

"Give me ten minutes, I'll help you look."

The bolt was non-reflective black, about the size of an overly thick Cuban cigar, and there was no telling precisely what routes he had taken through the woods and swamps. There was about one chance in a million that we would find that bolt. I wearily crawled out of my sleeping bag and pulled on my cold wet uniform and boots. I grabbed my weapon and shivered my way over to the hooch that he had set up while I was getting dressed. He was already in his sleeping bag.

His voice was weak and beaten. "Never mind," he said. "I don't want to look." He was too cold and tired.

I said nothing, limped back, took off my uniform and crawled into my sleeping bag. Sweet dreams.

A few days later during a weapons inspection a TAC was holding the M-16, "*TROOP!* Where the *fuck* is your bolt! You disassembled your weapon during land-nav."

Goodbye.

SURVIVAL

Letter to Richard White:

Next week promises to be extremely challenging . . . not eating for at least 4 days straight . . . last week a guy caught a dog, my chances of getting any food are slim to none. Your letter will be appreciated, then consumed . . .

DRIVE ON

Phase-1 included survival training. Like parts of my childhood, survival training would have been fun if not for the part about being hungry. My grandfather had taught me all the traps and snares that were taught in Phase-1, and more, so that part was easy.

We learned various ways of catching fish, like throwing a hand grenade into the water, but we didn't get to try it, which disappointed me. I had shot fish as a kid. If you put a stick in the water first, you can see which way the light defracts. The fish isn't exactly where it seems to be, but the stick will orient you to the aimpoint. Find a fish, aim, squeeze the trigger . . . *Bam!* A geyser of water shoots into the air leaving you soaking wet. Find the fish and eat it, then use its guts to catch more.

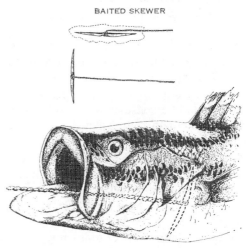

BAITED SKEWER

Of course, it's not smart to go around shooting fish and wasting ammo if you are in enemy territory. We learned more sensible ways to fish, like making hooks, and learning about certain plants that poison the fish. I made my first fish basket. That's right, I learned how to make baskets in Special Forces. I asked an instructor if we would also learn to knit. *"Very funny, Yon! Pushups!"*

One of the most pervasive nicknames for SF is "snake eaters." *Hey, I resent that!* I never ate a snake unless I was hungry. During a survival class an instructor was passing a rattlesnake over to another TAC, and explaining "This is the proper way to handle live snakes" when it bit him on the thumb, *"Ouch!"*

I wanted to yell, *"Pushups!"* but it didn't seem appropriate.

He calmly disposed of the serpent and changed the focus of the class to how to treat a snakebite. I really liked those SF guys! Camp MacKall was a secluded site away from Fort Bragg, so it would take some time before he could get to the hospital. A medevac helicopter landed outside and flew him away. Years later I saw him overseas and he barely recalled being bitten. "Oh, yeah, I remember that."

How the hell can you forget being bitten by a rattlesnake? Pushups!

Survival skills can be useful for many situations, such as the aftermath of a hurricane or earthquake. The instructors preached that if you are near water, you have no excuse but stupidity if you starve to death. Well, that sounded kind of harsh to me, but military directness is refreshing.

Another good place to gather food is the roads. Road pizza seems the most popular term. You can eat dead animals, or food from dumps even after it is rotten, if you boil it. Don't mind the maggots; they are edible, too. A friend who is a survival, resistance, escape and evasion instructor gave me the key to successful survival in six words: "Boil the shit out of it."

You must boil such food for at least *10 minutes, adding one minute for each 1,000 feet of altitude.* The problem is, you can kill the germs, but some leave behind toxins that need more time to destroy. If you come across canned food, vegetables, or meat, and the can is swollen, or a glass container's top is bulging, or if the contents spurt out when you open it, that food should be considered *deadly*, loaded with the botulism toxin. As with road kill, something like that should be eaten only in an extreme emergency. Once you open the can, that toxin will spread around, and even if you boil most of it, it takes only a microscopic amount to kill you. Better to just throw it away, unless you are absolutely starving to death.

So, those road-tenderized possum pancakes may be chow. Obviously, if you are eating road kill to survive, you are probably in enemy territory evading capture, so sneaking up on highways for supper can be dangerous. Besides, it's much better to learn ways to catch live food, or to identify and test potentially edible plants. Everything edible is milk and honey if you are hungry enough.

One of the absolute necessities in any survival situation is safe water, so we learned various ways of collecting and purifying water, and for transporting water. For instance, one survival tool that good soldiers are *never* without is condoms. A condom can be placed inside a sock for support, and used as a canteen.

Condoms are one of the great survival tools. Especially in this day and age. It was said that a good soldier could go his entire life without irresponsibly bringing children into the world, if he observed some simple precautions.

A vigilant trooper could avoid nuisances like herpes that remind him of one night stands that weren't worth it, or even that much fun. Those who got herpes never seemed to just laugh it off. The TACs didn't talk about that kind of danger in SF training because the men were mostly older, but over time the older soldiers passed the essentials of avoiding sexually transmitted diseases down to the next generation.

Sometimes I would ask them more about life itself than military matters. Throughout my time in the Army, I considered some of the old-timers more like fathers than leaders. I wanted to do right by them, not so much because I could get into trouble if I did wrong, but because I wanted to show them that I could measure up. I took them at their word. I knew they were teaching me what I needed to survive in a tough world. That's an important message for military leaders who don't already know it. Some of the young soldiers under your command do not fear your wrath. If they respect you, they fear that they will not measure up to your standards. That was me.

The instructor asked how many people had condoms with them, which I thought was a dumb question because there were no girls around. Sure enough, a couple of the Rangers had condoms. This, and countless other incidents, sealed it for me that Rangers are like gun-toting Boy Scouts. The good ones are always prepared. They always had at least five bucks, too. *Always.*

There are many uses for condoms. In shark-infested waters a condom can be a barf bag for seasickness. A condom can waterproof sensitive items, keeping fire tinder dry. It can cover the end of a rifle to keep water and dirt out. Two or more condoms and a "Y" shaped stick can make a slingshot, but with about enough killing power to kill an aggressive humming bird. (For slingshots it's better to use surgical tubing, or strips cut from a tire tube if you can get your hands on it.) Condoms can be wrapped around ankles

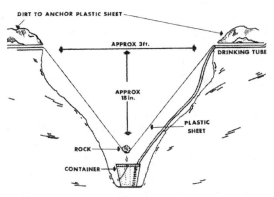

CROSS SECTION OF SURVIVAL STILL. HEAT FROM SUN VAPORIZES GROUND WATER. THEN THIS VAPOR CONDENSES UNDER PLASTIC, TRICKLES DOWN, DROPS INTO CONTAINER.

or shirtsleeves to prevent chiggers and other nasty bugs from getting inside, or as food storage containers, or to repair a leaking life raft. They make good waterproof covers for wounds. I could go on, but I'm sure you get the picture. It's better to carry the inexpensive heavy gauge types, except for sex of course, when soldiers should go first class. Veterinarians even use them as bandage coverings for snakes. It's important for young soldiers to be prepared with condoms, especially, they said, if the young soldier makes it through SF training. *Wow!*

Only later did I learn about "Groupies," that is, women who flock to and make themselves available to SF soldiers. They are called Groupies because SF units are called "Groups." By the time that I got to language school, and, later in college, being an SFer was like being a minor rock star. But, that was in the future.

After a few days of classroom training, it was time to go to the woods again. Each man was issued a flare to shoot if he decided that he would be happier in another line of work. The flares were so big that they took both hands to shoot, and they rocketed high into the sky. They were bright, made a loud *Whooosh* when fired, and could be seen for miles. The flares also made good signals for conducting combat operations at night; you can see them despite explosions and automatic weapons fire.

When for any reason a student fired his flare, it was over—coffee and donuts, no second chances on this test. (I heard of a student in a later class who shot his flare when he came upon a road and found a car accident. For reasons like that, he would not be shipped out. In SF, using common sense is essential, while rigid thinking is a sin.)

The TACs kept a twenty-four-hour vigil and they would immediately go find the student who shot his flare. They showed us the nice big tent with cots and chow waiting for those who decided that SF was really not for them. No harm done. It took a lot of guts just to try, and a man should be proud for trying something so difficult. Medevac helicopters were always at Bragg on standby for soldiers who got hurt, because soldiers are constantly suffering bodily harm in the training areas around Bragg.

The TACs were up to their old Jedi mind tricks again. They showed us how easy it would be if we just shot that flare. They reminded us that we probably wouldn't make it through the rest of the course even if we survived survival, so it only made sense to go home now. Besides, the weather was turning bad. They might say, "You can be drinking beer downtown tomorrow if you shoot your flare. Remember, this is how you shoot it." And they would quickly prepare a flare and shoot. "That's all it takes. You can tell everybody that you were doing great and you got hurt. Nobody will know. You're not quitters because no quitters ever made it this far. You've proven yourself in the toughest land-nav course in the U.S. military. Special Forces isn't for everyone. If you decide that you would rather do something else, it takes a lot of courage to shoot that flare—a lot of courage. And that goes for the rest of the course. It takes a lot of courage to say that this isn't what you expected. We all make mistakes. A lot of good men decide that this is not for them."

The night before we were put out alone, we were *hungry*. I hadn't eaten for over a day and even before there was never enough food. Actually, it was not so much the lack of food as the strenuous training that burned away my reserves. My body-fat was so low that I could see veins in my stomach. I could have done well again in junior bodybuilding contests at that point.

They gave us a little goat to eat the night before we went out alone. And when I say "a little goat," I mean the goat was walking around when they led him to us. But I only got a handful of meat because there was not enough to go around.

Few people have been truly alone. Sure, the vast majority of us have been what we usually call "alone." But how many people have spent time in the wilderness *a-lone?*

It is far different than a city slicker might imagine. Being alone, really alone, means no television or radio, no book with which to intertwine oneself in the thoughts of another. During survival, we were allowed to carry a Bible, so we were not entirely alone. And we had a flare to summon help, so humanity was never far away.

At other times, it has been an eye-opening experience for me to be totally alone in the wild, for many days and nights, with only my thoughts, with no flare to shoot, no book, and no other person to talk with. Being alone can induce more fear than jumping from a jet into the night sky, or standing with your toes hanging over the edge of a giant cliff, the wind whistling and gusting from behind. There are only the sounds of the wilderness and your own heart and breath. At first, the silence can be thunderous. It is at these times that I have become aware of how separate I am from other people, yet how intertwined with them. Such moments make me realize how much I prefer to be in the company of others.

At survival, we were allowed to take a sleeping bag, thirty feet of parachute cord, a knife, a pack of matches, a Bible, and an M-16 with no ammunition. The TACs issued a solemn warning that if we used the Bible to start a fire, we would be kicked out, and that they would check the pages to see that none were missing. (Which I now realize was only bluster, because they had no time to check.) Others have said they didn't get a Bible or a sleeping bag, depending on the time of year they went through. Every class was different.

We were each issued a live chicken or rabbit. They warned us that if you only eat rabbits, you will starve to death. The condition even has a name: "rabbit starvation." You could get plenty of calories, but if you didn't get certain other nutrients in your diet, your body couldn't burn those calories.

At survival, there were exactly enough chickens and rabbits for there to be one per man, and the TACs took us out to the woods and released the chickens and rabbits at once. The students were running around trying to get something before it escaped, which was exciting for a few moments.

The creatures had no chance for escape. I spotted what appeared to be the biggest rooster and dashed through the melee of animals and men, who were running around bumping into each other, and pounced on the rooster as if it were carrying a football. I got up from the ground and tucked the angry rooster under my armpit. I threatened to break his neck if he pecked me.

He pecked me.

He called my bluff.

Then the TACs drove us in a big, green Army truck further out in the woods, stopping now and then to put somebody out. Contrary to popular belief, we didn't parachute alone into the Amazon jungle and have to fight our way out for a month—it wasn't so intense, which disappointed me.

They put me out and drove away. I tied my angry rooster to a tree and named him "Pecker." They warned us not to name our food while it was still alive.

The problem is, being alone can be like starving. (Hence the phrase, "Starving for attention.") Some soldiers find that they would rather keep their dinner as a pet. Many have never killed anything bigger than a mosquito, and despite the rugged image, the title "soldier," and, despite the fact that they will jump out of airplanes, many are not good killers.

This was a serious test. To kill, or not to kill.

The TACs said that in the past some who wanted to be Green Berets had made friends with their bunnies, and gave them cute names like "Fluffy," which made it harder to kill them. After all, what kind of sick person can kill something that is soft and cuddly, eats from your hand, and is named "Fluffy"? Some soldiers even shared their sleeping bags with their bunnies. Fluffy rabbits are tricky like that.

But, the soldiers knew that if they didn't kill little Fluffy, they would fail the course. So there was the rule that you had to kill it; you had to eat it, and you had to keep its head and feet to prove that you didn't let it run off. Steve Shaulis later told me that, while on survival, one candidate actually searched out and found another, and paid him in rabbit meat to kill his rabbit.

I cannot fathom why someone who lacked enough killer instinct to *eat* would want to be in Special Forces. Maybe a rabbit had saved his life by pulling him out of a burning house. Maybe the soldier could have killed a rooster. I don't know.

At the other end of the spectrum, they didn't want people making rabbit-headed walking sticks, or making horns for their hats with rabbit feet. Mutilating the dead is not a sign of a healthy human being.

Pecker was the only food I had for a three-day stay alone, and he never looked at me with eyes pleading for mercy. I was not starving for attention, and he was not cute like a rabbit, of which I had killed and eaten many. I was hungry, he was chicken. I thanked him for his energy.

Before nightfall, I had built a lean-to, firewall, and fire. The weather was cold and wet. In the darkness I lay next to the fire in my sleeping bag. I was hungry, despite my chicken dinner that included everything edible down to the bone marrow, but happy to get a break from the TACs. I paged through the Bible and found it was filled with useful philosophy. Out in the darkness came snow, then rain, then snow and rain. It seemed unseasonably cold. I saw the distant glow of some flares going up the first night—"goodbye somebody, thanks for the energy." I talked to myself to break the silence of having no other voices. The next morning I went out looking for something to kill or pick. It was still cold and raining.

I built some traps and snares, made a fish basket and kept a written log, as instructed. The TACs had warned us about wild dogs in the area. Did they warn the wild dogs about us? I made spears, and piled up some fist-sized throwing rocks, and scattered the spears and rocks around at various tacti-

cally important places, like my water-spot. If any of those dogs came my way, we were going to have a serious fight. I planned to eat any that I could kill.

I heard barking in the distance; it sounded like a dinner bell, so I stalked off into the wilderness, but they kept moving and I didn't catch one. Finally, I recognized an edible plant, some sort of tuber, and decided to have a meal. I picked some and headed home. Chow time—I scored!

Later I learned that one guy caught a puppy, another caught a stringer of fish, and yet another got an owl (don't ask me), for which the TACs went apeshit but didn't kick him out. We were not allowed to kill things like Bald Eagles, or chop down trees. Killing a dog is the next worst thing to killing a human; some of my best friends were dogs, but hunger has a way of making the wild ones look a little different. I wondered if the TACs would kick me out for catching a dog.

While I had been out hunting, the wind had whipped up some embers from my fire and partially burned my sleeping bag. I suppose it was cosmic justice for the man who would eat a dog, though I'd had mixed feelings about catching one. My sleeping bag was still burning slowly, not really in flames, more like the embers of a cigarette, when I found it.

Since I was soaking wet, I jumped on the bag to put it out. When I stood up, I had down-feathers stuck all over my wet uniform. I looked like Big Bird.

I thought, *You dumbass, you broke a sleeping bag! What kind of idiot breaks a sleeping bag?*

The Native American blood running through my veins was obviously not enough to see me through. What an embarrassment. It was going to be a rough night. I had broken my sleeping bag, and I was going to freeze. I dried my uniform by the fire and then stuffed feathers in my pockets and tried to salvage what I could.

I had cooked Pecker the first night because I figured that he was getting skinnier by the hour and I wanted to burn his energy before he did, so now I only had my tubers to eat, and what was left of my angry rooster.

I spent much time making traps for animals and didn't catch a thing. Eventually, I knew, chow would walk into one of my traps which were baited with the less edible pieces of the rooster. Catching animals was not a problem, but I was hungry now.

Oh well, I thought, *this is part of the fun.*

I had a strange, recurring fantasy, in which a woman rode in on a horse, carrying a red and white checkered blanket and a big picnic basket. The fantasy was intrusive. Only the details changed, and the detail that most riveted my attention at that point was the food.

In my dream that night, she was clean and warm and had a new sleeping bag. It was big enough for two, and the giant picnic basket was filled with all kinds of food and a gallon of milk. I'd have given twenty bucks for a slice of buttered bread and a cup of milk at that moment.

And then came a chilling thought: *What if she finds me roasting a dog?* What could I say? A *car* hit it? Just the idea could ruin a budding relationship.

Back to reality, alone. That night I boiled the tubers with the last of Pecker. It was rooster tuber soup, and if I weren't so hungry, it would have tasted even worse than it sounded. The weather was icy cold, but my sleeping bag was still partially functional. I was afraid that they would kick me out for being so careless with the fire and sleeping bag.

The rain kept coming, but the lean-to I had built with deadfall was sound and kept me dry by the fire. At least I was doing *some* things right. My stomach started to hurt and I was shivering. It got worse. I had eaten poison.

I stuck my finger deep into my throat. I could only vomit pain. I kept trying but it only burned my throat. I drank all the water I could hold. I stumbled in the darkness to the creek for more water to dilute the burning poison, to slow it down. I kept going into the woods a few feet away and tried to excrete it. I was miserably cold. I drank more and more water. After some hours, I was completely doubled-over on the ground in pain. My muscles were cramping. I was at Heaven's door and afraid I might never meet that girl.

It hurt so bad, and I was so cold, so tired. I would've been hungry if not for the poison. I was alone, so alone. Shivering and shaking, while the accumulated fatigue and weight-loss from Pre-Phase and Phase-1, and the weakness from having little food over the last several days along with the general lack of sleep, all teamed up with the poison. I needed medical attention soon. When I passed out I might die. I fought and fought.

But I didn't need to worry about falling asleep. I was in too much pain and too cold, so I figured I could forgive myself for what I felt I must do. At least I'd made it really far and it was not because I wimped out, I thought; this was a medical emergency. Writhing in agony. I thought of the girl. There was no shame in surviving—this *is* survival.

Whooosh! In the distance, a flare rocketed into the sky. It was over for somebody. But not for me. I survived, one minute at a time.

I suppose the poisoning was not so bad; I recovered quickly and was back on track by late the next day. It could be said that I completely flunked survival training, but since nobody was there to see it, and I didn't bother to log it, and the TAC who picked me up forgave the sleeping bag affair, I survived and got to go to Phase-2.

Letter to Richard White:

> [I hope you] come see me at Bragg. I'll buy you the most expensive (well, almost) dinner you've ever had . . . got 2 paychecks stacked up so you probably won't break me . . . I can see it now. We starve ourselves during the day . . . go to the most expensive restaurant in . . . 100 miles . . . and eat Big Mac's and . . . wait a minute! Wrong restaurant! We'll eat lobster, steak, oysters, caviar, tartar sauce, mustard, etc. . . Then go outside and punch each other in the stomach, throw up and start all over . . . Let's do it! It's a mission! What comes first? That's right, not final exams, not court martial, mission comes first! I'm getting fired up. I'm about to smash a window or something!

PHASE-2 WEAPONS
THREE MONTHS BEFORE THE MURDER CHARGES

WHILE MANY WOULD disagree, Phase-1 (with a few noteworthy exceptions) was not what I would call extremely difficult. It was simply a matter of motivation, mental outlook, and painstaking preparation. As in sports and almost everything else, winning or losing, success or failure, is mostly determined during preparation, and the "test" is often only a demonstration of what one can or can't already do. Usually the competition or the test doesn't make or break you.

I succeeded in Phase-1, but had been prepared for much more difficult problems. Many others felt that Phase-1 should have been tougher. We were expecting something like Ranger training, but we received something subtler. Most of us, myself included, did not realize that we had been tested in a different way. After all, they were not looking for new Rangers in Special Forces.

Anyway, I made it to Phase-2 and the harassment of Pre-Phase and Phase-1 ended abruptly. We got a weekend off before beginning Phase-2. When I came to formation on Monday, an instructor said that there were too many soldiers in the class. The extra people were mostly recycles or people who came from another branch, like Navy SEALS, Marine Recon, or Army Delta Force soldiers who were there for the specialty schools of Phase-2. The instructors had to eliminate some people.

A major from the Phase-2 cadre, whom I had never seen before, arbitrarily conducted a uniform inspection. I was pulled out of the class for not wearing my jump wings, which I had, in fact, not even bothered to buy. I knew I was Airborne—so what? Airborne Training simply wasn't tough enough for me to start parading around like an airborne peacock. I didn't have the luxury of patting myself on the back, and thereby setting myself up for failure. I knew from earlier (and painful) experience in sports not to get cocky. When I got cocky, I didn't train as hard, I didn't try as hard, and then I'd lose.

A $1 set of jump wings stopped me cold. I figured that since this was SF training, everybody who needed to know already knew that I could jump.

I was not a dirtball soldier who didn't take care of his uniform or shine his boots. My uniform and boots were STRAC (meaning well cared for). I was eliminated not by *character* but by trinkets—*personality*. The Army places emphasis on "I love me" badges.

Whatever the case, I figured, *badges, we don't need no stinking badges.* Badges are good motivators for a lot of people, and many of those people are in fact great soldiers. If that's what it takes to get the job done—bring on the badges.

But I wasn't wearing mine. I would be recycled and pick up the next class. Unless it was full. And it would be. I was young, so they would have me peeling potatoes or picking up cigarette butts to keep me busy for the months it would take to get another slot.

As a TAC drove us back to the unit, I felt sick, a feeling which quickly turned to anger. I was livid. *To hell with the Army.* If that's all they thought about our enlistment agreement, they had wasted their money and my time. I had enlisted in good faith and was doing my best. There were many young soldiers assigned to SF as part of their enlistment agreements. Many were cooks, clerks, truck drivers, or whatever. They sang a similar song and it went something like this: "My recruiter told me that there were no available SF slots, but that I could get in by being a cook (or whatever). Then it would be easy to volunteer for the Q Course. He said I could get on an A-team." If the recruiter had ever been in SF, or knew what he was talking about, he would know that was BS.

Likely, they had sometimes misled the kids to make their quotas. I met many people who were duped and sometimes I would ask: "What was your GT score on the ASVAB?" Everyone in the Army knows his GT like he knows his blood type and Social Security number. The duped soldier usually answered something like, "My GT was 83." It took a 110 to get into SF. I didn't feel sorry for them, because they hadn't done their homework, which I considered a part of Selection. A good soldier doesn't need to be told to study or to prepare, but figures out what needs to be done and does it without further consideration. The duped ones flunked by not making it through the first set of obstacles before they even took the oath.

Though they failed to do their homework, it was no excuse for the mugging they received. When a person walks into a bad neighborhood and makes a mugger's job easier, it's still wrong to mug that person. Although they acted foolishly, they are still people and should be treated justly. They and I were mugged.

Furthermore, since I was so angry at the Army that day, I didn't want to be in a candy-assed Army that thought shiny boots and uniforms that looked like rainbows implied proficiency or morale. The peacocks preached that starched uniforms and boots that shined like mirrors meant that a soldier was motivated—*Bullshit*—it meant soldiers were shining boots when they should be studying war. It meant that they were spending effort to look pretty when they should have been running and keeping fit. I'm not saying that soldiers should walk around looking like bums, but I am saying that shiny boots mean nothing. I didn't even like wearing a uniform. But if there was someone in the Army more motivated than me, I wanted to meet him and learn his secret.

After about a half-hour, I was plotting my way out of the Army.

Furthermore, the Army would not get an ounce of good work out of me for the rest of the time they held me prisoner. They hoodwinked me, and I wouldn't allow it to be a one-way street. Suddenly, I felt I was a *prisoner* and would find a way out. I would work my way through college without their money. Passion goes both ways. I was an angry teenager and on a roll . . . *Goodbye* . . .

But I got over it quickly. *It's not the Army's fault that I wasn't wearing jump wings; it's my fault.* I knew what they expected; it was clear. I had agreed to play by their rules when I took the oath. Sure, I was mad as a hornet, but I liked the Army and was considering making it a career. I shouldn't get mad at the Army for not being perfect. *How do I know what the Army should be like, anyway? I can't adapt the Army to me; I have to adapt to the Army—or get out.*

Within the hour my perspective shifted. *This is just part of Selection. I'll figure out a way to get back in that class. If I'm any kind of a soldier, I'll figure this out. I'll just hitch a ride back and wait until they go on break, then I'll walk in and find an extra chair, maybe in a closet, just cozy up somehow and look small. Yeah, I'll think small. I'll avoid eye contact. I'll slip in like a true SF soldier—infiltrate. Yeah, like Charlie.* The Vietnam vets talked about Charlie. Charlie was sneaky, clever and audacious. *I'll be Charlie. When somebody washes out, the danger-time will be over; the Phase-2 cadre won't notice—or care. I won't be on the roster, but later the TACs will think that they overlooked me and forgot to write down my name. Somebody will flunk and the TACs don't know the students' faces yet, it's only been an hour . . . . No. I have another idea. Sneaking in will be plan B.*

When the truck dropped the "wash-outs" back at the unit, I was simply going to walk in and tell the highest-ranking man what happened and take my chances.

The soldiers filed into the barracks as I walked to the TAC-shack. It was empty, but open. I walked in, sat down and waited. I used the time to refine the idea. *How can I pull this off?* Soon, a throng of TACs rumbled in and before I could say a word, SSG Pait asked, "Yon, what are you doing here? Why aren't you in weapons class?"

Sibley, Jenkins and Gritz were all there. I told the bold-faced truth as SF men are expected to do to other SF men, "Because I wasn't wearing my jump wings. Do you think I'm a dirtball?"

Pait looked at my uniform. "Yes. You're a dirtball, Yon. What's wrong with you? Buy some damn jump wings. Why, to hell with that. Come with me."

Pait snagged a jeep and drove me back to the weapons school. We walked into the class. He told me to wait in the back. He approached an instructor and they talked for a moment. Then SSG Pait found a chair—a chair that someone else was sitting in. Unfortunately for that soldier, he had made some mistakes in Phase-1. Pait said something to the soldier who didn't seem to realize what was happening. (Nor did I.) The soldier immediately got up and walked past me and through the door to the jeep. Pait said, "Yon, come here. Have a seat."

He marched out and drove away. I was very happy that he thought so much of me as a soldier—I would never disappoint him or SF. I was sorry that there was not enough room for both of us, and that for me to be reinstated the other soldier had to be recycled, even though he was wearing his jump wings.

I tended to blame the Army for what went wrong and credit SF for what went right. It was complicated stuff to sort out.

During Phase-2 we learned our individual specialties. There were five: Weapons (heavy and light), Engineer/Explosives, Communications, Operations and Intelligence, and Medic. I went through the easiest, Weapons (light). We learned approximately eighty different military weapons, mostly foreign. Complete assembly and disassembly, working knowledge, theory, shooting, etc. The truth is that I didn't care much for guns, though I owned a few. Of course, I would never admit to such a character flaw while on active duty. That is to say that I had no love affair with weapons; they are simply tools. I loved to shoot, though.

You learn a few things right off the bat. Silenced weapons are not very silent—at least most aren't. The "sexy" guns on TV are often garbage, and the weapons that the media often calls "high-powered" or "assault weapons" are frequently low-powered pea-shooters. As a rule, the media is simply clueless when it comes to weapons and military matters. The movie-makers, who have plenty of time to perform research, are usually no better because they know that audiences want to see fire blast from the barrel, and when people are shot, their mangled bodies are supposed to dramatically fly through walls and windows. In reality, when people are shot, they often just crumple on the spot.

My BB gun was as entertaining as any machine gun I ever met, but the automatic grenade launchers and rockets found the boy in me, and were more fun than my BB gun, blowgun, and slingshots combined.

When I was a kid, as boys do, we took out our aggression by having battles: orange fights, sandspur fights, and Polish cannon fights. We made Polish cannons out of steel cans, pipe, and tape. We did some not-so-fancy assembly work on the cans and pipe, and soon were fit to fight the other team. (See illustration next page.)

Polish Cannon

No offense intended to the Polish people; I lived in Poland long enough to get to like them, but that's what we called the contraption. In parts of Idaho it is called a "potato cannon," and no offense is intended to the people of Idaho. In New York, it is sometimes called an "apple cannon" and I certainly don't mind offending New Yorkers. In fact, I rather enjoy it; they offend me all the time.

Tomatoes are not recommended as ammo. I have used hand grenades as ammo while in the Army, but the improvised cannon was much stronger. When using hand grenades, make sure the pipe is only slightly bigger than the grenade, and remember to pull the pin before shoving the grenade down the pipe. While loading, should the lever accidently be released and fly off the grenade—*quickly* throw the grenade in a safe direction, and lie flat for a few seconds. This is important.

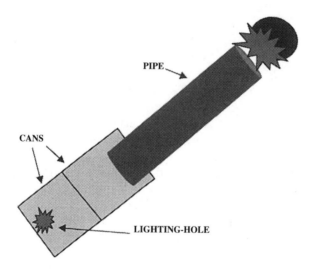

Shoots far, burns kids, breaks windows very well. The use of hand grenades as ammo is not recommended for normal neighborhood applications, and the cannon itself is not recommended as it may leave users in the burn ward of a hospital.

We squirted model airplane fuel into the little hole we poked at the bottom of the bottom can, and shook the contraption. Shaking got the fumes up inside the cans, then we inserted the projectile, for instance a small green orange, into the pipe. Technique was critical to lighting. Do it wrong and you would get a nasty burn. *Phuuump!* Cannonball away! They shot far, and were our artillery.

When pleasures such as jumping Evel Knievel style with our bikes, wrestling, orange wars and other pastimes grew tedious—there were the Bee Hives.

Bees and boys create a volatile mixture. We threw oranges at the hives to obligate them to chase us. Throwing oranges soon became too easy, so we took turns sneaking up and kicking the hives—then we ran like crazy. We had nothing against the bees. On the contrary, they were worthy opponents; that's why we liked them. After all, what kind of sick bastard picks on snails?

Someone got the idea of getting BB guns. The logical progression was as follows: Male children (or adults) + Weapons = War. There is nothing complicated about it, and taking away their weapons will not work for long; they just find other ways to fight.

It followed that Billy decided to have a BB gun war. I was the chosen opponent, but didn't have my gun. He chased me and I ran like—like a boy being chased by another boy wielding a BB gun! It was as though he were launching smart-bees at me, and that's about how it felt. A hit by an average BB gun stings/burns about as much as a normal bee sting.

Billy ran faster than me, so I was taking some hits and crying for him to stop and leave me alone. **"What's wrong with you!"** Wrong thing to say. My words renewed the moving battle, and the chase continued through many yards until finally he cornered me at the junction of two big fences. He was stinging me all over, giving it to me good. I was taking direct hits. There were three choices. Fight my way out, climb over the fences while taking multiple hits, or weather the storm until he ran out of BB's. I chose climbing the fences.

He stopped firing and showed mercy, for which I am today grateful. But he had started something. . . .

I worked and saved my money. Meanwhile, I picked out a powerful BB gun that I could re-cock very quickly. The mechanism slid straight back like a pump shotgun, so I could keep it mostly on target while re-cocking. Almost every day I went to the store to admire this implement of war. My imagination was running wild. I was going to shoot him into a piece of Swiss cheese.

Finally, I accumulated the money to buy my dream weapon. It came with some important instructions and warnings that I promptly used as my first target. I practiced, practiced, and practiced. I spent all my money on BB's. I learned to shoot so well that I didn't need the sights. I shot instinctively.

When I squeezed the trigger, I didn't need to look and I knew exactly where the BB would hit and when it would hit. I could throw a can in the air and plink it more than once before it hit the ground. In my mind, I was "The Rifleman" (Retrospectively, I was "The BB Boy").

I was down at the lake and there were two doves on the white sandy beach. A brisk wind blew off the lake while I shot around the doves. The BB's were kicking up the sand. The doves couldn't figure out what was going on. I was just having fun. I had shot a few birds at my grandparents' house, but felt guilty, so I stopped. I shot near the doves just as the wind gusted. I hit one.

It was flopping around, bleeding. I dropped my cherished gun in the sand and ran to the dove. I had shot dove with a shotgun, cleaned them and eaten them with no remorse, but now I felt miserable. I almost cried, except boys were not supposed to cry.

I picked up the dove. It bled on my hands and just looked at me. It innocently cocked its head back and forth, as if to say, *"What happened to me? Thank you for coming to help."* Then it died.

It was accidental, but what did that matter? It was dead and I had pulled the trigger. Its mate flew down the beach and waited. It would not leave. It just waited and waited and waited, walking around, back and forth, while I buried its mate in the sand. And when I walked off, it was still waiting.

When I practiced with my BB gun, the dogs tagged along. There was a medium-sized jet-black dog in the neighborhood. The kids called him Joe, or, to use his formal name, *Joe the Dog*. Joe was like any other kid in the neighborhood. I grabbed my BB gun, called for Snoopy and Schultz, and together we set out to find Joe. We couldn't find him so we walked to his house and rang the doorbell. A woman answered the door. I looked up, smiled big, and asked if Joe the Dog was allowed to come out. There were a lot of grown-ups in the house behind her. When she looked down at Snoopy, Schultz and me holding the gun by the barrel, slung over my shoulder, she put her hand over her mouth, turned around and burst into laughter. I almost bolted.

She left the door wide open and walked back inside. Soon the adults were in an uproar, coming to the door to look at us. I was thoroughly embarrassed, and with my white hair, probably looked like a strawberry with whipped-cream on top. But I got what I wanted. Joe came out wagging his tail, probably happy to escape all those silly adults, and we four took off to the "desert," where I practiced, practiced, practiced next to the lake. You had to be careful bringing the dogs around the lake, because alligators had a richly deserved reputation for eating them.

Eventually, Billy started another BB-gun battle. I responded with a blistering counterattack, dispatching a swarm of BB's, scoring multiple hits. He was stunned by the onslaught, dropped his gun and covered his head. His crown looked like a furry bullseye, so I shot it. He covered it up with his arms. This was war. I was going for the kill. The BB's continued to sting his arms and body. They were devastating, I thought. I would teach him who was boss, and would shoot until he cried for mercy; only then would I cease fire.

But Billy was no quitter and was not dead yet. He opted for a brilliant tactic. He counterattacked and assaulted through the steady stream of stings, rushing directly for me.

Yikes! The BB's aren't stopping him!

I tensed up but kept shooting and popped the last round into his body at almost point blank range. He was on me, but the fight in him seemed to seep out of his stinging head and body, and the battle ended without further injury.

It was the last great battle in the BB gun era. As an adult looking back, I sat one afternoon in my grandparents' home, my old BB gun leaning against the table inches from my right elbow. The gun felt so light in my hands that I figured it would not even make a good walking stick because of the risk of it breaking. When I cocked it and pulled the trigger, the pressure release sputtered like the sneeze of a tiny kitten. The BB's practically rolled out of the barrel.

Billy recalls that battle. He said that after that, he knew it was crazy to attack someone who would react so unpredictably. Isn't that strange. I thought *he* reacted unpredictably. The truce heralded the end of the BB war.

SPECIAL FORCES WEAPONS TRAINING, PHASE-2

I LOVED TO watch grenades blowing up all over the place. It was excit-
ing stuff. The ammo was "free" and plentiful. I was unpleasantly surprised
that mortars didn't make the same sounds as in the movies, where they go
phuump. In reality they go **Wham!!!** The larger mortars are bone-rattlingly
loud.

Soon I could walk up to a pile of parts from, say, ten disassembled
weapons from various countries: Machine guns, pistols, submachine guns,
assault rifles, WWII weapons, pre-WWI weapons, flame-throwers, or what-
ever, and quickly reassemble all the weapons, put them in working order,
and perform function checks. I found the best way to reassemble a big pile
of parts was to first separate them into individual piles, then begin re-
assembly one weapon at a time. Though one should never disassemble a
weapon at night unless it is malfunctioning, I could take apart and reassem-
ble some weapons by feel and sound, with my eyes closed.

When a machine gun is fired too much it will overheat and malfunction.
Parts expand at different rates from heating at different rates, and if they get
too hot, the parts don't fit and the gun begins to jam or do strange things.
Most modern military weapons work so well that they will fire until they
become hot enough to melt the barrel. They will literally glow orange-hot.
Soviet AK-47 assault rifles can get so hot that, while shooting, your front
hand can get burned just holding onto the wood. Mine did. In case you are
wondering, American weapons tend to be superior to most foreign weapons,
but there are exceptions.

Over time, I learned to tell the difference between the sounds of a Soviet
AK-47 and an American M-16, as well as other weapons. Not just the dif-
ferences in the way they sound when fired. That's easy. I'm referring to the
sounds made when they are carried. For instance, when a soldier acciden-
tally knocks his rifle against a tree or drops it, the weapon makes a distinc-
tive noise. When he lets the bolt go forward to chamber a round, it makes a
certain noise. After you have heard it a thousand times, it's easy to ID the
weapon just as you know the voices of the people you spend time with. At
night, when many weapons are firing, you can tell the difference not only by
the sounds and different rates of fire, but by the distinctive muzzle flashes.
Contrary to what is usually shown in the movies, where M-16's produce a
giant fireball when shot, the weapon makes no flash. Sometimes a few
sparks fly out the barrel, but, for the most part, you see nothing.

They are designed to be like that. AK-47's and most other weapons give
off more light. Some, in fact, do make bright flashes, which has some obvi-
ous drawbacks. Soldiers shoot at flashes. Also, the flashes destroy the night

vision of the shooter, so there are incredible disadvantages for soldiers who carry them, glamorous though they are. And the flashes don't add power, because they are merely propellant burning in the air after the bullet is away.

When performing a reconnaissance of an enemy camp, it can be useful to get the enemy to shoot at you at night. This will allow you to determine how many of the enemy there are. Also, if they are particularly untrained, you may get lucky and they will shoot at you with their machine gun(s). You can count muzzle flashes and make a sketch of their defensive positions as they fire. A more highly trained enemy will not fire at a small probe in the night, since such firing will give away their positions. Instead, they will throw hand grenades if they think you are close, or shoot grenades from their grenade launchers when they think you are far, or use mortars if they have them.

A problem with weapons that are fired too much in a short period is called "cook-off." Cook-off occurs when the gun overheats and there is an unfired round in the chamber. A round consists of a bullet (the part that flies and kills people), a metal casing, some gunpowder, and a primer that ignites the gunpowder when struck by the firing pin. When the trigger is pulled, the firing pin strikes the primer that is on the bottom of the round. When the bullet exits the barrel, it flies through the air on its way to a target. Usually it flies at supersonic speed, depending on the weapon and ammo. When a gun overheats from firing, a fresh round in the chamber can become superheated to the point that it cooks-off—fires—even when the trigger isn't pulled.

With machine guns, sometimes a soldier must open the gun to clear a malfunction, and, if he hasn't waited for the gun to cool, the round can cook-off in his face. One day we were pushing some machine guns beyond their nominal limits to learn what their limits really were. A soldier next to me was letting loose with his powerful, fast-shooting Belgian Mag-58 machine gun, M60 or whatever, when it jammed. A few people saw what he was about to do and yelled at him, but he couldn't hear. He was wearing earplugs and there were lots of automatic weapons firing all around. Too late. ***Bam!*** It cooked-off in his face. Several of us ran over to do first aid, but he did not suffer so much as a scratch. The range was an interesting place.

Despite the technical side, how to maintain weapons and fire them, the course was actually only kindergarten-level training, though vitally necessary, for weapons and tactics. Knowledge of weapons' capabilities and their proper employment is the real meat of the matter. Proper use is a skill that is only mastered during conditions of prolonged war. After all, you are never *really* employing weapons in peacetime during training. Fighting is not a one-way street—it's interactive—like fist fighting. In many karate classes the instructor only teaches students to perform certain moves as if the enemy will always cooperate. In fighting, you must always assume that the other guy is just as smart or smarter than you, and just as tough or tougher, and that you have to give the fight everything you've got.

As with most matters, whether sports, business or military, the real weapon is the mind that guides the visible weapon and the hands that hold it. You can give one person a machine gun and another a butter knife, and it comes down to the way the weapon is *used*, and luck, as to who lives or dies. Of course, the machine gun has many distinct advantages over the butter knife, but the butter knife has advantages, too. A machine gun can't kill silently or be sneaked into a theatre. The key is to deny the enemy the use of his advantages while playing to your own. War is an art (and a science and a business).

We learned about grazing, flanking, plunging and interlocking fire, the cone of fire in the beaten zone and the maximum ordinate, and many other interesting and oddly named things.

When a round is fired parallel to earth, the maximum ordinate is the highest point it travels; this is reached two-thirds of the way into its trajectory. The term Danger Close means, for our purposes, that when troops on the ground call for a fire support mission—as in the case of artillery or air strike—friendly troops will be dangerously close to the target. The lessons to learn went on and on.

There is a popular misconception that a bullet, or a sabot round, speeds up when it leaves the barrel. This is only true if the bullet has a rocket in it, in which case it's not a bullet. Another misconception is that when a bullet is fired straight up, it comes down at the same speed that it leaves the barrel. This is not quite true, but there is some validity in that assumption.

If you were standing on the moon and shot a bullet straight up, it would return at the same speed. Very fast! That's because there is no atmosphere worth mentioning on the moon, and is also due to some mathematical quirks of gravity. However, on Earth, the atmosphere greatly retards bullet flight. This is especially so when bullets are traveling at supersonic speeds.

When a bullet from a distant rifle passes nearby, the *Snap!* is unmistakable and that supersonic Snap! bleeds energy from the bullet very quickly as the energy transfers from the bullet to the air. Even sub-sonic rounds lose energy quickly due to air resistance.

When a bullet is shot straight up on Earth, it will often return with enough force to kill a person. That's why people are sometimes killed on New Year's after drunk and foolish people run out into their yards and fire their guns into the air at midnight. If you are on the highway, you may see some cars pull under a bridge for a few minutes at midnight on New Year's so that they don't get shot. In the U.S., the Fourth of July is also a good night to catch a stray bullet. And when you see foreign soldiers firing their automatic weapons in the air for some celebration, as they so often do, you know two things: 1) They are stupid; 2) you should seek cover for a few minutes.

Another misconception is that bullets rise when they leave the barrel. There is some truth to this, but, technically speaking, the bullet begins to drop, or at least slow any upward trajectory, the instant that it leaves the barrel.

Whenever I have heard that statement, I like to ask: *Does that mean that if you fire the rifle upside down, so that the trigger is on top, the bullet still rises? Or does it head to the ground faster?*

The reason that the bullet apparently rises is that when aiming at a target, you are not looking *through* the barrel, but *over* the barrel through the sights. In other words, your sights, which are sitting higher than the barrel, are *not* pointed exactly where the tip of bullet is pointed. Actually, there are two points along the trajectory of the bullet where the bullet crosses the place that the sights are pointed. Those two places are "zeroes."

Many things affect the flight of the bullet, prominent among them, rotation and wind speed. Most weapons have grooves cut inside the barrel to cause the bullet to spin so that it will stabilize. But the spin makes the bullet drift to the left or right depending on the direction the grooves spin the bullet. This also makes the rifle jerk to the left or right because every action causes an equal and opposite reaction; this is the same reason that weapons recoil. Grenade launchers "kick" hard, and after some shooting your shoulder can get sore, but an M-16 has no "felt recoil" because the weapon is cleverly designed with internal parts that absorb the kick. You can literally put the butt of an M-16 on the tip of your nose and fire it and it won't hurt. (Don't try this with a shotgun.)

As you can see, there is a lot to know about weapons and tactics. It takes years to acquire a respectable level of knowledge and skills, and our course was merely an introduction. Special Forces snipers, and other well-trained professionals who work with expensive "sniper systems," must train and study for a long time before they can brag "one shot, one kill."

Some people are not familiar with the term "sniper." The following definition will cover most of what they do: Snipers creep around with special, high-powered rifles, take their time, fire few bullets, wound or kill people with most of those bullets, and, if all goes well, return in one piece with an abundance of information about the enemy.

A military sniper is not the same as a police sniper. Police usually conduct "point sniping." That is, the shooter may have to hit a kidnapper who is holding a pistol in one hand and a baby in the other, with one well-placed head-shot before the man can react. Military snipers practice point sniping extensively, but also practice harassment, which basically means getting any kind of hits, thus denying the enemy freedom of movement and peace of mind.

Harassment sniping can be used to delay an enemy. At times, enemy militaries have even chained their drivers into their trucks so that they cannot get out and run away, thereby leaving a blocked road with lots of empty trucks while the snipers call in an airstrike on the abandoned convoy.

Snipers often have pinned down sizable units who are too timid to hunt down the shooter(s). The snipers generally go out into enemy territory in two-man teams consisting of a shooter and a spotter. They are actually both snipers, and they take turns with the rifle to remain fresh, which allows them to shoot better. They often go out without direct fire support. Shooting is only half the snipers' game; they must be skilled in camouflage and tactical movement. They must also be patient and stable emotionally because to get the best shots takes a lot of work and iron nerve.

If you can see an enemy, he can see you. If you can shoot him, he can shoot you. You can imagine the type of person that it takes to have the guts to willingly sneak up on a large unit and start shooting. And the sniper team knows that if they run into a well-trained unit where morale is high, once the shooting starts, they are going to be aggressively hunted. Sniper teams are lightly armed, and, with only two men, don't stand a great chance in a full-on fire-fight against a surging enemy. When possible, the snipers engage the enemy from across some sort of natural barrier, such as a river, a ravine, or from cliffs, to make getaway safer.

The best snipers learn numerous tricks. For instance, they might fill a sock with sand and put it in the armpit of their firing arm to lessen the thump of their pulse in that arm. Few people can put the cross-hairs of a scope on a man's chest, and, while lightly squeezing the trigger, be composed enough to control their breathing to the point that they can kill a man practically between their own slow heartbeats.

Great snipers are great stalkers. There is an art to stalking. It's generally better to move directly toward your target, because lateral movement is much easier to see. In approaching the enemy, whenever possible, it's also good to do so from the least-expected direction.

Good soldiers are naturally unpredictable and are audacious. If you look at a piece of terrain and say, "The enemy would never come from *that* direction," beware. There may be a soldier thinking, "With any luck, they won't expect me to swim across that crocodile-infested river and climb that insane cliff in the middle of the night just so I can shoot one of them."

As a rule, those who make it through sniper training are above-average soldiers with above-average intelligence. In some guerrilla warfare environments they are worth their weight in gold.

Target selection is critical for a sniper. When possible, snipers first kill other snipers, who are, understandably, their worst enemies. After all, who could better conduct counter-sniping than one who thoroughly understands the weapons, tactics, and mindsets of other snipers?

Then snipers go for priority targets such as high-ranking leaders, big weapons systems, and the operators of those systems. A patient stalker may watch an enemy unit for days before going for a kill. This makes emotional stability in snipers even more important. After watching people for a long period, and becoming familiar with them, the sniper may lose the will to pull the trigger. He must remember his mission. While watching the enemy, he is also responsible for gathering intelligence, so he must be observant and know what to look for and how to interpret what he sees.

In garrison, most military types salute officers. In the field that can be a fatal error. When the junior person accidentally salutes, it's obvious that the other is the officer. *Bam!* With a single bullet, a sniper can eliminate a highly-trained, experienced officer who took years of training, and considerable resources to create. Therefore, snipers learn methods of identifying leaders. For instance, one may be wearing a pistol, binoculars, and a nicer uniform. Also, he likely is not hauling gear around or digging a foxhole. Like a queen bee, he tends to be a center attraction and older than the rest.

At the range, it was lunch break and mail call. I got a "draft notice" in the mail (actually my Selective Service registration; there was no real draft). I'd already received a couple and I just threw them away. I found it amusing to receive a "draft notice," that's what I called them, while I was in the middle of SF training. So, with no further thought I whipped out the lighter that all good soldiers carry (along with a pocketknife, money, and some condoms), and set it ablaze. A TAC yelled at me not to burn it, but it was too late. I held it over my head and did a jig while I shouted in the middle of the crowd, some of whom had been in Vietnam,

"Hell no, I won't go! Hell no, I won't go!"

And I didn't—I was never drafted into military service. I was drafted for guard duty that night. Attention draws fire, but everybody had a good laugh. All night I walked around with a little shotgun guarding a semi-truck full of ammunition, and the next day, when we were shooting that ammo, I was feeling a bit groggy.

RABBIT HUNTING:
BE VERY, VERY QUIET

OUR GRANDPARENTS NEVER argued in front of the kids. Occasionally, I might detect that they disagreed on something, but it was like a summer breeze, not Hurricane Della. I asked Granddad if he ever argued with Granny. He said that sometimes they disagreed but it is normal that people don't always get along. As long as a husband and wife love and respect each other, there will be no problems that can't be fixed. A family can work through anything if there is love and respect.

He knew little about science, but whatever I saw anywhere else, I listened first to my grandfather. He knew how to live, which was more important than any science I studied. I didn't always agree with his beliefs, but I respected them, because I respected him.

Granddad and I would walk alone. We were a team, and he was my true father. He had taught me since I was tiny how to be a good man, and that goodness of heart is more important than material things. He was right. I was special because he told me so, and I believed him. He didn't tell me what to do, but he taught about good and bad, right and wrong. He said that it was up to him to teach me about life and how to live; it was up to me to do right.

Granddad worked hard. Sometimes I worked with him in the garden, and later as a teenager he hitched me up to the plow like I was his horse. Farmers may scoff at that statement: *You pulled a plow?* Yeah, right!

It was just a little plow that made a single furrow in the soft soil. The rows were not long, but it sure was hard pulling. I was always trying to show that I could. I would grunt and groan and my legs would burn like fire.

We dug a well. Dig, dig, and dig. Soon my hands were blistered and stinging because gloves were for sissies. The leather pair that Granddad gave me were still on top of the water cooler. I was trying to impress him by being tough. He didn't say a word, but he wore his gloves, and at the end of our digging his pile of sand was much higher than mine. We never hit water, but I learned to wear gloves.

Born in the lap of poverty, Granddad was a pack rat of the highest order. He could see potential uses for the rusty nails we pulled out of the warped planks that he sometimes hauled home in the back of his old white pickup truck. He saved the old nails, screws, nuts, bolts and sundry unnamable other small parts, in old coffee cans—which he also saved. He kept the old planks and plumbing pipes, some of which seemed as old as he was, in one of the three sheds that he used for storage. Granny called it pack-ratting.

Granddad called it saving money, or having stuff to fiddle with.

Granddad's three sheds were bulging at the seams, so he decided that he needed more room. Billy and I helped tear down his best shed. Of course, we saved every salvageable nail and straightened them out with a hammer. We built the new-improved shed, which was big enough to house a family of ten in Central America. I tried to keep up with Granddad while we worked, but he drove me into the dirt.

He was made of iron. When he saw that I was tired, he would tell me to fetch us something to drink. Or he might say that he didn't need me now, but I should come back in a half-hour or so, and he would need me for something else. Granddad allowed me to keep my dignity. Good thing, otherwise he would have had to bury me in the garden. He was the kind of rugged that only hardworking people know.

One day when the new shed was finally finished and I was tinkering alone, I discovered a chunk of metal. Somehow I concluded that it might be magnesium.

Oh boy! Magnesium!

I'd read in a science book that magnesium burns brightly. I shaved some off and lit it on fire.

My God! Fire! Bright, bright, blinding fire like a flashcube that refuses to go out. Fire in the new shed.

I was trying to put it out, but it consumed itself—and the big tool-shed was spared.

Granny was a great cook and I was normally starving when it came time for the blessing. Granddad prayed like a poet. And when we visited, he knew when he could pray a long time and when he needed to cut it short. It came down to the hunger level of the kids. The food always smelled so good, and my mouth sometimes watered like one of Pavlov's dogs'; it took everything I had to keep from starting early. At the end of his prayers, Granddad would say, "and thank you dear Lord for this food and sanctify it for the use of our bodies and to thy service. Amen."

"Amen." Once I piped up and added: "Rub a dub dub, thanks for the grub."

"Michael!" Granny looked at me with a little smile. Granddad said in his Southern drawl, "Pass the 'taters."

He taught me to hunt when I was old enough to shoot. The first rule was that without good cause, it was wrong to kill an animal, in fact, it was just plain meanness. Never kill anything unless you absolutely have to, or for food. (The rule didn't apply to moles or snakes.) Also, it was not good to kill animals in the times when they may have young. He said that to kill a mother meant that the babies would all starve to death. I could relate to that.

As for rabbit hunting, just walk slowly and be ready. It's easy. You don't have to worry much about things like wind direction and odor discipline. It's not like hunting polar bears that hunt back. Anybody can hunt rabbits. I could kill rabbits with a slingshot or even a rock if I had to.

There were two kinds near the house: marsh rabbits (a smaller version of swamp rabbit) and cottontails, and each exhibited behavior peculiar to its kind. When a marsh rabbit sees danger, it normally hunkers down and waits for the danger to pass, or if it can get to water, it will jump in and hide, submerged but for its nose. And they swim around. Sometimes I would see just how close I could get to a marsh rabbit before it hopped off without my firing a shot, but when they did take off, they dashed for cover. The cottontails, however, bolted and zigzagged at the first sign of real danger.

Billy had a great gun for hunting marsh rabbits and cottontails simultaneously. It had two barrels. The top was a .22 rifle and the bottom was a 20-gauge shotgun. I kept the selector on the shotgun because if I flushed a cottontail a quick blast was needed, but for a hunkering marsh rabbit, I quietly switched the selector to rifle and killed him with a single bullet. The reward was eating rabbit few hours later and telling my grandfather how I bagged him, as if it had been an African safari. "There I was. . . ."

"THERE I WAS . . . "
FORT BRAGG, PLAYGROUND OF THE ELITE

THAT'S THE JOKE, here's the reality. Bragg is a giant base including the 82nd Airborne Division, Psychological Warfare units, and many others. Delta Force takes up a tiny space; Special Forces is tucked in there with the rest, and there is even a Burger King on base.

The area is crawling with service members, and as international as can be. Soldiers bring back wives from every corner of the Earth and, when they retire, many settle around Bragg. It is a sea of current and former service members, fast food joints, used car lots and myriad pawnshops—as well as strip joints.

I made my way to a sleazy strip joint.

Phase-2 for the Weapons specialty lasted two months and we had the weekends free. I drove with a couple of classmates down to Fayetteville (a.k.a. Fayette-nam). We strode into a girlie bar and took a seat. I hadn't been to many bars, and still looked all of fifteen. As I sat there drinking a beer, my friends wandered off to ogle the strippers. I was too embarrassed to stuff money in a G-string while some strange girl wagged her butt in my face, and there wasn't enough beer in the joint for me to fall in love with one of the waitresses, so I moved and sat further back where they wouldn't notice me watching as a non-participatory-voyeur.

Soon, a pretty girl came and sat beside me on the left. She started talking through her pouty lips and professionally sultry eyes. "Hi," she said, touching my knee. "I'm Candy."

"I'll bet you are," I said with an unintentional sarcasm that must have been canceled out by the music and dim light. Her perky little breasts seemed barely restrained by her tight halter, and her stomach was as flat as mine, minus the muscle. Looks-wise, she seemed a knockout.

Though I had seen some prostitutes around Fort Benning while I was a drill corporal, I had never actually met one to my knowledge, so I didn't know how to handle this girl who seemed my age, and about two hundred times more worldly. I was not interested and told her politely, "No thanks."

Had we met in the mall, and she were dressed differently, I would probably be stumbling through some kind of introduction, trying to ask her to the movies, thinking she was baseball, apple pie, and home-cooking all rolled into one. But now I wanted to get lost and get away. She kept pushing. I said, "No thanks." She pushed. "No thanks, thank you for asking." She pushed and she pushed. Her dad must have been a used car salesman, or I must have looked half rich and the other half dumb—she just wouldn't quit. Maybe it

175

was just after payday and she figured my pockets were full.

Some of the girls around Bragg are experts and can milk young soldiers dry of every penny. They just sit there and talk about anything the soldier wants to talk about and look pretty while the soldier buys them drinks at some hormonally elevated price. It's amazing, because only the densest or most self-deluded would not see what is happening. But men have a natural response to women who are interested. Some men can't tell plastic from gold; others don't care. That, on top of the soldiers being young and often spending long periods without seeing a woman, and having a pocket full of cash, makes for an interesting scene. It's entertaining to watch—from a distance.

I wasn't going to buy her a drink, but she was a persistent tease.

"What do you do in the Army?" she asked tilting her head, brushing her hair behind her ear as if she had waited her entire life to meet me. She reached over and traced a vein on my left forearm, which actually felt kind of good. For a minute I thought . . . *she doesn't really like this job. She must have had a really bad time to land in here. She just needs a chance.*

Gross! I pulled back my left hand, brushed her hand off my knee, and looked her in the eye, "Look, I'm not gonna buy you a drink."

"I didn't ask you to buy me a drink! Why are you so uptight! Do you have a girlfriend back home? Is that it? What do you think she's doing tonight?"

"Leave me alone!" I barked like a drill sergeant. ***"Get outta here!"***

It worked, but I made a little mistake. A group of three soldiers were sitting at the next table. *Paratroopers.*

They heard me yell and saw the girl get up and stomp off. One of the soldiers, about my age and a little bigger, was drunk and meaner than a Texas rattlesnake. He stood up and grabbed the girl by the arm before she got away.

"Is he giving you a hard time, Honey?" he asked, swaying as he stood.

"No," she said, "everything's fine." Gritting her teeth, shooting a killing look at me.

The soldier was wearing his "Death From Above, Airborne" T-shirt when he staggered up and stood over me like a coconut tree swaying in the breeze. "Are you giving her a hard time?"

He was drunk-drunk. . . .

"No," I said "it's all okay. No problems."

He kept on. Making a show of apparently backing me down. I was still sitting down, and there was a razor sharp pocketknife in my pocket. I never cut anyone before. I carried it because all good soldiers carried a pocketknife, a condom, and five bucks.

I'm not sure exactly what my mistake was. Maybe when I backed down I made too much strong eye contact. Maybe the mistake was that I was talking to a drunk man who wanted to fight someone smaller so that he was sure to win. He, like many other bullies and unfulfilled fighters, just wanted to beat somebody up. And when you submit, or appear to submit, they see you the way a cat sees a mouse.

I didn't want to fight, but if I had, I would have already hit him. People who posture for five minutes, talking about how they are going to whip each other, are a laugh. That's like declaring war on a country and bombing it with leaflets, after which the enemy responds with insulting letters. Real fighters get on with business and it is scary; usually at least one gets hurt.

But if I got into the slightest trouble I would be kicked out of SF and maybe even sent to his unit with him. I'd tried too hard to get this far, and I wasn't going to blow it now. SF tolerated no discipline problems, especially in the beginning, when they watched our every move—the younger men, in particular. In the "real" Army a DUI, a positive drug test, a fight downtown or whatever, would spell problems. A good Army doesn't let its soldiers run around like hooligans and our Army cracks down hard on hooligan-behavior, though many great soldiers were, or are, hooligans of sorts. So it is a two-edged sword. As for SF, the tolerance level for childish behavior was non-existent. After all, if a soldier will not control himself in downtown Fayetteville where everyone is watching, how could he be trusted with sensitive and delicate operations?

So I was getting scared that I would be beaten to a pulp—this guy was here to fight—then kicked out of SF. I was looking for my escape. The paratroopers were sizing me up as a punching bag—I knew the look. My buddies were nowhere in sight.

I said, "Excuse me, I gotta hit the latrine."

I stood up to leave—the other two got up and approached.

Adrenaline.

"Waitress! Bring my friends a drink."

Tactical error on my part that I only realized later in Maryland—the offer to buy a round apparently was not interpreted as a sign of conciliation, but of submission.

"We don't want no fucking drinks," said Death From Above.

Men can be very childish, and I harbor no pity for a drunk who picks a fight. And it is foolish for a drunk to pick a fight with a sober man. He telegraphed everything. He glanced at my jaw on the left, took a quick breath, his body tightened—here it came. His slow, drunken punch made it about halfway and I hit him with a few hard punches in the face and jaw. He was so drunk and slow that he tripped on his own feet and gravity did the rest. He fell to the floor. Looked like a knockout, but there was no time to dally. Before his friends reacted, *Zoooom,* I was out the door. There was an adrenaline-packed chase, but I got away and made a link-up with my friends. I had narrowly averted disaster. This time.

Back in class.

Light Anti-tank Weapons (LAWs: Pronounced "laws") are used to knock out armored vehicles and small tanks. The LAW packs a serious punch with its specially shaped explosive charge that blasts holes through armor with an exploding jet of focused, white-hot gas. When a LAW round penetrates an armored vehicle, the searing gas leaves a little hole only about the diameter of a pencil. The gas is so hot that it melts and pushes the armor inside the vehicle. The molten armor followed by the jet of gas kills the occupants in an explosion of lava-like metal, often detonating ammo and fuel. But for all that killing power, LAW rounds are small: the rocket itself weighs only three pounds, and it contains only two-thirds of a pound of a high explosive called Octol.

The round is designed to kill with technique, not brawn. The warhead comes with a pressure-sensitive piezo fuse in the nose that arms when fired. It arms, not immediately, but after nine meters of flight (less than thirty feet). Like other military weapons, it's made so that if you accidentally shoot a nearby tree, with luck you won't be killed or dismembered by the explosion. Hitting a nearby obstacle is common during the day, and extremely common at night. Sometimes when you fire a grenade launcher, for instance, the grenade hasn't traveled far enough to arm and it simply bounces off and lands on the ground unexploded. Duds can be extremely unstable and dangerous. There is a standing order in the Army—*Do not disturb unexploded ordinance.* There is a reason for that order. "Duds" are deadly and kill people around the world daily.

A soldier from an airborne unit was out on a range. He picked up a dud LAW round, told a funny joke and thumped its nose. The round exploded and blew his guts out. An acquaintance in my weapons class was pulled out for a couple of hours to identify the body of his brother-in-law. He came back, described what had happened, and went back to work.

When a young college student does something childish, the school authorities may call his parents. Who knows? Maybe they will even suspend him or kick him out of college. When a young soldier does something childish, or just doesn't pay attention to his surroundings for a few seconds, he may be sent back to his parents in pieces. It's hard to imagine how many military people have died due to the most trivial misunderstandings, oversights, or just plain failure to follow instructions.

The dead soldier had betrayed his wife's trust by taking foolish risks. He killed the father of his own baby. He was just a young man like many others who were growing up in an unforgiving atmosphere.

Goodbye.

Phase-2 was over. Those remaining went to Phase-3, where we began to learn what Special Forces was all about.

GUERRILLA WARFARE

Letter to Richard White:

> [I am] in Phase-3 now and it's . . . an eye opener. Today we had 12 hours of class [scheduled] but they cut it to 10 . . . been a long day.

Unfortunately, many of the Phase-3 lessons were classified, though it was mostly stuff you could learn in a good library. But since they trusted me, I am bound to confidentiality.

"Secret" information is often widely available. Smart militaries are constantly trying to hide their true capabilities. Where they are strong, they often want to look weak, and vice versa. Frequently when training is classified, it is merely to hide capabilities and the information itself is not sensitive.

Some of my training was not classified, and this training was the most interesting to that point, consisting of introductions to unconventional warfare and guerrilla warfare (UW/GW) concepts and demonstrating why the motto of Special Forces is: *De Oppresso Liber:* To Free the Oppressed. That sounded like a worthy endeavor.

First, the instructors gave a basic overview of the structure of Special Forces. In the big picture, SF consists of Groups. At the time there were three active duty Groups: the 5th, 7th, and 10th. A fourth was soon to be activated and named 1st Group. Each Group was responsible for missions in specified areas of the world. For instance, the 7th Group handled activities in Central and South America, so soldiers in the 7th developed the skills needed for the region, such as language, jungle, and mountaineering skills.

As of this writing there are five active duty Groups: 1st, 3rd, 5th, 7th, and 10th. The 1st handles the Pacific region and Eastern Asia. The 3rd takes care of the Caribbean and Western Africa. The 5th is responsible for Southwest Asia and Northeastern Africa and had served with distinction in Vietnam, among other places.

The 5th and 7th were stationed at Fort Bragg, while the 7th had a forward-deployed battalion, about fifteen A-teams, in Panama. Due to the buildup of Special Operations Forces, the 1st Special Forces Group was being reactivated at Fort Lewis, Washington. The 10th was something of an anomaly, having two battalions at Fort Devens, Massachusetts, and a battalion forward deployed in Bad Toelz, West Germany, as well as a section in Berlin that was classified at that time. Though the 10th Group's primary area of responsibility included Eastern and Western Europe, its state of readiness was high enough that the 10th sometimes picked up missions that were out of its areas.

A Group consists of a vast array of support personnel including doctors and lawyers, pilots, intelligence specialists, psychological operations people, cooks, clerks, drivers, communications specialists, and many others. Those people's lives revolve around supporting the teams. There are women in Special Forces in some support positions, but they do not go through Selection nor are they, to my knowledge, used in combat positions as of this writing.

There are three types of *teams:* C, B, and A. The C team is the headquarters detachment for the battalion, and there are about three C-teams per Group. Company-level support and headquarters comprise the B-teams, so there are about nine B-teams per Group. Many soldiers on the C and B teams have not been through Selection.

The heart and soul of the unit are the A-teams. An A-team usually consists of twelve men, all of whom have been through Selection, many having college degrees and foreign language skills. The lowest rank on an A-team is supposed to be sergeant and the highest is normally captain. The officers generally do not run the A-teams, which are led by enlisted men who are responsible to the Team Sergeant, who is normally a master sergeant.

Each of the specialties (weapons, engineer/explosives, communications, operations and intelligence, and medical) is represented on an A-team, and ideally each man is cross-trained so that when someone is killed, injured, or otherwise unavailable, there is always one, but usually two or more people who can do his job. In effect, there are two complete six-man teams per A-team.

The A-teams conduct combat operations and such, but most of what SF does during peacetime is not directly combat-related, though it is just as important. For instance, teams sometimes administer humanitarian aid and today they are helping to clear minefields around the world in various countries where so many children and innocent adults are being maimed and killed every week. Teams help in nation building, aiding countries that need help with their infrastructures, and more humane concerns, such as basic hygiene, inoculations, and helping to build schools.

After learning some basic facts about the structure of Special Forces, we learned some definitions. Special Operations come in various types. Some examples include DA, or Direct Action; often this means a team hits a target. (These days, that's more SEAL, Ranger and Delta Force territory, though guerrilla warfare is filled with direct action "sub-missions," and Special Forces is the only military unit assigned to conduct guerrilla warfare.)

FID, or Foreign Internal Defense, generally means training foreign police forces or militaries. There are many other types of missions, such as counterguerrilla warfare, subversion, setting up escape and evasion networks to smuggle downed pilots out of enemy territory, psychological operations, counterterrorism, antiterrorism, etc.

Missions are further classified as overt, covert, or clandestine.

Overt means open, "in their face." No attempt is made to hide who we are or what we did.

Covert means the mission, such as hitting a target, is overt, but the identity of the operators is concealed. A covert mission should be carried out in such a way that our country has plausible deniability. If someone points fingers, the politicians may cast the blame elsewhere, and generally just say, "Who? *Us?* Nope, we didn't do it. Furthermore, we are surprised and offended by these unwarranted allegations. Your country would not be having such problems if the majority in power halted its oppressive governing policies, and wanton disregard for human rights against those minorities within your own population, and made moves toward a more democratic system of government." Deny everything and make counter-accusations.

Clandestine means that everything possible is hidden, including the identity of operators, and the fact that anything happened. A reconnaissance may be clandestine, as may certain types of sabotage.

Infiltration and missions come in colors.

White means that the host country is aware of and complicit with our presence—the work is conducted in "broad daylight." An example would be the Special Forces humanitarian work in Haiti.

Grey generally means that the host country is complicit, but the activities are all or mostly secret, like those in El Salvador during the Eighties.

Black might mean secretly conducting operations in an enemy-controlled country or area. An example might be found in Iraq, where agents were fomenting resistance against the existing government in a joint Special Forces-CIA operation. Any time the U.S. conducts guerrilla warfare, the CIA is heavily involved.

Going in *sterile* means that Americans will carry nothing to connect them to the U.S. If someone were killed and left behind, the U.S. could either deny everything, or, in a best-case scenario, because of the absence of definite identifying data, the enemy might not even suspect our involvement. Perhaps no U.S. equipment would be carried—the operators would have foreign boots, foreign footprints, foreign bullets, no dog tags, no ID. In places where U.S. equipment is being used, it's okay to carry U.S. gear. It is nearly impossible to send people that are truly sterile. For instance, tattoos can be give-aways, as can dental and other medical work. Most American men are circumcised and most foreigners are not, and, in many countries, the people are of different stock than the mostly Latin, European, and

African who fill our ranks. A black man can hardly pass as Polish, and a European can hardly pass as Asian. If you were going to send spies to Teheran before the rescue attempt, it would be important to try to mimic the physical appearance of the locals.

The best one can do is to go in as sterile as possible. Going in black and sterile very well could mean—if one were captured—being tortured and possibly shot as a spy.

In any type of conflict, there is some spying involved. One difference between guerrilla warfare and conventional warfare is that guerrillas must do much of the intelligence collection themselves, so we learned some basic field craft such as how to operate in discrete cells, and some basics of clandestine communications.

There was one instructor who kept repeating the party line over and over; he seemed an angry man, and perhaps that is because he was Czech and the Soviets had rolled over his country. In the early days of SF, many of the soldiers were of foreign birth, so they spoke the native languages fluently. Some of them came to SF with the hopes of liberating their own lands, and some of those types were still around.

Of course, I only vaguely remember his words and so I must fill in the blanks, but the angry Czech hated to see the young faces sprinkled among our group of future SF. He barked over and over, "You young soldiers better listen up! This is very basic material. Don't walk out of here thinking you are some kind of CIA spooks, because you are not, and if you should grow up to become real soldiers, or real spies, you'll know what I am talking about." I thought, *Who wants to be a spy?* Yeah, it's interesting stuff, but why build paranoia into your daily list of things to do and be?

He didn't stop there. It seemed that every day he told us what we were not: "Even if you pass Phase-3 to graduate, don't think you are some kind of Rambos. You are not. That's all bullshit. That's the movies. This is reality. Consider yourself a newborn. The best that you can hope for is to graduate, then get on a good A-team with soldiers who will teach you to change your own diapers." I thought, *what a jerk.*

He kept up the barrage: "I see some corporals and privates in this class. As you know, the lowest rank on an A-detachment is supposed to be staff sergeant. I don't know what those pencil pushers in Washington were thinking when they had the brain fart that blasted open the door to let you in, but I assure you that we are not here to hold your hand. If you can't pull your own load, there's the door. Use it.

"Phase-3 will be the most difficult training so far. At the end of these classes, you will be assigned to a twelve-man A-detachment consisting of your fellow students. Your team will be tasked with a complex mission. Each member of an A-detachment is responsible for planning different aspects. Together you will plan the mission, and you will be graded as a team, and as individuals. You will 'briefback' your plan, and will be asked many questions. During the briefback, the team explains its plan in intimate detail to the Commander, and must be prepared to answer questions ranging from 'what are the blood-types of your team members?' to 'explain your escape and evasion contingency plans.'

"The 'brief' back may last all day, or perhaps only a half-hour, depending on the mission and the Commander.

"Each team member must know the mission backwards and forwards. If you fail to plan, you plan to fail, and you will flunk this course. It's never too late to flunk. I have seen students wash out on the last day because they thought they were home free.

"After the briefback, if you pass, you will conduct a low-level, nighttime parachute infiltration into the country of Pineland in the Uwharrie National Forest. The drop zone will be small and surrounded by trees. Here in Special Forces, we like to jump at night. Night is our friend. With any luck, you will not be skewered in the groin by a tree branch, because it can be hard to see the trees at night, and judging wind speed can be difficult. If you survive the jump, your team will link-up with a guerrilla force which is resisting the oppressive government of Pineland. You are to organize the 'G's' [guerrillas] into a cohesive and effective fighting force.

"The two weapons specialists will instruct the G's in various aspects of weapons, including maintenance and tactics. This is where you youngsters will have a hard time. Most of you have never been in an infantry or Ranger unit, so your work will be difficult, but you will be expected to take charge and perform. The two detachment engineers will instruct the G's on demolition techniques, and will construct basic sanitary facilities such as slit trenches, which will be your latrines. The two medical specialists will look after the health of the G's and the team, and will give classes on emergency medical procedures. The communicators will have to successfully send and receive all of their scheduled messages, and successfully encrypt and decrypt the same. Every course at least one communicator calculates his antenna length incorrectly, or makes an encryption error, or does something stupid that gets him kicked out or recycled. Listen up communicators! Your job is critical to the success of the team. Let's keep those eyes and ears open, and do what you learned in Phase-2.

"The intelligence specialists will make contact with the local spy network inside the auxiliary and underground forces to gather information about the enemy situation and your targets. Hopefully your team will not be compromised during those encounters, but that comes down to you thinking, and paying attention. And luck.

"Finally, when the G's are ready, you will begin combat operations, which will consist of destroying specific targets. For extra credit, if you detect enemy forces you may attack them, but those attacks are expected to be well-planned, well-executed, and successful. You must *successfully* attack your assigned targets. If you do not succeed, the entire team can fail this Phase. Generally speaking, it's better not to go around attacking the enemy during this Phase, because the main point is to complete your assignments, but strong team initiative will positively affect your grading.

"Soldiers from the 82nd Airborne Division will be guarding your targets, and I assure you that they are looking forward to meeting you, and catching you. Any 82nd soldier who catches an A-team member will be given a three-day pass, and some of those soldiers have done this exercise on numerous occasions. They like nothing better than to brag about how they stopped you, tracked you, or attacked your base camp at 0300 on a rainy night and stole some weapons.

"The enemy will conduct counterguerrilla patrols. Don't get caught. There will be helicopters searching with special equipment, including night vision. Obviously they will spot campfires from miles away. If you would like to fail Phase-3, you can do so by starting a campfire. The civilians in the area love to play this game, and if they see so much as a boot print, they will call it in. This will be a very difficult exercise, and will last for almost two weeks. If one man fails to carry his load, you can cause a disaster for the team. Do you youngsters think you are ready for this?" The Czech glared at a soldier sitting in front of me and asked, "How old are you soldier?"

"Nineteen," he answered, and "Yes, I am ready for this."

That triggered another tirade from the TAC. "There is a thin line between arrogance and confidence, and a thinner line between confidence and over-confidence. I saw a soldier come through here just like you with the last class. He had top scores in Basic Training, Phase-1 and Phase-2. He was cocky just like you. He flunked Phase-3. Fell flat on his ass. This exercise is unstructured. Nobody will be looking over your shoulder. Anyone can perform when they are being told what to do, but each team member is expected to be both a leader, and a follower, and he is expected to shift gears between those roles with the greatest of ease." The Czech again glared down at the soldier, "And you think you are ready for this? We'll see, won't we?"

His blood pressure started rising higher, and his voice got louder, "The Soviets are experts at guerrilla warfare. *Experts!* That makes them experts at counterguerrilla warfare, and practically anywhere in the world that you may be deployed in that role, you will be up against the best, or at least the best will be right behind them. On this exercise, I will be out there with the 82nd, advising them on how to catch, stop, and harass you. And believe me when I say, I *love* this job."

I couldn't tell if the TAC was just trying to scare the young guys, or if he was serious about hunting us down. Better assume that he was serious.

Well, we survived the Czech offensive, and all the talk about the Evil Empire, and the classes about how many KGB and GRU agents were snooping around the world. Just the friggin classes were enough to plant the seeds of paranoia. The Czech and the others made it sound as if the communists all had devious mentalities by their very nature, as if it were built into their cells, right in there with the mitochondria, always spying, snooping, plotting, scheming. It's part of who they are, just as slithering around is part of being a snake. And by God, I thought he was full of it, and that these Green Beret instructors were starting to strain credibility, and just maybe they were a little wacko.

The poor Czech must have been incredibly frustrated when people didn't believe him, or, like me, thought him paranoid, when he knew what he was about. He seemed to be using scare tactics, but my days in those countries were still a long way off, and later I knew that he was right, but this was still Fort Bragg, North Carolina, Phase-3.

After a couple of weeks of classroom work, the TACs broke us down into twelve-man A-detachments for the final test. Those who were left were nervous, as was I, because people often got injured here.

Phase-3 would combine the skills previously taught. Those who had cheated at land-nav in Phase-1, or didn't study their other lessons well enough, might get lost in Phase-3, or would be deemed not ready, and—Goodbye. If you passed this, you'd magically become a "Green Beret." If not, thanks for playing, have a nice day.

My team was issued a mission for the exercise known as Robin Sage. The mission was to infiltrate the enemy country of "Pineland," link-up with the guerrillas, train them, and then hit some targets.

Robin Sage has been refined into a masterpiece. Some of the "underground" and "auxiliary" forces that we would deal with were actually civilians who live in the area. Some were retired SF who had been in real UW/GW situations and they promised to make life interesting.

I heard the story much later of what happened to a captain when he went through Robin Sage and got snagged by the local police while meeting with some civilians who were "aiding the guerrillas." (Such civilians are generally called the auxiliary.)

This is how I remember the story.

The intelligence specialist on the team arranged a secret meeting with members of the auxiliary to gain information about the enemy and a local target. But the auxiliary contact would agree to meet only with the Captain who was the Team Leader. He would not exchange information with a subordinate. This is a fairly ordinary request. Good team leaders can wean members of the movement away from having to meet directly with the top for every little exchange, but this takes time. Still, it is very important to maintain good relations with the local population, especially those who are involved in the movement. Without them, the war is lost.

So the meeting was set. The Captain was to come alone. It was to be held in an old barn near the edge of the forest just after dark, in a secluded area where it was unlikely that the enemy could approach without being seen.

It was about an hour after sundown when the Captain left the woods and walked toward the barn. He pushed open the door and found two men on their knees examining a map by dim lantern light. There was a third man who had been standing guard outside in the shadows, watching the overgrown dirt road that approached the barn. One of the men stood, welcomed the Captain in, and pointed to an old crate that the Captain could use as a chair.

The meeting began. Within minutes, the police burst in. At first, the Captain must have thought that it was just part of the game, and that he had blundered and gotten caught. One of the police officers was a sergeant, close to forty, heavyset, and well over six feet. The second was pale faced and didn't look old enough to own a firearm.

They wasted no time throwing the Captain to the ground, handcuffing him behind his back. He could have fought and tried to get away, but since they were real American police and this was North Carolina, he hesitated. They grasped his arms with some force, lifted him from the dust, and marched him out the door. The younger officer walked off into the darkness and returned about five minutes later with the patrol car, its lights bouncing up and down on the rough road.

The older officer looked to one of the "auxiliary" men and said, "Good job Jimmy."

"Nothin' to it Billy. Had to be done."

So it was a setup! The Captain must have felt like kicking himself. He knew better than that. He should have brought backup, and set up security.

The younger cop stopped the patrol car in front of the barn. They tossed the Captain's M-16 and gear into the trunk and shoved him into the back.

Maybe the Captain was wondering if that meant he had flunked the course.

As they drove to jail, the sergeant accused him of raping a local white woman. The black captain proclaimed his innocence, but the white police were not listening.

"Shut up back there before we pull this car over!" barked the sergeant.

"You filthy scum," the driver said. "I go to church with that woman. She has two children!" The sergeant's anger escalated into rage as the car sped down the back road.

"Call Fort Bragg," the soldier kept saying. "I am here on a training mission. I am a commissioned officer in the United States Army!"

The sergeant wheeled around, "Boy, I'm not gonna tell you again to shut up!"

But this was not just any Army captain. He had not been the commander of some obscure motor pool in charge of oil and tire pressure. His credentials would likely have included commanding troops in a combat unit, or he would not have been allowed to volunteer for Special Forces where he was now leading an A-team during Robin Sage. Men like that are not accustomed to being handcuffed and tossed into the back of a cruiser like some young thug.

To the police maybe he was just a black man wearing camouflage, not a college-educated Army officer with a Top Secret clearance. What do a couple of backwater cops care about that? They had no intention of calling Fort Bragg. They knew he was an Army officer, as was later shown.

"You raped a good woman last night. We got our ways of dealin' with shit like you."

"I demand that you contact the Special Warfare School!" Whatever was going through the Captain's mind, he wasn't in a position to demand anything.

At the station they locked him in a cell, still handcuffed. As the heavy door slammed shut and locked, the younger officer said, "Turn around and put your hands up to the door." The policeman reached through the bars and unlocked the cuffs.

"I would like to make a phone call."

At that, they laughed and walked away down the hall.

By their tone, the Captain believed that something bad might happen. Maybe he was thinking: *"Are these some of the good ole boys of the Christian Militia?"* The Captain must have heard the safety briefing two dozen times: *Hazards in the area include poisonous snakes such as rattlesnakes, copperheads . . . other hazards include brown recluse spiders . . . and the Christian Militia.* A.K.A. the KKK.

After the Captain had spent a couple of hours sitting alone in his isolated cell, the two policemen returned. The younger one removed the handcuffs from his belt.

"Step up to the door."

"Did you call Fort Bragg?"

"No," answered the sergeant.

The younger one snarled, "You don't ask the questions around here. We do."

By now the team would know that he was missing, maybe even that the police had snagged him. They would contact Fort Bragg via tactical radio. The cops couldn't keep up this game forever.

"Step up to the door. I am going to cuff you," commanded the younger cop.

"I am waiting right here. I am not going anywhere." Smart move, but it didn't do much good.

The sergeant removed the nightstick from his belt and pointed it at the Captain. "Boy, we *are* going to cuff you."

The Captain must have sensed the futility of token resistance. Why get beaten, then handcuffed, when you can just get handcuffed? Pride and stupidity can be like Siamese twins, but the Captain did not allow himself to fall into that trap. He stepped up to the door and turned around to be handcuffed behind his back.

"Turn around soldier boy. I'll handcuff you in the front."

Strange.

The policeman clicked the cuffs around the Captain's wrists and locked them in place so that they would not tighten and cut off the circulation. The sergeant was still holding the nightstick down by his leg, as the other unlocked the cell and grabbed the Captain by the arm.

On the way out, there was a phone call for the sergeant and he stopped to take it. The younger officer continued to escort the Captain to the patrol car, when he realized the sergeant had the keys to the cruiser. The policeman told the Captain to wait by the car, as he ran back to grab the keys.

The adrenaline must have been pouring into the Captain's veins. He knew how bait and ambush ruses worked. Maybe they were baiting him to escape so they could kill him? But if he stayed there, they would get him somehow, he was sure. There were woods just across the street. If he could make it, well, he was a fine physical specimen, an athlete. The police did not appear to be in great shape. It would be a race, but after ten seconds he could be out of sight. He went for it.

He dashed, across the street towards the woods, *"Halt! Halt!"* An officer commanded from behind. Just a few more steps and he would be in the woods. He didn't stop. The cop didn't shoot.

After some miles he came across a road and spotted a store. There was a payphone outside, so he sat down and observed from the darkness. People pumped gas, bought soft drinks and some used the phone. Which was good. That meant the phone was working. He didn't see any unusual law enforcement activity. There were no helicopters around. It was just a normal Tuesday night in Backwater, U.S.A.

He didn't have change, but the operator would patch him through collect to Bragg. The Captain needed just two minutes with that phone.

He made a dash to the payphone, trying to conceal the handcuffs. A flurry of communications later he learned that his "disastrous capture" was a story concocted and executed by the TACs. The police were in on it. They gave him the chance to escape and he took it, but they didn't think he would actually get away. He was more slippery than they expected.

The police were about to return him to the barn where a TAC would admonish him to be more careful whenever he meets the auxiliary. You never know when the auxiliary might be compromised, and they might lead you into a trap. The lesson: the Captain should have posted better security to watch for the enemy.

The Captain, the "rapist," told me the story while we were skiing in southern Germany, where he was the captain of a real A-team.

Some people would take incredible offense that such a thing occurred to a black man, but it also happens to whites and others. As far as I know, events like that are extraordinary, but the TACs were equal opportunity offenders, and would strike wherever they thought you most vulnerable, because that's what happens in the real world. Being Jewish, for instance, could be a death sentence for an American soldier if he is caught where they hate Jews. For that matter, some countries might not allow American soldiers to enter their country if they are not of the right religious or political affiliation. The fact is, we have to check a lot of our political correctness and American views on how things are, or should be, at the border. Our object is to complete the mission, whatever it is, not remake the world in our image.

This was not Disney Land. This was all about adaptability and out-of-the-box thinking. Also, above all, it was about teamwork. There was no telling what they would throw at you.

We planned our mission. It was to begin at night.

INFILTRATION, LOW-LEVEL PARACHUTE JUMP

THERE ARE MANY ways to infiltrate a country. You can slip in by submarine, surface ship, raft, scuba, parachute, foot, horse, helicopter, ultralight aircraft or any other way you can think of. Other times, teams have filtered in as tourists, businessmen, workers, etc.

There are three main types of parachute infiltration: HALO, HAHO, and Static Line. HALO, or High Altitude Low Opening, is the most glamorous way to go. The jumper exits from, say, 20,000 feet wearing an oxygen mask, and pulls the ripcord at a very low altitude. At night, an experienced ear on the ground can recognize the sounds of the parachutes opening.

HAHO, or High Altitude High Opening, can be used to cover vast distances without sending an aircraft near the drop zone (DZ). The jumpers exit from high altitude wearing oxygen masks, immediately deploy their main canopies, then steer many miles to the DZ, maybe over an enemy border. This can be a good method because the team can exit from a commercial airliner on its normal flight track, with no one the wiser, and soar to the DZ. A problem with HALO and HAHO is that the aircraft must fly so high that they will appear on enemy radar and can be shot down.

On static-line jumps, used for lower altitudes, there is a "static-line" which hooks to the aircraft. The parachute is pulled out automatically. A monkey can make a static-line jump. On the other hand, if a team must infiltrate by parachute deep into enemy territory where air defense is a problem, and the area is beyond helicopter range, the team normally must do so by static-line. The aircraft can fly low and avoid radar, giving the team a chance to get in undetected. One of the problems with this method is that more people get injured, especially during nighttime jumps, and, unfortunately, night is normally the best time to go in.

For our "visit" to Pineland, we had planned the mission, done the briefback, and been given the go ahead. It was about 10 P.M. when we roared down the runway at Pope Air Force Base. The team was completely camouflaged, and loaded down with combat equipment. The night was very dark.

As we lifted off the runway, my heart began to pick up the pace. There were whining sounds as the landing gear retracted into the belly of the beast, and thuds as it locked into place and the skin of the aircraft closed around it.

Soon, we were flying low, avoiding radar so as not to get shot down. When we approached the drop zone, the pilot would level off and we would parachute into the darkness with more than 170 pounds of combat equipment, including the parachute and reserve. After we jumped, the aircraft would immediately dive, as in combat, to avoid fire-control radar.

Multiple teams were infiltrating. We did not know when or where the other teams were infiltrating, or their specific missions, but we knew that they would be out there. Our structure was "cellular" so that if we were compromised and somehow got captured, the enemy could not break us and find out what the other teams were doing. (Obviously, for training purposes nobody would get any digits cut off, or body parts smashed with a hammer during interrogation. Our only real focus was our own team, and passing the course.)

We were flying "nap of the earth," which means flying low-level, using the terrain to mask the aircraft from enemy radar, at about four hundred feet above ground level, and if we'd been flying much lower, we'd have been hedge clippers. Motion sickness tends to occur on such flights. Some think that motion sickness is related to mental toughness; they are wrong, and many millions of dollars have been spent on researching the causes of the affliction. Even astronauts get it, and a couple of my teammates were becoming nauseated.

MC-130s normally have the same distinct smell, and a special overwhelming sound. The experience envelops all of your body and senses: it is action and noise and smell and vibrations rumbling through your body, flying over the earth at near-treetop level with combat equipment, parachutes, sweating men, and a strange air-conditioning system that often creates streams of fog that drift down from the ceiling, as if they were thick trails of cigarette smoke that sink instead of rise. The high-performance aircraft was as loud as a locomotive, so we wore foam-earplugs.

We were pounding down water to over-hydrate ourselves. Anything could happen on the DZ. We might lose all our equipment during an ambush and be forced to evade until we reached a rally point. There was no telling when we might get water again, and you can only go a short time without it. So, lots of water, but not *too* much; it would throw our electrolytes out of whack. The urinal hole in an MC-130 is often the final stop before infiltration.

Some of the hazards of this night's DZ included its small size, and its being surrounded by trees, as well as having a power-line and a river-hazard nearby. I was near the end of the stick. A stick is a group of jumpers that jump on the same pass. The stick was composed so that the first six men out had all the specialties of the team represented, which meant that the second half was a mirror image of the first. We also kept a jumpmaster at the end just to have an extra set of eyes looking over everyone. The main reason I was near the end was that I was the least experienced, so—just in case—the most expendable. On a small drop zone, being near the end can result in landing in the trees.

On a CARP (Calculated Air Release Point) infiltration, the timing of our jump was based on the aircraft's sophisticated navigation system. The release point would depend on the system calculating *precisely* where it was. The pilot would make only one pass so everything had to work the first time. CARP is dangerous because it takes the jumpmaster out of the loop in spotting the DZ; most of the experienced soldiers thought that jumpmasters were much more reliable than computers for this job. We had all heard CARP horror stories about teams being dropped miles off course, or landing in a lake or landing in a . . . *Stop thinking about it. It won't do any good,* I told myself.

Sometimes we exited from the doors, other times the tailgate, depending on the aircraft and the mission. On some missions, for instance with the Rangers or 82nd Airborne, missions that SF are rarely involved with, jumpers go out both doors at once so that more can get out in a shorter time. A faster exit keeps the unit together, which is very important if they have contact on the DZ, and it allows for faster assembly on the ground. Ours would be a tailgate jump. Most soldiers prefer going out the tailgate because it's easier to just walk off the ramp than to jump out the door.

On CARP the jump signals are red and green lights. It starts red, then turns green, then red again. You should only jump on green. Red means danger, you are past the DZ, or jump conditions are otherwise hazardous. But even the smallest delay, just a stumble, meant the end of the stick might go on red. Trees are a hazard. Soldiers have been horribly injured in the trees, and having made tree landings myself, I can say that they provide a special thrill that I would rather not repeat. Power lines are the same. I heard of a soldier who drifted into a power-substation and went up like a mosquito in a bug zapper. Sometimes people accidentally land in water and drown before they can escape their equipment. (In serious water hazard areas, jumpers wear little CO_2 inflatable preservers.) At night, rivers look like roads and it is difficult to avoid obstacles that you can't see, like barbed wire fences, until you hit them. This is not Fort Benning jump school with extensive, safe drop zones during broad daylight. I would like to say that it's not as dangerous as it sounds, but it is.

Before the mission, I had washed my uniforms several times without soap and hung them outside for a few days. I had not showered with soap, or used anything else with the smell of "civilized society" since we began planning. If this had been real, if possible we would've eaten only the local foods of the target country. When our bodies sweated and emitted the usual odors, we would more closely approximate the local smells. You can smell a cigarette from an incredible distance; I'm reluctant to say how far because it obviously depends on the conditions and the nose, but I have smelled them from more than a hundred yards, and once found a base camp with my nose. If several people smoke, the odor intensifies. Maintaining odor discipline has other advantages besides keeping you from getting killed. Mosquitoes have sophisticated tracking systems for sensing and trailing their intended meal. They are attracted to, among other things, soaps and colognes. It's nice to be clean and smell pretty, but if you don't like mosquitoes or getting shot, you are better off without perfumed soap.

And now we were rumbling into the night, flying low, taking hard turns, going up and down. If I had had money, I would soon be starting my second year in college, probably would've been at some party or studying in the library, but I was here and this was it. About to make the cut to the big leagues, roaring through the night like a freight train.

I only weighed about 145 pounds, so my 170 pounds of equipment had a mind of its own. Every move required a struggle with all the straps, gadgets, weaponry, and whatnot.

The aircraft was loud; we had to shout to hear one another, and there is something about loud noises mixing with fear that makes things worse.

At about thirty minutes before the drop, the pilot switched off the white lights and the cabin glowed with dim red lights. This allowed our eyes to adjust to darkness. Sweat trickled down my face, and a bead of it hung off my nose. Some team members were shouting to hear each other, others were using hand signals.

Crewmember shouts, "Just passed PONR."

Everyone relays, "Passed PONR."

Point of No Return. Mission is a GO no matter what, even if the plane is shot down, as long as the team is sufficiently intact to complete the task. (On a training mission the PONR is not as important as during a critical Direct Action mission or Special Reconnaissance, but we still observe it as a matter of procedure.)

At about six minutes out we stood up and did final checks of each other's equipment. An extra SF man was on-board to help. He would not infiltrate. He walked by to collect everyone's earplugs. We would leave only footprints on the DZ.

Fear—it was there, but I had no time to savor it. Imagination and time are the soil and fertilizer that fear needs if it is to flourish. Conditioning, procedures, and action would keep it in check tonight. I was focusing my mind, rehearsing what I was about to do.

Focus. Procedures: What if my chute malfunctions? *Pull reserve.* What if reserve malfunctions? Ambush on the DZ? Go over reference points. Aircraft will be heading 135 degrees at 120 knots, 800 feet above ground level on exit. Reference point: village 14 kilometers at about 10 o'clock, town 19 klicks at 3 o'clock. No moon.

The wind is another good way to tell directions during descent and on the ground, and it was blowing 6 to 10 knots from the west. It's partly cloudy, 70 degrees, relative humidity 30%, 15 minutes ago. Rally point at

RG90447618, northwest corner of DZ. Initial enemy reaction time, 35 minutes—90 minutes in force. First "go to hell point," which is where we all link up if everything goes to hell on the DZ, is 100 meters up the left branch in river Y, 2 klicks at 289 degrees. Final equipment checks.

Approaching the calculated air release point, the pilot slows the aircraft to about 150 knots to lower the ramp, or the combination of the high speed and open ramp will create dangerous aerodynamic conditions.

The aircraft slowed, and the ramp made a low rumbling noise as it opened, revealing the night. The eerie red-glow from the cabin lights met the darkness at the tailgate and the fresh night air swirled around inside the aircraft. The four engines were shifting, making different noises as the pilot frequently turned and adjusted altitude to hug the undulating terrain below.

Out the tailgate, as we rumbled through the darkness skirting the small communities, some lights broke up the night. The lights flickered from the distortion caused by turbulent air racing around the aircraft, like heat waves in the desert.

An Air Force crewmember wearing a big green helmet got the message on his headset from the pilot. The crewmember, who was wearing a parachute in case he fell out, held up his green-gloved finger to our jumpmaster signaling "one minute." They made eye contact, the jumpmaster signaled with his thumbs-up, then with his pointer finger and yelled, *"one minute!"*

"Standby!" shouted the jumpmaster.

We shuffled to the tailgate, the first teammate near the edge.

The plane shot up sharply from four hundred feet to eight hundred and our knees buckled under the strain as our loads became heavier. At jump altitude, the plane leveled off. The pilot throttled back to jump speed, 120 knots. Aircraft quieted down a bit as engines were throttled back. Bodies swayed backward with the changing airspeed. Out the back were only darkness and splotches of light, eternity.

Red light. Red light. Tension. The jumpmaster was busy. Thirty seconds. Red light—Red light—Red light—Red light—Red light—Red light. Green light!

"Go! Go! Go!" Shuffling to the rear. Teammates were stepping off, falling away into the night. Two teammates were still in front . . . ***RED LIGHT!*** . . . The Air Force crew chief held up his hand to stop the soldiers from jumping but they kept going . . . One more step and I would be off the ramp. I fell away.

The air slammed into me like a wave. *"Onethousand twothousand threethousand!"* The canopy was deploying above me. It felt normal, no need to check, but I did anyway; that's how we trained. Good canopy.

The aircraft shot back to lower altitude to avoid radar. The pilot would continue to pop up and down like a dolphin to mask our insertion point. The direction of my descent was made clear because I knew the flight path and heard the sound of the retreating aircraft.

For the Air Force, MCRTB: Mission Complete, Return to Base. Silence enveloped my team.

I reached up and found the steering toggles. While drifting through the darkness, for a moment I glimpsed the silhouette of a teammate just below and maybe thirty yards away. Cool air across my sweating face. I identified the reference points. We were on target.

It was too dark to see the ground or any trees. My weapon was strapped to my left side, and the rucksack was attached near my waist. If you land with your rucksack still attached, you can break your legs. (You can also break your legs without it.) The rucksack has a lowering line and you release it so that it dangles and lands away from you. I was afraid to land in the trees that surrounded the drop zone, but it was a little late for that.

At about two hundred feet I yanked the quick release straps and the rucksack fell away and jerked at the end of its line. I steered into the wind. Feet and knees together, I prepared to do a PLF (parachute landing fall).

The PLF is a special way of rolling on landing to reduce the chance of injury. Unlike sport jumping, where you often stand up on landing, this type of combat parachuting was designed to get you to the ground as quickly as possible, balancing the danger of being a target in the air with getting a broken body when you land. Sometimes, if the winds are high or gusting, the landing is more like an "impact." Many soldiers have been killed in various ways on landing. (I now understood why some people proudly wore jump wings.)

My rucksack hit the ground and a second later so did I.

I did a bad PLF, landing on my M-16, and nearly broke a rib. I was having difficulty breathing for a while because I got the wind knocked out of me. I expected a nasty bruise, but knew that I had better be okay. I was not going to quit.

In the darkness, the team members headed for the rally point where we were to "cache" our parachutes and helmets, then don our patrol caps. Contrary to popular belief, Green Berets do not wear green berets in the field.

There was a team member in front of me. It was very dark but I could see his Ranger eyes—which consisted of two pieces of luminescent tape—glowing on the back of his helmet. His Ranger eyes suddenly disappeared. *Karuuumph!* He fell into a hole and broke his leg. So close and yet so far from graduation. He had only two weeks of running around in the wilderness harassing the enemy to go. I always felt bad for the ones who got injured. It was just the luck of the draw.

Goodbye.

Our team leader was a captain from the Canadian Army in what amounted to their Special Forces. His code-name was Maple (surprise) and he was exceptionally squared-away.

Infiltration is usually exhausting. We moved most of the night to get as far away from the drop zone as possible. We set up a patrol base at a pre-designated spot that we picked out during isolation with the aid of a map and an old satellite image. We button-hooked back on our own trail in case someone was following us. In other words, the patrol base would overlook the trail we left. If someone found our trail we could either ambush or slip away—our option. When moving, teams will often leave a couple of people behind to wait for "ghosts"—to make ghosts. It's dangerous business to track a good A-team, or any good infantry unit.

Tactical movement is normally slow and tedious. Creep along. Stop. Look, listen, smell, think. Often, you hear something moving in the dark. If it just keeps trudging along, it's likely a human, but not a good soldier. If it keeps trudging along making noise, it's not hunting anything that can hear, and it's not worried about being hunted by something that can hear. Good patrols of soldiers walk slowly and deliberately. They, like a hunting animal, move forward a short way then stop, look, listen and smell. They keep their heads still when possible and, like a tiger, look for movement, or anything that does not feel right. They anticipate what the enemy might do just as a tiger knows that its prey goes to waterholes.

The next day we were to link up with the guerrillas. This would be a critical encounter, equally important and dangerous. We made it to the linkup point in the woods, but knew there could be an ambush waiting, so approached with great caution. Maple went forward to establish contact and confirm that these were in fact our G's.

We covered him with automatic weapons, loaded with blanks of course, just in case something went wrong. If the captain took off his hat, it was a signal that this was a setup, and we would open fire on the guerrillas. It's possible that the enemy knows you are coming, and may send soldiers disguised as "guerrillas" to meet your team.

Whenever a team links up with new G's there is an uneasy break-in period while everyone gets to know everyone else, when they watch every move the team makes, sizing us up. It is essential to seize the psychological initiative. Not by being bullies. That will never work; they have guns. Your course of action depends on the situation and the people involved, and making the best choice can be difficult. If the team is able to establish rapport, it can operate together with the G's as one big team, united in a common cause.

Soon we were at their camp. They were a mess, a motley crew, some of whom looked like they had never stepped off concrete before. The guerrillas consisted of soldiers from various non-combat units. A few were happy to be there and had volunteered to do this. Others must have been sent out as some form of cruel punishment, and they acted like they would have shot us in the back of the head if given a chance.

We began trying to establish rapport. Sometimes you have to perform a strange ritual. Other times the guerrilla leader throws his weight around. Maybe he will demand money or weapons. Or he may demand that the SF team be subordinate to his authority, or that we leave. We couldn't call a taxi even if we wanted. This sensitive time of establishing rapport can take much patience and the team members must be very steady. We are, after all, there to do a job. If one team member loses his patience, it can blow the whole thing. The situation is not eased by the fact that everyone on both sides is carrying automatic weapons.

Establishing rapport was difficult at first but we did it, and then we began giving the guerrillas classes in basic military tactics, weapons and so on. After that we were to go operational and hit some targets with the guerrillas.

Maple sent me on a recon of a target with two G's. One G refused to put his boots on. He stood there and defied me, like a bratty child sassing his mother. He was going to wear his running shoes despite the fact that the recon would take us through miles of dense North Carolina wilderness.

No problem, I thought.

We were out on the recon and needed to cross a road. If I could avoid it, I would not run across the road because the roads were heavily patrolled. There was a big pipe under the road, with a creek running through it. The area was covered by dense vegetation, and there was a healthy patch of stinging nettles growing near the culvert. Just what I was looking for. Time for a little attitude adjustment. Since the G with the attitude had obviously spent little time in the woods, I figured he probably didn't know what stinging nettles looked like.

Stinging nettles are good to eat if boiled, and medically are used as an antihistamine. However, the plant delivers a burning sting and dogs that have been over-exposed to them have even died. As for people, it just hurts.

It was the middle of July. Earlier, during a tactical movement, we had called in a medevac helicopter when a G collapsed and was in danger of dying from heat stroke. Now, my G had his trousers rolled up.

Oh, this was going to be cruel alright, but sometimes you gotta be mean to get the job done. Without boots he was in greater danger of an ankle injury or snakebite. I told him and the other G to wait and that I would dash for the culvert. When I got there and determined it was safe, I would signal for him to run to me. Tactically, it would have been better to walk, but the running was part of the ambush.

I ran through the stinging nettles and into the culvert under the road. It was nice and cool inside. The creek was a natural air-conditioner. Then I signaled for him to run to me and he trotted through the patch of pain. Immediately, he knew that he had problems. His ankles started to burn. The burning must have been intense because it was a big, healthy patch. Of course, I didn't say anything smart like, "I *told* you to wear boots." I helped him wash his ankles in the creek and the cold water soothed the pain. I scooped up some handfuls of mud and caked it on the stings, and he started to feel better.

The object was not to beat him down, but to bring him around and show him the right way to do things. After that, he became enthusiastic about our missions, and much more inclined to follow orders.

Some days later I was suspicious when the TAC assigned me to do a recon. Maple, the Canadian captain, or the Team Sergeant should normally do all mission tasking. Anyway, the G put his boots on and we set out to recon a PZ (pick-up zone).

Along the way we encountered a muddy road. The G wanted to cross it, but I gave the hand signal, *Stop!* I didn't want to leave footprints on the road, on which there were fresh car tracks. Still, we needed to do the recon so we searched up and down the road for a way to cross. All mud. We pulled back into a thicket and I started to think like an Indian. Nothing came to mind and the G didn't offer any usable ideas. Thinking like Tarzan didn't work. There were no vines to swing across the road, and no friendly elephants offering to carry us.

Sitting down, I took out my maps and plotted a different route. As I refolded the maps, a vehicle pulled up. It stopped and four men got out. We hugged the ground and stayed quiet as mice. We heard them talking. They were looking for our tracks! *The TAC set us up!*

The men were there to track us down. Very dangerous for them, and for us. Ordinarily, in a guerrilla environment, the guerrillas operate far away from where they live. If the enemy can locate the G-base, rocket attack, artillery, air strikes and massive waves of infantry may come its way.

There are various methods for destroying guerrillas, one of which is to locate the main body, contain them, and force them into decisive combat. Therefore, guerrillas generally only converge into large groups for short periods of time and for specific missions. Their network is cellular, and the small, decentralized guerrilla bands operate mostly as they see fit and take little instruction from above.

The men on the muddy road were conducting counterguerrilla operations. Finally, after they walked up and down looking for signs, we heard mutters of disappointment. They got in the vehicle and drove away. No problem. We made our way back to the G base and I went to the TAC who was sleeping in a hammock that he had strung up between two trees.

"Excuse me Sergeant," I said. "I finished the recon. Are you ready to debrief?"

He pulled the baseball cap from over his eyes, swung his boots to the ground and stood up.

"Yep," he said, "Go get the Captain and Team Sergeant so they can hear this."

A couple of minutes later we four were standing around a small table that a G had built from an old piece of plywood and some tree branches.

"Let's hear about it," Maple said. "Any enemy activity?"

I slung my weapon over my back, and spread a map on the table. "Yes sir. There was some activity here." I pointed with a pine needle to the spot on the map. "Four soldiers seemed to be searching for tracks. Their uniforms looked like 82nd Airborne, but I couldn't be sure. Didn't catch their ranks. Carrying M-16s, driving a civilian vehicle. I didn't get the model. That was at 1535 hours. Seemed weird, sir. Like they knew we would be there." I glanced at the TAC and Maple responded with a subtle nod; the Team Sergeant, a Vietnam vet, cleared his throat.

The TAC was looking at the map, trying not to grin. "Do you think they caught any sign of you?" he asked. "Do you think you may have compromised this base camp?"

I cleared my throat, "No. I decided not to shoot them because it was so close to the base, and we were only on recon. But they were definitely looking. Maybe they caught a sign somehow else. Maybe this location is already compromised."

At that, the TAC grinned openly and slapped my shoulder. "Good job. Finish your debrief with your Team Leader and Team Sergeant, then go get some sleep. I've got another recon for you tonight."

It seemed that I spent most of my time teaching weapons classes, or running recons. They worked me hard, but my own private G hung in there. I called him "Nettles" and he seemed to like the name. He was my aide when I taught classes, and volunteered to go on practically every mission, night and day, rain and shine. By the time it was over, he wanted to come to Special Forces!

After a couple of weeks of running around out in the woods having a blast, we crouched in the fog next to an LZ (landing zone) waiting for two Blackhawk helicopters to come and take us home. I was on security watching the LZ with NVGs (night vision goggles) and was worried that the helicopters would not land because it was so foggy. They would be coming in without lights, the pilots flying with NVGs.

I was very hungry. I had run out of food the day before and sure hoped that they would make it. If there is one thing that builds tension, it's a hungry belly and knowing that you are depending on people you have never met to come get you. So you sit there and strain to hear the sounds of helicopters in the distance. And when you finally hear them, you hope they are yours and not somebody hunting for you.

The helicopters swooped in from the darkness, but the fog was too thick for the choppers to land. Soon the sun would start to show another day, but for now it was just dark and foggy. I was very disappointed as the two helicopters hovered above the fog. I thought that they were afraid to land. But they hovered until their rotor-wash blew a hole through the fog, then landed without incident. The signal was given and the team ran over and climbed aboard. Since I was on security, I was one of the last. When I jumped inside I saw all the instruments glowing in the night through my goggles. But when I pulled my goggles off, the cockpit appeared blacked out because it was lit to be seen with goggles, and the pilots, too, were wearing NVGs. As we roared away I fell asleep.

Maple had been a good team leader. I learned a lot from him, and the exercise was challenging all the way around. I wished it could've lasted six months. It tested you mentally, emotionally, and physically, and required one to use his "whole self."

I passed all the tests. I made it.

I was the only one from Basic who was still around. Rob and Steve, who were on other teams, made it, too. There were a few other young men, but most were older soldiers including ex-Rangers, a few SEALS who were just passing through for the training, some Marines, and some foreign officers, and soldiers from regular Army units.

A few days later I officially graduated. Present at the graduation ceremony was a Special Forces commander named Colonel Donlon. When I was almost four months old, he was a captain in Vietnam earning the Medal of Honor. I was not particularly impressed by medals, but was awed by qualities that I feared I would never be able to match, though I hoped that I would never have to endure what many of my predecessors had. More impressive to me than their bravery was their loyalty, which in many cases cost them their lives.

No matter how well I did at Fort Benning and Fort Bragg, there were Major Howards and Colonel Donlons and men just like them all around. I felt like a pygmy among giants, and now those giants were going to rely on me to perform.

But I *was* there, and SF didn't normally put nineteen-year-olds on A-teams. Those like me who had made it mostly got menial jobs. Maybe they would get on a C-team, or a B-team. It was a big surprise when Steve

Shaulis and I got orders for the 5th Special Forces Group at Fort Bragg. I hadn't yet been assigned to an A-team, but I was told that I probably would be. It was strange—it was incredible.

It was all just beginning. Or, perhaps, it was all just ending. How could I know that I would soon be standing on the beach in Ocean City, my life passing before my eyes.

Steve and I headed for Maryland to celebrate our graduation.

What a strange journey. It was only getting started.

ROLLING THE DICE—
ON THE BEACH IN OCEAN CITY

TO BE HUNTED for murder is a frightening thing. Maybe it would be less frightening, and less burdensome, to have actually committed the crime for which you are being hunted. At least, then, in your guilt, you would know that you had it coming.

But I was a teenager, shaking, preparing to die, or take what came. If the police only knew the fear that twisted in my belly, they would know that I was ready to surrender and face justice. If they would only give me a chance to explain, if a judge would only listen, they would know the truth. With blackness and the ocean to my back, I walked toward the police. Would I be beaten? Shot? Would I ever see a courtroom?

They were a nervous-looking bunch. Or maybe they were angry. Any second I expected a bullet to thud into my chest, and that would be that. Game over. I would fall face down in the sand, my blood would be absorbed by the beach, and I would be the second man to die tonight. No mess. No trial. No expense or burden on society. Goodbye.

Together they stepped off the boardwalk, slowly converging on me in a small crescent formation. They left a clear shot so that nobody would be caught in the crossfire but me. So it would be a hail of gunfire, not just a single thud. To them, as I walked out of the darkness, I must have been a perfect silhouette, similar to the targets they trained with. Only I had a real heart and it was still beating. Furiously.

The ocean and darkness, safety, was behind me. Again, the powerful urge occurred to bolt into the night. I could just swim out into the ocean and maybe find a boat anchored, or swim parallel the shore for a few hours. Later, I could slip into a dark area on shore, hoping that the darkness and the swells would hide me. It would be a long shot. With luck, even with police boats or helicopters arrayed against me, there was a chance that they wouldn't spot me. I had a fair chance. The question was, *Will they kill me?* The act of running away might draw fire.

I decided to risk it again. Trembling. I walked forward, toward the light, so the police could see me clearly.

Moments later they were within speaking range when an officer asked: "Are you Michael Yon, Special Forces, Fort Bragg?"

"Yes," I answered.

A police voice commanded: "Get down on your knees."

I obeyed instantly. My knees buried in the sand on the beach.

"Put your hands on top of your head," commanded another voice.

My hands slowly rose and my fingers interlaced as if some unseen pup-peteers were directing this earthly show from the darkness above.

My eyes avoided contact with the police, and focused on the beach in front. The police were jumpy, as if the puppeteer who controlled their strings was new to this line of work, and had a nervous twitch.

An officer unsnapped a pair of cuffs from his belt. He stepped behind me and clicked the cuffs on my wrists behind my back. Two officers grabbed me under the armpits and told me to stand up. They searched me top to bottom, including the spinal crease in my back, and found nothing. I was unarmed.

They handled me gently; never pushed or shoved me. I was surprised when a big policeman asked if the cuffs were too tight.

I answered, "No. Thank you," and took that as a good sign.

Then a policeman behind me locked the handcuffs in place to prevent the bracelets from ratcheting further and cutting off my circulation. If the cuffs aren't locked in place, during the course of normal transport they continue to tighten down, but if they are too loose, exceptionally supple people can slip out. The metal is hard against your flesh and bones, and when your hands are bound behind your back, your belly is exposed and made vulner-able, which carries its own flavor of fear.

An entourage of policemen escorted me past the crowd of people that had assembled on the boardwalk. The gawkers silently parted and inspected me as we walked through. For them, it was just an unexpected diversion, and free at that. They would go home having seen a "Green Beret" arrested on the beach for some unspeakable crime. A crime that he must be guilty of, or he wouldn't be handcuffed with an entire police force dedicated to remov-ing him from circulation. The gawkers would see it all again in the papers and on television. For me, the bad dream had only begun.

The police led me to a cruiser. They put me inside, carefully holding my head so that I didn't smack the roof of the car as I slid in. There were four powerful policemen in the car, any one of whom could have crushed me. Two of them sat in the front. The two biggest sat in the rear with their arms intertwined in mine, ready to break my arms if I provoked them, a big black policeman to my right, a big white policeman wearing paratrooper boots to my left. A car filled with police behind and in the front. It was a little parade.

Before they drove me away, the officer in charge, who was a major, came to the back of the car and read me my rights. Then he shut the door, and through the open driver's window, ordered the driver to observe radio silence. He said that if there were any problems, they should pull over, so police from the other cars could pile out and help. They were only being careful, but they were overestimating me, even if I possessed any inclination to try anything. After all, I had turned myself in.

As we pulled away from the curb, the cruiser seemed ominously confin-
ing. The ride to the police station was not long in miles, but every block we
covered separated me further from the freedom that I surrendered on the
beach.

The big, black policeman to my right asked for the second time if my
handcuffs were too tight. I was happy just to be alive. He was very consid-
erate. As a black man, he must know what it's like when people presume
knowledge of his character before he even opens his mouth. He must know
that if he were to get into trouble, he would not be just *any* man in trouble,
but a *black* man. Even many of his own people would make negative
assumptions about him, suspecting his actions and his motives. But that is
what we do, isn't it? Group people. We group them into tidy little piles, so
that we don't have to think about them as individuals.

A WOMAN NAMED VIOLA

WHEN I WAS a kid, before everything went completely to hell, we had maids. Black maids. Dad had hired a woman of African descent named Viola. She was big, maybe two hundred pounds, and loud; she spoke her mind, and sometimes talked like a black preacher, and together we often listened to black preachers. Most of the white preachers I had heard, the ones who came to our church, or preached on television, just didn't inspire me. I didn't feel anything when I listened to them, and my only prayer was for the sermon to end. But black preachers were different.

The radio dial would find the voice and stop:

"*'Oh*, **yes!** brother, *dif-fer-ent.* Oh *God* in Heaven reach *down* and grab my hand—reach down and grab it, please oh Lord—and *lead* me to the promised land. I am *ready* for *you* Lord, ready ***now!***, waiten' for *you!* to take my *hand* and lead me out of this *mis-er-y!'*"

By now I would be getting fired up!

The good ones strike chords deep inside, and are inspiring, resonating. The best are like great singers, or poets, or writers. Great artists know pain and suffering and fear and despair and hate, and if they are lucky, they know that love and hope will prevail if that is what they want.

A person can study writing for a lifetime, get a Ph.D. in literature from the finest university, and quote lines and authors from sunrise to sunset, but all will be mimicry if he hasn't experienced what he writes about, and felt the feelings he wishes to describe.

When a soul wants, needs, desperately to communicate with others, it might sing, or write, or preach. And when a soul is sincere in its need to communicate, others feel it and join up because, after all, deep inside we are all human, and we are one.

Viola's manner was different from anyone's I had ever known. In some ways she seemed fearless, so long as you didn't talk about alligators, snakes or the Devil. When we went fishing together, I was not allowed to talk about snakes, or gators. *"Hush up,"* she sometimes scolded without looking at me, "or you gonna have to sit in that ol' hot car while I catches my suppa! This is your suppa too. I know you wants to eat, skinny as you is. Now hush up 'bout them snakes and catch us some fish."

It seemed every time I put a worm on the hook, she was watching like some all-seeing Black Goddess of the baiting process. When I experimented and did it differently than she or Granddad had taught, she wouldn't say anything. Nothing. And when the fish stole my bait, she just glanced at my empty hook, lifted hers from the water to check, then set it back down, and

205

the red and white cork found its place as the sinker straightened out the line. I was sure there was a better way to bait a hook than any she knew, but I never found one, though Lord knows I tried.

Viola would say, "Michael, you little blonde-headed know-it-all! You the one that digs them worms. You can fish with them worms any way you wants to. Why don't you just take a handful and throw 'em to the fish and make it easy? Them fish loves to see you comin' with a bunch ah worms. They know they suppa is heah. *Hehehe.*" Slapping her knee, and wiping her eye as if she were crying, *"hehehe."*

And I would practically always end up swimming or looking for snakes. Viola would say, "You come back outta that watah. Stop playin' 'round them weeds!"

The first day Viola had come to work, she was talking with Dad by the fireplace in the living room. They were talking about whatever it is that new maids and Dads talk about, when Billy and I got into a fight. Viola reached over to the coffee table while still talking with Dad, rolled up a newspaper, bolted across the room and smacked us both over the head like we were a couple of puppies messing on the carpet. She **shouted**—scolded—"If you act like niggers, I'm gonna treat you like niggers." I could have dropped dead.

Having established the pecking order, she went back to talking with Dad who just laughed like the new sheriff was in town to clean up Dodge City.

"'Scuse me Mr. Yon," she said, "I won't put up with no young'uns who don't know no betta and don't know no authority. If you wants me ah workin' in this house, I'm gonna put ah stop ta that nonsense. I will put this house in order. Ain't gonna be no fightin' in my house. Uh uh. No siree. No fightin.' God didn't put them little childrens down here to be actin' like baboons. You need to raise them young'uns respectable, and little boys is the worst."

I could have dropped dead, again. There was no place to hide from the truth when Viola was around. Now that she had my respect, we soon became friends in the way that boys and grown women can somehow relate. She smoked a pipe with Half-and-Half tobacco, and when I asked her what Half-and-Half was, she said it was half tobacco and half marijuana and she would laugh in her special way. *"Hehehe."* Then she would try to keep a straight face and say, "I'm serious. It's half marijuana. You don't believe me?"

"No."

"Hehehe."

"Do you drink beer, Viola?"

"No. And don't you never start none of that nonsense. No drugs neither. They calls it dope because you gots to be a dope to do dope. Don't be a dope on a rope. It'll tie you in knots and won't let go. Ain't no knot tighter than a dope-knot."

She talked in pictures. You could see her words in your head as she spoke. When one of the kids acted up, she would tell us to act right or she would sit on us. "Don't make me sit on you. There won't be nothin' left but a little grease spot." Every time she said that, I could imagine being turned into a little grease spot. She meant what she said, mostly, and she used her authority sparingly, but when she did, we listened.

She was a genuine American black woman from her skin to her soul, and the kind of strong that only suffering can make. She lived in a shack, with a dirt yard and a garden out back. Often I rode my bike to her shack, which had the appearance and size of an old tool-shed. The front door was two steps from a busy four-lane road. (Yes, *two* concrete steps—very, probably illegally—close. It strains credulity to think that someone lived that close to a major road, but it was so. When the road had been widened from two lanes to four, she obviously didn't have the money to pick up the place and move it back, and they didn't make her move out, but there is no doubt that when you are poor, you better watch out, or get run over.)

Viola might have been poor and very different, but I loved my time with her. She was as real as they come and could tell stories all day long. "True enough," she would say while finishing a story, moving on to the next one. I suppose "true enough" meant that even though "embellishment" of the facts had occurred, it was still true enough to deliver the message. And her stories always taught you something. Otherwise they were not worth telling. They had to be riveting, and thought provoking. Those were the rules of story telling.

Viola was uneducated and came down from Alabama with a doctor and his family to take care of his children, and through the years she had had a big hand in raising numerous sons and daughters of doctors around town. Though she was uneducated, even a kid could sense a deep, natural intelligence in her. There was something special about her. I loved Viola.

Her mind seems just as quick at sixty-six as it did more than twenty years ago. I spent a couple of hours with her recently in her little house in a dangerous part of town. She told me to be careful of my car out front, which "Might get broken into." Her former shack next to the four-lane road had an electrical problem that led to a fire. Her new place, though small and simple as ever, was as ever, clean as clean gets, and she fed me as much as I wanted to eat, all washed down with iced tea. She pulled the tea from her old refrigerator, a bungy-cord holding the door shut, and we drank the tea from old mayonnaise jars as I listened to her stories.

Among "real" Southern women, black or white, there is an unspoken rule that if you love them, or at least respect them, you eat their food. How much you eat indicates the degree of your regard. Saying that you are not hungry when food is offered is acceptable, of course, but somehow you know it hurts a Southern woman to hear that. I showed up with an empty stomach.

As I sat on her hand-me-down furniture with its blanket covers, I was reminded of those many years ago, and her old furniture that creaked and moaned as you moved on it. That furniture had holes and in all probability, had literally come from the roadside or a dump. But her house was always tidy, and she was proud of what she had and who she was. She was rich; she just didn't have any money. Though materially she was very poor, she was much happier than my father.

My grandmother, my mother's mother, says that Viola warned her time and again that she should take us away from our father. To me, he wasn't even my father. I considered Granddad to be my father. Granny tried to take us, but the man called "Dad" was stupid with the wrong kind of pride, the kind that doesn't admit when it's wrong. Viola had talks with Della and Dad, and told them that it was wrong to fight in front of the kids. Imagine that. The maid taking charge and being heard.

That was Viola. She'd shot her own husband, Josh, in the arm when she caught him fooling around, just teaching him a lesson. Shot him with a pistol, by God! That was years and years ago. He'd been shot twice before, and it was the second time that he'd been shot over another woman. The first time was an accident, when a man was running out the front door just as Josh came to visit. The man's wife was trying to shoot her husband over another woman, and Josh caught some pellets in the chest.

When I was a kid, we sat at Viola's house and talked about everything we wanted to talk about. I must have told her a hundred times, "I really want to know what it's like to be black." She would answer, *"No you don't."* It was more like a warning, *"Jes be happy you's ah little white boy. You got some hard times behind you and more ahead, but you jes be happy."*

When Viola took me fishing, we first drove in her big old car to places to dig worms or catch crickets. That was my job. Then we sat together in creaky, folding lawn chairs and fished for shell crackers and bluegill, while she read the papers, smoking her pipe. I read, too, and she told me that I should read the paper every day—"but don't believe everything you read."

"Viola, that doesn't make any sense," I protested. "Why should I read the paper if I can't believe it?"

She folded her paper, dropped it on the grass, and reached down to pick up her cane-pole to check whether it still had bait, then set it back down. "Michael, you little blonde-headed-question-askin'-boy, them fish ain't ah-bitin' today." She sucked in on her pipe, crinkled her eyes, blew out the smoke while staring out over the calm lake as the sun set orange in the west, and answered. "Well, you cain't believe all of it, but you cain't walk around blind all the time. It's better to see fuzzy than be blind. Know what I mean?"

"Sort of."

"Jes remember what I say. You gonna see it someday." She sucked in another load of smoke, and the mosquitoes started biting.

Only about nine years later, I was sitting in the backseat of a police cruiser that belonged to the good citizens of Ocean City. The big black policeman was to my right, the white one to my left. There were cops in the front seat, and in the cars ahead and behind.

The thought of a long prison term was sinking in. It seemed surreal. Like I was out of my body and only watching all this happen from above. Any minute now I would wake up in my bed, sweating, but safe.

No, *this is real.* This is not a nightmare. *Real.* A thousand thoughts blasted through my mind. *Army. Green Beret. Dead man. Prison.* And I kept going back to: *How will I explain this to Granny! How will I explain that I was in a bar? How will I explain the fight? How will I explain any of this!*

I had just completed one of the most difficult accomplishments of my life to date. I had trained an entire year to get into Special Forces. I had avoided disaster, injury, all the pitfalls, and now, scant days later, I was about to be charged with murder. The police holding my arms were real. I felt their power. They didn't talk. They maintained radio silence, as ordered. Silence. Only breathing and driving.

When the car stopped at the station, the police holding my arms waited for the men from the other cruisers to get out and converge on our car before taking me out. Then they all escorted me into the station quietly, respectfully; the little parade marched on and ushered me to a small room to await something. I didn't know what, and I wasn't asking any questions. There was nothing to say.

When they took the handcuffs off, a policeman unholstered his pistol. He didn't point the weapon at me, but he assumed a good shooting stance and positioned himself with a clear field of fire. I looked at the pistol. It was a .357 magnum. I had seen what a .357 magnum did to a goat a few months back. The policeman had only to raise the pistol, point and **Bam!** Game over. Suddenly I wanted to get into a jail cell where it would be safe.

They handcuffed me to a special chair. I sat there in silence while three or four policemen guarded me as if I could magically melt the handcuffs and drift away like smoke, escaping out an open window. Policemen filtered in to have a look. I was as strange to them as they were to me. Truly, they must have thought I had magical powers. How could they know that it was only an accident? I just sat there and breathed rhythmically. Heart beating. That was good. I wondered by what strange chain of events I had arrived here. What had I done wrong in life to earn this? *What now?*

The police spoke to one another in muted tones. Soon they un-cuffed me from the chair and cuffed me again behind my back. We walked out of the room and ended up in another where the major, who had read me my rights, asked if I wished to waive my rights to speak with an attorney or make a statement.

I spent eighth and ninth grade at Westwood Junior High, home of *"The Westwood Warriors."* One of the Warrior teachers, a civics teacher, ironically, taught one of the most important lessons about American justice that I ever learned. It only lasted a few minutes, and it was unrelated to whatever he was teaching, but it stuck with me because he talked about the matter with obvious emotion. We were studying laws and liberty, or some such lofty matter that I figured would never concern me, when the teacher told us that if we were ever arrested—*NEVER* tell the police *ANYTHING*, except your identity, until you talk with an attorney. *NEVER, NEVER, NEVER.* He was totally committed to conveying that message, practically yelling at times.

An angry cop may threaten you with years and years in prison if you don't cooperate. He may threaten and scream that he is a close friend of the prosecutor and the judge—and finally the jailer—and that he will make sure that you get a big, nasty cellmate named Bubba for the next twenty years if you don't cooperate. Then the nice cop comes in and tells the mean cop to settle down and go fetch three soft drinks, and he even buys one for you. "What would you like," he asks, "Coke or Pepsi? The machine has some other flavors, too. *Root Beer?"*

Then the Good Cop who just sent the Bad Cop to fetch you a soda, tells you that if you just give a little help, he will see that you get off, or at least that you get a lighter sentence. And when you talk . . . .

The civics teacher warned, as I have rarely been warned before: *NEVER tell the police ANYTHING until you speak with an attorney.*

There are certain immutable laws, for instance: 1) Never point a gun at anyone whom you do not potentially intend to shoot—no matter how "unloaded" the gun is; 2) never jump off a cliff if you don't intend to follow through with the landing; 3) never talk about your legal case until you talk to an attorney.

In the civics class, of course, hands shot up and the sensible "kid" question was asked: "What if you are innocent?" (That's like asking, "What if the gun is unloaded? Then is it okay to point it at people?" If you talk about your legal case to the police, you are pointing the gun at yourself.)

The teacher's response was fervent and without qualification. Your **innocence** is **irrelevant** to the issue. It wouldn't matter if you were the Pope and were in a different country when the crime occurred . . .

NEVER, NEVER, NEVER . . .

Remember—the police are experts at getting information out of people. They train for it. They watch videos and learn about body language, and take classes on human behavior that teach them how to get people to talk. And they do it every day at work. Some of them are very good at their art, which is good for us when they are keeping us safe, but when a dolphin gets caught in the net, that dolphin better keep quiet or he might end up in the can with the tuna. Most people have no experience being caught in the net, so the match is very lopsided. The newly netted person is a rookie in the ring with the pros. The best thing he can do is *nothing. Keep quiet.*

It's not for the police to decide innocence or guilt, but obviously they already think it is likely that you are guilty or you wouldn't be under arrest. It's not perfect, but due process is your best bet. If the police try intimidation, don't cave in. They would not bother threatening if they knew everything. If they knew everything, they would know you are innocent (assuming that you are).

And there was the Code of Conduct with which service members are compelled to comply:

Article V

When questioned, should I become a prisoner of war, I am required to give name, rank, service number, and date of birth. I will evade answering all further questions to the utmost of my ability. I will make no oral or written statement disloyal to my country and its allies or harmful to their cause.

So, thanks to my civics teacher and military training, I refused a phone call offered by the police at 0314hrs (Who was I supposed to call at that hour?) and gave this interview at 0315hrs:

Det. Glenn Hager
Det. Robert Bokinsky

Michael Phillip Yon

Det. Hager: Mike, for the record I'm going to read your Constitutional Rights. You were read your Constitutional Rights on the scene by Major Cropper. For the record, I'm going to read you those rights again, ok? Number one, you have the absolute right to remain silent. Do you understand that?

Michael Yon: Yes.

Det. Hager: Anything you say or write may be used against you in a court of law. Do you understand that?

211

Michael Yon: Yes.

Det. Hager: You have the right to talk with a lawyer at any time before any questioning, before answering any questions or during any questioning. Do you understand that?

Michael Yon: Yes.

Det. Hager: If you want a lawyer and cannot afford to hire one, you will not be asked any questions and the court will be requested to appoint a lawyer for you. Do you understand that?

Michael Yon: Yes.

Det. Hager: If you agree to answer questions you may stop at any time and request a lawyer and no further questions will be asked of you. Do you understand?

Michael Yon: Yes.

Det. Hager: Do you formally understand the rights that I just read you?

Michael Yon: Yes.

Det. Hager: You do? Having that in mind, do you wish to waive those rights and speak with us now?

Michael Yon: No.

Det. Hager: You don't? You wish to have an attorney?

Michael Yon: Yes.

Det. Hager: Ok. Our interview is now ending. The time is 0316 hours, same date, same persons are present. End of interview.

That was the third time the police read me my constitutional rights. They were being more than fair. So far.

That night seems so strange as I write these words. I contacted the Ocean City Police Department and talked with Lieutenant Bokinsky, whose office even today is next to Officer Hagar's. Lieutenant Bokinsky knew me immediately, even remembered my middle name off the top of his head, and we talked for quite some time about sports and kids and whatnot. He remembers that night well, and actually volunteered, without prompting, that the police thought I was not guilty of any criminal misdeed, but that when they had asked if I wanted to talk about it, I recited to them what my eighth grade civics teacher had said. Now, writing this, I find it amusing that a fire-breathing "Green Beret" would so readily fall back on advice given by one of his eighth grade teachers, and I find it illuminating of how important school teachers can be in preparing kids for the world. Talking with Lieutenant Bokinsky, especially when he told me about some of his ideas on justice, I get the strong impression that he is a stand-up man. He seemed like the kind that I would be happy to have as a friend.

At the time of my arrest, however, he was the enemy, and the chief investigator, and I was about to be charged with murder.

Once you are accused of such a crime, you are never again innocent in the same way, not for the rest of your life. Many people will hear the accusation who never hear the rest of the story. And when you ask for an attorney, the police do not think, *there's a smart one;* they think, *there's a guilty one.* Ask a cop. Of course, if you don't know the cop, likely you will only get the robotic and politically correct answer that "everyone is considered innocent until proven guilty." That's a sick joke. Once accused. . . . Unfortunately, "Where there's smoke there's fire" is almost universally believed, even by good people.

That night in Ocean City, as they escorted me away from the interview, the major in charge asked me if I was okay. He *seemed* genuinely concerned. Maybe he was trying to get me to open up and talk. My natural instinct was to think he was sincere and that he realized already that I was not the bad guy. Which was irrelevant; he was on the other side.

I was not going to talk. The major was a policeman, and though under normal circumstances we would be on the same side, at that moment there was no friendly ground. This was war. My life was at stake. I could die in prison. If I tried to leave without permission, "to escape," they would do everything possible to stop me, including kill me. When you reach the point that you cannot freely walk away without being killed, you are at war, and no matter where you go, you will always be standing at the bullseye until the war is over. Both sides were operating by wartime rules: this was deadly serious.

I looked at him and eked out the closest thing to a smile that I could, straightened up, and said:

"Trained to keep cheery."

My own words immediately lifted my spirits. I could assume the role of a teenager who was in deep trouble, or I could assume the role of an American soldier who would keep the faith. When I said, "Trained to keep cheery," that sealed it. Soldier. Take it like a man.

When some people are arrested they cry—as if they were crying to their mothers. Others scream and hiss and fight. None of that behavior will get you set free.

My experience in youth and in the military had long since stripped away any remnants of a smart-mouthed or cocky attitude. There are times to stand up and fight, and times to shut up and do as you are told. The smart thing to do is to treat the police respectfully, show your personal dignity, don't draw attention, and seal your lips. If they hurt your feelings, get over it. If they scare you with threats, that's natural. Suck it up. Keep quiet.

We left the detectives, and two uniformed policemen escorted me to another room to take my fingerprints. First they roll your fingers on the ink-pad, then the card. The officer rolling my fingers was nervous and botched the impression a couple of times. He had to start over. I learned to take prints in the Army. In certain unconventional warfare circumstances, it is critical to ascertain people's identities, and if you aren't careful, the prints smudge on the card. As he crumpled the second card and tossed it in the trash, he asked me to lift out the waistband of my shorts. The other policeman gave him an odd look and he explained, defensively:

"He might be carrying one of those stars."

The big policeman was talking about a steel throwing-star that young karate-guys like to throw at trees. I was no longer handcuffed, so I obliged by lifting out my waistband. I was carrying no weapons.

Finally, the officer got a good set of prints. As I wiped the ink from my fingers with some special goo and a rough brown paper towel that he handed me, the nervous officer said suddenly, *"Stop!"*

I stopped cleaning my fingers. The other officer looked strangely at him again, to which he replied, "Should we check for skin samples under his fingernails?" They stared briefly at one another.

The nervous cop looked at me and said, "Never mind."

They were firm but continued to treat me well. They took pictures: front and profile, as on the show *Dragnet*. That was it for procedures. It was time for my first night, or what was left of it, in jail. It was about 4 A.M. and the sun would soon rise over the ocean while the gulls roused from stupor and began another day of begging and stealing from tourists and sunbathers.

The local jail was full, but they cleared out a cell. This caused some prisoners to be crowded into a nearby cage. A couple of thuggish-looking guys started to complain, but the big cop told them to shut up and do as they were told. They shut up and did as they were told. I had a private cell—or as private as any place can be that is under constant surveillance—they put a camera on me.

I lay down in the bed on my back and stared at the ceiling of my empty cell, listening to the other prisoners jabber. They were drunk or high or both. *How could they still be awake?*

I was finally safe. A feeling of euphoria swept over me as I drifted off to sleep.

MARBLES, BULLIES & BAD DREAMS

Marble playing has yet to enjoy the respect that it deserves. There are no cheerleaders dancing flirtatiously, no shoe companies sending free shoes— or even marble companies bearing free marbles.

Marble competition is not in the Olympics. I can only attribute this to the fact that marble players reach peak form at the age of twelve. Precisely at twelve. After that, you are a teenager, and marbles are for kids, or so they say. Despite the brief duration of his renown, a great marble player enjoys respect among his peers and evokes fear when he enters a game. The lessons of competition last a lifetime, and the game can be dangerous.

We played for keeps. Some kids had lucky shooters that they never bet. They would trade their sisters before gambling with their best shooter. I had a shooter for a year or so, until I figured that after enough practice, every marble was lucky, so long as it wasn't too lopsided to aim. The luck was in the thumb.

We played before school, during lunch, and while we waited for buses to go home. Often for our last game, we bet "all the marbles in our pockets." Sometimes I rode the yellow school bus home from Jewett Elementary, a school for sixth graders only, with my overstuffed pockets spilling out cat-eyes, bumble bees, luggers, clear, green, and red crystals, ball bearings, and unnamable others. But all too often, I stepped on the bus empty-handed, so when I got home it was *practice, practice, practice.*

I practiced and played so much that I developed a painful case of "marble-thumb." Some kids stopped when their thumbs started hurting, but mine just got luckier and luckier. Finally, I was winning so many marbles that I began lugging my loot home in a purple cloth bag with a gold drawstring.

I started giving them away. Sometimes I boiled water and dropped in a handful, which caused them to crack like a 3D spider's web, but they stayed together. You couldn't play with them after that; they would break. I gave those to girls. You had to be careful which girls you gave marbles to, or they might take it the wrong way.

Finally, I got a little business sense and started trading for lunch tickets so that I could eat twice. But I could only eat so much, so I lost my business sense and used them for slingshot ammo. Talk about power! Billy killed a rabbit with a lugger. Hit it square in the head.

Most kids were good sports but others were sore losers. The worst played like junior lawyers, and cited vague transgressions of the rules while refusing to hand over the goods. Some junior lawyers got socked by junior boxers. One boy took losing so hard that he sometimes slipped into the restroom to cry.

Some would even try to jinx your shots. Jinxing was against the rules, but they did it behind your back. Others simply went crazy when they lost too much—stomping, spitting, threatening and cussing. They, quite literally, lost their marbles.

I was on my knees in the sand, playing a left-handed game—"lefties" as we called it. I am not left-handed, but I practiced both ways so that I could play both ways. Unknown to me, I had a secret admirer. I had given her some boiled crystals, a high honor. She wanted to give me something in return. As I took aim and got ready to shoot—*Crack!* **White flash!** She sneaked up and kicked me square in the eye.

It felt like she hit me with a mallet. On my back, writhing in pain, holding my eye, I couldn't see. Marbles spilled out of my pockets into the sand. As I squirmed, still shocked and not knowing what happened, she stood over me and said, "That's because I love you," and ran away.

The fear of losing my eye jerked me to my senses. The other boys came around. When I took my hand away and opened my burning eyelid, there were gasps, *"uh-oh"s* and *"oh my God!"s* as they huddled for a closer look. One kid-doctor said that I would need a glass eye, and on that note, my knees felt weak. *A glass eye!*

The good news was that I could see, albeit not as well as before I blocked a field goal kick with my face. And there she was. Red-headed, sitting on the ground about twenty yards away. *Blurry* .

Her hands covered her mouth as if in surprise at what her foot had done. As I walked closer, some of the boys screamed from behind for me to beat her up, to punch her. But her eyes loved me from head to toe. I knew she loved me. She told me every day. She wrote notes in some kind of code that I could never figure out. She drew pictures of us holding hands. In the lunchroom she dropped extra food on my plate. And sometimes she threw rocks at me.

The story was that her brain swelled when she was a baby, causing brain damage. She was in special classes. With certain exceptions, she was a nice girl, and powerfully built; she terrified some of the boys, and could be a little dangerous to those who foolishly mocked her. If a boy made her cry, she liked to reciprocate, and probably that is why they were yelling for me to beat her up.

I walked over. She didn't run away, or seem afraid of me. I showed her my eye, and asked her to *please* not kick me in the *eye* again because it hurt. The boys were going crazy from the safety of their pack. "Get her! Get her!" they shouted. But I wouldn't hit her, and she screamed at them to ***"shut up!"*** and they did, the bunch of lily-livered cowards that they were.

I got a good shiner, and the eye itself was bloodshot and looked like a mutated cherry. It was a mess, so whenever I talked with other kids I shut it so they didn't stare in horror.

After that, I played marbles like a wary squirrel collecting acorns on the ground. I asked my friends to warn me if they saw her coming.

Mrs. Stephenson was my sixth grade homeroom teacher. I liked and listened to her because she liked and listened to me. I was pretty certain that I was one of her all-time favorite students. Maybe *the* all-time favorite. In retrospect, having lost my mother, I bonded with a couple of teachers, though I never said it to them. Mrs. Stephenson knew of my uncontested reign in the marble world, and had even come out to watch us play.

One day she caught me sitting at my desk in her classroom writing colorful things in a textbook. Cuss words. She swallowed any trace of anger, if there was any, but her motherly voice softly sang a hymn of disappointment when she asked me to stay after class. As the class continued, I suffered the full burden of her disappointment. My blood seemed transformed to the thickness of molasses, making my heart ache with a cruel pain as it protested having to pump the wretched life through my unworthy body. A body that would defile a textbook—school property—with cuss words! In *Mrs. Stephenson's* classroom, of all places.

Besides the fact that I was unworthy of life, she would report me to the office and they would call my dad, I thought. But she surprised me. After class, sitting alone in front of her desk, she said that she expected more of me. Normally she was happy to talk with me, but she seemed hurt and said only that she was disappointed and asked me to please erase those things so that the next student would not be distracted. She said that when I used cuss words I made myself sound dumb.

It was amazing what I would do for people who treated me decently and fairly, and gave me the chance to correct myself. Others would have punished me for writing bad words in the book. But if the object was to get me to stop, to change my behavior and not just punish past behavior, she knew how to do it. Had she used punishment, she may have egged me on, having taught only that "the price of getting caught is such and such."

I got lots of whippings at home when I was a kid. I remember the pain at times, as if I were lashed to a tree and flogged. And when I screamed, Dad would say, "Shut up, you're only making it worse," and when I reflexively blocked the belt from hitting my legs and butt, it only stung my arms and hands, and earned me more. Some lessons were taught by beating, as if one's body needed to be beaten so that the mind could learn.

The belt never taught me to be good. Pain only taught me to avoid pain. There is a subtle yet simultaneously giant difference. After all, when the punishment is delivered, all debts are settled. But with open-ended *disappointment* of someone you respect, there is true cause for suffering that does not disappear with the sting, and reason to prove that you are worthy and are not a disappointment.

Mrs. Stephenson's way was that of a mature woman. The ultimate tool in shaping behavior is not the rod, but the heart. Spare the rod, spoil the child. *Phooey.*

If she had sent me to the principal, the punishment would have been forgotten that day when the sun went down, and I would merely have classified her as "one of them." That was more than twenty years ago, and although she could not know, I never again disappointed her by defiling a book.

Maybe thirty percent of the students at Jewett were black and the rest, with few exceptions, were white. There was racial tension besides the normal childhood tension. Some blacks spit out the poison words: "honky," "cracker" or whatever, and some of the whites spewed their own venom delivered in all the well known forms, like "spear chucker" or "porch monkey." The word "nigger" was by then off-limits except in the private circles of the light-skinned, and among some blacks, who called themselves niggers all the time.

As I walked down the hall between classes, rattling with marbles, a white boy was in Mrs. Stephenson's classroom picking on a black girl named Shirley. Mrs. Stephenson was not there. The boy was a rough, dirty kid who liked to pick on people. His parents probably sported one of those stupid "My son beat up your honor student" decals. It's low enough for a boy to pick on another boy, but only slimy scum picked on girls. That's how I saw it then, and that's how I see it now.

I didn't know they were fighting, and walked into the class just in time to see Shirley's hand arcing down as she lunged to stab the brute with a pencil.

As the pencil came down, I raised my left hand in reflexive self-defense, and it plunged into the back of my hand. Life is like that, you know. One minute everything is okay, the next minute you are knee deep in boiling water.

My hand came back with a yellow #2 sticking out.

There it was.

In front of my face.

My mind registered, *A pencil is sticking out of my hand.*

A *pencil* is sticking out of my *hand.*

It didn't even hurt, yet. I looked at the pencil, looked at a wide-eyed Shirley—she must have surprised herself—dropped the books from my right hand, and yanked the pencil out of my left.

I screamed at her: *"YOU STABBED ME!!!"*

Blood ran out of my hand onto the floor. The bully vanished in the face of real violence. Shirley started crying and apologizing and she hugged me and I pushed her away and I felt bad for screaming in her face and pushing her away and my hand was bleeding and it hurt and I was scared so I handed her pencil back and walked out.

I nervously walked to the restroom and washed my bloody hand. It stung and ached, but had seemed worse when the pencil was sticking out than after. The bleeding was not so bad; a bloody nose was three times worse both in pain and blood. And that was that.

The Bone-Breaking Fight, which I will soon explain, would occur in sixth grade, but I experienced plenty of action in earlier years. When I was about ten, there was a kid in the neighborhood named Phelps. Phelps always seemed self-centered and stingy.

He had a rough sidekick, more like a hit-man-in-training, who was about my size, named Stony, of all things. Stony did not live in our neighborhood; he came from somewhere tough and mysterious. Most of the kids were afraid of him. Stony looked rough, his head was shaved, he was always dirty, and he liked to fight. When he walked into a room, people took note, and when he walked down the hall, girls and boys alike stepped aside. He was pure meanness. Nothing but trouble.

As an adult, I can only try to imagine the man who named his boy "Stony." Maybe he was holding a cold can of beer in his hand when he said, "We'll call him *Bud*. No. **Stony!** His name is Stony!"

And Stony worked for Phelps.

I went through a period when I walked with my thumbs through my belt-loops like a cowboy. I walked pretty funny sometimes and I liked to walk funny because it was fun. I was walking home from school with my thumbs through my belt-loops when Phelps came up with Stony and challenged, "Why do you walk like that? Think you're *cool* or something?" Yikes! I felt the fear of the fight brewing.

They were obviously in an attack mode. Kids don't hide it well and I was by then an experienced fighter. That experience made me all the more fearful. This is serious stuff, fighting. The object in a fight is to cause immediate damage, and to win decisively. And I had lost a few. Sensing danger, I tried to talk my way out, "Uh, what do you mean?" I didn't do a very good job.

Phelps commanded his little bulldog to attack: **"Get 'im Stony!"**

In a scene fit for Hollywood—it may as well have been gangland Chicago—Stony eagerly pounced. That body of pure meanness and trouble latched onto me, and the fur began to fly. It was the usual tangle; there were elbows, knees, fists, grass, sand, and profanity; there was no hair-pulling because Stony didn't have any, and I didn't have much, either. But Stony didn't know that I did this practically every day at home, and my brother was a giant boulder compared to Stony. Compared to Billy, Stony was slingshot ammo. Stony was an image of pure hell, but mere images don't do well in Show Me Country.

I ended up on his back, holding his head, smashing his face in the dirt and he was crying, flailing and screaming as if he were being burned alive. When I let him go, he got up bawling his eyes out, bleeding around his teeth and nose. It was a nasty sight. All that dirt and blood on his teeth, tears streaming down dirty cheeks as he spit out soil and grass. And to see Stony crying after I had beaten him, *Wow!* I was euphoric. *I beat Stony! The toughest white kid in the school!* Sure, there were black kids that were judged to be tougher because they acted meaner than Stony, but not many. I felt like I had conquered the white world.

He ran away and left Phelps standing there. Alone. So much for unit cohesion. I only had some little bruises, and when I looked at Phelps, anger filled my body. I was primed for the fight, and had plenty of energy left after Stony ran away. I felt that I had Stony's left over energy, too.

Phelps was standing there scared as a squirrel that suddenly realizes the dark cloud it is standing under is actually a hawk's shadow. He tried to talk his way out. I was so mad that I could have chewed rocks and spit gravel. After all, I had been really afraid, and fear is a bottomless well for anger. The crossing guard by the road saw us and said, "Come on. Time to go." He must have enjoyed the fight. Some men like to see boys fight. I had been there before, too.

Since we lived in the same neighborhood, Phelps had to walk home the same way I did. I suppose he didn't think his strategy through; he had counted on a sure win. As we walked, I figured rich-boy Phelps probably paid poor-boy Stony with some marbles or milk-money to beat me up.

Phelps was offering me all kinds of stuff and when we got in the orange grove on the path home, he was talking as fast as he could, almost like an auctioneer. He was trying to cut a deal on some marbles in exchange for safe passage, I think. I remember thinking that this was just not right; Phelps was not attacking me and I had whipped Stony. I shouldn't beat up Phelps. I was thinking that as I beat the crap out of him. I beat him soundly and twisted his arm; I was afraid that if I didn't do something he would come back with two "Stonys."

Yeah, this was Show Me Country. Don't step in the ring expecting mere words or reputation to see you through. *Show* Me.

On a different occasion in elementary school, a kid was picking on me and a big crowd had gathered. The choices were either to fight, or, since image was important even in Show Me Country, to eventually face other bullies who were surely watching. He put up his dukes and prepared to box. Boxing was alien to me. I was more of a brawler. I followed his lead and put up my dukes.

POW! Right in the nose—*my nose.* It started to bleed. That punch came *so* fast. A black kid broke it up, then the bell rang and we had to go to class just when it was about to get really good. My nose was hurt and bleeding, and my ego was hurt even worse, but I had learned a valuable lesson. I learned then that someone could force me to fight, but no one would ever again get me to fight the way he wanted me to. He could force me to defend myself, but not by *his* rules.

Finally, The Bone-Breaking Fight. There was serious pugilistic action in sixth grade. Tough guy "#100" found me, and this being a different school, there was a new batch of students, many of whom I had never met.

I didn't know him well, and why he picked on me is a dark mystery of the bullies, but he had a reputation for toughness, and it may have stemmed from a marble dispute. I don't know. But trying to figure it out, I would say that it stems from my actions not being in accordance with my physical appearance. I looked like I *should* back down. I looked like I wouldn't, or couldn't fight. I was nice to the girls. I smiled, said "hello," and came complete with fairly good manners. Ruffians just didn't see the other side, and they must have thought it safe to push me out of line, take my food, take my money, my marbles, or make a fool of me so that they could look big. They thought wrong.

Well, the origins of my opponent's angst are murky; maybe he was one of those "my kid beat up your honor student" boys like Stony, but what happened is clear. I began to climb a tree by the bus stop. He reached up nonchalantly and pulled me down by my foot as if he were plucking a tangerine from the tree to throw at a passing dog. Fear jolted me as I lost my grip and fell, *Karuumph!* into the dust. It hurt. He let go of my foot and stood over me laughing.

The adrenaline poured into my bloodstream. I felt the spring tension. I stood up and brushed myself off.

Then he had the audacity to taunt me and say that I could not hit a kid with glasses. What kind of bully wears *glasses*, anyway! He must have grown up in a weird neighborhood if kids with glasses, or kids with braces, or kids on crutches—or anybody—could pick a fight and not expect to get hit. Part of fighting is getting hit. That's just the way it is. If you can't take a punch, don't start a fight!

I am as certain as of tomorrow's sunrise that he did not expect to get slugged. He left himself unguarded, parading like a peacock, as if eyeglasses were a brick wall of protection, or as if blustery words would protect him.

There was no rule against hitting stupid people. He was trying to back me down in front of the other kids who now encircled us, the way they always do. "Come on," he said, motioning at his chest for me to push him. If he wanted a pushing match, he was in the wrong arena.

He made the mistake of stepping forward and trying to push me backwards, and when he moved into range *WHAM!* my right fist landed in his face with stunning impact.

There was serious contact.

Square in the eye.

His glasses broke and flew away in two directions.

He fell to the ground.

He was on his back. Holding his face and crying as he kicked his feet. I was ashamed for him and all his drama, but my hand hurt sharply as if my pointer-finger knuckle had been smashed with a hammer. The bus drove up and I ran off with my books and marbles and jumped onboard.

Mrs. Stephenson never heard about it. No teachers saw it, and nobody told. So that was that. Except for my hand. It swelled, and I knew that it was broken. *I'm in real trouble now.* Dad wouldn't mind me fighting back—in fact there was the rule that I had to fight back against bullies, or face him. But I didn't want to complain or reveal that it was broken. I figured that he would be as angry with me for breaking a bone as he would be for breaking the TV. So I simply acted like nothing was wrong.

At school, it was hard to write because I couldn't hold the pencil, and when I tried with my left hand, the resulting script was illegible "chicken scratch." So, I scrawled with my right the most physically painful words I ever wrote, and walked around for a week or two with a broken hand before Dad noticed. After I explained, he was only upset that I hadn't told him.

X-rays. A cast. Within a few days the shining white shell of plaster that covered my hand and forearm disappeared under schoolhouse graffiti: names, pictures, stickers—it looked like a piece of luggage that had traveled around the world. I hated it.

The nicest girls at school avoided boys who fought as if such ruffians emitted a wretched, foul odor. And most of them did. Meanwhile, I was walking around with a cast that reminded everyone that I broke my hand on a kid's head. A glasses-wearing kid. Glasses that were now taped together. He got a black eye. It was remarkable that we didn't get into trouble except for our own injuries. And it was hard to play marbles with a cast, though I did find a way to shoot by balancing the marble on the plaster.

Soon the cast was driving me crazy, what with all the itching and zillions of people asking how I broke my hand. How do you explain that you broke your hand in a fight without coming off as a heathen? People will automatically think you are covering something up if you say *he* started it. Even with a zillion witnesses. After all, *he* got the black eye: *you* got the broken hand! Case closed.

I never said that I couldn't fight well; only that I didn't start it. I hated that cast! Every day people would ask, "How did you break your hand?" Finally, after I figured it had been on long enough, I cut it off with a steak knife. My right wrist had withered and was skinnier than the left. My hand was stiff and white. Dad got mad at me for cutting off the cast, and so did the doctor. But it was off, and stayed off.

I played marbles until I turned thirteen, and that was the year the grizzly killed me.

Because we stopped paying the rent several times over the years, we got evicted or "run off" by landlords, and had recently moved into a nice, two-story condominium on one of the nicest lakes around. The community was known as *Casa del Sol*, and Dad liked to point out that that was Spanish for House in the Sun. Or maybe it was House *of* the Sun. Anyway, it was Spanish.

There were sailboats that I somehow taught myself to sail without getting my head knocked off by the boom. And I had a flipper-boat only big enough for two people, with a small outboard motor that I used to navigate all around the "Chain-o-Lakes," which is a series of more than a dozen Central Florida lakes connected by canals. I would ride in my boat from one end to the other, and when the bad weather and lightning came, as it often did, I just pulled up to shore somewhere and sat down until it passed.

At *Casa del Sol*, there was a swimming pool along with a gym. Eviction, or moving, or whatever it was that we did, was a strange thing in our family, since sometimes we landed in a nicer neighborhood than we had left behind. I don't know how the man called Dad managed to get the lights turned on, but he did, though sometimes they, along with the phone, would get shut off, but they always came back on.

For me, the bad part about moving was leaving my friends behind. The good part was that I met new friends and eventually, after we had lived all around town, I could tour on my bike and see friends all over Winter Haven. Later I bragged that there was not a street in Winter Haven that I had not traveled—which is a big claim—and I set out with a map just to make sure. I rode my bike a lot. It kept me out of the house, now a condo, and there was good reason to make myself scarce.

Through the years Billy was an incorrigible bully, a persistent abuser. I could do little right by him, and he needed no excuse to take out his own frustrations on me. The years since our mother died had been for me a period of constant vigilance.

Like a time bomb, Billy needed no outside disturbance to set him off. His clock ticked away inside, and when it ticked around to some random moment, *surprise!* it was my time, fight time. If I wasn't handy, he searched me out. He seemed especially programmed to locate and humiliate me in front of my friends—most especially girls.

Sticks and stones may break my bones, but words will never hurt me.
I agreed with the sticks and stones part. I disagreed with the words part. Billy used both. His sticks and stones were his legs and fists. His birthday was on Halloween, appropriately enough.

It is very difficult for the smaller child when he sees only two choices: endure beatings and constant humiliation, or retaliate with such over-whelming force and ferocity that someone gets hurt. There was the option of running away, but that was like running into the jungle to face unknown terrors. Our size difference was such that I was not able to simply subdue him, and any halfway defense resulted in more battering.

If I chose to truly retaliate—*hard*—I might have a chance at walking away without broken bones and scars. And I knew about injury. By now, I had broken five bones in my hands. (The other four had been from a nasty go-cart accident.) I had also undergone emergency surgery on a finger for a bone infection, which I am told was done without anesthesia when I was about nine. I don't remember that so much, and it seems rather incredible, but I do remember the torture of getting the bandages changed.

I was well acquainted with pain and fear. When bullies picked on me, it was not only a matter of being humiliated as it would be for some kids; my world was bloody, broken bones, life-threateningly real.

Billy would not cave in to threats. Far too many people threaten who can't or won't back it up, and they dilute the words of those who will. When I threatened to clobber him with a bat, he beat the hell out of me. But he misunderstood my threat, which was actually a warning. I stupidly wasn't holding the bat when I had threatened to use it. Oddly enough, I still loved him for some reason. Too bad for me that for years I showed more respect for his well-being than for my own. If I had to do it over again, I would have ended it earlier. I would have used the bat, which may seem harsh, but not when you consider the alternative: the deer rifle that my dad kept in his closet.

After enduring more than a half-decade of constant bullying and abuse, I was reclining on the couch, reading a book, when Billy barged in the door with a friend. They must have been bored or I must have looked inviting; they decided to beat me. Each of them had a solid thirty pounds advantage, so it was two big kids against a small one. I was outweighed by about double my weight plus sixty pounds. They were about two years older, about a half-foot taller, and stronger.

To put that into perspective, it would be like a one hundred pound boy fighting a two hundred sixty pound monster that has four arms and legs and four hands and feet. It also has two brains, so it can think like two separate fighters, but in fact is a single being, like a stampeding herd, or a mob.

The fight was on. I was losing.

I begged the monster for mercy, failing to realize that *asking* for mercy was not the way to get it from a demon. Demons must be fought. I was taking a pounding. Mostly body shots; if Billy banged up my face, he would have to answer to Dad. Inevitably, they knocked me down and piled on. I couldn't breathe under their weight. They were laughing and having a jolly old time; my body felt ready to explode, both from the terror of it, as well as from not being able to breathe and being pummeled.

One minute I was reading physics, the next minute I was fighting to breathe under two hundred sixty smothering, life-crushing pounds. My life went from calm to full-on combat with virtually no warning. I was afraid I was going to die, and sometimes when they held me down I couldn't breathe. Those times when I was suffocating were terrifying beyond all possibility of description. I knew that if they wanted, or if they got carried away a little too long, I would suffocate. The terror was explosive.

This went on until, somehow, I escaped.

The only direction to run was upstairs, which was not good. It meant that I would have to climb out a window and jump off the roof, and they could still catch me on the ground. I ran into Dad's closet hiding, afraid, hurting and crying. Not baby crying. My "feelings" were not hurt; I was in fear for my *life*. The tears flowing were those of terror and confusion. I truly didn't want to kill them. But I was going to, and that was confusing.

I was holding Dad's deer rifle. It was there. So I grabbed it from the corner in the closet.

This was it.

I choked and gasped for breath. Tears flowed and the world was a blurry fog.

God, I didn't want to kill them.

I reached up and pulled a box of high-powered rifle shells from the closet shelf. My hands trembled as I fumbled with the bullets. Some cartridges dropped in the darkness on the carpeted floor. I knew the rifle well enough by feel that I managed to load five rounds into the magazine.

Loaded, cocked, safety off.

The only thing left was to point, and pull the trigger.

I hid in the dark corner behind the clothes, pointed the rifle and waited. When they came through the door, I would shoot them. Finger on the trigger, I waited. My body shook uncontrollably, and my trembling finger was in danger of blowing a hole through the wall.

I have a right to live. To live without constant fear. To breathe air without suffocating. They would kill themselves by coming through the door. Nothing existed outside of the moment. No past, no future. Just live, or die.

Is a thirteen-year-old child holding a rifle—a boy who has not yet sprouted a man's hair on his skinny body—justified? Justified to *kill*?

Imagine being beaten several times a week for almost half your life. Imagine feeling helpless, and unable to breathe. To better gauge how it feels, one may wish to perform an experiment: Find a man that is two and a half times your size—or use two people. Put a pillow over your head and have him lay on it for a minute.

A full minute.

Try to suck air from that pillow for a minute while someone punches your leg muscles. Make sure that the punches are hard enough to leave bruises.

A full minute.

After becoming comfortable with that—and you will not, but maybe you can take the next step—tell him to stay as long as he wants while ignoring your muffled cries. Tell the man that you wish to be at his mercy. His complete mercy. Have him bind your hands behind your back, and tie your feet. Tell him not to pay attention to your screams—unless he wants to. Pick a man whom you do not know who has a nervous-twitch—that's my brother's friend—he had a nervous twitch. Make it *real!*

Remember to explicitly instruct him to make you feel *helpless.*

Tell him not to stop until you are *panicked.*

Tell him not to stop at all, if he doesn't feel like it.

It is a form of violent rape.

Is it okay to defend yourself against two people bursting into your home and raping you?

Sometimes I see on the news that a child has shot another child. Many people reflexively react in horror: "That Goddamned little *monster!* Throw him in the electric chair, like the adults!" I always wonder if the kid who did the shooting was like me. A good kid, but feeling helpless.

Tell an adult?

Sounds good—it never worked—I tried it countless times.

Go somewhere else and avoid the confrontation?

Get real—I couldn't run that fast, and I lived in that house.

I was in the closet, holding the rifle.

Silent, only sobbing and gasping, no threats, no warnings. Words were over. This was deadly combat. Kill or be killed. My mind was bathed in a distilled fear. My finger was trembling with all the energy it needed to kill the raping monster.

In my mind, they were already dead. They had only to complete the action.

I heard the door open and shut downstairs.

They walked out.

I had killed them in my mind, but it was as real as if I had pulled the trigger. I stayed in the closet for a long time, until I knew they were gone and not trying to trick me. I unloaded the rifle and put it back, and sneaked out the back into the woods next to the lake where I sat down and sobbed alone, for hours.

And then there was the grizzly.

Billy and I drove out west in a jeep. Deep in the wilderness on a dirt road. He was driving. He stopped and we got out. We carried shotguns. We walked away from the jeep, maybe a hundred yards, when we saw two grizzly-bear cubs.

Stop . . .

Their mother is here somewhere.

We slowly backed up to the jeep. *Crash, crash, crash* the huge mother grizzly burst from the woods a hundred yards from us. She charged faster than a racehorse.

We turned and ran for the jeep.

Billy ran faster, so he made it first and cranked the engine. I was almost to safety. Only a couple of feet from the jeep. Billy drove away. I lunged for the door but missed. I screamed:

Stop!

Please Stop!

Billy Stop!

Oh my God Billy Stop! Stop! Stop!

I ran as fast as my legs would take me, screaming Stop!

I turned and saw the raging bear. Snarling, ferocious, with giant teeth and claws. She charged like a wave of death. I ran frantically down the dirt road. As Billy drove away in front, I heard the grizzly closing the distance behind me. She gained quickly. I ran as fast and hard as I could. At the last moment before she got me, I turned around and shot her three times with the shotgun.

Bam! pump

Bam! pump

Bam!

No more ammo.

She didn't slow down. I dropped the gun, turned to run, and made a few more steps until she had me. With a single crushing swat from a massive paw, her claws ripped away my shirt. Blood and meat flew from my back. I was wide open. I fell to the ground and she was on me. I fought and fought, but she ripped me to pieces with her teeth and claws.

Looking
down
as
I
floated
up,
I saw the jeep driving away from my lifeless body

The grizzly finished her work and was walking back to her cubs. My body lay in the road. Face down, torn, bloody, dead.
I died

I woke up

I must have slept only an hour or two. My eyes opened to a new world, six years later in Ocean City. There was silence. The other prisoners seemed to be asleep in their cells. No snoring. Just the quiet. I sat up in the bed, swung my feet to the dark floor and sat there, looking around. Dim light seeped into the cell from the hall.

There must be a guard out there somewhere. He's probably watching me through the camera. There was a camera on wheels that they placed to monitor my cell. What did they think? That I was going to tunnel out with my teeth the minute they turned around? I was just flesh and blood like them. I pushed out of bed and stood up on the floor. The cell came complete with its own toilet, which was probably more for the guards' peace than the inmates' comfort.

They had taken my shoe strings. In a military situation, this is sometimes done so that if a prisoner tries to escape by running, he will run out of his boots. As for civilians in a typical jail, prisoners occasionally commit suicide, and shoe strings are an easy route to hanging.

You don't have to hang yourself from a pipe. Years later, I had a Special Forces friend who was suffering greatly from various personal demons. Demons that, as far as I could guess, he picked up in Central America, in combat. He must have been into something serious: there was a picture of him in his quarters on base, along with his team, with the vice president in the Oval Office receiving an award. Someone told me after he died that the award was a Silver Star, awarded for valor in combat.

One night, while I waited for him at a restaurant, my friend hung himself with a belt by tying it around a doorknob in his quarters. Not far from the picture of his team in the Oval Office, he simply knelt down and leaned into the belt. They found him on his knees, dead. He was a good man.

But I was in jail and suicide was not on my list. The place was silent, except for the sounds coming from my heavy breathing as I exercised. Pushups, sit-ups, mountain climbers and any other exercise I could think of.

My right hand was sore from the punches I had landed. I opened and closed it, flexed it, examined the flesh, and kneaded the bones of my right hand with the fingers of my left. It hurt but, amazingly, was not broken. A boxer's gloves are made not only to protect his opponent's head and body, but his own fists. Fighting is brutal to your hands. It seemed a miracle that the hand wasn't broken the night before: hitting a human head on the hard parts is almost like punching a bowling ball wrapped in skin. It's heavy and hard.

I worked up a good sweat exercising, and a couple of hours later had some kind of sandwiches for breakfast. The military teaches that if you are captured, never decline food. The enemy won't waste time with poison. They don't need to trick you to kill you. Not when they can just drag you out and shoot you, or bludgeon you to death. The sandwiches were bland and dry but I wolfed them down, along with cartons of milk and orange juice.

The police have many tricks that will cause people to admit to crimes, whether they committed them or not, and to talk when they should keep quiet. The same tricks are used by military interrogators with POWs. Their first stab at getting me to talk, at least that I detected, had been only hours earlier. After reading me my rights, the major asked if I was okay. That's intended to be a conversation starter.

"Trained to keep cheery," I had answered.

If I had engaged in conversation, undoubtedly he would have verbally hooked and jabbed like a boxer, searching for weak points to exploit. Police undergo special training in proven psychological methods of destroying defenses and going for the kill by tricking information from suspects. That's what we pay them for. I was a teenager in the ring with veteran lawmen. As with soldiers who are tasked to protect us, we want police who are at once capable of being Robo-Cops, who will lock horns with violent criminals, but who are temperamentally more like Sheriff Andy Griffith. We want lions with a conscience. People who will fight crime with a voracious appetite, while walking that thin wire and preserving justice, as well as treating others as they wish to be treated. We want Supermen and Superwomen.

The second trick that I detected—and who knows what I missed—was at the Ocean City jail that first morning. There was a window with bars, outside of which seemed to be the police motor pool. I couldn't see out the window, but heard car doors opening and closing, and engines starting. Some police were out there and they began talking loud enough for me to hear. A voice asked about the recent excitement.

"So what happened last night?" asked the voice (as if he didn't know). The camera peered into my cell, so others must have been watching me on the monitor as I got close to the high window to listen.

The second voice responded, "He used that Green Beret stuff and it worked too good."

The first voice asked, "How much time do you think he will get?"

"Maybe fifteen or twenty years," answered the second voice.

Sounded like a lot of years for a simple fist fight, and I figured they were trying to get me to talk to prove my innocence. No way. I would only talk to a lawyer, and none was in sight. The only people to whom I must prove my innocence were going to be the judge and jury. I guess, technically, the prosecution had to prove my guilt, but they had lots of supposed evidence: Green Beret, Bar, Fight, Dead.

The police are clever, which is a good thing when they are fishing for dangerous sharks, but a horrible thing when someone, like a frolicking dolphin, accidentally gets snagged in the dragnet. The voices chatted some more outside the window, conveying veiled threats in an attempt to frighten me. Finally the men walked away. With the camera rolling, they knew that their payload had hit the target. They probably built that window specifically for that reason, and they probably used the trick on a daily basis. Some military interrogation centers are built to allow prisoners to quietly "overhear" distant conversations between guards. It was all the same.

I was scared alright, but they would have to do better to get me to talk.

I gave them a reply. I moved to the center of the line of sight for the camera, and started doing pushups and sit-ups.

NEVER GIVE UP

KEEP YOUR STRENGTH. Keep a positive mental outlook. Know that you are not forgotten. Keep the faith that your family and friends are doing all they can to help you. They want to be reunited. Make humor in your situation. Secretly mock your captors. Of course, I wasn't a POW, but the little training I had in that area was all I had, besides my own common sense.

I exercised my body, and waited, and exercised and waited. *How long will I be locked in this cage? A year, while it goes to trial? Will there be a trial? Ten years?*

My captors charged me with two crimes:
1) Assault with intent to murder
2) Second degree murder

The murder charge alone carried a possible sentence of twenty-five years to life in prison.

How was I going to hire a lawyer? I joined the Army for money for Christ's sake! That's like begging in the ghetto. I couldn't even afford a cheap car without spending the bonus that I had invested for school. How much does it cost to hire a lawyer in a murder case? Fifty thousand dollars? Would the Army even pay my measly monthly salary while I was in prison? Doubtful. Would they demand my enlistment bonus back? Probably.

Of all the evidence that was gathered then—or ever—there was no derogatory evidence whatsoever, and there was overwhelming exculpatory evidence.

But the charge was Murder.

On this road, the only signs were flashing:

Penitentiary
Next Exit

Bail was set at five hundred thousand dollars. It might as well have been five hundred million. I joked to myself at the awesome gravitational power of the black hole that was sucking me in. *So much for being home by Christmas,* I laughed to myself. *Keep your spirits up.* This was serious trouble. Five hundred thousand dollars bail, a murder charge, and the other felony charge, which seemed slight in comparison, but which could also cost me years in prison.

The police allowed me to make some calls to the outside. First, I called the Army. *The Army.* And worse yet, I thought, *Special Forces.* The police had already contacted the Special Warfare Center at Fort Bragg and, by then, I figured, the commanders were seeing it on the news over their morning coffee. Phones were ringing. Wheels were turning as they saw that one of their young "Green Berets," one they had chosen to trust with a secret clearance and all that expensive training, had managed to splash himself all over the news. This kind of negative publicity has a bad impact on the Army. Even I, as a nineteen-year-old, knew that I could become a casualty of Damage Control, meaning justice was at risk.

Now it was my turn to deliver the news. I pressed the phone receiver to my ear and listened to it ring like a little klaxon in a distant office at Fort Bragg. In the Army, phones are to be answered on the second ring. Somebody answered in a sharp military voice on the second ring, "Charlie Company First Special Warfare Battalion, Sergeant 'Smith' speaking, this line is not secure, how can I help you, Sir?"

The operator queried him, "I have a collect call from Michael Yon in Ocean City, Maryland, will you accept the charges?"

"Yes," answered the sergeant.

"Go ahead, sir," the operator said to me.

"I have a little problem, sergeant," I said, "I am in jail."

"We heard."

"Well, they charged me with murder. I won't be at formation Monday morning." At times I have been accused of being a master of the obvious. The sergeant was agreeable to my missing formation, and told me the commander had been informed. There was nothing else to say.

"Anything else?" he asked.

"Nothing I can think of," I said, "I'll keep you informed."

"Okay."

"Goodbye," I said, wishing that I could escape with my words through the phone lines.

"Goodbye," said the sergeant, "and good luck."

I hung up the phone. *Well, that wasn't so bad,* I thought.

The Army's first concern is the Army. If it suited the Army's best interest to defend me, it would. If not, I was on my own. That is not a criticism of individuals in the Army. It is a statement of fact concerning any organization that is more concerned with the whole than the individual. A large government organization, or big business, is a machine. Machines don't care about people. We are the inventors and operators of the very machines that consume us. Our contrivances trade and spend our lives as freely as if we were marbles. When there are lots of marbles, the machine forgets that each person is a human being. Human life is degraded to fodder, to lunch money, to slingshot ammo. And if I was not an asset to that machine, I was a liability. The machine is programmed to eliminate liabilities like defective marbles. Nothing personal. Just Damage Control. (D.C.)

There seemed to be all kinds of "evidence" against me. I was a "Green Beret," I was accused, and I had asked for a lawyer. That appeared to be some seriously damning evidence.

The Ocean City police were generous and allowed me to make as many collect calls as I needed. I called Richard White. As a college student, there was nothing much he could do physically to help—unless we were talking escape—but his moral support was a huge boost.

When I was finished with my generic calls, a policeman said, "Tell me if you need anything. I'll see what I can do."

Another officer asked, "Did you get enough for breakfast?"

Despite the storm looming and all the torpedoes that were still chasing me, and the fact that I was sealed in a jail cell, I felt like I was riding first class. But I didn't ask for anything. One never takes privileges or accepts favors from the enemy without a very good reason. Nothing is free.

I hadn't been able to reach Steve Shaulis, but he reached me. He was out there, searching for a lawyer. Steve was in my corner. I wanted to tell him not to call my family, as if the delaying tactic had any value. I didn't want to worry my grandparents. Especially Granny. But it was too late.

Steve remembered my hometown in Florida and started calling all the "Yons" listed until he found my dad. My sister, Susan, later said she answered the call that night, and she knew that something was wrong the moment she heard Steve's voice.

ESCAPE

ONE NIGHT DURING eleventh grade, the verbal abuse at home crossed a new border when the man called Dad finally found a way to hurt me. He called me a "fag" because I never brought home a girlfriend. It was like getting punched in the stomach, only worse.

Even by that age, I was secure enough in my masculinity that I didn't care what homosexuals did, but I surely did not like to be accused of being one. I often suspect those who gratuitously point fingers of hiding something.

When I was younger, and asked questions about girls, it was a subject for jokes and teasing. If I said that I liked a girl or was even seen looking at one, my father and brother kidded me unmercifully. So I learned never to talk about girls and to avoid looking at them when Dad or Billy was around.

Also, I did have a real problem talking with girls when I was younger. Not because I was shy per se; I was anything but shy, but perhaps because my mother was not there to teach me, I did not learn the subtleties by which women communicate. When I was younger, I once asked a babysitter how to get a girlfriend because there was a girl at school that I wanted very much to get to know. The babysitter just told me, "Be nice to her." But that didn't work. I was already nice. It takes more than that. Time and again, I saw girls, then women, walking off with the wrong male who could talk a good line. I was more like Tarzan, King of the Jungle: "Me Michael; You Buffy!" If she wanted a sweet-talking, sensitive, modern male, that was somebody else.

During my high school days, the man called Dad would stagger in late at night, drunk, forgetting that he'd left the car lights on, and the front door open, and rouse us out of bed to lecture us about things that made no sense. Next day at school I could barely keep my eyes open.

That night, his drunkenly calling me a fag was just the latest affront in years of abuse and neglect. Hunger was common in our home at this time. It was not the kind of hunger that emaciates children, but more subtle; one would never have known that I was hungry. When I visited friends' houses and saw their refrigerators and cupboards full of food, I would think, *I'm gonna make a lot of money when I grow up.* Wealthy people often have a closet in the kitchen seemingly jammed with every type of cereal, and every kind of soup you can imagine, and giant refrigerators filled with enough food to pay the rent for a month.

At our house, there might be a half dozen eggs, an empty box of cereal in the trash along with an empty gallon of milk. But there would often be a tasty report from Susan that "Dad called and said that he'll be home in a couple of hours with some sandwiches." *Yeah, right.* And Susan knew better, too. We never went for days without eating, but the number of missed or meager suppers and breakfasts, before we started making our own money, could not easily be tallied.

Instead of punching him in the mouth for calling me a fag—he wasn't worth it—I grabbed a duffel bag. While he was drunk in the living room, probably ranting about how the niggers and Jews were being allowed to ruin the country, I quietly loaded the duffel with some cans of food that were around, pots, pans, and utensils, some clothes, and a few books, then slipped out the front door into the darkness and was gone.

We lived on the outskirts of town at the time, and I was headed downtown to stay the night in The Gym before making a plan. I wanted to finish high school, so I didn't want to leave the area altogether.

I had walked about six miles and was cold and wet, carrying the over-stuffed duffel bag. I was not trying to be stealthy, and had not been on the lookout for the police. When they spotted me, nobody said "Halt!" or anything, for that matter.

Quietly, the police surrounded me in the darkness. Because of my duffel bag, they thought I was a burglar.

Cold and alone. The wet, desolate streets shined black against the lights and a moon that was fighting through the clouds. It was silent, except for the sound of my footsteps, the clanking in the duffel bag that was wearing into my back, and my breathing. The police were converging in a loose, moving perimeter. I still did not see the eyes that stalked me from the darkness.

A police car drove by a couple of blocks away. I was so lost in thought, it had not occurred to me that I must look like a burglar. But after I saw the police car, it didn't take an astronaut to figure out what was happening around me. I didn't want to talk with them and had committed no crime. The Gym was only a few blocks away. If I could just get there, it would be okay. I might even work out for an hour.

I bolted down an alley. Pots and pans and cans of food clanked in my shifting duffel bag as my heart banged away in my chest. They must have seen me run. I heard a car nearby accelerate hard, and another police car passed the other side of the alley with its lights out. I stopped and listened in the darkness.

A car stopped, then another.

There were voices and more cars. I slipped inside a dark recess between two buildings, but there was no way out. I pressed tight against the cold concrete, wishing that I could flatten myself invisible. Maybe if I were still enough, they would not see me. If I could only hold my breath, they might just walk by. If I forget them, maybe they will forget me. It was a silly idea, but the only one I came up with.

They crept down the alley with flashlights and careful footsteps. The county had a high incidence of violent crime. The fear of getting shot caused my adrenaline to surge, and I was ready to bolt, but I was surrounded. The police narrowed it down to the area between the buildings. I held my breath, and it's true that when one is being hunted and is hiding, one's heart really does seem loud enough that others might hear it pounding.

A voice commanded, "Come out with your hands up!"

"I'm unarmed. *Please* don't shoot me," I answered meekly.

A voice commanded sternly, "Come out with your hands up; *DO IT NOW!*"

I answered compliantly, "Okay, I am putting down my duffel bag and coming out."

I stepped out to face them. The white beams from their flashlights caused me to squint painfully. Out with the handcuffs and on with the search. A policeman dragged out my duffel bag and looked inside with his light.

"What are you doing?" asked the stern voice from behind a light.

"Moving," I answered into the light.

Apparently there had been no robberies reported that night. Nobody tried to push me to confess to a crime. Other than that, I just gave them my name and address. What was I supposed to say? That I was *running away?*

I was ashamed that my father stayed drunk, and that home was a psychological war zone. I did have my dignity, and clung to the self-image created in my first years of life. That was who I was. I came from a great family. Very happy. We had dogs and cats and a squirrel named Chipper.

I had a great mother. She taught me to hold my breath underwater and how to swim. And she had prepared me for the road ahead before leaving. She loved me and I still loved her. What I was enduring was only something that I had to survive one day at a time. I wasn't running away. The man called Dad didn't own me. The police didn't own me. And nobody could make me live like that. I own me, and I was moving.

The police had captured my body, loaded it into a car, and driven down the deserted road. Tomorrow was a school day. Probably my friends were all asleep. The radio crackled with sharp voices and strange police codes as the car passed by The Gym on 3rd street. A few blocks later it pulled into the station.

They locked me in a cold room, without bars. An interrogation room. They called Dad but he didn't come to get me. A smart move on his part. Likely they would have arrested him for DUI if he showed up. But locals still seemed to look at him in the old light. Many, many times when someone heard my name, it was, "Oh, you are Billy *Yon's* son" with a kinder, softer voice. Doors flew open, and people talked to me as if I were something special. Dad had made a lot of friends in his earlier life, but I rarely met my father as I grew older, just the thing that inhabited his body. My real father was a very good man, but I remember him only from my first seven years.

And there were those who said, "I knew your mother, she was a very nice woman." I wanted them to tell me everything about her and I wanted to know who she was. But they seldom said much after that, and I didn't ask. I wanted to, but didn't.

Several times through the years, some of my mother's old high school friends who had moved away called to talk with her. When they called, I had to tell her friends that she had passed away. And on each occasion they asked who I was and there was shock in their voices and one woman cried as I stared at the wall, holding the phone to my ear. And now she had been gone for nearly ten years. It seemed like a thousand.

At the station, I was soaking wet from the rain and sweat and began to shiver. I tried to sleep on the floor, but it sucked the heat from my body like a vacuum. From my amateur physics, I figured that plastic had a more favorable coefficient of heat conduction than tile, which is just a fancy way of saying it "feels" warmer because it transfers thermal energy slower, so I pushed some plastic chairs together and curled up in those. But that didn't do much good. I was just cold and soggy. It doesn't matter how much you read or study, cold is cold, and wet cold is the worst, but even worse than that is to be cold, wet, hungry and locked up for nothing, and not much to go back to even when you are released.

All night I asked for a blanket. Always politely, as was my way: "Can I *please* have a blanket?" Unseen voices talked outside the room. There were no windows. They ignored me while I shivered, alone. They never responded one way or the other. A *Shut-up!* would have been better than silence. At least I would know where I stood, and that they cared enough to hate me. At least to hate me is to acknowledge me. I wasn't even worth that to them.

Maybe the police forgot that run-*away* is not run-*to*. I had no idea where I would end up. When kids run from a wolf, they are not concerned about where they are going—just about escaping the wolf. Kids don't want to run away. It takes a great deal of pain to make a child flee into the hungry jungle alone.

When a kid runs, he or she should not be punished if picked up by the police; that just means there is another wolf for the kid to fear and escape. Most such children are refugees from a war at home, or are simply neglected, and are not intrinsically bad. Kids are not born bad—or if some are, they are very few. I can only base that on my intuition, but I strongly believe it.

Often people speak contemptuously about our young ones, and like to start sentences with peremptory disdain: *Kids today.* . . . What about kids today? Why are kids today any different? It is doubtful that kids have suddenly genetically mutated. No, the proper statement is, *We Adults today,* who are responsible for raising our children. . . .

I say this with certainty—of all the evils perpetrated in the last two thousand years—gigantic wars, concentration camps, torture, slavery, atomic bombs—no kid born in the last fifteen years was responsible. No kid born in the last fifteen years produced violent movies to show to children—merely for the sake of making money—or designed chemically enhanced cigarettes, then created manipulative advertisements, to hook children—for the sake of making money. No kid born in the last fifteen years designed alcohol advertisements. No kid designed violent video games and sold them by the millions. Boys, by their very nature, have a marked tendency toward violence in certain situations. That is part of being male. Why encourage that tendency? It's more than strong enough already!

And as for all those money-making products that are shoved down kids' throats, piped into their ears, and fed through their hungry eyes; some business leaders will say, "We are only giving our customers what they want."

A crack dealer could make the same rationalization.

Does a good mother give her little boy ice cream every time he asks for it?

I am sure, as a matter of intuition, that the majority of "bad kids" are simply surviving any way they can. They are taking their cues from human nature and from us. After all, if a child grows up around violent people, violent TV, violent video games and song lyrics that tell him to shoot people who piss him off, what do we expect? When we plant corn, we expect corn to grow. When we plant poison ivy, that is what we will get.

I harbor some passion for this subject.

I have no training in auto mechanics, but some things I know from driving. I know that a car engine needs gas and oil to run. I have no training in psychology, but some things I know from living. When those children who are stumbling around, lost in the darkness, see a beacon of hope, they will flutter to it like moths to a light. If that beacon of hope is a pimp, they might become prostitutes. Good kids, given bad circumstances, often become prostitutes. If that beacon is a drug dealer, so, too, might they turn to drugs. Likewise, good kids do become drug abusers and sellers. Good kids do join gangs, and become gangsters. In order to live, one must first survive. And in a survival situation, popular morality can become blurred, suppressed, or merely rejected if the child feels cast out.

I have heard the arguments of the soft-bellied men-of-means protesting the building of basketball courts for inner-city kids. I want to scream when I hear those arguments, but I know that would be counter-productive. When you scream into people's faces, normally they stop listening, just as I tend to stop listening when someone screams at me.

Sports provide a great beacon of hope for many kids. It did for me. For a precious few, it provides a way up and out, and they become role-models. Not always good role-models, of course, but I am sure that the net effect is positive. Even a moderate level of sports achievement can go far to instill self-esteem in our little ones. And self-esteem that is earned through any kind of achievement is worth more than money in the bank.

But if our message to our own child citizens is that they are not worthy of our love, then they will not love us. When we would rather build bombers than basketball courts, and when the children do not answer the call to defend us and our precious property, of which they own little if any, we have no right to cry. And we have no right to cry when we breed violence and must defend ourselves from our own citizens. Adults run this country. We have no right to cry that what was handed down to us is broken. We are here. Now. This is what we have to work with.

The violence. It causes me to wonder about the man who had the *Death Before Dishonor* tattoo, who was wearing his shit kickers. In retrospect, and after having gained more experience, it sounds as if he were saying from the voice of *fear*: "I would rather kill than be put down again." What could have made him so angry? He began as we all did, a little crying baby, sucking nourishment, probably giggling and smiling that little baby smile when his mother held him to her face and he smelled her breath.

It is wrong to cry out that we are victims of society. Seeing oneself as a helpless victim, a leaf carried by the wind, without free will, is a loser's rationalization. To be a winner, one must take charge of one's life. Through luck and through searching, I found a few genuine beacons, people worthy of the name *mentors*.

The first night I spent in a jail was as a runaway. The man called Dad picked me up the next day, and that was one of the first days, up to then, that I ever missed school.

The second night that I spent in jail was in Ocean City. I was feeling the euphoria of having survived. I felt exhilarated as never before. I had defeated an aggressive, larger opponent in hand-to-hand combat. I didn't feel euphoric because he was dead—it was the threat, the fight, and the chase that caused the evolutionarily determined chemical release. When the fight was over, the natural painkillers were still in my blood.

Usually when someone who has killed another person describes the experience, that person says it was horrible. If a person killed another while driving drunk, I imagine that in that setting, only a deeply disturbed person would feel euphoria. But I had faced—and defeated—a dangerous opponent. There is a tremendous difference. The "popular" thing to say might be that I felt horrible about the whole episode, but that would not be true. Much later I did, and likely for different reasons, but evolution has ensured that we each are superbly equipped chemically to flee or to fight, and that night I had done both.

When our bodies prepare to flee or fight, our oldest animal instincts take charge and suddenly we are transformed into something else. The experience is like being outside yourself. Fear, like Power, is its own right, and it makes its own rules. In true life and death fear, if you don't panic or freeze, you may well become action incarnate. It can be as if there is an autopilot and the ordinary, everyday "you" is only along for the ride. Your being has instantly transformed into something like pure energy and all that energy is focused tight, like a laser, on one objective—survival.

If normal daily life is akin to a leisurely drive in a slow car, in intense fear, suddenly your slow car is a high performance racecar. Instead of an ordinary curve, the broad highway is suddenly transformed into a treacherous mountain road, with hairpin turns, and giant cliffs. The car's accelerator is mashed to the floor. There are no guardrails. No time to check the map. You can't see what is around the next curve. No time for thinking. No brakes, and no breaks. One mistake—you die.

And you, the normal driver, have been pushed out of the way. Richard Petty slid into the driver's seat and took control as you watched from the backseat. You didn't even know he was in the car and now you are knocking bumpers at 200 mph. Or, more aptly, in flight you become the gazelle or even a shadow, or in fighting you become a fierce lion. Flight or fight can be summed up easily: utter and immediate fear for your life—a galaxy beyond any fear that we normally feel. It can be very exhilarating, even addicting.

Likely, in the modern era of our allegedly civilized nation, most people go through their lives without ever feeling their evolutionary inheritance take charge.

By turning myself in, I had sacrificed an incredible amount of control over my freedom, which now rested largely with the state of Maryland. When the survival chemicals wore off, anxiety set in. I thought surely Special Forces would boot me out while the Army slammed the door, but the only doors I would hear slamming behind me would be heavy, and metal.

Getting your finger cut off sounds horrifying, until you realize it could be your head. Suddenly, a finger doesn't seem so important. *I've got more where that came from!* Facing murder charges makes most things look trivial. I was facing twenty-five years to life in prison for the murder charge alone. *Goodbye, Special Forces. Goodbye, Army.* All that effort at Basic and at Selection, on the very first Friday night after my efforts finally came to fruition—zip. *Goodbye college money, goodbye freedom.*

Hello prison.

I was sickened by the possibility that people would think I was a murderer. The strangest thought of all kept popping in. *How am I going to explain to Granny and Granddad that I was in a bar?* And then—*A man is dead and I'm thinking about how I'm going to explain that I was in a bar? Have I lost my mind?*

I was confused that I had felt so euphoric after having killed a man. And the churning anxiety I felt was not for him; it was for losing my freedom and all the rest. I thought that maybe I was crazy. I didn't join the Army to kill people. That's not my idea of fun, but I am here to tell you, and many vets will concur, killing someone who is trying to kill you in combat can leave you incredibly high. It is an evolutionary inevitability, part of who we are as humans.

The Army didn't teach me how to deal with my feelings after killing someone. I had learned and practiced how to kill people, but they never told me how I might feel when it actually happened. It would have helped to know. Nobody asked, ever. I had no inkling that a feeling of euphoria is normal; we don't talk about these things, or at least the Army didn't.

How the enemy is killed makes a big difference in what effect it has on the killer. Bombing from high altitude in airplanes is said to be rather clinical in comparison to dog-fighting with an enemy pilot. In bombing you don't see the actual killing, and often the pilots and crews are in relatively little danger themselves. (Even when, at other times they may be in great danger, they still usually don't see the aftermath of their work.)

In dog-fighting, the personal danger level is higher. When the pilot hits the enemy jet and sees the metal flying away from the fireball he created, he knows that he may have just ended another human life. But he also knows that the man in the other jet is not a hapless *victim*, but an *enemy* who was doing his best to kill him, a fact which changes everything.

On one end of the spectrum, some people have an incredibly difficult time taking human life. On the other end, some find it addictive and intoxicating. Killing someone at close range, with a pistol during a police shootout for instance, is likely to have a powerful effect on the killer. I'm not talking about lining people up against the wall and shooting them; I am speaking of combat where the personal risk is severe. Kill or be killed. The closer the range and the greater the danger, the more personal and the greater the effect.

Hand-to-hand range is the closest, the most personal, the most inescapable—you *know* that you did it. The effect can be very, very intense. Even in a situation where killing is perfectly justified, the act often leaves some survivors feeling like criminals, while others become so addicted that, as with any drug, they go back for more and more.

Personally, I felt like a criminal after the euphoria wore off, even when I knew beyond all doubt that what I had done was an accident, and justified. Without someone giving me a road map to my feelings, I did a natural thing and set about dehumanizing the dead man. After all, under normal conditions I have a hard time with killing humans, so why not just label my former adversary with a nickname that is not so human?

Dehumanizing human beings can be a bad mistake, but in waging war it can be indispensable.

In World War II the Germans were called "Krauts" and the Japanese were "Nips" and so on. In Vietnam the natives were called "Slopes," and "Dinks," and lots of other *things*, rather than humans. It's easier to live with yourself knowing that you hit a village of sub-human Slopes than it is to flatten a village filled with men, women and children.

I have talked extensively about this with a police officer friend of mine. He provided valuable feedback on the police perspective. He admitted that the police, too, dehumanize suspects, calling them anything other than men or women. A skinny woman in the wrong part of town is automatically labeled "crack whore." Not a woman, not a human being with a story, sad as it may be.

A crack whore effectively has no rights, because she is "not human." We care about dogs more than crack whores. Male suspects are called things like "scrots." If an article appeared in the paper that said, "Crack whore raped by five Scrots," who would care? It's unlikely such an event would even make it to the paper, that's how much we care.

I have a friend who saw an old man stagger and collapse on the street. Usually, nobody cares about an "old drunk," but my friend told her husband to stop. Her husband protested. She made him stop. She jumped out to check on the old man, and discovered he was not drunk, but very ill. They rushed him to the hospital. Later, she learned that the old man merely needed some medicine, but that without it, he would have died.

So, too, was I being dehumanized. I was no longer the nineteen-year-old seeking college money who was secretly trying to overcome his own demons—but a "Green Beret" charged with murder. The city police handcuffed my wrists and shackled my feet, loaded me in a car and drove me from the city jail to the county jail. On the road, we passed free people, good citizens.

It was a hot Saturday and crowds streamed along the roads to the beaches. Bikini-clad college girls would be frolicking like otters on the sand where I was arrested, and where I was supposed to be frolicking, too. Meanwhile, others we passed on the road stared at me handcuffed in the backseat like I was some sort of dangerous animal. It's impolite to stare at people, but okay to stare at animals.

One guy drove up beside the back window of the cruiser. He grinned and gave me the finger. Taunting me, the helpless creature in a cage that he was sure he would never have to face. He reminded me of Lizard.

A feeling of intense anger at being mocked for my misfortune by this punk swept over me. I was an American soldier, specially picked to defend this country, including his sorry ass. I mouthed, *F- You* and forced a smile, or at least managed to show some teeth. To which he repeated his hand gesture with some force, pumping his hand up and down as if that would hurt me more. He screamed obscenities that I could not possibly hear through the closed windows and the air rushing outside. I stuck my tongue out, at which he sped away. Along with the little victory, a warm feeling replaced my anger. In a situation like this, one should savor every morsel of pleasure, and the encounter was very gratifying, in a silly sort of way.

We arrived at the county jail, drove past the fences and the barbed wire and into the jail compound where there were more men with guns, and big metal doors. There were buttons to push and intercoms to speak into, but soon we were inside, where I was to be signed over to the jailers. I was no longer a free citizen, but a prisoner who had to be signed for, like a package. Signatures and paperwork were exchanged, and, out of my earshot, the policemen had a conversation with a jailer. Then the policemen left me as they returned to the sunlight. The place felt like a dungeon.

The jailers promptly took over. First, they searched me. I expected a cavity search, like those shown in the movies, but there was none. The jailers reminded me of drill sergeants minus the pushups, but they were rather pleasant toward me, compared to the other prisoners in the area.

To the others they spoke in commands like, "Step over here" or "sit down!"

To me it was: "I need to ask you to step over here, please" and "thank you" after I complied. The treatment given me by the police and the jailers was very good—except that I was in the dungeon charged with murder and that other felony of assault with intent to murder.

The guards issued me an orange, short sleeved prisoner's shirt and pants similar to medical scrubs. The material was thick and rough on my skin. They took my clothes and inventoried my sparse belongings. Jailers have to be particular about their inventory sheets. For instance, if a prisoner is wearing a gold necklace, the jailer doesn't scribble on the sheet: "1 Gold necklace" but, "1 necklace, gold in color." Otherwise, the inmate can cry that he was ripped off and got a cheaper necklace back. You will get your property back when you are released, if it isn't seized for some legal reason. With luck, your clothes will still be in style. As for me, the only jewelry I ever wore was a watch, and my dog tags, of course.

My weight was listed at 165 as per the initial witness descriptions that continued to be used without anyone actually checking my weight. In fact, I weighed about 145. Blonde hair, green eyes, Address: **Charlie Company first Special Warfare, Fort Bragg, North Carolina.** One guard examined my dog tags and dropped them in a plastic bag along with my Florida driver's license. Another asked me to sign for it.

After the preliminaries were settled, a relaxed guard escorted me through the jail to my assigned cell. By now it must have been obvious that I posed no threat, and the guard treated me like a guest as he gave me a walking tour. There were prisoners mopping and moping about. More big doors, lots of prisoners, and loud metal sounds clanged and banged throughout this place filled with unnamable smells, and lots of testosterone gone awry.

We arrived at my cell and the guard unlocked the door and opened it. He asked me to step inside. The heavy door shut behind me and locked.

"If you need anything, just ask," said the jailer, and he walked away. They were suspiciously pleasant with me.

And there was a cellmate. A nameless, faceless creature that looked at me, then looked away, feigning disinterest. He was curious, with intelligent eyes. I walked over, sat on my bunk, and initiated contact.

"Hello," I said.

"What's up, man?" he asked.

I looked around the cell.

"What are you in for?" he asked, as if he didn't know. He looked at my hands. It seemed that everyone who met me since the fight automatically looked at my hands. As if they were magic. The skin was scratched and marked all to hell, as though I had tangled with an angry tomcat. The abrasions and cuts came from all the thorns, vines, and just living in the wilderness for two weeks during Phase-3. One can often surmise that a soldier has just returned from the field by such tell-tale marks.

I didn't answer his question.

"Hey man, I am only making conversation. What are you in for?" he asked again in a Northern accent. His manners were pushy in a way that Southerners often find rude, even when they are soldiers.

"Murder," I answered in a soft tone, almost a whisper.

I figured he was a policeman or at least a snitch. He small talked around for awhile, clearly trying to draw me out. I wasn't much for conversation, so I just listened and finally there was silence.

Eventually, I asked a few questions about the jail. "How many inmates are here?" "When are visiting hours?" "Is there a gym or a track?"

He used any opening to try to inconspicuously lead the conversation over to my charges. He wanted to hear about the fight that he admitted having heard about on the news.

"So what happened?" he asked.

"I am not going to talk about it," I replied more forcefully, making strong eye contact.

"Okay," he said, "I understand man. You're right, too, you gotta be

careful who ya trust in here," he continued, "So where're you from any-
ways? You got an accent from down South, yeah?" and he kept trying to lead
me back to the fight.

"Listen," I said with finality, "I am not going to talk about me, my case,
or anything other than right here, right now. Do you understand?"

"Yeah, man," in a nervous tone, showing me his palms; "I don't want no
problems, okay?" He was backing up, "I was just tryin' to make small talk."

Anybody who asked about the case who wasn't my lawyer could only do
harm. I probably didn't know the term "snitch" at the time, but I knew
instinctively that he was the enemy.

A snitch is another prisoner who will pass on information about you, or
even testify against you later at trial, in order to gain favors, which some-
times even include being released from prison. Snitches would hardly seem
trustworthy witnesses, given that many of them are already felons, and that
they can get their own sentences reduced by concocting stories, but they are
used frequently in our criminal justice system.

Heaven forbid that you should ever be imprisoned, but if it should hap-
pen, do *not* tell your cellmate your story. There is already "evidence" against
you, otherwise you would not be there. You are the accused. And since you
have asked for an attorney, you are almost certainly guilty in their eyes. But,
then again, they already "knew" that you were guilty or you would not be
accused. At this point, the police are *not looking for evidence to clear you,
but to convict you.*

There is no expectation of privacy in police cars, or police stations. Their
phones are usually tapped, and listening devices are often installed in rooms.
A basic rule for handling POWs is to separate them so that they cannot con-
coct a story. If your captors are allowing you to talk, either they are incom-
petent, or they are up to something. *Never assume that the enemy is
incompetent.* Smugness will cost dearly.

My cellmate with the intelligent eyes was either a snitch, or a cop. There
was no doubt of it in my mind. That night when the lights went out, I slept
lightly, wary of him. I did not think that he posed a direct physical threat,
but I didn't even want to talk in my sleep with him around.

When I did fall asleep I had dreams of prison or the electric chair, and
whatever it was shocked me awake. I still had dreams from childhood that
shocked me awake; now there would be more. Whatever I dreamed about,
maybe it was the fight and all those police with guns, or the dead man's
angry face staring at me cold from the morgue, waiting for me, I don't know,
but the hands reaching out from the ether left me turning fitfully in bed.

My life seemed like the cruel joke of some angry or crazy God who was
trying to confuse me. Each time he would give me just enough room to get
marching in the right direction, then spring a trap. A lion trap. But the trap

would be just less than powerful enough to kill me. Yes, this God was cruel, I thought. He wanted to see suffering, moaning and fighting down in the pit. Maybe he was trying to make a lion. Or maybe he was trying to break a lion cub, to tame it like a house cat, before it matured.

There was no food or water in this cage. Others brought the food. If you got sick, you would have to take what treatment was offered you. In case of fire, you must wait for others to open your doors, or you will face the flames, alone. If you die in the hole in the dark wilderness, nobody will come looking, nobody will care; they will simply heap the dirt on your body, wipe their hands and the sweat from their foreheads and move on. Forgotten before supper.

All that hard and dangerous training was for naught. My college money, and the $5,000 bonus would be gobbled up the moment an attorney walked through the door, if the Army didn't swallow it first. But that was trivial. What's money at a time like this? What woman would ever marry me if I was convicted and sent to prison? I might as well have a foot growing out of my head. I would die a lonely old man, or an accused young one. If I got out of this alive, I would never look at the world the same again.

FELONY SELF-DEFENSE

DURING THE SUMMER of my fourteenth year, I got a job clearing beaches and building docks around the lakes. In Florida, white sandy beaches next to a lake are not natural. The freshwater beaches must be constantly maintained or nature will reclaim what is hers. The edges of lakes that are not cleared are more akin to a jungle, with thick vegetation.

Thanks to innumerable depictions of white, sandy beaches and Mickey Mouse advertisements, there is a common misconception that alligators are endangered, or even rare, as if Florida were one big theme park. Let's lay that misconception to rest. While Florida is a great place to live and vacation, gators reproduce readily, in quantity, and are found in great abundance throughout the state. Official estimates say there are more than a million gators in Florida, and I met lots of them. (I'm not talking about the football team.) The largest that I have seen appeared to be about fourteen feet long. There is nothing on which to base this estimate except my judgment; gators that large are not safe to approach with a tape measure.

I had seen one nearly devour our family dog, Schultz, who later had simply disappeared, and I suspect that he was eaten by a particular gator that was about six feet long. One problem with the people-gator relationship is that many people like to feed the gators, which is illegal. Gators are *great* hunters, and don't need help finding food, but when people feed them, gators lose their fear of humans, and this leads to dogs being eaten, and people being killed. I once encountered an old man feeding a gator from a dock. He was tossing in marshmallows and the black beast was gobbling them down.

"Why are you feeding that thing?" I asked. "I swim in this lake!"

The old man just chuckled, kept tossing marshmallows, and answered, "I know which gators I feed, and I know to watch out for them. Go swim somewhere else."

Well, nobody else knows which gators he feeds! And fifty years after the man is dead and buried, those gators may still be prowling around the lake, waiting for some kid to venture too close.

I saw gators practically every day. They looked frightening and occasionally, though not often, killed people. Children are the most vulnerable targets of the giant water lizards. To be devoured by a gator seems infinitely more frightening than to be killed in, say, a car crash. Maybe it's because gators are so ugly, or because they lunge from the water, and that part of being killed by a gator involves drowning. Personally, I would rather be killed by a lion than a gator, but that's just a matter of taste.

There I was, with my brother and our Boss, clearing out weeds for some rich people on the edge of the gator-infested Lake Hamilton, keenly aware of the danger present. When I say gator-infested, I mean that there were at *least* hundreds in Lake Hamilton, though few would be what I would call monster-gators. The place was grown over like a crocodile scene in a Tarzan movie. There was also an abundance of turtles and snakes. Since we found several snakes each day, we brought guns along for the false feeling of security they provided.

One afternoon, unknown to us, we were being stalked by a monster. We had cleared a working area in the lake that was about the size of a one-car garage, and had piled the water-weeds on the shore. The black gator was slowly moving in, the way I had seen them do many times as they stalked their prey.

Alligators are very powerful. A swat from a gator's tail can break a man's leg. Yet they stalk effortlessly, and with the grace of a housecat. They are masters of stealth and surprise. Even a monster gator can swim almost imperceptibly on the surface, barely rippling water. When it is close, it silently slips below the surface, leaving tiny ripples like those of a few raindrops hitting the surface as its eyes and nose submerge. When stalking, the gator is patient, slow, and silent. It slips in like a submarine, a black beast invisible in black water.

There were three of us working: the Boss, Billy, and I, and one of us was the intended victim of a gator that weighed hundreds of pounds and was over twelve feet long. Its leathery-looking back was hard as rock. They say that you can put a gator to sleep by rubbing its belly, but that's a difficult trick if the gator is planning to put you to sleep by crushing your bones and filling your lungs with water. (And gators don't really go to sleep; they pass out and will die if left in that position.)

This stalking gator had all the advantages. Its angle of approach was camouflaged with thick weeds, and we were working hard in the hot sun while watching mostly for snakes, not gators, which usually leave people alone—this being a noteworthy exception. Billy and the Boss were in waist-deep water working about ten yards apart from each other. I was about twenty yards away from the Boss and surrounded by weeds; Billy was between us. The scene looked like this:

Swimming, pulling cattails here:
```
xxxxxxxxxxxxxxxxxxxxxxxxxxxxxxxxxx
xxxxxxxxxxxxxxxxxxxxxxxxxxxxxxxxxxxxx
```
↑
Giant Gator?
Me—↕10yds—Billy—10yds—Boss—10yds—Dock
↓
SHORE

I had been swimming out into water that was above my head and diving down to the base of the weeds, maybe six feet down, pulling the cattails out by the roots, one by one. I found the base of the cattails by feel, keeping my eyes closed, because after only a few minutes of work, the otherwise clear water was silted to zero visibility. At the base of the cattail, I planted my feet on the bottom of the lake and pulled up the root. Some came easily while others seemed stuck in concrete. After pulling one out, if I had enough breath, I would feel for another and try to get it before surfacing. It was hard work, and marginally similar to pearl diving, though considerably less exotic.

Green, uprooted cattails floated on the surface with their white roots and little bunches of pink snail eggs attached to their sides. When I had gathered enough, I would swim to shore, pushing them in front of me, and throw them on the heap.

The Boss was about thirty years old and was the gator's target; he drew the unlucky lottery ticket in one of life's biggest games: survival. A violent, frenzied, bone-crushing finale was unfolding. When a gator grabs large prey, it seizes it in its jaws, and often violently spins underwater, drowning it.

The Boss waded a few yards through the weeds and murky water to fetch a rake where he had set it down only a minute earlier. The vegetation was so thick that the tools wouldn't sink into the water.

Maybe the gator had been resting on the bottom, waiting, and maybe it had surfaced to take a look because the water was so murky.

As the Boss grasped the rake, he spotted the twelve-foot gator, only a foot from his hand.

He froze.

Eye to eye with death.

Just him and the gator. If the gator lunged. . . .

The Boss was standing in waist-deep water, so it was not possible to easily run away, and besides, at that range, even on land the gator would have him.

Billy and I were still oblivious. Even so, by the time we could get to the guns—and if we could manage to kill the gator without shooting the Boss—it would probably be too late.

The Boss backed up a couple of steps, then *screamed* as if he were being eaten alive. A man's scream evokes a special chill, and I will never forget the sound the Boss made that day.

He skirted the gator, and began plowing through the water as fast as he could toward the shore. But gators are incredibly fast and agile in the water. To the Boss, the water must have felt thicker than jello, like he was in a nightmare and could not run fast enough because his legs would not work, as it slowed his escape and he screamed so horribly.

I was swimming in with a load of cattails when he screamed. I didn't

Grandmother Eason holding baby Callie, my mother.

Mom was "just" a Great Mother.

William A. Yon

The wedding.

First birthday with Billy.

Mom, Billy and me waiting for the Apollo 11 launch.

One of our many fishing excursions.

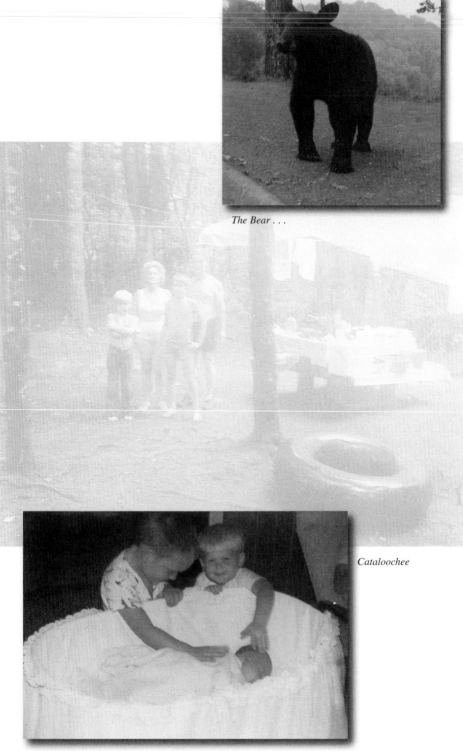

The Bear . . .

Cataloochee

Baby Susan arrives. She was fantastic!

Billy feeds Susan, while I stand guard with rifle and pistol.

The Yon Family

Susan at The Great Sidewalk.

Susan choking.

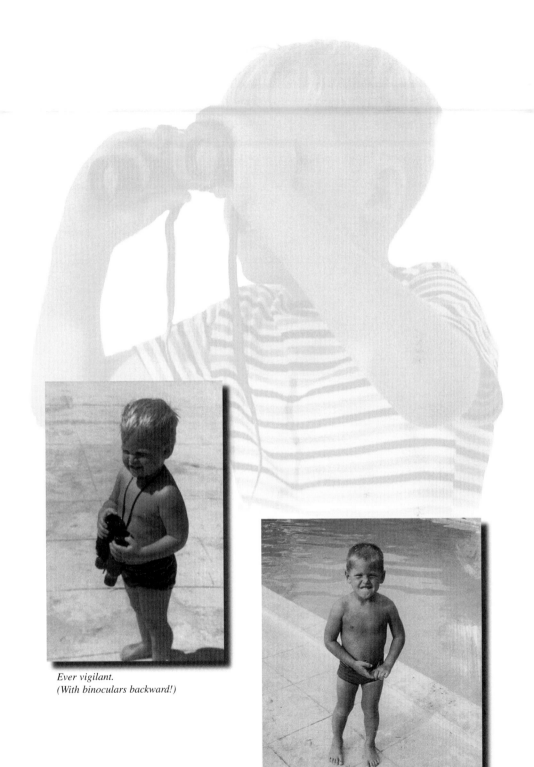

Ever vigilant.
(With binoculars backward!)

Tadpole training was rigorous.

"Let me tell you about Godzilla women . . ."

Early combat training.

Ethel and Phillip Eason

True love really exists. I know because my grandparents said so.

THE FIGHT against birth defects is for everyone—not just the mothers. And while mother is out marching, daddy is probably going to be in the kitchen. William A. Yon, whose wife has served as Area Captain in the Northwest Section for the past three years, is more than willing to do his part, and get help from his children, Billy, seven, Michael, five, and three-year-old Susan.

Mom was adventurous. She enjoyed scuba diving and alarmed family and friends when she announced her desire to parachute!

Early astronaut training.

The "Dark Years," clinging to sports and books.

Getting stronger in the 10th grade, with help from Mr. Cuddie. (Lifting 205 pounds.)

Jim Cuddie—NO NONSENSE, a demanding coach.

Mike Yon, a sophomore at Winter Haven High School, lifts 250 pounds. Yon has been lifting under the supervision of Cuddie and competes in the 132 pound weight class in the AAU.

(The actual weight in the picture is 225 pounds, not 250. Reprinted with permission of Winter Haven News Chief.)

15 years old, 117 pounds.

15 years old, 133 pounds.

Mike Yon is the 17-year-old manager of The Gym of Winter Haven Inc. He has been lifting for three years.

(Reprinted with permission of Lakeland Ledger.*)*

With friends John Harrison and Al E. Gator.
We released Al after the picture was taken.

Richard White

With brother Billy and the tail from the stalking gator.

Just do it?
Just did it!

A winning team:
Susan and Misty
bring home a prize.

Misty, the horse I rode to school.

Steve Shaulis

Mike Yon

BASIC TRAINING

1 PLT 8 CO 7 BN
INF TNG BRIGADE
AUG-82 FT BENNING GA

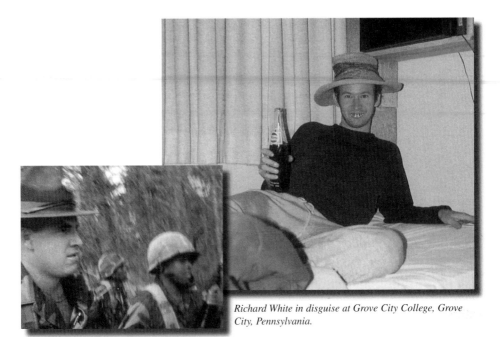

Richard White in disguise at Grove City College, Grove City, Pennsylvania.

Sergeant Wood during road march.

My second accident with an army truck. The sergeants got really upset that time.

Parachuting in Zephyrhills, Florida, with Richard.

Jumper exits C-130 at Fort Bragg, NC.

Snapshot while floating down.

Jumpers entangled. Neither was injured, but they loved the picture!

Special Forces training.

Lots of character is built at Fort Bragg—and many characters are humbled.

Training, training, training. . . .

"Silenced" weapons.

Enemy anti-armor weapons.

Phase-2 training.

Top: *Enemy assault weapon.*
Bottom: *Friendly assault weapon.*

Another enemy weapon.

'You don't kill someone over a haircut'

By JAMES LILEJEFORS

Self portrait. A photo Charles Scott took of himself shortly before his death in Ocean City.

Steve Shaulis one day before the murder charge.

Surviving one day at a time.

San Francisco as seen from DLI. (With black
and white infrared film.)

The day after the accident in California, peering
over the edge at Yosemite.

Canada

North to Yellowknife.

In the team room at Fort Devens, Massachusetts.

Mike, winter warfare.

Climbing near Conway, New Hampshire.

Communications specialist Bob Wallace constructing a boobytrap.

Demolitions specialist, Ray Shadel with a boobytrap.

Medical training.

A-team practicing infiltration. (Gerald Trainer, facing.)

Granddad sends a picture from home.

ODA-052. Winter warfare training, Utah.

I *said* don't shoot! It's already dead."

...ger relaxed and I raised my cheek from the shotgun, keeping it ...my shoulder. It looked dead. Kind of.

...red the shotgun and uncocked the trigger, and Billy did the same

...oss was afraid to get back in the water. So was I, and I wasn't going ...work until I *knew* it was dead. Gators are very resilient. Billy pro-...at he wade out into the water and hit it with a rake to make sure it ...d, while I covered him with the gun. After he confirmed that it was ...e would pull it to shore by the tail. However, because of the angle I ...ot cover Billy from the dock. He would be in the line of fire. I would ...go with him in the water, and cover him with the over and under, ...had two shots (though, in retrospect, the 12 gauge would have been ...r choice). The Boss did not try to stop us, and still seemed dazed by ...se encounter with the giant reptile.

...e-handles are pretty short, so Billy would have to get close. He knew ...was a good shot, but he was afraid that I would flinch and miss, or ...y freeze if there were more drama. So was I. And though the word ...gun" carries with it the suggestion of overwhelming, deadly power, an ...wise powerful weapon can feel like a BB gun in your hands at ...ents like this.

...e fear was present in Billy's voice when he said, "Make sure you shoot ...makes a move."

...Okay," I said.

...trained the shotgun on the gator, aiming at its eye. As security, I moved ...into position first—perfect military procedure—not bad for a couple of ...agers, but through no design—it just seemed appropriate. I kept the ...tgun pointed at its eye as I stepped through the water, praying that I ...uld not trip and drop the gun. I was about fifteen feet away, easy striking ...tance from me to the gator and from the gator to me. Billy moved in, ...med with only a rake.

"Are you ready Michael?" he asked from beside me.

"Yeah," I said.

"Be careful," the Boss offered from the dock.

Billy kept his eye on the gator.

Billy reached out and hit the beast on the head with the rake and it ...nstantly sprang to life. It jerked its head violently to the side, splashing ...water everywhere, and made a frighteningly loud hiss, mouth wide open, ...displaying lots of teeth. Billy was on his way out of the water at record speed.

"Bam!" I fired the shotgun, then clicked to the rifle, ***"pow!"*** Both ...seemed hits.

252

Glenn Watson did three tours in Vietnam, was picked for the second rescue attempt in Iran and, finally (perhaps his most challenging assignment), taught me to drive.

Bad Toelz, Germany.

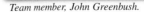
Team member, John Greenbush.

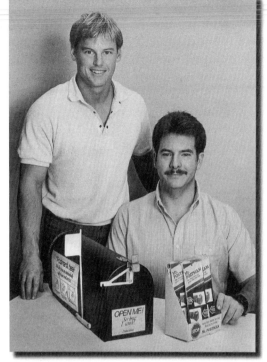

Back home after five years in the Army. During college, John Harrison and I started our first business. (We did very well until we lost all our money!)

Second business in Poland.

know what he was screaming about, but wha
Maybe he had stumbled across a big cottonm
never seen him panic over a snake.

I gulped some air, closed my eyes, and
swimming to the shallow water where I stood a
and weeds to shore. I crashed through the "jung
ing my arms and body.

Meanwhile, the Boss had actually made it
screaming *"Gator! Gator! Gator! Gator!"*

I made it to a shotgun and dashed out onto th
beast. Billy had made it to shore, too, and stood rig
over the water and weeds where we had just been.

And there it was.

"It's *huge!*" I said to Billy, my voice quivering.
Adrenaline was in my veins and I was moving in fo

Billy had his combination over and under 20 gau
had a 12 gauge single shot. I opened the breach and
that was loaded for snakes, and loaded a rifled slug. I
cocked the trigger with my thumb.

I pulled the shotgun to my shoulder and took a bea
yards away.

Killing a gator was a felony, for they were still cons
What a joke, I thought. They were about as endangered a
working illegally for the Boss who was the only adult in
think about the law. I was fourteen, what did I know abou

The Boss said, *"Don't shoot! Don't shoot!"*

Billy was aiming, too, but we both hesitated at the Boss
We still had work to do, so we had to get back in the wa
seemed rather limited. The Boss could forbid us to kill it, an
new jobs. Or we could kill it and go back to work.

I looked over at Billy, then reacquired the bead and squee

Whamm! There was a sharp pain as the 12 gauge stock witho
slammed into my bare shoulder. Billy fired his two shots, w
high into the air like a geyser.

"Stop shooting!" the Boss screamed.

I was sure that I'd hit it, but when I'd fired, the monster had
below the surface just before Billy shot. Billy and I reloaded a
Finally, it surfaced again, and I took a bead.

"Stop shooting!" yelled the Boss. "People will hear. Do you
to jail? I don't! Stop shooting."

I was looking straight over the barrel and my bead was on the ga
and my finger was squeezing and about to launch another slug.

"Mike
My fin
ready on
I lowe
with his.
The B
back to
posed th
was dea
dead, w
could n
have to
since i
a bette
his clo
Rak
that I
simpl
"shot
other
mom
T
if it
"
I
out
teen
sho
wo
dis
ar

I retreated so fast that I nearly ran out of my skin.

A few minutes later, the wounded gator tried to swim under the dock. I gave Billy's gun back and grabbed the 12 gauge, and, putting the barrel of the shotgun a couple of feet from the top of its head, I squeezed the trigger *Ka-whamm!* Water splashed up all over the dock and drenched me. The blast left a hole about the size of a silver dollar behind and between its eyes. Game over. This time it was the gator that drew the short straw.

It took all three of us to drag it onshore. As close as we could measure, it was 12'3" long. We axed off its tail and took it to our grandparents' house.

Granny nearly had a fit. "Why, for heaven's sake, did you shoot that gator?" she asked us.

"Self-defense, Granny!" Billy answered.

We skinned the tail, and she cooked some that night. She put the rest in the deep freeze, with all the turtles and fish, out in the utility room next to the Mason jars filled with squash, green beans, black-eyed peas and all the rest.

My next serious "gator encounter" happened at night with Richard White.

SURF-N-SUDS

STEVE SHAULIS WAS still in Ocean City staying with a friend. It had been less than twenty-four hours since the fight, and it was now Saturday night. While I shared the cell with a snitch, Steve had returned to the night-club. That sounded a little crass when he first told me, but when I thought about it, it seemed a natural thing to do.

Steve said that the Surf-n-Suds was packed, and that the only topics of discussion were The Fight and The Green Beret. He said the band was cracking jokes: *"People are dying to get in here."* Apparently, the action had left the crowd in an excited mood. I wonder if the bouncers had learned as big a lesson as I had. Maybe the next time someone asked for help and kept coming back, they would pay attention and do their jobs.

That night, the moon made its normal circle while I sat in jail. It seemed almost unimaginable that a week ago I was creeping through the wilderness with the guerrillas and my team, preparing to hit a target. It might as well have been a thousand years ago in a different universe. All that incredible effort, the risks, the reward, seemed snatched away by the hand of fate.

Sunday morning was the second day in my new world. The sun rose again over the Atlantic; people returned to the beach and frolicked in the hot sand, splashing in the waters from which we supposedly came. Maybe some kid had found my Gilligan hat in the trash and thought he hit the lottery. By now, the balloon I had released might be hundreds of miles away, caught in the branches of a tree, or maybe floating over the Atlantic.

For me, there was the jailhouse breakfast. After that, at regular times we were released to exercise or to watch TV. There were monstrous prisoners— huge criminals, real murderers and rapists.

It's an eerie feeling being locked in a cage with dangerous criminals. It's sort of like swimming out into an alligator-infested lake at night. You don't know what to expect, and likely you will not see it coming. The rules are those described by Darwin: *survival of the fittest.* And the luckiest.

In the TV room, the inmates avoided eye contact with me. When I looked around they looked away, but I had the distinct feeling that all were watch-ing me as they talked quietly among themselves. It felt like eyes were watch-ing me from the dark. They could see me, but each time I looked around, they disappeared.

It was a human zoo. Many of those who surrounded me functioned on a different level: a more basic, animalistic level, stripped of most normal man-ners and considerations. The wrong kind of eye contact could lead to vio-lence. A big man approached in the chow hall and asked what happened.

I looked him in the eyes, and said, "I don't want to talk about it."

He said, "Okay buddy," and left.

I was extremely alert, and wary that someone would test me. But the prisoners had seen the news and seemed afraid. The press liked the story because it had two special twists. First, there was a man killed with punches. Second, a "Green Beret" did it. I was lucky to have the fear generated by the story working for me; some of the prisoners were twice my size, and only time would tell whether one or more of them would test my media-manufactured reputation.

There were chairs in the TV room. I sat down in front of the screen. The inmates were watching corny morning talk shows. Then there were shows like *Green Acres*, which were fine by me. I used to watch that and *Gilligan's Island* all the time. I liked Mary Ann more than Ginger. I could never bring Ginger home to Granny.

Later, back in the cell, my curious cellmate said that I had taken the chair of King Kong, the biggest, meanest animal around. He was the alpha-prisoner. The cellmate warned me that nobody dared sit in King Kong's seat, and that they were all wondering what was going to happen. I did get some strange looks when I sat down, but nothing came of it and King Kong never mentioned it.

Within forty-eight hours, Dad had rushed up from Florida to help. I always knew that he wanted to be a good father, for what that was worth, and he was with me in my time of need. Though good intentions, or at least words suggesting good intentions, don't mean much to a kid who suffered for a decade.

He asked for power-of-attorney to help with my case. With that sweeping power-of-attorney, he could do anything on my behalf, from signing checks to buying cars, or whatever. I granted him this power-of-attorney, and, by the time it was over, he had quietly stolen the five-thousand-dollar bonus that I had invested toward college. I would never see it again. He had liquidated my investment and taken the money. He managed to hide the theft for about a year.

If he needed it that badly, I would have given it to him. It was very strange. For a time after this, I was very angry and embarrassed, though I was the only one who knew besides him. Finally, I forgot about him. I held no grudge but, as far as I was concerned, he'd died. I still wish, though, that I had known my true father, the man people said he was before my mother's death.

This was the long road to college. There were dangerous hairpin curves, bone-jarring potholes in the dark, police lights, guns, bad guys, cages, and lots more to come. On nights when I might have been delivering pizzas, I was jumping from airplanes, riding in helicopters, or creeping up on targets.

On days that I would have been in college classes, I was in Army classes. On my convoluted path to school, there were some parts of the journey that, once begun, there was no way to simply step off.

FREEDOM FIGHTERS

THERE WAS NO money to hire an attorney of the kind I needed, and there was no rich relative to step in and rescue me. Fortunately, Steve Shaulis' father was an attorney. He did not normally work with this sort of case, but he saw that I was in dangerous waters. He saw that saving me from smashing onto the rocks would require the skills of a serious criminal defense lawyer. I was literally facing the possibility of spending my life, or at least much of my productive life, in prison.

The criminal defense lawyers who stand before judges and juries and wage verbal combat for human lives are the elite of the legal world. They are, in fact, its warriors. As the famous Wyoming attorney, Gerry Spence, likes to point out, when human life is at stake—it *is* war.

It does us no good to maintain a stock of military warriors to fight for our well-being abroad if we do not have a good stock of lawyer warriors to lead our never-ending fight for freedom here.

After seeing the image flash across the screen of a handcuffed suspect who is charged with some hideous crime, it is easy for us to cry out: "To hell with a trial, get on with the hanging!" And some reporters, ever searching for their shocking stories, canvass the accused citizen's neighborhood knocking on doors for sound bites. We hear things like, "But he was such a quiet man. He never caused any trouble." Our jaded ears, burdened by years of hearing of crime, translate those words into something like: "He's just like all the rest," and too often we conclude: Case closed. Away with him.

There are believers in justice, however. Through a chain of calls, a lawyer named Daniel Long agreed to at least listen to my side. Steve Shaulis' father told me that Mr. Long was coming down to the jail. Mr. Long was a state representative, and was said to be a formidable attorney. When I got word that this man, himself a member of the government, was willing to listen to me, it felt like Christmas and my birthday wrapped into one.

There I was, poor as a scarecrow, and, worse yet, a feared Green Beret (though then clad in prison orange). Yet a man stepped out who had never met me but was still willing to listen. What could he gain other than knowing that he was serving justice? Likely, if he sided with me, *the accused,* he would be seen as another of those oily-tongued, liberal-minded lawyers who help criminals evade their due punishment by invoking silly technicalities.

I was labeled the "bad guy" in this case, and it is not good politics to risk siding with the bad guy, even if the cause is just and the label is wrong. There was the inherent conflict of interest between justice and politics, and

257

Daniel Long was a politician, so there was more at stake than his time.

I didn't know what to expect, and my first impulse was to keep my mouth shut even though he was an attorney. Which was a mistake; a client should tell his attorney what he or she needs to know (though I realized that I was not yet his client; he'd only come to listen). When we sat down to talk through the thick glass, he asked about my treatment, which I said had been good, and he asked if I needed anything. *I need a good lawyer*, I thought. But this was no time for levity, even if it was to keep my spirits high.

When Mr. Long got down to business, I could tell that he was intensely serious. His initial question was something like: "What did you tell the police?"

That was easy. "Nothing," I said, "except my name and military unit," which, under the circumstances, was equivalent to my address. Mr. Long was pleased with that, and I was pleased that he was pleased. He began with other questions. I was already having a hard time remembering even simple details. For instance, "What kind of beer were you drinking?"

That was difficult to remember, not because I was drunk, but probably because more vivid impressions cluttered my memory, and I had no brand loyalty. It is easy for perfectly innocent people to contradict themselves. Actually, it's difficult not to do, but when people contradict themselves, it looks like they are manufacturing a story. Which, actually, they are. That's how our minds work. Our memories are dynamic and plastic. As it happens, some of my earliest memories, ones that I could check, have turned out to be remarkably accurate, whereas I've discovered that other memories that are more recent can sometimes be far off the mark. The edges get worn, details are forgotten or smoothed over, and retrospect tells its own story.

But there was a murder charge looming. Twenty-five years to life. The little details were important. Unfortunately, just because many years of one's life are on the line doesn't mean that one will remember better. Mr. Long asked about the details of the fight, which even by then were blurry because of the speed at which the events unfolded, and my adrenaline-induced haze. A great deal had happened in a short time.

If you walk through a crowd of people at the movie theater, after the show you may not remember a single face, unless someone specifically stands out, and even then you will likely remember little more than a general impression. What type of shoes was that person wearing? For that matter, what color shirt did *you* wear yesterday? During your first conversation yesterday, what did you specifically hear and say? Your adrenaline probably was not pumping, but even with that advantage, you likely will not remember many of those occurrences distinctly.

You don't know in advance that you will need to remember these things on penalty of your life. Highly stressful situations usually catch one completely off-guard.

I do know that many of the witnesses' statements coincided with my memory. Each witness' perspective was different; however, they made not a single statement against me. In fact, they provided abundant corroboration of the account of the night's events that I would ultimately give.

Finally, Mr. Long had learned what he needed to know, although I had not mentioned that I had gone into disguise. For some reason, I was embarrassed to tell the whole story.

Mr. Long was reassuring and said things were looking good, which eased my anxiety greatly, but I was still charged with murder, and still in jail. Mr. Long strongly warned me not to talk with anyone about myself or my case, whether in jail, on the phone, anywhere or anytime. He said goodbye, and a guard took me back inside the zoo.

Knowing that a good attorney was now in my corner gave a tremendous boost to my morale. He knew that I was poor. Realistically speaking, I couldn't pay him anything more than the $5,000 that was not yet stolen. Mr. Long took the case, but I had failed to mention the details of my evasion, and it left me with an uneasy feeling that I had not laid all my cards on the table, though the omissions seemed insignificant when compared to what I was facing.

Many innocent people go to prison regardless of the facts. A *USA Today* article in November, 1998, stated: "Since the Supreme Court reinstated the death penalty in 1976, there have been 486 executions. During that same period, there are 75 known cases of people wrongfully convicted and sentenced to death."

The well-written article by Kevin Davis goes on to say that one man spent eighteen years on Death Row before being cleared, and that factors leading to false convictions "include faulty eyewitness recollections, perjured testimony from jailhouse snitches and false confessions made under duress. . . ."

Mine was not a death penalty case, but if such an incredibly high number of people are falsely convicted and sentenced to death, one can only imagine how many are convicted of lesser crimes and suffer decades in prison.

At the county jail, besides those who might be wrongly imprisoned, there certainly were *real* criminals all around. Big criminals. Black guys, white guys, Mexicans. The place looked like a tattoo parlor, and there were many ominous tattoos. Lots of savage-type people. *What if they gang up on me? What if the dead man has friends or family in here who want revenge?* He had seemed like the criminal type. His friends might've been all around me. *I don't know who they are. They can ambush and kill me.*

The clangs and rumbling thuds of weighty, metal doors echoed all about, and the voices of prisoners talking about whores and drugs and violence and other jails completed the atmosphere. There were more muscles in the place than in any gym I had ever seen. It looked like a professional football team had been incarcerated. And then there were the skinny drug-freaks, and the middle-aged men who looked like they were in for drunk driving or for not paying child support. Many people spend time in county jails for offenses like driving on a suspended license.

The prisoners talked about judges and lawyers. They talked and talked and talked and talked. ***Shut the hell up!*** I wanted to scream.

But I was getting more education by the hour than I got by the month in high school. Within forty-eight hours I knew, or at least had heard, which jails had the best food, where the jailers were lax, where they were "dicks," and where the air-conditioners worked and didn't work.

They talked about the law—and "experts" were everywhere. It was like law school, only from the working end. They complained about the illegal things the cops did, or how their lawyers didn't give a shit, or how they got ripped off by some lawyer. Some prisoners were truly in the trenches of society, and their lives sounded like one long siege, a running battle that went on endlessly. Jail was literally part of their rite of passage, along with the crimes they'd committed. Some knew that society had hated them since the day they were born, so they must have decided to return the favor by hating and abusing society until the day they died.

As for my education, for the time I spent in jail I might have earned one college credit hour in pre-law (working end), one in sociology, one in criminal behavior—and might have been able to toss in a few credits for psychology. Sometimes education gets dumped over your head like a bucket of cold water.

The prisoners seemed to know everything about the judges, too. To prisoners, the judges are next to God. A criminal who, on the street, may be the meanest, vilest and most contemptible thug around, who may beat his whores and steal drugs from his illegitimate kids and slit your throat for the watch on your wrist, when it comes to the judge, is humble. Or he is a fool. The judge doesn't own your soul, but when you are a prisoner, he or she does own your body.

A silly thought came to mind as I sat there. I knew that it was silly, but at least it was something to chew on. I imagined an assault force from Fort Bragg would swoop down in a wave of helicopters at about 0300 when all were asleep, blast through the walls, neutralize any resistance, blast the door off my cell, and fly me to liberty.

I had been thinking about escape off and on since the moment I had turned myself in. Not because I actually planned to do it, but because it was the military thing to think about. After all, the Army compelled me to memorize the Code of Conduct.

Article III

If I am captured I will continue to resist by all means available. I will make every effort to escape and aid others to escape. I will accept neither parole nor special favors from the enemy.

Well, I wasn't going to help a bunch of prisoners of this type to escape, but it gave me more food for thought.

Article VI

I will never forget that I am an American fighting man, responsible for my actions, and dedicated to the principles that made my country free. I will trust in my God and in the United States of America.

My gut churned.

By Tuesday morning, my fourth day in jail, the investigation was going full blast. An officer went to the dead man's last employer, the Tijuana Junction Restaurant, located at 7 Caroline Street, Ocean City, Maryland.

The owner, Mr. Terry Boyd, forty-five, described the assailant to the investigator as a trouble maker, a difficult person to get along with, and as being very volatile . . . Mr. Scott was pretty loaded the night of the incident . . .

The day of the incident Mr. Boyd said that Mr. Scott was with a couple of friends and he had heard that his friends had previously gotten Mr. Scott out of a couple of fights . . . he believed that Mr. Scott was upset . . . because of a phone conversation with his sister. . . . Mr. Boyd stated that Mr. Scott didn't have any close friends that he knew of but he did hang around with his brother. . . .

The policeman then took statements from employees. Susan Stewart, thirty-three, said Mr. Scott had come into the restaurant one day and "begged" for work until she'd hired him.

Two days after Mr. Scott was employed . . . he became very hostile towards the other employees. Mr. Scott's personality was described . . . as being, "very antagonistic towards employees, always hyper, and that of being a menace."

[Scott was] very offensive, the type of person who was difficult to explain (things) to, and, lastly she said underneath his outward appearance that he was a "sad" person.

The day of the incident Ms. Stewart said that Mr. Scott was throwing equipment and other objects around in the kitchen . . . By 3:00 p.m. Ms. Stewart asked Mr. Scott to leave because of the way he was behaving.

Later that day Mr. Scott returned for his check. All throughout that day . . . Scott was agitated and was taking orders slowly.

Ms. Stewart said Mr. Scott constantly picked on people but never really threatened them. . . .

Another employee, Erica Fath, eighteen, when asked about Mr. Scott's attitude and personality, replied that he would act differently at different times.

She said that he could be friendly but most of the time was very temperamental and "took stuff the wrong way." He was very "defensive," and didn't get along with anybody and couldn't take care of himself.

[He] acted like he was going to throw things at me . . . he scared me. The day of the incident . . . [he] appeared to be uptight . . . [and] was with 3-4 friends . . .

Ms. Fath believed that Mr. Scott was going to be fired the next day.

Another employee, William Haskins, forty-one, said that Mr. Scott was difficult to get along with . . . [He] liked to run the show . . . [Haskins] only knew Mr. Scott for 1 week.

While the police and others had an opportunity to investigate the facts, back at the jail they shackled me to a bunch of inmates and drove us from the county jail to the courthouse.

I was unaware of the details of the investigation, and was trying to ease my mind by thinking of all this as just a training exercise. Strangely, when it's training you try to pretend that it's real, and now I was trying to pretend my new reality was training.

They brought me before the judge. I was standing in front of a man through whose words flowed the authority and incredible collective power of the citizens of Maryland, awaiting my first judgment. I looked up at the man who was sitting up high. *Very* high. The judge looked down at me and spoke with authority. I listened quietly.

Legally speaking, I was in it alone until Mr. Long, who was there beside me, stepped in and said something.

Mr. Long had seen that I was overcharged. *Assault with intent to commit murder?* How, especially with all of the witnesses, could anyone justify that? According to attorneys that I've consulted, people are often overcharged. But when those criminal charges are piled on your head, it's natural to become afraid, and some people crack, start talking, and admit, though innocent, to a lesser crime because they fear the more serious charge.

As for the *second degree murder*, again, Mr. Long asserted, that the charge was not supported by the evidence.

The courtroom was filled with other prisoners who were awaiting their own solemn words from the judge. This was only a hearing, not a trial, but it was serious business. Each prisoner would go and stand before the judge, who would make decisions about each case. In the courtroom there were lawyers with their clients, and some family members of prisoners, like my former father, sitting on the pew-like benches, alongside some others who seemed to be gawkers, or reporters. The atmosphere was somber and serious, like that of a Catholic church service.

But this was a Maryland judge looking down at me, a soldier from a different state, who, upon my first day in Maryland, had been in a fight and caused a man to die. The judge knew that I would leave Maryland if he released me. If he opened the door, I could slip through the fingers of justice and be gone. I assumed he would just keep me in jail until the trial.

I felt sick, and my stomach was wrenching tight, his words were oozing out so slowly. The judge barely acknowledged my presence in his courtroom—*just tell me!*—I wanted to scream, but remained silent.

What if he doesn't like soldiers?

He peered down at me over his glasses and rendered his judgment. He dismissed the charge of assault with intent to murder. As for the accusation of second degree murder, he reduced that to *involuntary manslaughter.*

He kept talking, now looking down at his papers, writing something. He reduced the bail from a half-million dollars to nothing, and released me on my own recognizance. *Wow!* He decided to release me despite knowing I would leave the state.

Obviously the judge was much more even-handed than the persons who had reflexively accused me. I was alive. Free! The gate keepers had been ordered to open the door and let me out. The fear and anger that I had felt at being charged with murder was at once replaced by a warm feeling that there really *is* justice. By now there was a stack of witness statements that

263

made it obvious the man I'd accidentally killed was menacing, and that I had repeatedly asked for help and walked away from fighting. The witnesses were solidly behind me.

Despite the manslaughter charge, it was a huge relief that the murder charge had been dropped. With the judge's words, the tidal wave that washed me into the jail had made a major retreat. But that still left the threat of the felony charge of involuntary manslaughter, a very serious accusation which carries a maximum sentence of ten years. The problem is, once the system has made an accusation, it is very reluctant to admit its error and simply let you walk.

A legal accusation is a two-edged sword. After the finger is pointed, both the accused *and* the accuser are under serious social pressure. The accuser will have done serious damage to his or her own credibility if the allegations cannot be proven. When citizens are accused by the state and stand trial, if the state cannot prove the case, the citizens are not found *innocent*, but *not guilty*, which still carries with it the implication that the accused was guilty, but was somehow able to avoid successful prosecution.

Mr. Long's reputation as a good lawyer was entirely deserved, and he made quick work of slowing the momentum that had been building against me. The judge's favorable ruling was reported in the local news, but not always accurately. In the following article the passages enclosed in brackets indicate errors in reporting. These particular mistakes are minor, but they go to show the many errors that creep into the news even when the reporter has no agenda other than reporting the facts.

Murder Charge Reduced

SNOW HILL—Murder charges against a 19-year-old soldier accused of killing a man in an Ocean City bar fight last Friday have been reduced to manslaughter and he has been released on personal recognizance.

Worcester County State's Attorney B. Randall Coates said he decided there was insufficient evidence to prove the second degree murder charge resort police first filed against Michael Phillip Yon of Fort Bragg, N.C., in the death of Charles William Scott, 23, of Hanover, Pa. [A different article said that he was from Maryland.]

Police said Scott was dead on arrival at Peninsula General Hospital Medical Center in Salisbury after he was carried unconscious from the Surf and Sands [Surf-n-Suds] nightclub where the two were involved in a fight. Coates said the cause of death has not yet been released by the state medical examiner's office.

A second charge of assault with intent to murder filed against Yon was also dropped. Coastes [sic] said the $500,000 bond set by a Worcester County court commissioner was reduced to personal recognizance after military authorities guaranteed his return, Coates said. No trial date had been set.

According to Coates, Yon was in Ocean City on leave [I was not on leave] at the time of the incident Friday after completing Basic Training [it was SF training] earlier in the day [it had been several days].

The errors in the article above were not important, but in other instances the mistakes were blatant and misleading. Every article about the case that I read contained errors. Also notice that the state did not say that I was wrongfully charged with second degree murder, but that there was "insufficient evidence to prove the second degree murder charge."

James Lilliefors, an accomplished writer, was so taken with the case that he was still writing about it a year later. When I was released, he wrote an article for the *Maryland Coast Dispatch* titled:

Bar death charge reduced from murder to manslaughter

Michael Phillip Yon, the 19-year-old Green Beret charged in the death of a patron at the Surf and Suds bar late Friday night, was released from the Worcester County Jail. . . .

[The] State's Attorney . . . conceded it was possible the charge would be changed once the autopsy was received in about three weeks.

. . .

According to a spokeswoman for the Fort Bragg Special Warfare Public Affairs Office, Yon, who is from Winter Haven, Fla., had been on pass with another soldier in the resort when the incident occurred. She said his classmates at Fort Bragg described him as "a friendly guy". . . .

. . .

According to police reports, Scott was knocked unconscious . . . was carried outside by a bar employee and two customers while the evening's band, Drawbridge, continued to play, and patrons danced . . .

"It was all over in about four seconds," [and] . . . "most of the people in the place didn't even know what had happened."

In fact, Scott's younger brother, who was with him that night, did not know Scott had been struck and killed . . . and later went to the city police department asking for information.

. . .

Yon fled the scene immediately after the altercation, according to a police spokesman, and an all-points bulletin was issued for his arrest.

. . .

[The State's Attorney] said at first it was feared that Scott may have died of a broken neck, and that the employee and two patrons who moved him may have contributed to the death . . . [it was determined that the] cause of death was not a broken neck.

. . . "It's also been suggested that he died of aneurysm (a blood filled expansion of a blood vessel). If he had an aneurysm, he could have died whether he was struck or not."

[The State's Attorney] stated that it is conceivable, though not likely, that the second degree murder charge would be reinstated, as well as the charge of assault with intent to murder. Yon has 30 days to request a jury trial.

"At this time we have insufficient evidence to hold him on the murder charges.". . .

Yon . . . was expected in North Carolina late Tuesday, after stopping in Annapolis to talk with his attorney, Danny Long.

. . .

After the judge's ruling, guards took me back to jail and filled out the necessary paperwork for my release. I returned their jailbird clothes, and they returned my shorts, T-shirt, and my dog tags.

From Maryland, I headed down to Fort Bragg to await a trial date. I expected to be entering the jaws of an angry Army, and a Special Forces that would say: "See what happens when you let kids go through Selection?" as they tossed me in an Army jail. Maybe I was better off in the Maryland jail.

Now, there was the state of Maryland and the United States Army and Special Forces to deal with. And the media. And my poor grandmother. She must be going crazy with worry, I thought, though I'd called her several times to say that all would be well.

Steve had waited for me to be released, and drove me back to Fort Bragg in his white Datsun pickup. Meanwhile, rumors about the original incident were growing. One rumor was that Steve and I were in uniform, sporting our green berets, cruising for "chicks" and showing off. The man was said to have knocked the beret off my head, so I killed him. The truth was that Steve and I both *avoided* uniforms, and I was generally out of mine within a half hour of getting off duty.

We were free as a summer breeze between Maryland and Fort Bragg. When we arrived, the Special Warfare School was waiting, but not as we expected.

FACING THE MUSIC,
FORT BRAGG, NORTH CAROLINA

THE WORLD IS strange and things change in an instant. It had been five days since the fight. While the wheels of justice started turning, and public outcry began in Maryland, Steve and I drove to base.

I was to report to the sergeant major and commanding officer (CO) at Charlie Company of the Special Warfare School. Surely, I thought, they would lock me up while the Army dishonorably discharged me. The Mexico option was still there, and, after having seen two jails in the last four days, it was something to think about. I was innocent, but what does that matter, *really?* Still, something inside told me to face justice and trust in the system.

I had a Secret Security clearance and had already been receiving some classified training. I couldn't keep that clearance, much less stay in the Army, if they thought that I was unfit for duty. That is, in this case, if they thought that I chose not to control my temper. The press hadn't bothered to learn the real story; they never called me—not that I would have commented—but the people at Fort Bragg would dig deep.

We young soldiers had been duly warned to avoid trouble, and I had seen what happened to the few who ran astray. They were thrown out of Special Forces. When one serves in the Armed Forces, one serves in a totalitarian regime, a machine. If the Army machine locked me up, that would be that. I would languish in an Army cage and await my trial in Maryland. I heard that treatment of prisoners at Army facilities was rough.

On the other hand, if the Army discharged me, the officials in Maryland could order me back to sit in their jail to await trial. Of course, I could have avoided all the trouble by just running away and never coming back. But that would mean I could never contact my family again, and I was unwilling to do that. I would simply face justice, I decided. I would face it as a soldier and a man.

First things first, I had to report in. I sneaked into the company area and into the barracks to my locker, dialed in the combination and pulled out my best camouflaged uniform, one of the couple that hadn't been destroyed and sewn up like Frankenstein's monster by my own hand during training, and did a quick shining of my boots. I wasn't much for ridiculously spiffy uniforms that proved how much time you wasted on unimportant details, but now wasn't the time to roll in like a dirtball, wearing shorts and a T-shirt, trailing manslaughter charges in my wake along with the bad press that was bound to follow.

I stepped out of the barracks, pulling the green beret over my bristly short hair. The green hat and the image of a super-soldier it evoked were my biggest liabilities with the public. I walked down the few stairs to the street and over to the Headquarters building (HQ). In less than a minute, I was standing in front of HQ. I took off the beret, stuck it in my left thigh pocket, took a deep breath, then walked in to see the sergeant major and the CO. Time to take my medicine.

Inside the un-air-conditioned building, a sergeant sat behind an old, green, metal Army desk. He only acknowledged my presence by clearing his throat, then looked at my uniform, at my hands, and into my eyes. He said nothing. He pointed to the sergeant major's door, which was shut.

I stepped over to the door, cleared my throat, and knocked three times in the military fashion. You learn how to knock in Basic Training. There is a certain cadence and force involved. Don't knock too hard—he will take that as a challenge to his authority: Not too light—that means you've got no guts: Not too fast—he might think you're anxious or don't know your place. I'm not sure what too slow means. I knocked just right.

Knock—*I'm not challenging your authority*

Knock—*I've got guts*

Knock—*Here goes*

A voice called from behind the door, "Enter."

I opened the door, shut it behind me, and came to the position of parade rest in front of the sergeant major's desk. With my feet shoulder width apart, my hands in the small of my back, and my eyes straight forward, I started to report in, but he cut me off, "At ease," said the sergeant major, another Vietnam veteran.

Then he started in, "What in the hell happened over the weekend?"

The question was rhetorical. The sergeant major knew that I couldn't discuss the case with anybody but Daniel Long, my attorney.

In Ocean City the police and prisoners were intimidated, but such was not the case with the sergeant major. I suppose after Vietnam, there's not a lot left to surprise you.

After some discussion, during which he emphasized for my own good, and the good of the Army, that I not talk to anybody about anything concerning the case, the sergeant major gave me a private room to live in while the Army machine began its investigation. It seemed I was getting private rooms almost everywhere I turned. I had one in Basic and in the city jail (though I had to share one with a snitch at the county jail), and now I had a nice, big room on Smoke Bomb Hill at the Special Warfare School. However, by the sergeant major's implication, things would get ugly if I was not squeaky clean. For the time being I was free to come and go as I pleased.

Steve had orders for the 5th Special Forces Group that was just down the road. When he reported in, they put him on an A-team. It was a scuba team, so he began preparing for the scuba course in Key West, moving forward in his Army journey.

His team members wanted to know what had happened. They had heard the rumor that we were up there in uniform, and they already knew that it wasn't true, or Steve would not have been put on an A-team. An unfortunate thing about rumors is that they are usually filled with the bad stuff. It makes for better gossip. For instance, nobody, that I know of, except for the witnesses, the police, and those who read the witness statements, heard until now that Steve had actually treated Mr. Scott for shock.

Steve was under orders not to talk about the case, so he could not confirm or deny anything. But the fact that he was put on an A-team, given his involvement in Ocean City, was a strong vote of confidence from the Army that we were clean.

As for me, during the first week or so nobody bothered me. I just walked around and thought. I didn't wear a uniform. I got up in the mornings and did PT with the new class of candidates. The TACs were smoking the new-comers' bodies in Pre-Phase training and taking no prisoners during PT. The course was not too standardized or rigid, and the TACs could dish out discomfort largely at their whim. Maybe they were trying to eliminate all the young soldiers by shocking them into a reassessment of their choice, I don't know, but people were quitting in droves.

After PT, I wandered around the main post, and out into the woods, and watched the Army machine clunk along. Helicopters were flying all the time, artillery was booming in the distance, there were the sounds of distant machine guns, and jets flying over with soldiers parachuting out. During the hot part of the day, I took fifteen-minute naps in the woods. When darkness fell, flares dropped over training areas as soldiers did battle drills, and I walked back to the unit.

At night, as I dragged in, there was always a cluster of soldiers that had decided that Special Forces was not for them. They sat around the barracks smoking and joking, waiting to be sent back to wherever they'd come from, while the others kept going and pushing. When I walked by the quitters, there was silence, and I stayed away from them.

In my bed in the dark, staring at the ceiling, I reflected that I was facing ten years in prison. Thinking of how I got there, I thought about the good times of my life. I hardly slept, but would doze off for a few hours. Then another day would begin.

Night and day, I kept thinking about an enchanted place called Cataloochee.

CATALOOCHEE

(CAT AH LOU CHEE) IS THE transliterated version of a Cherokee word. One of its meanings is said to be "wave over wave," a reference to the mountain range's resemblance to the rolling sea. It is a beautiful place, part of the Great Smoky Mountain National Park in western North Carolina, and for me a place of magic.

Many people know of the Cataloochee ski area, and the Cataloochee Ranch, but relatively few know the park nestled on the other side of the mountain. There are few signs announcing it, and the park is hard to find on a map. Even some of the people living in nearby towns have never heard of the park. It is about six hundred miles north of Winter Haven and the drive there always seemed to last forever.

My first visit to Cataloochee occured just before Susan was born, when the bear had charged and Dad had scared it off. Eventually, Susan was married there, in a little white church, while I was away in Poland.

After our mother passed away, Dad didn't travel far, but our grandparents vacationed in Cataloochee twice a year for more than fifty summers and falls. They had brought my mother along since she was a baby, and later they brought us, her children, while Dad stayed home.

The park is secluded, and the final sixteen miles of gravel road over the mountain is slow going, but once we rolled in, the two weeks seemed to flash by like a summer dream. Remnants of the early settlers take one back to another time. They are reminders of the preciousness of our time in life, and that there really is no time to waste.

There is the Caldwell House, whose attic is filled with bats, where, when I climbed through a hole in the ceiling of a closet, a shaft of light revealed hordes of them hanging upside down in the darkness. Around the park, old cemeteries sit at the top of steep climbs. The pallbearers must have been horses; the walks alone leave one winded, and the dates on the stones go back to the last century. The number of infants' and children's graves tells its own story of primitive medicine and the struggle to survive in harder times.

Other places there are filled with apple trees and masses of blackberries. We picked them by the bucket, and caught salamanders in the creeks. The park was teeming with life.

Our grandparents' marriage seemed ideal; they loved each other and it showed. Granddad filled notebooks with poems to his bride, and could tell a story like few others. In fact, our strongest form of communication was through story, and I have rarely seen his rival in the art of telling. Every night in camp was the same when it wasn't raining—with the fire crackling, Billy or Susan or I would start the journey with, "Granddad, please tell us a story."

Granddad would say something like: "I've done told you every story I know." Then he would pause and stir the fire with his stick. He never stirred the fire aimlessly like we did. He adjusted the fire to replace the smoke with flame, then would say, "Well, I reckon I know a'nothern." And he would begin.

"SERGEANT" YON

FACING MANSLAUGHTER CHARGES and ten years in prison, I continued to wander around the woods at Fort Bragg, wondering what kind of mess I was in.

Certain areas at Bragg were designated "Off Limits." Some of those places were impact areas for artillery and other explosive ordinance, or old impact areas littered with duds. Unexploded ordinance was everywhere. If you walked into an active impact area, you could find yourself in the middle of an artillery barrage, or practically any other type of fire you could think of, except torpedoes. You could blow yourself up by stumbling across a supposed dud.

One method guerrillas use for obtaining explosives is to remove them from unexploded ordinance, like dud bombs. Risky business. An experienced guerrilla who attempts to disarm a new type of bomb will make one painstaking move at a time. He will perform a single action, then walk away to write or explain what he had just done. Then he will make sketches and explain his next move. He will repeat this tedious work until the bomb is disarmed—or he is vaporized.

This way the guerrillas can, by trial and error, figure out how to disarm various types of ordinance. Of course, the enemy knows this, so sometimes the enemy drops "duds" with boobytraps. When the guerrillas try to disarm them, it's *goodbye*. And the guerrillas may take the explosives and crawl through a sewer system to attach a bomb to the bottom of a manhole cover. When the intended target drives or walks over the manhole, *goodbye*. The trickery men employ in killing each other is limitless, and terrifying.

While I wondered and wandered around, the Army seemed to have temporarily forgotten about me, but they had not. No branch of the armed forces is compelled to exercise the same due process that the military protects in the civilian world, nor does it take chances with people who may give it a black eye in some future incident. Neither the Army, nor Special Forces, would allow a man to receive such specialized, expensive training if that man showed a propensity to misuse it. If the military had the slightest indication, or even suspicion, that I might have been guilty, or just unfit for duty, that would have been enough. *Zero defects allowed.*

The zero defect mentality is asinine, but that's the way it was and is. The mentality does not actually create zero defects, it merely seeks to cover them up, where they continue to fester under the surface.

After some time, the military came to a conclusion independent of the civilian side. It wouldn't have surprised me if they had distanced themselves, in doing their imitation of Washinghands, D.C. (Damage Control). But if the Army D.C.-ed, it would likely be interpreted by the public as further evidence of guilt.

The Army's conclusion: If the state of Maryland drops the charges, *you are welcome here*. The Army, in effect, had stood by me by not dropping me like a hot rock, which was chancy on their part.

Having fully expected to be kicked out, I was ecstatic that they still believed in me given the potential bad press, which was to be expected, when it went to trial.

The Army gave me no help with Maryland. I was on my own, but fortunately, not alone. There was the lawyer, Daniel Long, who had placed himself between the wolves and me, for which I was very grateful.

That was two major obstacles down; the Army and SF. One big one to go. While the system ran its course in Maryland, I was at the Special Warfare school. My orders for the 5th Special Forces had been canned.

Since I was unemployed and just wandering around, I asked SFC Sibley for a job. He gave me one of the best and most educational jobs that I have ever had, assigning me as a "junior TAC" to help the TACs with the new class. Instead of promoting me to an acting corporal, this time they promoted me, a private, to *sergeant*. SFC Sibley simply handed me the stripes and said, "Good morning *Sergeant* Yon." And that was that. Yet, though the new job carried the responsibility of a sergeant, it went without the pay. The payoff would be in experience.

Now, I was a nineteen-year-old (real) Special Forces (fake) sergeant. Just as when I was a platoon leader and a drill corporal, I felt the heavy pressure to measure up in real life to the plastic title that was hung around my neck, and the fake stripes on my collar. It was a joke, I felt, but at this rate I would be a phony sergeant major in another year, and possibly playing general by the time I was twenty-two, give or take a couple of years.

When soldiers at Fort Bragg saw the stripes, along with my baby face and green hat, there were some strange looks—as if they thought I were impersonating a soldier. I got stopped maybe a half-dozen times by officers and sergeants who wanted to see my ID card, and then I had to explain the stripes with a letter I carried around everywhere with me.

Others recognized my name tag, and often said "Hello." Unlike the rest of the world, the soldiers knew that if I had done something wrong, I wouldn't be walking around Fort Bragg with those stripes. SF is a small community and word spreads fast. As it became obvious how much restraint I had used, although it was generally agreed that I had screwed up by not leaving and avoiding the fight altogether, I was given special treatment.

But, at the same time, there were those who said that the man got what he had coming. They said that I let him push too far before I stood my ground, and had I reacted sooner, maybe he would have walked away knowing that I *would* fight. And if he hadn't walked away, what was the difference? The result would have been the same.

We are taught since childhood that it takes more guts to walk away than to fight. However, as with most "rules," there are exceptions. It only takes more guts to walk away when you think that you can *win*. It takes no courage to walk away from a fight that you think you might *lose*.

If a person were to "valiantly" avoid every confrontation in life, that person likely would be pushed around and taken advantage of on a regular basis. There is a time to stand your ground. *When is that time?* Well, that would be very hard to say, and every instance is different, but the important part is not to be an active participant in escalating the problem when there is a reasonable chance for peaceful settlement.

Aside from the philosophical aspects, no matter how many times I explained that it was all an accident and that I could not say much because I could not discuss the case, the Maryland event always seemed in the back of their minds since they continued to treat me so differently. Whereas earlier, the senior enlisted men and officers paid no more attention to me than to the others, now when I walked into a chow hall I often heard, "Hey, Yon. Sit over here."

The first few times I just kept quiet and listened. I spoke only when spoken to. They talked back and forth, told Army stories, and when I started talking, they answered just about any question I asked.

Sometimes groups of NCOs went off post to eat and invited me along. I would be sitting with people who had been in the Army ten, fifteen, or even twenty years. Education-wise all those informal chow sessions with the older soldiers started adding up. To me, it was: "Learn while you eat." This was truly Twilight Zone stuff. I was still facing manslaughter charges, but being treated like I was being groomed for bigger and better things.

Some congratulated my self-restraint, but the more I tried to downplay the actual fight, the more they believed the opposite. They seemed to think that I was a closet Kung-fu king and, as time went on, more and more the "silent warrior" image hung around my neck.

Soldiers my age from other units started asking what they needed to do to get into Special Forces. "How did you make sergeant so fast?" they would ask. In the beginning, I told them that I was only an *acting* sergeant, but then a TAC heard me and pulled me aside.

"*Sergeant* Yon," he said, "You can't tell soldiers that the stripes are not real." He tapped the rank on my shoulder and continued, "You are a sergeant. You are just not being *paid* as a sergeant, and when you tell soldiers that you are a private, they will not respect the rank, which undermines the authority of other sergeants."

He was right, I knew. I had learned the same lesson as a drill corporal. But it still made me feel hypocritical to be wearing stripes that I had not earned.

Young soldiers continued to flock to me and ask how to get into Special Forces. As usual, I told them: "First, make sure that you want to do it. *Very sure.* Then train very hard. Don't show up like it is going to be a little jaunt through another Basic Training. Do your homework. It's up to you. Good luck, I hope you make it." Yet, it felt wrong for me to dispense advice since I had only made it through the Qualification course and had never been in a real Special Forces unit. What did *I* know? Very little, actually.

But I did know one thing: If someone plunged in without first doing his homework, he was still too young in experience for this environment. Through the years, many young guys have told me that they were "thinking about going SF." Often, they launched into the normal comparison, asking me which is tougher. "Is it *SEALs*?" they asked. *Rangers? SF? Force Recon?* Whenever someone started comparing incomparable things, I told him that SF is not the toughest, and that he probably should try something else.

CAUSE OF DEATH

THE CAUSE OF Scott's death[2] was stated on the autopsy that I received about one month after the fight:

Diagnoses:
1. Head and neck injuries

    a. subarachnoid hemorrhage of brain
    b. brain swelling marked
    c. intraventricular hemorrhage
    d. subdural hemorrhage of the cervical spinal cord
    e. laceration of skin below left eye,
    f. contusion of left lower lip; abrasion of shoulder

Opinion:
[Mr. Scott] died of head and neck injuries. . . .

BLOOD: ALCOHOL 0.16%
DRUG SCREEN, BILE&URINE—negative

His blood alcohol level was 0.16%. Putting that into perspective, in Florida the legal limit for driving is half that, or 0.08%, unless there is an accident, in which case the limit halves again to 0.04%. (For many states the legal limit is 0.10%.) After consulting various law enforcement people experienced in administering breathalyzer tests, I found the consensus to be that 0.16% for one person might be slobbering drunk, while another might just be starting to show signs of drinking.

As for me, I was feeling tipsy but not "drunk." The police asked after my arrest if I would voluntarily submit to a blood test, but I declined under the never-say-anything guideline. I was not operating a vehicle, so I presumed that they had no authority to take the sample, and they did not push the issue.

We all know that alcohol clouds the judgment and lowers inhibitions. It has the magical ability to turn an introvert into a rock star, a quiet accountant into an aspiring prize-fighter, or a proud company man into a weepy fool. As for me, I was the happy type: telling jokes, dancing, and generally having what I then considered fun.

---

[2] I was reluctant to include the following material out of respect for the dead, but proofreaders continued to insist that the inclusion of the cause of death was important. Finally, I saw their reasoning was valid.

Every night, all across the land, people drink and become violent. Alcohol lowers one's ability to realize the image he is projecting, and what signals he is sending. Mr. Scott's body language had spoken for him that night.

The witnesses, to my knowledge, did not see him throw his punch because it didn't travel very far. But they did see me grab his right shoulder with my left hand. To an experienced eye, that was an indicator.

When I saw him prepare to punch, I grabbed his shoulder and pushed hard, throwing him off-balance. This is a basic self-defense move; the assailant cannot deliver a powerful blow when he is not balanced. His punch was slow, probably due to the alcohol, and since I was primed and afraid, I was faster.

It was said that I hit him four times, but I only remember three blows, and, based upon their statements, it's clear that the witnesses, too, were unsure. Different witnesses often "recall" different things, and in times of crisis, the variations are likely to be even more pronounced. The truth usually is somewhere in between.

My opinion of the cause of death: Alcohol, a freak accident, and most of all *stupidity*. A man was out to pick a fight, the bouncers did not do their jobs despite being asked to do so many times, and I didn't leave. None of us were entirely free of responsibility.

THE LITTLE INVASION

ALMOST THREE MONTHS since the incident in Ocean City.

20 October, 1983 (on or about), A future friend and his team got an intelligence warning of a potential terrorist strike and immediately left Beirut, proceeding to a secluded camp for safety.

23 October, 1983, Beirut, Lebanon. A truck containing approximately 12,000 pounds of explosives detonated, killing 241 Marines, injuring more than 100 others. The team returned to Beirut to help.

24 October, 1983, Fort Bragg, N.C. I was on my back in bed looking at the old ceiling, listening to abnormally heavy air-traffic. I looked out the window and saw another gigantic C-5 Galaxy transport jet roar low overhead into the night. Steve came in from 5th Group and said something was up. *No kidding!*

We jumped into his Datsun pickup and drove to Pope Air Force base, flashed our ID's to the Air Force gate guards and headed on base. There, the soldiers and airmen were obviously loading up for war. People were carrying weapons, and they were quickly preparing their camouflaged vehicles for air transport by taping glass and rough edges, and strapping things down. The camouflage-clad people scurried around, sergeants barked orders, officers huddled. Even rookies could see that this was not a training exercise.

Air-traffic was thick with C-5 and C-141 transport jets stacked up like it was rush hour at the Atlanta airport. I had never seen the military mobilize before and it was a sight—exciting and electrifying. There was energy in the air and soldiers were running around like ants. Army ants. Fire ants. Somebody was about to get stung, but who? We drove back onto Bragg to see which units were mobilizing. The 82nd Airborne was out with combat gear. Weapons were already issued, rucksacks were packed and in formation as the leaders went down the lines and conducted pre-combat inspections. The 82nd is a big, formidable unit, and I wondered what unlucky people were about to be attacked.

Wow, we thought, the U.S. was going to war. *Must be either Lebanon or Grenada.*

Something was up in Grenada. There had been a small article in the paper about an amphibious Marine unit down there on exercises, plus other snippets of information. But the bomb in Lebanon may have triggered some military response. Jimmy Carter had been replaced in the White House by Ronald Reagan, so it could be anything.

We drove back to Pope Air Force Base, which was just next door. There were some parachutes out near the aircraft. Somehow Steve and I figured they were going to jump into Grenada. We thought about stowing onboard a jet with the 82nd paratroopers and jumping with them. That'd be easy enough; they would have extra parachutes on board and if anyone noticed we weren't in the unit, our uniforms showed we were Special Forces, so we would say it was classified and that they never saw us—how's that for a quick plan? In all the confusion, we figured we might get away with it. It is difficult to understate the value of audacity.

Fighters are not lap kittens purring away the hours waiting to be fed. They are hunters by nature, and we wanted badly to join this hunt. It was not to be.

We were disappointed at being left behind, and went downtown and waited to hear about Operation Urgent Fury when they got back. When the 82nd returned from their little field trip, we found that some of the men who had washed out of Selection had gone while we'd stayed home. The irony was not lost on us. I learned to like the 82nd soldiers and discovered that they were a lot of fun—except when too many young ones got together; they could quickly get out of hand.

It turned out that the unit we saw loading to fly to Grenada did not jump in, but the Rangers jumped into Grenada from so low that they did not even use reserve parachutes because the DZ was hot (under direct enemy fire.) Some people say that American boys don't have the fighting spirit. I doubt that those people met many of the soldiers and other military members that I knew. Later, we heard that others got the same idea about stowing onboard an airplane, but to our knowledge nobody did.

And I just waited and waited for the indecisive system to sort itself out. I remembered good times in the past, and hoped for more in the future.

SERPENTS AND MOLES

THERE WAS GRANDDAD'S tale of the railroad man who lost his head. Somehow he slipped, and the train cut it off. On some nights, people said, you could still see his lantern swaying down the tracks as his body looked for his head. That happened somewhere in Georgia, and though there were no railroad tracks in Cataloochee, there were still plenty of ghosts. It seemed that spirits were always either looking for something, or trying to talk to the living.

Sleeping outside, there were many sounds that came from the darkness. *What is that . . . a bear? . . . or just a raccoon?* You didn't even think about leaving food out overnight in Cataloochee; if the bears or some other creature didn't get it, the raccoons would. Of course, to them it wasn't stealing; the park was their home as much as ours. If they found food, they took it. Everything belonged to nobody. Everything belonged to everybody. Those were the rules.

There were lots of squirrels, but at night they slept in the trees. During daylight, I sometimes "fished" for squirrels by tying food on a string. When they came down for it, we played tug of war. A determined squirrel is a squirrel unstoppable by normal means. They are incredibly persistent problem solvers, and if they want your food—watch out.

Every night we roasted marshmallows or hotdogs, while the moths fluttered in from the darkness to bounce off the lantern. There were big moths and little moths, but most of all, lots of moths. When we turned off the lantern, they disappeared, and the night creatures again took over.

There were crystal-clear mountain streams, footpaths and horse trails, and lots of wildlife. I often thought of living there forever. Cataloochee seemed a different universe, and, in a sense, it is. I imagined that it smelled like Heaven must smell. It smelled like life, forever and forever. It smelled like peace. If you journey to Cataloochee, you probably will not forget that smell, and sometime after you leave, you will encounter a scent that will draw you back into that valley.

There was a special place on Cataloochee Creek, near the campground, where I used to sit every year and watch the water flow over the rocks. The creek was big enough to float down on innertubes, but shallow enough to walk across in most places. Leaves floated down the little whitewater rapids, and the creek seemed to speak to me, telling me that everything would be alright. I drank the water and it was the best I ever tasted. I splashed it all over my body. I ducked my head underwater and held my breath for as long as I could, just as I used to do in the same spot with my mother.

I would sit on the bank for hours, chewing on twigs, watching the birds fly, and the hornets zooming like little jet fighters. The squirrels were usually scampering around, chasing each other, or foraging. It was a very special place for me. I could see my mother standing there with me in the water, splashing back and forth. We had sat at the spot together. The same old trees still hung over the water. Sometimes the rain dripped from the leaves into the stream, and I lay on the rocks on the bank, wondering where she was.

Through the years, we slept in tents, then a camper, and, finally, a motor home. For protection against the mountain rains, Granddad would tie a big, square piece of clear plastic, probably fifteen feet in length and width, over the picnic table between the trees. I loved the rains, and resisted all of Granny's attempts to reel me in. Usually, Granddad seemed on my side. Granny was loving, but a little over-protective when it came to safety. But, being good grandparents, they kept a united front.

During the heavy rains, the forest seemed to roar. Granny worried that I would be swept away by a flash flood. She warned, "you never know how much rain fell up on the mountain."

When it was not raining, flies prowled and buzzed around. Some got "trapped" in the clear plastic that hung high over the picnic table. They trapped themselves the same as flies get trapped at a window trying to buzz to the light. Granddad said that the flies are the buzzards of the bug world, and that the hornets are the eagles. When a hornet stings, it burns like a cigarette, or an extra strong BB, but unlike with a BB, I get a quiver when I think of getting hornet-stung.

Granddad looked to the plastic that hung over our heads. "See those flies up under tha' plastic?" he said in his thick Southern drawl, "Watch. Directly a hornet'll come in an' get one. He'll catch 'im an' drop to tha' picnic table with 'im. Then he'll rip his wings off an' fly away."

That sounded like a scene from a space alien movie. It was hard to picture that a hornet was going to magically appear, grab a fly in *mid-flight*, wrestle it to the ground, or, in this case, the picnic table, rip off its wings— then fly away with the wingless prey.

Well, I've learned to keep my skepticism in check when proof is said to be on the way. And, more importantly, Granddad had always been right about this kind of stuff before, crazy as it may've sounded to me.

We watched. Not long. Just a few minutes. A hornet zipped in, made a pass at a fly and missed, but it turned instantly and air combat was on. Top Gun. It wasn't much of a fight because the hornet was much faster, more maneuverable, and ferocious, like a little lion with wings. Hornets are full-on, take-no-prisoners killers. The fly stood little chance. He may as well have been a lumbering 747 trying to evade an F-18.

The hornet darted around, made some kind of fancy move that would probably make a great slow-motion picture, and snatched the fly from the air. They fell about four feet to the table, and, in my opinion, their wings were not beating—it was like a slam to the wrestling mat.

We moved closer to watch the action. The hornet knew some kind of insect judo, and within a few seconds, the fly's wings were on the table as the hornet prepared its prey for take-off. The fly kicked its little legs. I admired its spunk, but this game was nearly over. A fly without wings is no longer a fly. He is a walk. Granddad said the hornet would fly the walk to the nest to feed the young. *Zooommm.* The hornet took off with its kill.

I saw this repeated many times. The wild is its own movie, if you just watch.

The streams had many uses. We kids, and others from the campground, would take tire innertubes and float down Cataloochee Creek all day, screaming and tipping each other over. Granddad taught me how to catch crawdads in the creeks by sticking my foot in the water. Crawdad is the "real" Southern word for crayfish, which look a lot like little lobsters with similar little claws, though in the Southern Appalachians they only grow to about the size of jumbo shrimp, maybe a little bigger. The crawdads would come out to eat my toes and I could just pick them up. Or, if I wanted to be fancy about it, I tied a chicken neck, or some kind of meat, and a pebble (as a sinker), to a string, and dropped it in the water. The crawdads would crawl out from under rocks, their pinchers reaching out in front, and grab the bait. When one started to munch, I gave it a few seconds to get a good taste so it wouldn't let go, then gently lifted it by the string and shook it off in the bucket of creek water beside me.

Granny went bonkers when I caught crawdads in Cataloochee and brought them back to camp. "This is a National Park! It's *illegal.* The Ranger will put us in jail or give us a fine. Don't catch no crawdads in that creek."

"*Granddad* taught me!"

We boiled them and ate their tails.

Granddad taught us the danger of putting stones from a creek or a river in or around a campfire. Sometimes they explode. He said that there is water trapped in some of the rocks, and when they get hot they pop like popcorn. Only more forcefully, and louder.

And yes, I tried it. I had to. But not in Cataloochee. I tried it on a different trip when there wasn't a camp full of people. He was right—it's dangerous. The rocks sometimes explode like a weak hand grenade and spray fire and sharp stone fragments everywhere.

If you find that you simply must try it, make sure that you have a hot fire, throw the rocks in, and get the heck away. Sometimes it doesn't work. But when it does . . . *Bam!*

During an annual trip to Cataloochee, we stopped at our Uncle Henry's farm in Baxley, Georgia. He raised tobacco and was a millionaire, though there was no way of telling except that Granny said so. Millionaires, of course, are mysterious people, to those of us who are not.

Uncle Henry was one of Granddad's older brothers and he had a number of workers living on his property in little shacks. They worked long, hard days in the tobacco, and when it was time, harvested the bottom leaves by hand. While we were visiting, I got the "opportunity" to work the tobacco, picking the bottom leaves off the plants, trying to keep up with the workers. A nasty, bitter taste collected around my lips as I worked, which Uncle Henry said was nicotine. Picking tobacco is an incredibly hard job, and convinced me that I was going to stay in school—I was not going to pick tobacco.

Back to Winter Haven: Granny and the F.L.M.K.

I hated to leave the peace and fun of the wilderness only to return home, but I often found short refuge at Granny's house. In her yard, I watched moles tunneling under her grass in search of insects. Unfortunately, for the moles, they pushed out the extra sand into mounds. The molehills were ugly, and bad for the lawnmower blade when I flattened them. *FRRRRaap!*

Granny decreed that the moles were unwelcome and had to go. Dead or alive. Granddad wasn't much for mole killing. In fact, the only creatures he killed without regret for their demise or gratitude for their nutrition were poisonous snakes (and all were considered poisonous until they were dead).

My dog Snoopy had shown fantastic talent as a snake finder. When she barked a certain way—*Alright! Snoopy found a snake!*

Then came the tense moments as Billy and I identified the snake as poisonous or non-poisonous. The ID process was often a shaky enterprise, no matter how many pictures we saw, or how many snakes we caught—and we caught them by the dozen. Granny had warned us a hundred times that snakes were deceptive. They play dead when they are alive, and somehow disguise themselves as friendly when they are poisonous. That is their nature.

Some, like black racers, were unmistakable, but Granny said that sometimes rattlesnakes are born black and without rattles. That sounded somewhat improbable, but she had been around a lot longer than I had, and you never know what kind of mutant nature will create in one of its experimental whims. Nevertheless, I concluded, if a rattlesnake was born around there, and it was black, without rattles, and without a rattlesnake head, then it was also born without fangs because it was a black racer, not a rattler. If it were born looking like a yellow rat snake, then it *was* a yellow rat snake. If it swam around and quacked, it was a duck . . . that's how I saw it.

If we were reasonably certain, meaning it didn't have rattles, a copper-head, a cotton-mouth, or otherwise look like a venomous serpent—we caught it. We could sell even a common garter snake for five bucks to some doctor's son who lived in town and never got to catch snakes. Boys like snakes. That is their nature.

Granny, more so than Granddad, detested and destroyed snakes with a lust and fury only matched by that visited on trailer parks by tornadoes. Billy and I often defended the snakes and would stomp around and protest all day when Granny killed them. Then she would say—every time—that even dead snakes had poison. "And you never know when they are really dead. Even with their heads cut off, they can still poison you," she would say.

Moles were not so deadly, but catching them merely to relocate them would be like catching, then transplanting, cupboard mice. Such an exercise is neither socially demanded, nor worth the effort—unless you were the mole or the mouse.

I didn't look forward to the idea of killing moles or mice, but I was not going to take a serious stand on their behalf. I would defend a snake. Any snake. I would defend a snake as a lawyer would, with heart-felt arguments about my client's innocence, and with rightful claims about how snakes were part of nature, made by God himself.

I would stand between the snake and Grandma's rake. I had done it many times, and even got swatted with the rake. I would try to delay the killing by any means, pointing out all the obvious signs that the snake was not poiso-nous. "Look, Granny! No rattles! No rattlesnake head! It eats rats! It eats rattlesnakes too, I think." I was arguing with the executioner. Granny read the Bible, and to her, snakes were serpents, though she called them snakes and admitted that some were harmless and helpful, and she would not kill a black snake.

Granny would yell, "*Hush* up and move yer fanny out of the way, Michael! Michael, move!" swatting at me with the rake, "he's getting away!"

Whack! Whack! Whack!

Another one bites the dust.

Granny didn't hate the moles so passionately, but I raised not a finger to defend them. There were no library books with colorful pictures of moles leaping out to catch rats, or showing moles being milked for the venom which could be used for medicine. Snakes had redeeming qualities, and value. I could sell them. Nobody would buy a *mole*, except maybe to feed to a pet snake, and a mole's place in the circle of life just seemed, well . . . unimportant.

So, when Granny declared war on the moles—not a malicious war, there was no mean spirit to it—saying that they just had to die, Granddad and I became her soldiers.

Moles were quick. At that time, I had never seen one alive. It was as if they only existed when they were dead. They spent their lives underground and through their persistence in tunneling, piled lots of sand in the yard. Those unsightly sand piles drove Granny crazy. So we began our mole hunting.

Granddad was the teacher. After a two-minute class in mole behavior, during which he taught that *it's best to hunt moles in the morning*, and our own practical observation, that lasted another three minutes—it was time to graduate to "mole killers." To guerrilla-ize our name, you could call us the F.L.M.K.: Free Lance Mole Killers.

When they work, moles toss out sand quite often, so their whereabouts are easy to pinpoint. Just find the freshest sand pile, and lay your ambush.

There are many methods for the killing of moles: cats kill them, but Granny didn't like cats. Poison kills them, but it kills dogs too—so no poison with Snoopy around. You can watch to see the mole toss out some sand, then run out with a shovel and toss the shovel-full in a bucket, hoping to find the mole inside the scoop of dirt, but that would do more damage to the yard than the mole. Even dynamite would work, but that solution came with disadvantages not only to the yard and the plumbing, but also the question: where could you get it?

Granddad showed me where to shoot by aiming the unloaded shotgun. At the right moment, just as the sand flew out of the hole, he pulled the trigger. *Click!* Now it was time for me to try, but with a loaded gun. Granddad coached, pointing out that timing and aiming are everything. "You gotta wait 'til it tosses out a little dirt. Keep yer shotgun steady 'til you see the dirt fly. Steady. Don't get tired. Steady. Steady." *Bam!*

Sand, dust, and clumps of grass flew up in the air. The grass wasn't so healthy to begin with, and now a little patch was missing.

As the sand settled to earth and the dust cleared, I said, "I missed."

Granddad said, "Oh fiddle, you didn't miss. Couldn't have. You shot at just the right time and you hit the hole. Let's have a look."

I pulled out my earplugs and we walked over. The blast had blown the mole from the hole to where it now lay on the grass. Sure enough, I had killed it. A mole. Killed with the technology of modern firearms. It was like hunting doves with surface-to-air missiles.

Despite the fact that Granddad had said that moles were small, I expected it to be about the size of a rat, or at least a mouse, but it was no bigger than a pair of fingernail clippers. I shot a mole with a shotgun shell that was bigger than the mole it killed, and I could have used the empty shell for its coffin—all for Granny.

The battles were not particularly difficult or risky for Granddad and me. The F.L.M.K. retook the yard from the moles.

Granddad often chewed on a twig, toothpick, or wooden matchstick, so he showed me how to make a waterproof match/toothpick holder out of two empty shotgun shells that were always around. He taught the important things, like how to make a slingshot, climb trees, tie good knots, sharpen a knife or ax, drive nails, and work in the garden.

Granny preserved vegetables from the garden in the Mason jars that filled the utility room where there was a deep-freeze and washer and dryer, though she liked to dry the clothes on the line because they smelled better. When we were canning vegetables, Granny would say, "You stay out of the kitchen when I'm cookin' with the pressure cooker. It might blow up and it'll hurt ya bad. It'll burn ya."

I sat in the rocking chair next to the coffee table where Granddad kept his *Farmer's Almanac*. Sitting there, I snapped the peas that we had picked by the bushel. I snapped until my fingers hurt, then we sometimes made butter or homemade ice cream.

In the South you can buy boiled peanuts on the roadside. Every so often, when Granddad and I were driving along in his old white pickup, we stopped for a bag. There was an old roadside stand down the road from the house. The stand was made up of a series of umbrellas and rickety tables, where an old woman sat day in, day out, in the shimmering heat.

She boiled the "P-nuts," (that's what her sign said), and used a Mason jar as the measuring cup. She sold the P-nuts in brown paper bags, double-bagged because they were wet, for a buck a bag.

She sold tomatoes, squash, carrots, and a dozen other things as well, all of which she weighed on an old spring-scale. But Granddad grew a lot of vegetables, so he only bought things that he didn't have. Granny boiled P-nuts, too, but there was something special about *roadside* boiled P-nuts. As we pulled away from the stand, I would dig into the bag, cracking them open with my teeth and sucking out the salty juice, then I devoured the meaty insides and flicked the soggy shells out the window.

It was a common sight to see turtles crossing the road. Billy and I always snatched them up. The story of the tortoise and the hare has some merit but, like all things, it should be kept in perspective. I never chased a turtle that was able to outrun me.

I knew how to get them out of their shell. Granddad taught me. Contrary to what a schoolmate said, a turtle can't be lured out of its shell with a carrot. Granddad's method involved a pair of pliers, a knife, and a jig saw. We reached into the shell with the pliers and pulled out his head, cut it off with the knife and threw it to Snoopy. But you have to be careful with certain snapping turtles that you sometimes catch while fishing; the mouth can still bite after the head is cut off.

After cutting off its head, we hung the turtle upside down for awhile to let the blood drain out, and finally cut the shell open with the jig saw. That's when Granny would walk out with a bowl for the meat; Granddad kept the liver for catfish bait.

As for the actual apprehension of a turtle, the drill was simple and no words needed to be exchanged. This was standard procedure: Granddad stopped the truck, I jumped out, grabbed the turtle, and put it in the bed of the pickup. Then, turtle soup, fried turtle, turtle stew. . . .

I liked fishing with our grandparents down on the Peace River in Florida. Granny would say, "You put on your life jacket, you might fall out of the boat. Watch for gators."

She would keep on: "Don't snag yourself with that hook; those barbs are hard to get out. Be careful if you catch a catfish; they'll sting ya and you'll have to go to the hospital. Watch for snakes; they swim ya know. Wear your hat or you'll get sunburned. Don't get tangled on that branch when you cast. Be careful."

She always looked out for us kids, though at times it seemed a nuisance. She said, "Don't throw rocks. One of your uncles [one of Granddad's brothers] got killed when he was a boy throwing rocks. He got hit in the head. The boys were just having fun."

Back at Granny's house, we were eating a rabbit, probably fried, that I shot in the garden a couple hours earlier for supper. Granddad was eating a tomato that he'd picked just before the meal when he stopped chewing to spit some lead shot on his plate. *Plink-Plink.* He chuckled, but didn't say a word. Some of the pellets had missed the rabbit and hit the tomato. After that, I stopped shooting rabbits in the garden.

To see Granddad around small children was heart-warming. Kids were attracted to him like moths to a lantern, and he forgot about everyone around except the little ones. He usually ended up on the floor playing with the babies, whom he would hold over his head, or crawl with. He could make train noises or hoot like an owl, and the kids loved it, squealing: "make the train noise again!"

As the adults talked about cows, corn, or tobacco, Granddad taught us all the important stuff: throwing rocks, climbing trees, making slingshots and traps, rabbit hunting, rabbit cleaning, turtle hunting, turtle cleaning, and of course, mole killing.

But, Granddad had diabetes, which stopped him from enjoying the cakes and pies that my grandmother made for the kids and she would often lament that he loved sweets so much. I had told him that I would become a doctor and find a cure for diabetes because I loved him. That's why I wanted to be a doctor, and I studied everything that I could about the human body. Diabetes had met its match.

I studied the human body for a long time, several years, but my studies drifted to various sciences and finally landed in physics. I probably studied various "physics things," like magnetism and such, for a year before I knew what I was studying. I apologized to Granddad for having lost my focus, but it happened by accident, I just drifted. From that I learned that one should only make big, long-term promises that one's heart will naturally follow, or risk drifting away.

TESTING, 1, 2, 3

AT FORT BRAGG, Steve was on his A-team, and I still had hopes, despite the pending criminal charge and my lack of a security clearance because of it. The older Special Forces men obviously believed in me. Rather than confinement, I enjoyed a freedom known by few military people; there were the sergeant's stripes, my own quarters, and a general feeling of "Do what you want."

After the new class had finished Pre-Phase a couple of months back, those who succeeded went to Camp MacKall for Phase-1. In my job as a junior TAC, there was work to do with the new class. I spent most of the time with James Gritz, but I also sat in the classes again with the students, and re-ran much of the training. I helped any students who asked for it, and spent a lot of time teaching them what I had learned. When it came to land-nav, besides helping to teach the technical parts, I must have said dozens of times: "Stay *off* the roads. *Don't* link-up and herd around like cows with other students. You won't be happy if you do."

Soon the candidates were out of the classroom and in the land-navigation course. One of the students was a future teammate of mine, Danny Howe, who later became the executive officer at Camp MacKall. He thinks he remembers, though he is not absolutely certain, that by the time this class finished land-nav, the number of students had dropped from around two hundred to about eighty, which would be very high attrition for that short period. I do not recall, and the Special Warfare School says that records to confirm the numbers were no longer kept for classes during that period. I do know that there was indeed a high attrition rate, and James Gritz and I were partially responsible for it.

Gritz came to me with a mission: *ambush cheaters at land-nav.* The goal of the mission, he said, was simply to enforce the rules by which the students had agreed to abide, and to keep people who can't navigate out of SF.

On the one hand I didn't like the idea that I would cause people to flunk, but on the other, the integrity of the course had to be upheld, and it needed to be done for the ultimate protection of everyone.

It is basic to most types of ambushing to "channelize" the enemy, that is, to cause them to travel along a certain route, or into a certain area. In many types of terrain, people will channelize themselves. Often they simply travel on roads and trails, which is the most basic mistake imaginable. Good ambush sites are usually obvious, for instance, intersections, or dry places between swampy areas that would likely be a route of travel. But other ambush sites take some intuition and studying of the terrain to figure out.

I had learned the basics during infantry training and at Selection, but there was a lot more, which Gritz set out to teach me. With some experience, one can read the natural lines of drift—knowing that people tend to travel the easiest routes—and predict places to catch them. Since the students were not allowed to use the roads, some of the best places to catch them were in swampy areas, where the temptation to use the road, or a bridge, for a short jaunt past the swamp was greatest.

We wanted to snag the road-runners, so we had to be wily. Gritz had me select places on the map that I thought, based on terrain, would funnel students. The first night we hunted for boot prints to see if I was right. As it happened, the soldiers were fairly predictable; after marking their destinations on the map, and looking at the terrain, finding their lines of travel was simple. So, that first night we switched from selecting ambush sites to actual ambushing.

The idea was for Gritz to hide in the bushes with night vision goggles. I would spring out from ambush and take the road runners down. At that point, Gritz would tear off his goggles and rush out to help me, shining a light in their eyes to blind them, and yelling, *"TAC!"* We didn't want to be mistaken for someone trying to steal an automatic weapon.

We could tell them to *stop!* but they would just run away. It's difficult to catch a man who is running through the woods at night. You keep running into trees and everything else that's out there.

Ambushing these soldiers was not a sport for the weak-hearted or indecisive. The students carried unloaded M-16's, and knives. I could get clubbed or stabbed when I pounced on a soldier from the darkness. A frightened, full-grown human male, especially a scared soldier, especially one of *these* soldiers, is dangerous game.

As we waited in ambush, Gritz whispered to me what he saw through his goggles. For instance, whether the soldier was carrying his weapon as he should be, or had his hands free. I couldn't wear the goggles for the tackle since they would get in the way, and I didn't peer through them because the green glow would hurt my unaided night vision.

I suggested early on that we tie a trip wire of green parachute cord across the road at ankle level, but Gritz vetoed that idea because someone might get hurt when we could "safely" tackle him instead. So I said: "Then let's tie it between the trees around here. I will yell at them to *stop!* and if they run for it, it's their fault." Gritz nixed that idea, too. This was to be a full-contact, lion-like takedown. I had to be quick and bring them down as if they were fleeing antelope.

I wasn't convinced that his way was the safest, since I had played football and knew that there was no way to tackle someone gently. At least with the parachute cord, I thought, only one soldier was at risk.

Tentative at first, I made mistakes and some ambushees got away into the darkness. Gritz was not at all satisfied with my apparent unwillingness to pounce out of the night upon a man who was carrying a knife and a club. But when they simply ran away, as he said they would, I knew that it was time to start hitting them with serious tackles.

One soldier that I hit from the dark screamed like he was being killed by a chainsaw, and others fought back, but they were carrying so much gear, unlike me, that they didn't stand a good chance. I found that if you hit them low and clipped their legs, their rucksacks took them down—*karuumph*— and then you just needed to quickly get control of their hands while their rucksacks held them back. After they hit the ground, it was more like pouncing on an overturned turtle.

Nonetheless, each tackle was still scary for me. Most soldiers carried big knives that they could unsnap with one hand, and the idea of a blade slamming through my ribs up to its hilt made this serious business. Getting immediate control of their hands was essential.

Gritz and I moved from place to place, ending up at an intersection of dirt roads far out in the woods. We concluded it was a good place for ambushes because there were land-nav stakes in the area, and it was an intersection, which was a natural danger area for travelers; traffic comes from four directions, so the intersection was a sensible place to set an ambush.

The site was a weather-worn junction of two dirt roads. There was a gully in the middle that was just deep enough for me to lie in and hide my body. This meant that I no longer had to run from the woodline. When they ran by the gully, I pounced.

Some ran straight over the gully, and I took them down from behind. Then Gritz would run from the edge of the woods to help me, telling them to stop fighting when they resisted. After a couple of close calls, I got worried that someone wouldn't see the gully in the darkness and might step on my face. So I changed tactics: if they were coming straight at me, I started hitting them head on. With some experience, I began to get the hang of it, and to look forward to this new "sport" with a certain zeal.

When my increased proficiency threatened to take the challenge out of the game, I decided to see just how uncamouflaged I could be and still succeed. I found that if I lay flat in the darkness next to the road, they usually would not see me if the moon was not bright.

Word got around, and cheaters became scarce. Certainly the Army would not have approved of our risky tactics, but we had done our job. Mission accomplished.

THIRD GRADE—THEN THE WORLD

ALMOST EVERY DAY as a kid I visited several different planets. At home, I was on Planet Turmoil. With my grandparents I was on Planet Fun and Discovery. Church was Planet Rabies, where the teacher thought *hydrophobia* had nothing to do with frothing at the mouth, and my own mind was Planet Philosophy.

Stepping slightly back in time in the progression of this story, I find myself at Planet School, the most enjoyable planet. In fact, I hated summer vacations, except for the parts that I spent with my grandparents, because I missed my friends at Elbert Elementary. The ***Elbert Eagles!*** The faculty must have had little warriors in mind when they came up with that name.

The teachers invited a city councilman to our third grade class. He was a big, black man. People were bigger back then. He was talking about citizenship, and I was impressed with him, as if he were the president. *Maybe he knows some astronauts?!* I speculated.

After his talk, I grabbed a piece of paper and my pencil and asked for his autograph, as I might have done with a ballplayer at the stadium in town where the Boston Red Sox held spring training. The teachers and the councilman were surprised that I wanted his autograph, and he looked down at me and smiled real big. He was nice and made me feel special. He signed his name and I thanked him, then he signed another thirty or so because all the kids lined up behind me.

Third grade was eventful. Once, a kid was sleeping in class with his arms crossed on his desk and his head resting on his arms. His eyes were wide open, unblinking—just staring and staring and staring. This went on for awhile, so I said something to him. No reaction, nothing—*dead!* A boy was *dead* beside me! I was afraid to touch him.

I told the teacher that I thought something was wrong with him. "Maybe he is *dead*," I said. She told me not to be afraid, he was just sleeping, and she woke him up. He was just sleeping? With his eyes wide open?!

At about this time, I started a riot.

At Elbert Elementary, the big classrooms were divided into quadrants called "pods." There were four separate classes with four teachers. The rooms were mostly separated by space and with little sound partitions. The teachers shared an office area, which was enclosed, with windows looking out over the students. When classes changed, we just picked up our trays of books and papers and walked to the next quadrant. I imagine there must have been one hundred and twenty students among the four groups.

One day, the teachers were late arriving because they were in a meeting, and a woman came in to tell us to sit down and wait, saying that our teachers would be there soon; then she left us alone. Big mistake.

Well, sorry. "Soon" would not be soon enough, I thought. It started when I balled up some pieces of paper and yelled,

"LET'S HAVE A RIOT!"

And it worked. . . .

Those turned out to be singularly inflammatory words for high-strung third-graders. The kids went completely haywire. They were throwing chalk, smacking other kids on their backs with dusty erasers, emptying trash cans, turning over desks, throwing books, writing on the blackboard—they even ransacked the teachers' offices, which I had opened. There was pure chaos that would make even the CIA proud.

The action was out of hand, and, startled by what I had caused, I tried to get everyone to stop, but it was like a stampede. I was grabbing students telling them to *stop!* but I might as well have been spitting on a house fire. I turned it on, but I couldn't turn it off. The kids were in a feeding frenzy, less like Eagles than little piranhas with blood in the water, and their food was mischief and mayhem.

The teachers would nail me to the chalkboard when they returned and found the pandemonium and wholesale destruction raging through the four classrooms. I was nervously trying to erase some cuss words from the chalkboard with a paper towel because the erasers were in use on kids' backs and faces.

The teachers opened the door . . .
stepped inside
an eraser flew across the room
and bounced off the wall next to a teacher
leaving a white spot.

The kids suddenly noticed the teachers.

silence

For a moment, the teachers seemed in a state of shock.

Then they went berserk, yelling at us to get to our desks, which was easier said than done, because the desks were mostly turned over, with books and marbles strewn all over the floor. The boys stored marbles in their desks, and cateyes were now rolling about everywhere. One kid had secreted away some milk cartons from the lunchroom and the milk was on the floor, burst open and sour. A girl held her nose and said, *"Grossss!"*

The four women teachers pulled themselves together, retreated to their ransacked office area, and closed the door for a private conference. Probably they were closing their eyes and counting back from one hundred, and thinking of all the reasons that they should not kill us. Maybe they were thinking: *We will lose our jobs if we kill them . . . go to prison . . . the kids are not worth it . . . if we can just beat them . . . everything will be okay. . . .*

We waited.

And waited.

And waited.

What are they going to do?

Finally the teachers emerged, and the tension in them was easy to see. Their composure must have been held together by frayed and failing threads.

They lined us up and paddled each of us with a rolled up magazine (which didn't hurt!).

They probably thought, *That'll teach 'em.*

I probably thought, *That'll teach 'em.*

They never figured out that I started it, luckily.

It seemed like excitement or crisis was around every corner. In prosperous times, my sister, brother, Dad and I were out in our big ski boat. For some reason, Susan was swimming out away from the boat when she gulped water down the wrong way. My dad, a would-be-action-hero, jumped in to rescue her. Susan, being a drowning kid, looked like the cat I once threw in the swimming pool, as she tried to climb on top of Dad's head.

They were *both* drowning!

Dad was fighting to breathe, going under and also swallowing water the wrong way. Susan was in utter panic. There was no swimming going on; they were clawing at the water, flailing, choking. They would drown within the next minute, I thought. They were maybe fifteen feet from the boat. I almost jumped in, but what could I do? Susan would just crawl on top of me. If Dad couldn't save her, how could I? Billy was starting the boat as I reached for the nearest floatable object. I still remember my dad's face when I clobbered him in the nose with a seat cushion.

They both lived, though barely, and Dad thanked me at least a hundred times over the years. He would say, "Michael, you nearly broke my nose with that seat cushion. You saved your sister and me. I'm so proud of you. Come here and give me a hug."

It's amazing how fast the world can spin out of control.

SPECIAL FORCES LAND

Most of the other young soldiers who made it through Selection, after completing all that arduous training, were driving trucks or performing some such menial work for the real SF teams. Unlike Steve, few were getting on A-teams. Meanwhile, I was eating breakfast each morning with a table-full of SF veterans, and spending my days and evenings with them, too.

After Pre-Phase and Phase-1, those remaining went to Phase-2, though there was a load of recycles and others joining the next class. While I anxiously waited to see the outcome of the manslaughter charge, my situation at Bragg remained as unsettled as ever, and I was free as a bee. I could have gone through the Phase-2 weapons training again, but I wasn't such a big gun fan, and besides, I had just done that course.

While working with James Gritz, I was allowed to study whatever I wanted to learn, so I started with Morse code, then attended a short mortar school—without official orders. This is not normal Army policy. Soldiers, including officers, do not wander around Fort Bragg and walk into a school because they *want* to. I did. If those who wanted to see me in prison knew that I continued to receive combat training on a daily basis, likely there would have been some fiery controversy. Mum was the word.

I wanted to attend the Special Forces medic course, but it was far too long, and I didn't have the prerequisite training. The preparation of medics is by far the toughest SF course, and the total initial training lasts about two years. In comparison, my weapons training was a brief and relaxing interlude.

The attrition rate among would-be Special Forces medics is extremely high, and for good reasons. They are not trained merely as EMTs or paramedics. They don't just patch the bleeding places and open airways, trying to stabilize the patient until he can get to a hospital. SF medics are trained as physician *substitutes*, but receive much more training in emergency medicine than most doctors. They learn skills ranging from pulling teeth to delivering babies, amputations to parasitology, anesthesiology, etc. They even learn veterinary medicine. Some knowledge of veterinary medicine is important because guerrillas, and others who need military or non-military assistance, tend to lead simple lives that often depend directly on their animals.

SF medics, as a group, are highly respected in a community where respect is hard to come by, and they are much like doctors who carry guns. It is a common occurrence on Special Forces teams for members to go to the medic instead of the doctor. I've even seen team members take their kids to the medics. On one occasion, a team member brought his sick son into the team room. The medic took the standard diagnostic measures, looking down the boy's throat, in his ears and so on, right there. The medics switch gears from being tough soldiers, and tend to be so gentle with patients, especially with kids, that you would think they were conscientious objectors. On this occasion, the medic took the father into the other room so the boy wouldn't hear and said: "Jesus Christ! We're not in the jungle. That boy is sick. Take him to the doctor right now!"

The medics often work side by side with doctors in various hospitals as part of their ongoing training, and, like all good soldiers, tend to be fanatical about their job. In fact, it is common for medics to leave active duty to enter medical school. They are truly a strange breed, and I always wanted to be called, "Mike Yon, Special Forces Medic, healer of the lame, soother of the pain." I could imagine the picture clearly: stethoscope around my neck, the room dimly lit by several flickering candles and an oil lamp. In my hands, I am holding a crying baby that I have just delivered, and handing it over to its mother, who is smiling gratefully. The father is thanking me in Spanish for waking up at two in the morning and walking ten miles to deliver their new baby. *"Gracias señor Mike!"* he says, *"Gracias!"* He offers two live chickens as payment, which is all that he can afford. At first I turn down the chickens with a *"por nada señor,"* as I look away and continue to pack my gear. But when he stands there silently, I realize that he is offended, so I take the skinny chickens, thank him, and hoist my rucksack for the ten mile walk back through the jungle. All in a day's work—hero of humanity!

But, regrettably, I never was a medic and never delivered a baby.

The first time I got hypothermia, Morgan Gandy, an SF medic, bailed me out by lending some body heat that he could ill afford to spare, but without which I would likely have died. During a training mission, our team hit a target. We were moving out through the night to get away. The weather was alternating between rain and snow when I caught a tree branch in the eye. So, there I was: a very cold Cyclops. While Morgan was patching my eye under a flashlight held by another team member, I mumbled through very cold, shivering lips: "Morgan, we are just two Florida boys in a winter Hell. We need to get to the jungle." He squirted some kind of gook into my eye, proclaimed that it would be fine until the morning, and patched it.

Later that night my hypothermia was becoming critical. Morgan and I shared a sleeping bag that we could not fully zip (for reasons not worth explaining, we were short one sleeping bag). Both of us were shivering uncontrollably, praying for sunrise. He kept shaking me to make sure I was awake: *"Mikey, are you all right?"*

"I am rrreally cccoldd. I willl livvve bbutt ttthis rrreally sssucks. . . ."

Morgan Gandy wrote from Panama.
He captioned the back of the photo:

TO MIKE,
  THE WEAPONS MAN

FROM MORGAN
  AN SF MEDIC

<u>BROTHERS</u>

But that was in the future. For now, I was at sunny Fort Bragg awaiting judgment.

Since I couldn't go to medic training, I decided to attend the two-month long Phase-2, Engineer/Explosives course. By showing up at the school, I was cross-training in a second specialty, and though SF soldiers spend much time cross-training in other jobs, few actually attend a second formal specialty school. I scored a minor coup by just walking in and sitting down in an empty seat. There were no official orders allowing me to attend the school: I just took it. I keep saying it, but I will say it again: audacity will get you everything! (Including into trouble.)

Some of the classes were classified and my secret clearance was still suspended, but I just sat in the class as if I belonged, secret clearance or not. None of the formal training that I informally took ended up on my records, but I didn't care. A diploma is a reward, like a trophy, and a marketing tool for the selling of human services. The enemy would not check for diplomas one way or the other. Normally, people check for diplomas only when you are asking to work for them. I didn't plan to ask an enemy for anything.

The course started with a math test. Soldiers don't usually just slap a bunch of explosives on a bridge and say, "*Yeah*, that looks about right. 'P' for plenty." There is some calculating involved; basic algebra skills are required.

In an earlier class, the instructors noted, there had been an FFI incident. Failure to Follow Instructions. The class had been downrange placing some big charges when a student prematurely hooked up the firing device and detonated the explosives. We were told that six men died and more were wounded.

If I recall correctly, it was at this time in SF explosives school that the following incident occurred: An instructor was showing us how to make some sort of charge. Caution and safety were in the air. Like rattlesnakes, TNT, plastic explosives, dynamite, and other high explosives tend to get people's full attention.

We were sitting in open air-bleachers at one of the ranges. There were maybe thirty of us. During the normal course of the class, the instructor made a charge, which he intended to detonate later. But this time, as he handed the charge to another instructor, somehow the pin on the fuse-igniter was jerked loose and the time fuse started burning toward the charge.

The instructor screamed for everybody to run. The bleachers emptied out immediately and soldiers were crawling over each other to get out of the way. I whipped out my knife, ran down, and cut the fuse—*cutting it didn't work!* A couple of other guys had the same idea and one said, "Cut it closer!"

Military time fuse has a waterproof coating, and the fuse had burned further inside than it appeared on the bubbling surface of the sheath. My heart skipped a couple of beats, and then I cut it again, further down the powder-train, closer to the charge, which was inside a steel box for some reason. Luckily, cutting closer worked.

The instructors returned, laughing and said that it was just a fake charge, a joke. *A Joke!*

That's not what I call a joke. As the students returned to the bleachers, my hands were shaking a little, but I was laughing it off as my thoughts wandered back to some earlier bombs.

THE HIGH SCHOOL
BIGGEST BOMB CONTEST
(NOT OFFICIALLY SANCTIONED)

The non-existent Bill Gurley had long since been elected a sophomore class representative and Richard White had turned his attention to more traditional boyhood pastimes, like making explosions—or, in Richard's case, giant explosions. Richard introduced me to a friend that I will call "Eardrums."

Eardrums was making some explosions of his own when he demonstrated the gravity of the situation. He was smart, outgoing, friendly, and as a teenager, was already a pilot and scuba diver. Everybody seemed to like him. He had an enviable reputation, and led the kind of life that makes for a stirring eulogy. He was the sort of kid that, if he were killed, many people would speculate on the sort of president he would have made had tragedy not cut him off at the pass.

The materials he used were exotic by high school standards, and, though the devices were cheap and simple to make, they were not your ordinary, over-sized firecrackers. They were powerful and deadly, but his "technology" seemed safe and well-conceived. His bombs worked by the mixing together of certain gases that were very reactive when combined in a container, and detonated by a burning fuse. To prepare a device, he submerged the container upside down in water, then displaced the water inside the container with the gases, so that the mixture was relatively pure. The optimum ratio of the gases was calculated with high school chemistry calculations.

These devices were exceptionally loud. For those who have not felt the shockwave of a high-order detonation, or heard it rumble away like thunder, something similar can be found at Fourth of July or New Year's firework displays. There is the type of pyrotechnic that—*phump!*—rockets into the sky trailing orange sparks, then detonates with a *White Flash*—delay—*BOOM!* I call those kind *"White Flash—BOOMs!"* For argument's sake, I would say that ten gallons of Eardrums' gas mixture was about as loud as a *White Flash—BOOM!* But subjective loudness is difficult to gauge for many reasons, one of which is that *White Flash—BOOMs!* are airbursts, and Eardrums' were surface bursts.

Though his original technique seemed safe, Eardrums made a critical error when he changed the material used to contain the gases. His folly was trying to simplify his bomb-making by injecting the gases into a black, plastic trash bag. Trash bags have a tendency to build up a static electricity potential which often discharges with a spark, just as when you walk across a carpet on a cool, dry, day and touch another person.

The teenaged pilot had sucessfully detonated some of these devices on his own, and that day wanted to show Richard and me what he had discovered. He'd made an explosive device and, as we drove to a safe place to detonate it, I actually held it on my lap in the front of Richard's pickup truck. I might as well have been holding an angry king cobra.

There were only the three of us. Richard was driving, Eardrums was to my right in the passenger seat, and I was in the middle holding the garbage bag filled with probably twenty or thirty gallons of gases. The device was not particulary deadly compared to others we made, but it was plenty big enough to cause three eulogies.

The windows were open, so the bag was fluttering as the headlights cut a path down the dark road. I used to say, in a joking way, "It's *all* physics, man." A grasp of some basic principles of physics can be invaluable, and life-saving. When I felt the bag stick to me, it occurred all at once how incredibly dangerous this was. My heart raced and adrenaline flooded my veins. I practically screamed, ***"Richard, Stop!"***

He stopped at once, and I explained. We jumped out with the bomb, taped a fuse to the side of the bag, lit it, piled back into the truck, and drove maybe an eighth of a mile down the empty road, then stopped to watch. We stared into the night, filled with anticipation, and suddenly there was a brillant *white flash*; the shock wave hit us—***Boom!***—and rumbled away like thunder.

Richard agreed that the plastic-bag container was a bad idea and we promptly labeled it *The Hindenburg*. We warned the pilot, Eardrums, about the serious hazard of his design and that a static discharge could have caused premature detonation.

Yet Eardrums did not heed the warning; he didn't believe the danger existed, arguing that if that were so, an accident would have already occurred because he had made many of the so-called Hindenburgs. It seemed incredible that someone who was trained to fly and scuba dive, who presumably would know that he could get killed due to the *slightest* oversight, and who had seen the power of the devices, would take such an illogical position.

Later, when he was filling a garbage bag, it Hindenburged. In his face. Though he was alone when it occurred, he managed to get help, which wasn't difficult given that the explosion occurred in a populated area nearly in the middle of Winter Haven.

He was taken to the hospital. The blast singed his hair, eyelashes and eyebrows, but luckily the device had no fragments, the lack of which allowed him to keep all his appendages. The over-pressure caused severe trauma to his eardrums, leaving him unable to pursue his former hobbies. No more flying or scuba.

He must have matured five years in five seconds. It was sheer luck that he wasn't killed. Since he had just begun mixing the gases, the device was still small, maybe only a gallon or two, he said. He also said that his last memory was of the trash bag fluttering against the release of the gases. The tiny blast blew pictures off a nearby wall.

Some kids just don't seem to get the picture until it's too late. I do not call him "Eardrums" to mock his condition, but so that any teenager who stumbles into this book will remember what happened. Scare tactics are like scarecrows—they are for the birds—but the truth may help to caution. Later, I had a girlfriend whose high school boyfriend built pipe-bombs. One detonated prematurely, blowing his hand off. He died within a few minutes.

As for the garbage bag devices, the gases burn very fast, and that's what an explosion essentially is—fast burning. But that particular mixture doesn't release a great amount of energy compared to the noise it creates. So, though his eardrums were shot, our friend got to live. Other explosives, many of which have much lower detonating velocities, give off considerably more energy, and would have blown his body apart. Had it been a garden-variety pipe-bomb, it would have been nasty. Relatively speaking, Eardrums was lucky.

Before the Hindenburg, my friend John Harrison and I used a system that was safe and simple. We detonated most of our devices electrically, considerably increasing the danger in some ways, but lowering it in others. Using electricity opens a big can of worms, all of which are planning to kill and eat the inexperienced. Electrical systems bring the danger of accidental detonation to a height exceeded only by that of radio detonation. But our devices were so good, and tested so often under safe conditions before arming, that we were confident we had worked out all the bugs.

To eliminate human error, we practiced procedures, just the way rocket launches are practiced, step by step. Sequence is important; if you accidentally do step "F" before step "E" your next step may be into the grave.

After lots of above-ground tests we decided to detonate a device underwater. It would be a little tricky. Sound is magnified underwater and an explosion can burst your eardrums, or, if powerful enough, collapse your lungs. That's why it's good to throw hand grenades into the water if you think a frogman is down there. However, while we were in high school, the threat of enemy frogmen was not a major concern in Winter Haven.

We selected a remote lake where nobody would be swimming. We prepared and waterproofed a device, then tossed it into the dark water with a long electrical cord attached so that it would rest on the bottom. If it were a dud, we would simply cut the cord and leave it. Within an hour it would be harmless.

3, 2, 1 . . .

John flipped the switch . . .

Thud!

It worked!

Bluish-white smoke bubbles rose to the surface and percolated away, confirming that we could detonate charges underwater, electrically.

In his own world, Richard was an adept bomb-maker so, naturally, the conditions were ripe for our Biggest Bomb Competition. Nobody in our group was allowed to say the word "bomb" or use the real names of any of the materials; we didn't want to go to jail. We used code words, as if making a sandwich. *"How much mustard and mayonnaise do you want to use?"* The closest that we would get to the word "bomb" was "device."

For the competition we divided into two teams. Richard and the pilot, who had not yet injured his eardrums, were on one team, and John and I were to be on the winning team (or at least that's how we had it figured).

Before the teams agreed to compete, we quizzed each other endlessly to see if the other guys were the dangerous, non-thinking types that could get us all killed due to carelessness or ignorance. In retrospect, our precautions seem laughable, but at least we were trying.

We set a date, picked a desolate location, and gathered the materials. Each project was a closely guarded secret; if we knew what the other team would bring to the duel, we would have been able to add more power if needed.

The night of the competion finally rolled around and we made our final preparations. Each side had tried to figure what the other was up to, but security was tight and we had no clue what they would bring. They arrived at the rally point in Richard's black pickup truck. John and I were shocked to see that the pickup was actually required to transport their very large device, which filled a fifty-five-gallon drum! Ours fit into the car trunk! If size was an indicator, things were not looking good for the home team.

From the rally point, we traveled to the remote location. We scouted the area to make sure we were alone in the night, then placed and prepared our respective devices. We separated the devices far enough so that when the first detonated, the shock wave would not damage the second and make it a dud, and we waited until the last moment to arm them, reducing the time-window of danger. Since theirs was to ignite by fuse, its timing was less predictable, so it made sense that they go first. I was to electrically detonate our device after the first explosion.

This was serious competition. Tension and excitement were in the air as the two fuses burned toward the drum, which sat quietly, silhouetted in darkness. While our eyes adjusted, we seemed to glimpse occasional sparks in the distance, or maybe it was only our imaginations that created the flashes—nobody wanted a dud.

Richard gave the countdown. They had it timed to the second.

3
2
1
0 . . .
    everyone holding his breath . . .

1!
2!
3!
4! . . .

I barked angrily to John: "They made a dud!"

A dumpster-sized, blinding *white flash* ripped the night apart and we were momentarily blinded. The SHOCK-WAVE hit us almost simultaneously, and ***Kaaa-Booooom!***—rumbled and echoed into the darkness. Within twenty-five seconds, everyone within a five mile radius who was outside must have heard it.

That was a nuke! Awesome!

The competition was going to be closer than we thought.

I could have simply touched the wires to the battery terminals, but that would've taken some of the fun out of it, so I quickly connected the battery to the firing box, unshunted the wires, and connected them to the terminals on the box.

"Ready!" I yelled.

"Fire!" came John's reply.

I flipped the safety switch to red "**ARM**," then the firing switch to red "**FIRE.**"

There was an uncomfortable delay . . . *Oh hell! A dud!*

There always seemed to be a delay.

Another flash ripped the darkness. This time it was not white but orange. A large fireball collected itself and mushroomed skyward as the shockwave thumped our bodies ***Kaaa-Booooom!*** and rumbled away.

Adrenaline pumped through us as we rushed to collect our equipment, which was just the box and long firing wire. I ran to the car, ripped the wires off the firing box and tossed it, along with the battery, into the backseat. John sped away behind Richard's truck as I hauled the wire into the car through the open window. We escaped down the dirt road into the night to our pre-arranged safe area—a McDonald's many miles away—where we would decide the victor.

Sitting happily inside Mickey D's sipping Cokes and eating fries, we had a difficult time deciding the winners. Their explosion was louder and brighter, but ours was more visually pleasing with its fiery mushroom cloud. We squabbled awhile, having unwisely entered the competition without first setting judging criteria—in the end, each side claimed victory—but we gained mutual respect.

During the following weeks, we considered having a second competition, but given the players involved, we were afraid that we would overdo it and the detonations would be picked up by seismographs or detected by Soviet satellites and misinterpreted as ballistic missile launches. Or at least that was the joke. In any case, device-making lost its appeal as we found other pursuits. We stopped after making a few more, including the Hindenburg in Richard's pickup truck. As a result, "Eardrums" was operating alone when he made the little Hindenburg that ended any hopes of him becoming the next Captain Cousteau.

But later, and despite the accident, we made one more big device that combined our ideas. We planned meticulously to make an earthshaker.

Unfortunately, things did not go as planned.

SPECIAL FORCES, DEMOLITIONS
SABOTAGE, BOOBYTRAPS

THE TWO DEMOLITION specialists on a 12-man A-team are actually called the "engineers" because one of their primary functions is not *destruc*tion, but to help *con*struct things like schools, irrigation ditches, sewers, and so on.

I stress from the outset that guerrilla warfare itself, despite its ominous name, is not about killing and wreaking wholesale destruction, it is about *getting what you want.* If we are searching for others to buy into our way of life—and we Americans do crusade for capitalism with a nearly blind religious fervor—the best way is first to treat others with the respect and dignity that people deserve, then *convince* them that ours is a better way.

There is a great deal of salesmanship in guerrilla warfare. Obviously, in Vietnam, when the egos of politicians got involved, and the fear of communism was so great, we seemed to have forgotten the carrot and replaced it with the stick. Most politicians and even some military leaders seem to have little understanding of guerrilla warfare, though they often use the term.

But persuasion is only part of the guerrilla warfare picture. Often a nasty government or other force stands against the people, and in those cases, where power is entrenched and tyrannical, killing and destruction may be necessary. Our particular demolition course largely concerned that aspect of guerrilla warfare.

The explosives school was comprehensive. One of the first lessons taught was simply a basic principle of Special Operations: When destruction is called for, strive for maximum damage at minimum time, effort, and risk. When assessing the value of a target, before considering one's ability to hit it, the target's value to the enemy should be considered. Also important is its recoverability, which is normally determined by the time it is estimated that the enemy will take to replace, repair, or bypass the damage.

As the years passed, we made field trips, touring dams, rail stations, radio stations, factories, and so on. Unlike the field trips in school where we learned how widgets go from A to Z, we now learned how to *stop* the process of widgets going from A to Z. We made those tours with engineers and experts who showed us what to hit. *De*struction was a lot easier than *con*struction, according to our *in*struction (In contrast to a burning time fuse, that's what I call a joke, though I don't claim that it was funny).

Sabotage is a thinking person's job. To do it well doesn't mean just blowing trains off the tracks. It means damaging the enemy's war-making capacity as much as possible, with minimum effort and risk. The word "sabotage" comes from the labor unions of France in the past century. A sabot is a type of wooden shoe, and during serious labor disputes, workers sometimes jammed sabots into factory machines, halting the widgets, and costing the rich people money. When the machines stopped, the owners were suddenly better able to hear what the workers were saying.

The resisters who sabotaged were called "saboteurs." Sabotage has long been a method used by the underdog to fight a stronger foe. Unions, in fact, engage in a type of guerrilla warfare either through such direct actions as sabotage, or when they simply persuade others to join their cause to work in a united front against their common foe. If they are particularly adept, later they may somehow build a bridge and work with their former foe toward a common goal. But, as with most powerful forces, when the pendulum swings the other way, it tends to be payback time. The tyranny of the union often merely replaces an old despotism with a new one.

An example of this in warfare would be what happened in Cuba in the Fifties. We aided the guerrillas, but when Castro took over, he merely replaced one heavy hand with another. This is risky business, this guerrilla warfare. Still, conducted correctly, it can be a much *less* violent means of revolt against oppression than overt war, and it is often the only means available to the underdog. We can arm and train guerrillas to fight, but if they are successful, some guerrilla leaders probably will become warlords. A guerrilla warfare strategy must be very carefully executed, or it can backfire. (I have often thought that we should employ some of our scientists and engineers to develop weapons with a "shelf-life." The weapons and ammo would begin to deteriorate after some amount of time. This way, we could arm guerrillas knowing that they will automatically be disarmed after a certain amount of time.)

To cause maximum destruction with minimum effort, good saboteurs don't stop at just blowing up a bridge. They wait until a train is crossing. And they don't blow up the first train carrying people, unless those people are soldiers, when they can blow up the next train carrying ammunition. One of the most important aspects of guerrilla warfare is to strive *not* to hurt the people that one is trying to protect and persuade; the mission is to protect, organize, train, and fight *with* them. A particularly useful characteristic of most tyrants is that they create enemies with their heavy-handed tactics. Understandably, their enemies become your friends.

A saboteur can inflict serious damage upon the enemy by disrupting production. Why damage electrical transformers, though it may be easy, when the saboteur can destroy the transformer factory? (*Then* go around shooting transformers.) In some countries, there are only a few types of cars, and only a few models account for the vast majority in use. Often in those countries, especially in current or former communist countries, a single factory builds the whole car, tank, train, or whatever, so makes a great target. Destroying the factory will halt production, and replacing parts will soon become a serious problem.

Just as people have hearts and brains, every target or infrastructure has critical nodes, the damaging of which can bring it down or cripple it. Telephones, for instance. It is senseless to try to destroy every telephone when the saboteur can instead hit the telephone company, which, in effect, is like taking out all the phones at once. Electrical and phone lines are easy targets. There is no need to destroy every radio or TV in a country if the saboteurs can simply destroy the broadcasting stations, which also makes the government look weak each time the evening news is only white noise. Even though they will normally get the stations back on the air quickly, the white noise is indisputable proof that the guerrillas are scoring victories.

The government must rebuild and then guard potential targets, which is expensive and demoralizing. The guerrilla's object is not to wage indiscriminate war, but to cripple, then destroy the enemy's will to fight. The object is to do things that will lead to victory, and "victory" must be clearly defined. Does *victory* mean completely overthrowing the government? Perhaps *victory* will be the institution of free elections, or to stop taxation without representation.

Some people, especially many of the millions who watched the smart bombs and cruise missiles during the Gulf War, think that unconventional warfare is outdated. Nothing could be further from the truth. LICs (low intensity conflicts) are a global fact of life, and the U.S. can't, for many reasons, go around shooting cruise missiles at factories and harbors.

This ability to fight in covert or clandestine ways, and to be able to counter the same within our own borders is important. The United States is particularly vulnerable to this type of attack simply because we have a lot of wealth to attack, and wealth is important to us. And we are vulnerable because our country is full of urban centers, rather than spread thin, like many less industrialized nations.

Also, we have social rifts that are widening and vulnerable to exploitation, and the United States itself is a candidate for eventually going the way of Yugoslavia if we do not make serious adjustments to the direction that we are now heading. This is deadly serious business. The "ethnic cleansing" that could take place here, given a population in which there are more guns than adults, and our underlying warring mentality, could make Yugoslavia look like summer camp. We cannot allow groups who advocate dividing our nation, as many militant and hate-mongering radical elements would like, to gain power. *Can't happen here?* Yes, it can.

We learned about conventional blasting techniques like blowing bridges, trains, or whatever. How to blow frozen lakes so that they are impassable, not that I had ever seen a frozen lake at that point. We learned how to destroy lots of other things. For instance, the "proper method" of destroying fire hydrants. After all, one rule of thumb is never to blow something up when you can burn it down, and when burning is your chosen method, it's good to take out the little fire hydrants that stand sentry. Guerrillas often plant a big time-delay bomb nearby to take out the firefighters, too, a tactic which causes them to not want to respond to fires. This is very demoralizing. (This ain't summer camp.)

Improvisation is invaluable. We learned other less dramatic methods of harming the enemy, such as teaching locals what they can add to the enemy's gas tanks that will damage the engines. Resisters working in ammo factories have been known to make dud ammunition by improperly assembling shells and bombs. They may improperly assemble tanks or aircraft on the assembly line, causing breakdowns. Trains can be derailed or prevented from climbing in mountainous regions by greasing the tracks.

After the Resistance is cultivated and motivated, their imagination and initiative can go a long way toward gaining victory. We only have to look at the Vietnamese guerrillas, who fought our country against seemingly hopeless odds, to see the power of guerrilla operations. The guerrillas, along with their obvious disadvantages, have some major advantages. For instance, they hit targets when they see fit. The big guy can't guard everything all the time, and whenever he drops his guard, *whammo!*, the guerrillas fade back into the woodwork.

One of the most important aspects of guerrilla warfare is this: *if the guerrillas are not losing, they are winning.* This is especially true when the guerrillas are fighting the United States; we seem to have a low tolerance for wars that last more than a few months. And though we don't mind causing massive bloodshed, the public at large normally seems ready to pull the plug when the first few drops of American blood are spilled. We want the guerrillas to play by *our* rules, which are the rules that favor us. We complained that the Viet Cong dipped their punji stakes in feces while, simultaneously, our bombers flew overhead and turned parts of their country into a moonscape. Realizing this, the wise underdogs avoid direct confrontation and decisive battles. If they can cause us to spend our precious money, and spill some blood, while at the same time making themselves appear "not worth it," we probably will go home.

Guerrillas must normally accomplish a great deal with limited means. When using explosives, it is vitally important to know when to do what, with what, and how. Lots of homework. There are many blasting techniques, just as there are numerous explosives to learn about.

Is the target underwater? What is the temperature? If the night is cold and dry, static electricity can spoil the operation by causing a premature detonation. Helicopters are a potential danger; rotors beat the air and build an enormous static charge. If you touch a helicopter before it lands, you can be shocked. If you are carrying unprotected electric blasting caps, you can be killed. If you are carrying explosives next to the caps, the helicopter and passengers can be destroyed. There are lots of interesting ways to accidentally die around explosives. But for all that, U.S. military explosives are safe if one studies the job thoroughly, and pays attention to detail.

U.S. military explosives such as C-4, TNT, and dynamite are made to withstand direct hits by high-powered weapons without exploding. During our first day at the range, the TACs had brought along a sniper rifle with which they shot various explosives. Nothing happened, except that the C-4 splattered like play-dough. Then we burned various explosives, all without exploding them.

To successfully blow something up, one must determine which technique to use, what type of explosive to employ, gauge how much explosive is actually needed, and understand how to safely detonate the charge(s). Last, but definitely not least, one must know where and how to place the charges, which is an entire separate study by itself, and enough to thoroughly frustrate a conscientious soldier. The final test for that portion of the course was called Calc & Place. (Calculation and placement of charges.) This test spelled the end of the road for some soldiers in the Q-course; if you failed the test, and the retest, *goodbye*.

The Calc & Place test consisted of a written portion that lasted, as I recall, several hours, with numerous simple algebra problems involved. For instance, one formula was $P=R^3KC$, or as it was called "P equals R cubed K C." (If a person joined the Army to avoid algebra, he should not go into demolitions.) Also on the test were pictures of bridges and other targets, such as railways. The students had to identify the vulnerabilities of the targets, and sketch where to place the charges—and what kind of explosives were preferred for a given target, and what technique to use. Finally, after the paper test, the students had to successfully blow up certain targets at the range, and the timing of detonation had to be correct to within a couple of seconds.

There was also the improvised munitions and boobytrap training, which was a jarring wake-up call. This part was classified, but in reality, like many classified matters, there was no secret to hide and the information was widely available. Nevertheless, they trusted me to keep my mouth shut, so I will only speak of it in general terms.

Innumerable substances can be made to blow up or burn, so the possibilities for boobytraps are limited only by the imagination of the maker. We learned about many potential explosives, for instance, improvised incendiary devices to burn down structures. These improvised devices often require improvised triggers, such as timers. A timer can be made from nothing more than beans and water. Put beans in a cup, add water, and the beans will expand. As they expand, they cause two wires to touch, completing the electrical circuit to the charge—***boom!***

IGNITER MIX

A rubber glove may also be used as a membrane for this delay. Pour some concentrated sulfuric acid into the glove and suspend the glove over a pile of igniter material. When the acid eats through the glove, it will drip onto the igniter and start a fire. A rubber glove will give a longer delay time than a condom because the material is thicker.

Some incendiary devices spontaneously burst into flames when various chemicals mix. A timer for a certain type of device can be nothing more than putting one of the chemicals into a condom. The chemical will eat

The rubber membranes for use in this delay must be without pin holes or other imperfections. The sulfuric acid must be *concentrated*. If only battery-grade sulfuric acid is available, it must be concentrated before use to a specific gravity of 1.835 by heating it in an enameled, heat-resistant glass or porcelain pot until dense, white fumes appear.

through the latex, mix with the other chemical, then burst into flames. Just the boobytrap and improvised munitions portion of the training, not including the regular blasting techniques, filled four books, and the books were quick to point out that these were only ideas to get you thinking. Still being a teenager, I found all this fascinating and read the books many times. The final test on the improvised portion of the class involved, among other things, successfully boobytrapping a desk so that when the target pulled out the middle drawer, he would be killed.

It's difficult to overstate how much fun it was blowing things to kingdom come. It was pure joy to build charges that consisted of maybe fifty pounds of TNT, and blowing up simulated parts of bridges, or practically launching cars into low-earth orbit with ammonium nitrate charges that we improvised, using fertilizer and other ingredients.

Even chicken droppings can be used to make explosives.

THE LAST DEVICE

A COUPLE OF years before the manslaughter charge, after a temporary retirement from the creation of bigger and better bombs, we pushed our luck one more time.

We decided to combine our skills to build a monster explosive device, and set the date for its unveiling to coincide with a Saturday night high school party that would take place on a ranch owned by the wealthy parents of a friend. There was a lake on the ranch that was large enough for us to detonate a major device on without the chance of someone being injured.

In fact, as we recall, when we performed a "reconnaissance" of the lake during daylight, we decided that if we couldn't have at least triple the distance deemed safe between the explosion and the observers, we wouldn't go on with the show. Since our planned "spectacular" was to be a surprise, we told nobody and set about our work.

Because the device would be heavy, we needed a method of floating it safely on the lake and keeping it dry, so we decided to float it on a car innertube, on top of which we strapped a wooden pallet. The device would sit atop the pallet.This was to be a covert operation; we would go in black, and at night. We planned to slip into the water in darkness from a secluded area near the woods and swim the device out to the prearranged location. If the wind was anything but calm, we would abort for fear that the contraption would drift ashore in the darkness.

The device itself was kept simple to avoid problems, and since our first and biggest priority was safety, we spent more time thinking about avoiding what might go wrong than anything else. There was no doubt that it would explode. Our problem was precise timing and location.

We constructed it in such a way as to minimize "primary fragmentation"—shrapnel—and the only secondary fragmentation would be from the pallet or the innertube, neither of which were much of a threat. By the time we were sixteen, we had already heard enough metal whiz overhead, and bury itself in chunks in nearby trees. We knew those trees could have been leg bones, or skulls, and were under no illusions about the "safety" of most explosions.

A seventeen-year-old mind should never be discounted. It often makes up in quickness what it lacks in experience. All those bubbling adolescent hormones are responsible for many of the wild things it conjures up. And, I can see looking back, we were certifiably crazy for what we did.

To prevent the device from being blown to shore, we made a cinder block anchor with plenty of rope to reach bottom. Eardrums was to drop us off on land, and pick us up later. We didn't consult him for design advice, but he was still good as a knowledgable support person. After his accident, he didn't even want to get close to an armed device.

Before detonation, Eardrums and John would be at the party. One of their jobs was safety; if anything went wrong and they saw our lethal device floating to shore, they were to make a swift, minimally incriminating explanation, and evacuate everybody. We figured it was better to go to jail as minors charged with building a bomb than to dismember and cook some of our friends when it detonated. We were responsible lunatics.

As if swimming in total darkness while pushing a bomb-carrying innertube were not sufficient cause for alarm, we also had to consider the possible hostility of our "hosts": *Alligators.* They hunt primarily at night, and there were no houses around the lake, so it was infested. The weather was warm, and there would be gator nests around the lake, and baby gators near the shore. And momma gators. And bull gators.

The lake was the home of some whoppers, so there was a real chance that one or both of us might be eaten. Then there were the countless snakes that inhabited the water, and the thought of being bitten in the face by a snake can be cause for alarm. Despite the dire possibilities conjured up by our sometimes over-active imaginations, we, being teenagers, joked about being gator bait or snake snacks, and decided to do it anyway.

We decided against using an electrical system for detonation because of the water and our method of insertion. A radio system was too expensive for our slim-to-vanishing budget, not to mention being fraught with hazards (though we were certain that we could overcome those). But there was no use to go to the expense and research for radio control of what we all agreed would be our final bomb.

We could have used a timer, but back then a timer meant an electrical device, so we settled on a set of burning fuses. We calculated the length of the fuses to allow us just enough time to get back to shore and to the pickup point, where Eardrums would come for us in his truck. As another safety measure, we made the fuses redundant: self-reigniting. In other words, the *three* fuses snaked around and crossed over each other so that if one burned out, it would be relit by another. The fuses were cut short to reduce the danger time that the device could float to shore, or that a boat would happen upon it, but we balanced that against giving ourselves plenty of time to swim away.

We would watch from shore. In the very unlikely event of a boat starting out, we would be forced to compromise ourselves by telling the people to stay away for a few minutes—if we somehow could manage to get the boaters' attention.

After detonation, the plan was that Eardrums would immediately whisk us away, and we would quickly dry off, put on our party clothes, and join the festivities as if we had nothing to do with the explosion.

After long and careful planning, we were confident nothing had been overlooked. We assembled the device at the last minute to reduce the danger time. Only one person worked on the hazardous parts, so that in case of accidental detonation, the uninjured people would be able to call an ambulance and douse any flames with the fire extinguisher and water hose that we kept running just in case. This was wishful thinking, really; if the device detonated prematurely, they would have been collecting us from the tops of trees with tweezers.

Soon it was ready, and I now know that the device was exceptionally safe, even by military standards. What could possibly go wrong that we had not already thought of (besides the gator/snake wild card)?

We rehearsed our plan, except for the actual swimming part, many times. It should've been simple. I was very concerned about the gator hazard, though Richard played it down as no big deal, despite his living next to a large lake, and the fact that gators often came up into his yard or on his dock. Or, perhaps, because he saw gators practically every day for years on end, he simply felt comfortable in their presence. I saw gators practically everyday, too, but was not at all comfortable swimming with them.

Execution:

Eardrums was to drop us off with his truck, but he began fidgeting and complaining as if he wanted to back out. We somehow convinced him that if the bomb were going to detonate prematurely, it would have done so already. The silliness of that argument didn't have to be explained to Eardrums, of all people, but he finally agreed, so Richard and I loaded the device into the truck.

It was dark. We lay low beside the device in the bed of the pickup. We made our way down the road, passing cars along the way, and finally reached the dirt road by the lake. A quarter-mile down the bumpy road, Eardrums turned off his lights, drove a little further and stopped. *All clear.* Richard and I were out and away in less than fifteen seconds. Eardrums drove away.

Darkness.

The party was raging maybe five hundred yards to our left, and fifty yards from the water, which provided still more safety buffers. The music was blaring and we saw lots of schoolmates in silhouette, with their bushels of oysters and kegs of beer. The party was reaching its climax as we moved to the edge of the water. We watched the lake for a short time and there were no boats—at least none with lights on—the wind was calm, the "mission" was still a *GO*. We carried the improvised raft between us, our masterpeice firmly secured and waterproofed on top.

The warm water was shin-deep where we sat down in the weeds, the tube between us. The edge of the lake was the most likely place to get killed by a giant gator, and that scenario was playing in my mind as we slipped black scuba fins on over wetsuit booties, which were our shoes if we had to run.

Richard whispered, "I'm ready."

"Ready here," I whispered back.

Richard laughed quitely and said, "It's *show* time," and tried to put his hand on my shoulder, but, in the dark, hit me in the nose instead.

"Ouch!" I whispered.

"Sorry 'bout that," he said.

"Didn't hurt," I said, faking a laugh, feeling the bomb with my left hand and my nose with the right.

We stood in the darkness and, with fins on, walked backwards, in approved Frogman fashion, into deeper water, crouching down, until we were about waist deep. From there we started our stopwatches and began to swim into the blackness.

We swam out into a silent lake that was so dark I could barely see Richard, who was a couple of feet away, against the dim light of the party. Behind the clouds, the moon barely lit the black water as our fins rippled the surface.

Occasionally, headlights from a new carload of students flashed across the lake and temporarily illuminated us, so we decided to swim with the innertube in tow so that its blackness would camouflage us. *What if someone catches a glimpse and figures we are a giant alligator? He might grab a high-powered rifle from his truck and start taking shots. What if a bullet hits the device! What if . . . Stop thinking!*

We swam further and further into the black water. If a boat were to magically appear, we would quickly detach the device and drop it into the water as planned. The fishermen might think that we were crazy for swimming with an innertube in a gator-infested lake at night, but at least they would not see the device.

We had arranged the system to operate without a light, so we were completely blacked out, though our faces were not camouflaged because we planned to go to the party later. We would listen to our drunk schoolmates at the illegal beer bash talk about the illegal bomb. We were quite the optimists.

Gators are basically living dinosaurs that scientists say have been around in almost the same form for well over two hundred million years. They have seen more full moons and comets reflect off their waters than mankind likely ever will, on this planet.

It follows that gators are great survivors and hunters, living in balance with their world. They have highly developed, exceptionally acute senses for detecting prey in the darkness, including the ability to sense even slight disturbances in the water, and they have excellent night vision. When you shine a light, their eyes glow in the night like little beacons; creatures with eyes designed to see in the dark have that eye-shine characteristic. It was a glimmering we were not eager to see that night.

Gators often swallow their prey whole, but if it's too big, they will violently rip it to pieces by shaking their heads or spinning in the water. Sometimes they hide their catch on the bottom under a log until it rots, or keep it between their jaws while it softens. Gators are not normally aggressive toward people, but this was nighttime and we were literally swimming with them. The threat they represented was very real. I was becoming seriously afraid, more so than I had imagined, and wanted to turn around. This was truly stupid, I thought, but we kept going.

The further we got from shore, the more intense became my feeling that at any moment my head would be crushed like a grape in the jaws of a massive black gator. Or maybe it would simply slip in from below and grab my legs or waist, or crush my rib cage as it pulled me below the inky surface before I could even scream for help. Screaming would do no good, and holding my breath would only make me drown slower.

My mind was racing: *What will I do if a gator gets Richard? Fight it? Swim like hell? Would I have the guts to go underwater and fight it to save Richard? This is such a stupid, stupid, stupid idea!*

The adrenaline machine was working perfectly as designed, but if Richard could do it, so could I. Besides, this was fun in its own strange, teenage-boy sort of way, and it was "training." We finned across what seemed an eternity of darkness, punctuated only by the occasional sweeping of headlights across water. The sound of loud music, probably the then-inescapable Michael Jackson, floated to us across the water.

Finally, we made it to our chosen spot. Our watches read that we had been swimming for fifteen minutes. We stopped, virtually in the middle of gator-land. We went through the much rehearsed ritual of preparing the device for detonation, which took maybe thirty seconds. It seemed like forever.

Final procedures: *Anchor's away.*

Richard asked in a whisper, "Is the anchor on the bottom?"

"Yes," I whispered.

Richard asked, "Is all okay?"

"Yes."

He proceeded as per plan and asked, "Do you see any reason not to light the fuses?"

"No. Proceed," I whispered.

"I will now light the fuses," he answered.

Richard pulled a lighter out of one of the three separate waterproof bags that were taped to the pallet. Each bag had a lighter, waterproof matches, and a small towel with which we could dry our hands. He dried his hands as practiced, and initiated the device on the first try. The lighter illuminated Richard's face and the device, as all three fuses sputtered to life.

I didn't know what Richard was thinking, but I was now afraid of two sources of imminent death: The gators, which I knew were all around, (they had to be, and I knew that *they* knew we were swimming in their home/supper bowl), and the very large device with several fuses hissing, spitting, and sparking in the night. The long fuses snaked around the tube in a special way so that we had enough time to return to shore, but also in such a way that a spark would not jump from a fuse and light itself closer to the device—which would cause premature detonation. And our *premature extinction,* though I prefered not to dwell on that. It causes one to wonder who is smarter: human beings, or alligators?

What if one of us gets a cramp and can't swim fast enough? I thought. We had considered that. Tough luck. The other would drag the disabled one as fast as he could and hope to get away.

As we swam to shore I whispered into the blackness to Richard, "Are you worried about gators?"

Through the darkness Richard made his trademark snicker-smirk, which was always accompanied by a cough-like noise. He whispered back, sounding like he was on his back with his face pointing up, "It's a little late to worry about that now."

"Hey, Richard."

"What?"

"Let's speed up the pace a little. Forget about the ripples, nobody will see us."

"Stick to the plan. Let's just keep this pace," he scolded.

"Why?" I prodded. "Are you tired and can't keep up with me?"

Again, I heard his trademark snicker-smirk. Richard was not afraid of gators, or at least he wasn't admitting to it, nor would he pick up the pace. Maybe he was sticking to the plan that we'd made before my adrenaline was pumping because he was genuinely savoring the experience. Plans always look different through the lens of fear, and it can take lots of guts to stick to plans that were made when everything was calm and quiet.

For me, the worst came when we were finally close to shore and had only about a minute to go, just one more minute of swimming. I was ready to ditch the fins and run a solid mile from the lake as fast as I could. But I kept my composure, and, since it was dark, Richard couldn't see my apprehension.

Several times I closed my eyes, turned over so that my belly was facing the bottom of the lake, and descended a few feet so as not to ripple the surface, then burst forward with hard fin kicks. Underwater it was completely black and silent, as if we were swimming in the digestive juices of a giant stomach. We could dissolve in the darkness and never be seen again, and after all the gator meat that I had eaten, maybe this was a time for cosmic justice.

Richard kept plodding along. Sticking to the plan. The &^%$#@! plan. I can't believe I helped make it! "Make sure you stick to the plan," I would say and Richard would look nervous as if he weren't sure he could do it. Oh, he could do it alright. *Too* well, if you asked me. Before I make another plan, I better make sure that I can stick to it, I thought.

We reached shore, and sat in the waist-deep water. We hunkered in darkness and weeds, and began taking off our fins. My hands were shaking and fumbling. Finally, fins in hand, we rose, staying crouched, and made our way the last few steps to shore. When we were about twenty feet from the lake, I could finally believe the gator threat was over.

Staying low, we made it to the prearranged spot where we were to be picked up immediately following detonation. We each checked our Casio digital watches to see where the countdown timers were in the sequence. Our timing was good.

The countdown timers were preset with the calculated eighteen minute burn time, and we had started them when Richard lit the fuses. There still was a minute or so remaining; I think the gator-threat hastened our retreat and we were ahead of schedule. Again, it seemed like forever.

"Please don't be a dud," I whispered to myself. I didn't want to swim back out there, but if it were a dud, we would. It would be hard to find in the darkness, so we would swim separately, dragging a string between us to snag the anchor line. And then there was the terrifying idea that it would blow the moment we touched it.

Don't be a dud . . .

The countdown:
14
13
12
11
10
9
8
please
please
please
don't
be
a

dud

ZERO . . .

nothing

+1
+2
+3
+4
+5

A blinding *white flash* shattered the darkness, and was immediately followed by a very large, orange mushroom fireball that had not yet gathered itself to rise into the night. For a moment dozens of gator-eyes flashed in the light, the water glistened with the rising fireball, and trees around the lake were illuminated. As this happened, the SHOCK-WAVE smacked us . . .

Kaaa-Booooom!

and rumbled away into the night. It would be heard for miles.

I sure hope Granny and Granddad didn't hear that. They lived about five miles away, but it was a possibility because they had heard them before, but of course I had to deny everything. Truth-telling is a virtue, but always telling the truth is just plain stupid.

The music stopped at the party. Flames spread in the area around the detonation, as we had planned, for further visual effect. Everybody at the party was focused on the burning lake, where flames assaulted the darkness and lit the rippling water. The pallet was completely destroyed, as if by a nuclear detonation on a small south-Pacific atoll, and only tiny, scorched pieces were found floating in the weeds the next day.

As the lake burned, we expected the imminent arrival of our hearing-impaired friend in his pickup truck. The people at the party were stunned by the explosion, which still illuminated the lake, as well as the shock wave that went beyond tickling their ears; it thudded through their bodies, as some later testified.

Eardrums was late, and we were getting nervous. Some partygoers thought that an airplane had crashed or a fishing boat had exploded, and jumped into their trucks, racing across a big field to check around the lake. Our linkup point was exposed simply because there was no good concealment near the road, and we depended on a speedy pickup for escape.

Eardrums was now very, very late. Headlights flashed and bounced across the field and we hugged the ground as several pickup trucks came straight at us, though they had not yet spotted us. *Where the hell is Eardrums! Something is wrong!*

Thirty seconds later the trucks were on us, blinding us with their highbeams and searchlights. We strained to see, but it was like staring into the sun. There seemed no use in running. They stopped and piled out of the trucks, and when they walked in front of the headlights, the shadows allowed us glimpses. Moments later, we were surrounded by eight or ten guys—*busted.* Their excitement level was very high—as high as their blood alcohol level—and one of them started talking violence, which quickly caught on.

We were outnumbered, wrong, and on private property. Some of them, who had probably never been in a real fight, now saw that they had an advantage and wanted to do some ass-whipping from the safety of the herd. Few men have the guts to stand alone, but any punk, any Lizard, can cast stones from a mob. There was little doubt we would lose if they attacked. I kept quiet, my hands to my sides.

Richard did the talking.

The situation was volatile. Very tense. This was Polk County, and violence was no stranger to these parts.

So there we were. Negotiating for our hides. Richard kept talking. The Big Mouth of the group was angry at Richard, and threatening from the safety of the little mob. Richard had never been in a fight. I told Big Mouth to shut up. Richard quieted me the way one quiets a friend, and kept talking.

Richard, the seventeen-year-old man who at the age of fifteen had brought Bill Gurley to office, brought the mood of the mob down to a manageable level, then someone from the mob told Big Mouth to shut up. They were siding with Richard. He culled the herd. Amazing.

Cooler heads prevailed, and fortunately Richard and I were widely liked. It was the alcohol, the excitement, and then Big Mouth's saber-rattling that started things down the wrong path. We went back to the party with them, and the event went down in history as the unchallenged highlight of a party that otherwise would have been deservedly forgotten.

It turned out that Eardrums claimed something akin to flashbacks or posttraumatic stress disorder when he saw and felt the explosion. He was too afraid to pick us up. Richard forgave him, but I felt betrayed at an important moment. With the additional perspective gained from a few years of experience, I do not judge him quite so harshly now, but I would never again willingly depend on him to overcome his physical fears.

Bomb-making was very dangerous and the joys it provided did not justify its risks. Most young bomb-makers have little understanding of the hidden dangers awaiting them, the mishaps that will splatter their hands all over their faces, blinding them with fragments of their own finger bones.

It wasn't worth it and I wouldn't do it again if I had a choice. Even worse, it didn't favorably impress any girls.

Perhaps the only picture left of that night is the drawing in my yearbook:

Maryland

Nothing.

To maintain the appearance of justice, the case was being dragged out, meaninglessly. I anxiously awaited the setting of a date for trial.
Just waiting.

ARMY TRAINING

THE CHARGE PENDING, I simply hoped for the best, and continued to prepare for a Special Forces team.

During Pre-Phase, I had befriended an Army sergeant who was scheduled to go through my class. Before one march he had secretly added weight to my rucksack as a joke. Well, maybe he thought that it was funny, but a joke like that is never finished until the favor has been returned. He had been injured during the course and was now waiting for a new class date. Sometimes he grumbled in a half-serious way that I was already wearing sergeant stripes when it had taken him years in an infantry unit in Panama to earn his.

"Yon, what's up with those stripes? How long you been in the Army now? A year and a few months? It took me *four* years to earn these stripes. I was bustin' my hump in that jungle down there when you was in junior high." Then he would launch into another jungle story about some guy wearing night vision goggles who walked off a cliff, and he would finish that story with a warning that I should be careful when wearing night vision goggles because they leave you with bad depth perception. Or he would talk about the zillions of biting ants or the trees with all the spikes that you better not run into at night. His stories were fun and interesting, but I was still looking for some way to return the favor of all that weight.

I would boobytrap his quarters.

"Killing" him with a boobytrap would be simple. A kid could do it. But I wanted to show some class. After all, he was a "real sergeant." By now I had made lots of boobytraps and we often set them for each other. Knock on the door—*Flash!* (We normally used flashcubes to simulate detonation.) Talk in a room—*Flash!* Walk in a room—*Flash!* Turn on your radio—open the window—turn on the lights—pick up the phone, the paper or what-ever—*Flash!* Boobytraps are scary business, but they can also relieve the tedium of the everyday routine.

I wanted to hit him in his own room, but in a special way that he would appreciate. So, a few nights later, under the cover of darkness, I struck. While he was out for the night, I climbed on his roof, wearing a camou-flaged uniform and ski mask. Sometimes it's better not to use camouflage paint because you can't remove it quickly the way you can a mask, dark clothes, and gloves. (On the other hand, camouflaged patterns are better concealment than black clothes that leave silhouettes intact, though SWAT teams wear black for intimidation purposes.)

I could almost hear the *Mission Impossible* music playing while I slipped through his second story window—this was as fun as blowing up cars at the range! I could have simply rigged his door, but he wouldn't give me any credit for that. One of our objects was to learn to improvise. Doors are every-where. Any booby can trap a door. So, I recon'd his room. There was a radio, but that would be too easy. I wanted to scare him. Keep him on his toes.

Hmm . . .

He must have showered and grabbed a pair of pants and a shirt that were hanging in his locker; the hangers and towel were on the bed, and situated in such a way . . . *I found the trigger.* Detonation would be initiated electrically.

I noted how they were sitting because I needed to replace the hangers and towel exactly where they had been. I grabbed them and headed out the window.

They had been sitting on his bed so that the towel separated the hangers. I would hook the battery to each hanger. One hanger would be positive, the other negative. The towel would separate them. When the hangers touched, they would complete the circuit and—*goodbye!*

I only needed to arrange the contraption so that any disturbance would cause the hangers to touch. I tested it, but it didn't work. *Huh?* I was sure that the hangers were conductive, so why didn't it detonate?

While closely examining a hanger, the reason hit me. The hanger had some sort of lamination around the metal, probably to keep it from rusting. No problem. I removed the lamination from the critical sections of the hang-ers and, for good measure, tested them several times to figure out what else could go wrong.

Finally, I crept back through his window—*Mission Impossible theme playing*—replaced, and then armed the device. It's funny how you can get a little nervous arming a boobytrap even when it's non-lethal. His towel and hangers were not exactly where he had left them, but unless he had a near-photographic memory, it was close enough. If he did have a photographic memory, I would lose.

I held a small, red-filtered flashlight between my teeth, making sure not to shine it at a window where a passerby might catch a glint. This was actu-ally a little dangerous. If a passing group of soldiers saw the glint of a red flashlight, or saw me creeping around blacked out in the night wearing a mask—they would instantly conclude: *Barracks Rat.* Thief.

This was SF country. TACs were around day and night, and soldiers who were waiting for a class, and those going through Phase-2, lived all around. I could imagine what might happen if they caught me. Either it'd be a full-on assault with fists—they could round up a dozen men in a minute with only a shout—or maybe they would ambush me from the dark. Suddenly this didn't seem like such a great idea. It felt a little like I was swimming out in that gator-teeming lake again.

As for the boobytrap, the device was armed without mishap. I turned off the flashlight, crawled out the window, and made it back to my place without getting caught. Doing stuff like this helped me forget about the manslaughter charges in Maryland, and soon I fell smugly asleep.

Later that night . . .
Loud, angry footsteps pounding up the wooden stairs startled me awake. It must have worked, I thought.
Bam! Bam! Bam!
Yikes!
That was not a friendly knock, nor was it a polite little knuckle rap to see if I might be awake—it was a fist slamming my door! Though I felt honored that he knew who did it, I couldn't help noticing that he seemed a little upset.

I answered the door with the most innocent, meek, sleepy hello that I could muster, holding my pillow like a teddy bear against my chest as if to say, *who, me? What are you doing here so late?* But he didn't give me the chance to say more than one mouse-like *hello*.

As I opened the door, he pushed his way through, carrying a six-pack of beer. He sat in my metal folding chair where I did homework on the wooden table. There were books strewn about on the table along with papers and pencils. I had been practicing calculating charges. My quarters always looked like a book-bomb had exploded, spewing books and papers all over. With a couple of swipes of his arms, all the books and papers that were on the table were sent flying to the floor. *Rather aggressive*, I thought. He plopped the beer on the table.

Then he just sat there.
And sat there.
And said nothing.
He came back to life just as quickly, pulling a beer off the plastic ring. The room was mostly dark except for the light streaming in from the open door, and the red glow of my alarm clock showing it was almost midnight. He threw a hot beer to—or at—me, but it bounced off the pillow that I was holding and hit the floor. It erupted and was squirting away in the darkness before I could find it and toss it out the open second-story window, to which someone down below yelled, *"What the f—!"* (Many soldiers think you can't hear them unless they cuss.) I peered out the window and saw a soldier sitting in the dark on the front steps smoking a sniper magnet, a cigarette. *"Sorry about that. . . ."*

I was not winning friends that night, but I was certainly influencing people.

While sitting silhouetted on the metal chair in my dark room, the angry sergeant pulled another beer off the plastic ring, opened it, *pishh,* and guzzled it himself. There was no hint of apology for dousing my room in hot beer or for clearing off the table.

"Don't worry about the mess," I said sarcastically as I flipped on the light and squinted. "I'll clean it up."

"Yon, you scared the *shit* out of me!"

"I thought you would appreciate that," I said, laughing.

He wanted to sound angry, but he was too "dead" for that, and the humor was creeping in despite his best efforts.

This time I had not used a flashcube, but a long string of firecrackers. He said that his place was a mess with all the firecracker paper, but I detected appreciation of my foray.

Mission accomplished.

Around the same time, I figured that Richard White needed some caffeine in his coffee to keep him on his toes. He had asked me to check the prices of Casio digital watches in the PX. (Post Exchange. A store on base with discounted prices.) I got back to him with the cost, $34, and he asked me to buy one. Technically speaking, it was illegal to buy for civilians in the PX, so the watch was his Christmas present. Or so he thought.

I did buy the watch, but took it out of the little white plastic box and replaced it with fun. The trigger consisted of a mousetrap cut to fit the watch-box, two metal thumbtacks, one paperclip, some tape, three inches of wire, a watch battery and a flashcube. It was designed so that the moment he opened the package, the box would fly open and the flashcube would blind him.

Richard was in the mail room at his college when the little package arrived. There were students all around and—*Gotcha!*

Richard still has the device and it still works.

The note inside says,

> Richard: If the trap closed consider yourself a casualty. It would be just as easy to rig with military explosives.
> [% chance you got hurt] if trap closed: 90% dead, 10% alive.
>
> . . . this was . . . only to train you! Feel special, or sick.

On the back of the mousetrap was written: CARLOS WAS HERE. The reference was to an infamous terrorist, then at large, who now is rotting away in a French prison.

Anything to take my mind off the charges.

WAR STUDIES

I QUERIED THE most experienced vets, asking them what they recommended I study. "What would help in a guerrilla warfare situation?" I asked. They gave lots of advice. First, they suggested, study the five SF specialties: Weapons, Engineer/Explosives, Medical, Operations and Intelligence, and Communications. Of course you can't even begin to learn it all, but at least familiarize yourself with the abilities and limitations of the other team functions, and learn as much as you can.

Mostly, they suggested that I first become highly knowledgeable in my primary specialty, weapons, because my future team would depend on me. They said that I should also study the history of guerrilla warfare, and the critical role of psychological operations. I took their suggestions and studied war at night.

The more I learned, the more awestruck I was at the breadth, complexity, and depth of warfare. I am continuously amazed to see civilians who read books and watch some movies, then suddenly think they are the next *Sun Tzu.*

It became apparent that I could study for the next fifty years and still only scratch the surface. I began reading what the old-timers, the masters, like Mao Tse-Tung, had to say about guerrilla warfare. Many of their hard-won lessons are locked in the pages of books, and passed down from old-timers to upstarts like me. Their political views are as irrelevant as those of a gymnast. I was not learning politics, but war. It didn't matter if I learned it from a communist or a Martian, because the ideas were universally applicable.

Mastering warfare is akin to mastering "science." "Warfare," like "science," is a broad term covering many diverse specialties, each of which is tremendously deep and wide in its own domain. Can anyone say that he has mastered chemistry, biology, physics? Each of those disciplines can be further divided into infinitely deep sub-domains.

Depending on who makes the definitions, warfare may be divided into Naval Warfare, (which has its own complex categories such as submarine warfare), Air, Space, and Land Warfare. Land Warfare is itself a broad term, and the complex mission of Special Operations Forces (which include Delta Force, SEALS, Army Rangers, Task Force 160, Special Forces and a few others) focuses on a tiny region of the spectrum.

As for Special Forces, our little region included things like counterterrorism, antiterrorism[3], complex strike missions, strategic intelligence collection,

---

[3]Counterterrorism refers to offensive actions such as hostage rescue, or military strikes against terrorists. Antiterrorism refers to defensive actions such as training people how to reduce their exposure to acts of terrorism.

foreign internal defense, etc. Again, these categories have no absolute definitions and are as inseparable as the smells in a bakery.

An Army manual provides a tedious but straightforward definition of Unconventional Warfare:

> UW includes but is not limited to, the interrelated fields of guerrilla warfare, evasion and escape, subversion, sabotage, direct action missions and other operations of a low-visibility, covert or clandestine nature. These interrelated aspects of UW may be prosecuted singly or collectively by predominantly indigenous personnel, usually supported and directed in varying degrees and (an) external source(s) during all conditions of war and peace. . . .UW is conducted to exploit military, political, economic, or psychological vulnerabilities of an enemy. . . .

The definition of the subcategory of UW known as guerrilla warfare includes the following: "GW is characterized by offensive actions with emphasis on swift, bold, violent action, and elusiveness, mobility and surprise. . . ."

The definitions just given are simplistic, but sufficient for this book.

As for the TV-image of the guns-a-blazin', non-stop shootouts every weekend or so, soldiers who are looking for something like that should head to a Ranger unit, or into the Navy to try out for SEALS. Or, another way to see action in the absence of war is to join the Air Force and try out for the PJs. If you stick around long enough, or are in the right place at the right time, you might get what you want.

Though Special Forces sees its share of direct action, especially during wartime, its job often revolves around more down-to-earth activities like Foreign Internal Defense—where, for instance, teams are sent to assist foreign militaries and police forces in training, or, perhaps, creating, or combating an insurgency. In some circumstances, if GW is prosecuted carefully and thoughtfully, the fighting can be ended or even avoided altogether. Smart people know that you fight to *win*, not to *beat* by overwhelming force. The distinction to be drawn is critical: *Win, not beat.*

Neither Delta Force, SEALS, nor Rangers conduct guerrilla warfare in the true sense. Insofar as active duty combat units involvement, GW is the sole domain of Special Forces. Many people, apparently even senior military commanders, think that guerrilla warfare is just running around in a jungle, swinging from trees and shooting people in the back of the head, or slipping behind enemy lines to do some dirty work, or perhaps occasionally assassinating a misbehaving foreign leader. While the image may provide some level of dark entertainment, this is not what guerrilla warfare is about.

GW is not Jungle Warfare. Nor is it Desert or Cold Weather Warfare. Jungles and deserts are simply among the places where war occurs. War is like cancer: where there are people, it can be found, but in different forms.

I have a theory that might explain why even so many military professionals get confused about certain GW-related definitions. The misconception that guerrilla warfare and jungle warfare is the same stems from several coincidences.

1) Vietnam: The enemy fought a guerrilla style war, often in the jungles.
2) Gorillas: Animals associated with jungles. Guerrillas are humans who sometimes fight in jungles. (The word "guerrilla" comes from Spanish. It is the diminutive of *guerra*—war, related to Old High German *werra*.)

Given the confusing coincidences: gorillas, guerrillas and jungles, the general lack of understanding of GW is understandable. In contrast, a textbook example of a *conventional* war, where militaries directly faced each other toe to toe on a battlefield, was the Gulf War, which happened to be fought mostly in the desert. So, the *strategy* was to fight a conventional war using desert warfare *tactics*.

On strategy and tactics: A strategy is an overall plan, the big picture. Strategic targets and objectives are very important. For instance, if an enemy military is dependent on an oil field and a pipeline to furnish much of its fuel requirements, the generals will want to do something about those targets. Why fight enemy tanks and jets when you can simply cause them to run out of gas? Strategic *weapons* are things like nuclear weapons, aircraft carriers, B-1 bombers and ballistic missile submarines. Big stuff.

Strategy should not be confused with *stratagem*. A stratagem is a ruse or deception—a tactic—used to outwit or trick the enemy. A peculiar habit of militaries (and many other large organizations) is to stop using deception when they find themselves significantly more powerful than their adversaries. In these cases, the powerful tend to be easily tricked by wily adversaries who do not bow down in the face of seemingly hopeless odds. The powerful tend to get smug because of their power, and they tend to feel insulated and untouchable. This major weakness is highly exploitable by guerrillas, something that needs to be remembered by Americans, who often succumb to a false sense of security, and a false sense of unchallengeable power. It seems that our cruise missiles and other gadgets have become our latest phallic symbols, but we should beware of this tendency to use sheer power when there are peaceful alternatives, and, when we must use force, we should do so as wisely as possible.

Tactics, tactical targets, and tactical weapons are the nitty gritty details of fighting. Tactics are used to achieve the strategic objective. A rifle is a tactical weapon. A missile carrying normal explosives is a tactical weapon. An F-18 Hornet is a tactical jet fighter/bomber. Digging a foxhole is a tactic for saving your life. A tactical target may be an enemy radar site that, when destroyed, will leave a hole in the enemy air defense, or a fuel depot that, when destroyed, will hurt the enemy, but will not threaten to put them out of business.

The line between what is considered tactical and what is strategic can be blurred at times, and can change quickly. A low-priority target today could become a very important target with a change in conditions. For instance, a bridge may not be particularly important until a massive enemy unit is preparing to cross it, a crossing which might lead to the capture of an important airfield and a waterway. For the Commanders, this is the ultimate game of chess, but one played with real lives.

GW strategy and GW tactics can be used just about anywhere: jungles, deserts, arctic regions, rural areas, cities, even in business. GW, like conventional warfare, is a *style* of fighting, just as boxing and Aikido are styles of fighting.

As for assassinating political leaders, such activities are illegal according to what our military lawyers said. Nevertheless, we have seen multiple attempts in which the U.S. has openly (apparently) tried to kill hostile foreign leaders ranging from Castro in Cuba, to Khadafi in Libya, to Hussein in Iraq, and most recently Slobodan Milosovich in Serbia, where war had not even been declared. Where should we draw the line between a political leader, and a military leader? And who really cares? They are the enemy, *right?* That we chose them as enemies is a separate matter—and the morality of the issue aside—perhaps killing the leaders would be "cost effective." But that's not the point; the point is that killing political leaders is illegal.

Of course, an enemy would look at our president and our Congress the same way, as hostile leaders, but we don't like that thought. Killing *our* leaders is not fair, *right?* Consider our reaction had the Vietnamese assassinated Nixon and set off a few car bombs around our country attempting to halt our massive, constant attack on their nation. Would we have overreacted and unleashed our nuclear arsenal on that poor little country on the other side of the world which was choosing communism after having been brutally exploited by capitalists? Or would we suck it up and say, *that's war and we chose to engage in it.* We like to feel untouchable, don't we? And our leaders like us to feel that way. But then what can we expect from leaders whom we elect based on the same principles by which Bill Gurley was elected? Façade. Marketing campaigns. We choose the tallest, the best looking, the most eloquent, and those who only apparently are the most sincere, who often seek the very thing they cannot be trusted with: Power.

The fact is, we are not untouchable, and we allow our leaders to delude us, and lead us by our own opinion polls. Talk about a dog chasing its tail. We do not run this planet, though clearly we want to. We are not omnipotent, but we are very powerful, even powerful enough to protect ourselves effectively, so long as we do not create enemies who wish, from the depths of their being, to seriously injure us.

It is hardly surprising that it is illegal to kill political leaders. The ones who start, control, and stop most wars have made it illegal to kill them, and they will continue to redefine and reinterpret the rules of war as they see fit. How likely is it that they will willingly submit themselves to the same exposure to risk as the rest of the world?

Every quarter, we sat through long explanations presented on such issues by lawyers. It was surprising what was permitted and not permitted in warfare. Knowing the rules was important, not that one can always follow rigid rules in a non-rigid world.

A fastidious person might crinkle his or her nose and say: "You just said you would break the law, like those immoral politicians." To that I say: "I do not seek the moral high-ground. If obeying the law means that I will be a dead, but law-abiding soldier, rather than a soldier who would normally follow the law but who wants to live—I would seriously consider stepping over the line." I am in no position to claim sainthood.

We learned that it was permissible to wear enemy uniforms or civilian clothes to evade capture or to conduct operations—but that you might be executed as a spy if caught. It was forbidden to use the Red Cross symbol as camouflage for military operations. It was forbidden to kill the people, seize or destroy the property of the Red Cross.

It was forbidden to kill non-combatants without a "good reason" (many examples of "good reasons" to kill innocent people were cited). It was illegal to assassinate people who have unacceptable political views, but who are technically non-combatants. This seemed like a sick joke, especially since many wars, such as that in Vietnam, have ideological roots.

For instance, religious leaders who may rally the enemy, but who do not carry a weapon or take part in military operations were defined as "non-combatants." There was a vast gray area, though. If a spy happened to be a religious leader, he was primarily a spy, at least by my interpretation. He was simply the enemy, and his religious views and affiliations were his business. Of course, the enemy would say the opposite, and if he were a preacher in my hometown, and on my side, doubtless I would argue that he was merely a religious leader and should not be considered a military target.

Nothing is certain about war except that it is insane and every bit as ubiquitous as cancer. Unfortunately, it has proven just as difficult to cure. There are liberal peaceniks who know that war is insane. For some reason, they seem to think that they are inherently more enlightened than the rest of us. There are those who would neuter the military and leave us exposed, which would be like protesting the rain by not carrying an umbrella. I can imagine an activist standing on his soapbox on a sunny day screaming at the top his lungs: *I object to rain! Rain is wrong! We should band together and toss out our umbrellas and our rain suits, and together we shall defeat the rain!* And on the horizon there blows a dark cloud, and there is the rumbling of thunder.

Often it is appropriate to reduce matters to their lowest common denominator. People can protest war all they want, but until there is a safe cure, we had better be willing to fight; until that cure is found, war is always on the horizon, never more than a day away.

Murder, torture, hostage taking, poor treatment of military prisoners or non-combatants all were illegal according to my books. It was illegal to fire on non-combatants, but if you were taking fire from a village, for instance, it was permitted to return fire even if it meant innocent people might die. In such situations, the response should be "measured." In other words, if you know that an enemy unit numbering fifty lightly-armed infantry is hidden in a town of ten thousand people, it would be a misuse of lethal force to call in a B-52 air strike to flatten the town just for the sake of destroying that unit. And so, it would seem a war crime that we flattened two Japanese cities with nuclear weapons, but it seems arrogant for me to sit here and pass judgment; I didn't have a seventeen-year-old son drafted off the farm to fight the Japanese after the sneak-attack on Pearl Harbor.

It was forbidden to pretend to surrender as a ruse for an attack; the enemy's sincere offer of surrender *must* be accepted. You are not obligated to ask for the surrender. You could kill the enemy, even an unarmed enemy, on site, without warning. Rape was forbidden and punishable by death. Looting was no longer allowed, but, as true of all the above, was still a customary part of war.

Okay, up to this point I agreed with the laws, mostly. There's no need to be animals while we wage war and kill each other, though often it is the meanest and cruelest animals that win. I could state the actual law here, but it is more accurate to state how I remember the law. We react to our memories and feelings, not to definitions from books.

It is illegal to cause unnecessary injury or suffering to the enemy.

Fair enough. I agree. But now it starts to get silly.

An example we were once given: The spirit of the law would make it illegal, for instance, to have backward facing notches on a knife used to stab an enemy soldier. The issue here is *unnecessary* wounding. It's okay to have *forward* facing notches. The reason for this is that, technically, the lawyers have concluded, when you stab somebody you are attacking, but when you remove the knife you are no longer attacking. Backward facing notches could pull your victim's guts out as you withdrew your knife. And so, it was concluded, backward facing notches cause unnecessary wounding.

Notches, splotches! Isn't war about killing? Department of *Defense?* Call it what it is, the Department of *War.* Well, I wasn't about to let that example slip by without comment. I stood up during a lecture and said respectfully to the lawyer (who was also a military officer): "Excuse me, sir. If you are trying to kill an enemy soldier, you will be so scared that you will keep cutting and hacking until he's dead. Therefore, the notches are actually more humane in that they make him die faster."

The lawyer chuckled and replied in kind, "If you've got backward facing notches on your knife, it might get hung up on his bones or in his uniform when you try to pull it out, and *you* may be the one who gets killed. You know what I'm trying to say. It is illegal to cause unnecessary suffering. When it comes to doing your job, you may have to kill people. I hope you do it well. But not only is it *illegal* to cause unnecessary suffering, it is *morally reprehensible.* It is *un*-American. It is *wrong.* It will *not* be tolerated in this military."

He'd made his point. I understood what he was saying, but the grey areas are always controversial. If everything were cut and dried, we wouldn't need lawyers, or soldiers—maybe.

However, in the successful pursuit of war, it is very important to cause the enemy to suffer, to break his resolve. For example, during the Gulf War, a conventional desert campaign, our military applied the type of psychological pressure on the enemy that would cause many to suffer from post-traumatic stress disorder. Some of those tactics included constant bombardment, with incredibly large bombs, and cutting off their food and water supplies. Also, it was considered very important to make the Iraqis *feel* like their own country was selling them out and did not care about their lives and well-being—much as our young soldiers felt in Vietnam when we sold them out. Feeling sold-out or abandoned leads to great mental suffering. It is certain that many Iraqi will re-live that war for the rest of their lives, but at the same time, it is certain that many of our people came home alive who otherwise would have been killed had the enemy been more enthusiastic, which was the rationale for dropping nuclear weapons on Hiroshima and Nagasaki.

All those laws were nice and made us feel better, because with them, we had rules by which we could kill each other, slaughter children, and destroy each other's countries in accordance with the law.

And we should never forget Vietnam, as much as we would love to. I respect those people who went there for me when I was just a kid. I have known many veterans of that war, and became friends with some while on active duty. I think that the political decision to wage that war was morally reprehensible and amounted to a massive war crime by the politicians. Most of the fighters were just kids. They were taught to trust their elders to know what was right. They did what they thought was expected of them.

Many citizens would be surprised to know that many of their Special Forces soldiers are against some of our country's violent actions when more peaceful solutions are available. Often the military itself is against violence and advises against it, but there are those, many of whom who have never served, who will resort to violence with murky intentions, or little fore-thought. Of course, there is a time for war. When our security and well-being is threatened, as by terrorists, it's time to fight and to fight very well. Ferociously. But at times we beat the hell out of little countries simply because they don't do what we want, and because we *can.*

It is worth saying again that the object of fighting should always be to *win*, not *beat*. Winning means getting what we want. If we want to discredit other ideologies because we think ours are better, we should demonstrate how much better they are. As for communism, I have since been to enough communist countries to know that the system is ridiculous insofar as it robs humans of their spirit, and turns them into drones, robots. The system sounds good on paper, though. Communism, in some form, will stage a comeback, and we will have to fight it again.

Can you imagine how many hospitals and schools we could have built in Vietnam, and here at home, for the price in money and lives that we paid to bomb and burn it all to hell? Those people didn't want to die any more than our people did. They didn't want to fight. We traveled half way around the world and *made* them fight.

In Special Forces, it is drilled into your head that violence is not always the way to get what you want. It is often counter-productive.

Philosophically speaking, the rationale for the "right" conduct of war can get very confusing, but some things were clear. As the years went by I real-ized the most frightening aspect of fighting: *There is an enemy out there who is just as smart, or smarter, than I am, and he is better trained. He tried harder and studied more. He is in better physical condition and knows his weapons. He is resourceful, tough and brave. But most frightening is that I know that he looks at me the same way I look at him.*

Since there was so much to learn about being a soldier, and I only had two eyes and two ears, I focused on GW during my free time. I found it endlessly fascinating. To my surprise, the art and science of warfare intrigued me; dur-ing my last year of high school I wouldn't have given it a second thought. I wasn't enamoured of the subject, and still believed that warfare was a prim-itive behavior taken to a horribly advanced level by its finest practitioners, of which, as in every discipline, there were few. But I had completely forgotten about college and physics for the time being. I enrolled in military correspondence courses and spent a great deal of time in the military libraries.

My commander knew that I wanted to get to an A-team; I told him every chance I got, but with the charges still hanging over my head, that was not yet possible.

Life was odd, and getting odder.

JUDGMENT DAY

THE CHARGES OF second degree murder and assault to commit murder had been dropped, and replaced with the single accusation of involuntary manslaughter. I have been told by attorneys that after someone is charged with a serious crime, unless there is a plea bargain, normally the person is headed to trial.

In court he stands accused before the judge and the members of the jury, and the prosecution launches an attack to prove its case. With luck, the defendant can afford a good, tough attorney who knows how to fight, and does so with the same intensity as if his or her own neck were on the block.

The jury would consist of citizens who had been summoned from their daily lives and paid a pittance to carry a burden so important that, without the collective service of juries across the land, our military would be a waste. The jurors' burden is to listen to both sides open-mindedly, and to do their best to dispense maximum justice, or at least minimum injustice. That must be very difficult. I have never served on a jury, but have often imagined the difficulty of putting aside my own mental baggage to render a fair decision. We all have prejudices. Even the purest among us cannot claim otherwise and walk away with credibility intact.

Often we hear of criminals set free on silly technicalities after the laws are twisted and contorted by some slick-tongued lawyer who fools the jurors. But few defendants can afford a legal "Dream Team," and the prosecutors and the police are professionals. The words of the accused usually carry little weight.

As a people, Americans are trusting, and we listen to journalists. We trust that our leaders are looking out for us, and that our writers are impartial—unless they clearly state otherwise—and that they are knowledgeable and truthful. Though we see exceptions practically daily, we still have this underlying belief that everything balances out, that truth always prevails, and Good triumphs over Evil. After all, good people expect good things, even after experience has, all too often, suggested otherwise.

There were articles about my case and about military matters that I would read in the future, where the journalists were blatantly wrong, or had little understanding of the subjects they covered. That is to be expected; this week a journalist may cover a legal case, next week a conference on global warming, and, a month later, a war in Kosovo. Their business is to sell stories—and controversy makes money. Due to public pressure, my case had dragged out for almost half a year. Some citizens wanted to hang me because I was in Special Forces, in their eyes, a damning fact.

The police knew I was innocent, and said so. The prosecutor knew it. The Army, too. Special Forces had given me sergeant's stripes, fake though they were. Of the witnesses, all made statements supporting my innocence, none made derogatory comments, and attorney Daniel Long examined the matter carefully. He questioned Steve and me, and after an investigator checked out our stories, defended me.

But politics was involved. I was merely a "Green Beret," saddled with whatever images that brought to mind. Maybe it evoked the picture of a man who had been dropped into the Amazon jungle and programmed to kill with those "secret punches" that are still advertised in some magazines. There is little wonder that the average person believes these "secret punches" exist. A published author recently asked, in all sincerity, if I must, being an "ex-Green Beret," register with the local police when I visit a new town. The answer is "no." Neither do SEALS, Delta Force soldiers, or anyone else except, perhaps, certain types of criminals.

Researching this book, I leafed through certain magazines and found large advertisements about secret fighting techniques taught to "Navy SEALS, Army Rangers . . . SWAT teams . . . FBI . . . CIA." One ad takes up four full pages, which, according to the rate schedule, must have cost $6,000-$8,000 per month to run. Likely, some people who read the ad are left shocked and paranoid about walking the streets. But finally it offers hope in the form of secret techniques that will "place you among the most viciously-effective fighters on the planet. . . ." For $97 plus $4.50 shipping and handling, you can get the two tapes and the secrets they contain, plus a bonus tape on knife-fighting.

Since our government has been shown inept at keeping nuclear secrets from the Chinese, this must be a good deal, *right?* Yes, I say, it is a good deal for the people who sell the tapes, each of which costs considerably less to produce than the price of a Whopper with cheese, for nearly a hundred bucks. These snake oil salesmen perpetuate and peddle the myth. The secret punches do not exist, but those imaginary blows do land real money, and the myth they help perpetuate was my problem.

So I waited, waited, and waited. Still no trial date.
Still no Judgment Day.

Fort Bragg

I waited and studied war until December, shortly before Christmas, when Daniel Long called from Maryland with news. The evidence would go before a grand jury. The people of Maryland would determine whether the evidence was sufficient to try the case.

So, a group of fellow citizens would examine the facts in more intimate detail, and though Mr. Long was confident they would come to a just decision, the night before the hearing I did not sleep. I waited in my room, alone, at Fort Bragg.

The next day, while I waited at Fort Bragg, ignorant of the proceedings going on in Maryland, the people made their decision. Would I stand trial for manslaughter and face prison, or would they vote to let me get on with my life?

GRAND JURY

THERE WERE TWENTY-THREE citizens on the panel. Apparently none of the dead man's family came to the proceeding, and since it was just before Christmas, nobody seemed to be paying much attention.

The *Daily Times* in Salisbury, Maryland, sums it up:

Yon manslaughter charges dropped

Worcester County State's Attorney B. Randall Coates has dismissed a manslaughter charge against Michael Yon after the Worcester County Grand Jury determined there was insufficient evidence against him.

Charges of second degree murder were filed against Yon after the death of Charles Scott, which was caused by injuries sustained in a fight that occurred in an Ocean City bar last summer. According to witnesses, the fight between Yon and Scott had been precipitated by at least four separate attempts by Scott to start a fight. On each of the attempts, Yon was able to avoid a fight by enlisting the aid of employees and patrons of the bar to calm Scott. Reportedly, Scott was taunting Yon because of his haircut, the result of Basic Training at Fort Bragg, N.C.

The original charge of second-degree murder was reduced to manslaughter by Coates shortly after the incident when information revealed that Yon had not acted with malice in the incident. Coates indicated that he believes the action by the Grand Jury was proper and, in any event, viewed the charge against Yon as an "impossible one to prove in light of the evidence."

It seemed rather anti-climactic. I was not sitting in a courtroom, watching the citizens file into the jury box after having come to a verdict. I did not see the women and men of the jury look over at me for my reaction as the foreman read the verdict, while the bailiff unconsciously rubbed the handcuffs on his belt. I did not see a judge sitting up high, looking over at the jury, waiting for their decision before he decided what to do with me next. No, what I saw was just an empty room at Fort Bragg, and the telephone by which Daniel Long told me that twenty-three citizens had set me free.

I went for a long run to celebrate, and to burn off a tiny portion of the accumulated tension.

LESSONS LEARNED

THE COURT FOUND no reason to order me to return to Maryland. After nearly half a year of anxiety, that was the end of it as far as the legal particulars went.

Finally, I became angry at the dead man, Mr. Scott. Angry at what he did, at his dying, and at his being human. So I began to dehumanize him. I told myself that he got what he deserved, and that society should thank me for saving it from him. If it had not been for me, I told myself, he may have killed some other innocent teenager, or one of those women at his job. I tried to convince myself that he was just a rabid animal that had attacked unprovoked, and I gave him the nickname "Wild Bill." After a seemingly endless barrage of questions about the incident, I began telling people that my assailant got what he deserved. I was angry about the stigma with which he left me. And it wasn't over.

TRANSITIONS

IT HAD BEEN a year and a half since my high school graduation and nearly six months since the SF course. Captain Weaver, the company commander, said that he was happy with my performance as a junior TAC and acting sergeant. As a reward, he had said that after the charge was dropped in Maryland and my secret clearance was renewed, he would approve any school I wanted en route to a Special Forces Group. Having been cleared of any wrongdoing, my clearance was immediately reinstated, and the captain was as good as his word.

Any school I want? That amounted to a blank check, one I needed to spend wisely. I wanted Ranger school, but that was not the right pick for now because, though it would have been good infantry training, there were other schools that could better increase my value. There were lots of choices: air assault school, pathfinder, or the Special Forces HALO parachute course. When I told some of the other young guys about the blank check, there was a steady stream of suggestions, mainly from their own wish list, like the SF scuba course in Key West.

But it was important to pick a course that made me as valuable an SF team member as possible. I wanted to get on an A-team, not collect badges, and though there were many good schools to choose from, only one would vault me up to the next level. So the choice was obvious: DLI, the Defense Language Institute in Monterey, California. It would be an intense course, and there would be no badge to show for it. But in addition to gaining a language skill, graduating from DLI proves that a person can buckle down academically and learn very quickly.

I had been asking the TACs about the options available, as well as which was the best Special Forces Group. They generally agreed that the prize was to be assigned to the 10th, which had the reputation of being the best-trained and on-the-go Group. In retrospect, I believe that to have been an unjustified supposition given that the other Groups consisted of the same kind of men.

I was not interested in spooky-spy stuff and short strike missions, which was my perception of the chief functions of the 10th; I was more interested in guerrilla warfare. I thought the 7th was the place to go, and Spanish was a key language for that Group.

While many were tripping over themselves to go to the 10th, I was zagging to the 7th, which was active in Central and South America, chasing guerrillas and drug dealers. I knew that they needed my help and couldn't do without me, and I wanted to test my guerrilla warfare skills (which were, of course, practically non-existent).

James Gritz knew a woman in Washington, D.C. who worked in one of those magical places where things happen. She controlled one of the proverbial "strings," and told Gritz over the phone that she would pull one to get me into the next available Spanish class. So he drove me to Washington, and almost before we could say "Hola!" we were standing in her office.

We exchanged pleasantries, then got down to business. She cleared some papers and a coffee mug off her desk, then unfurled a computer printout that stretched on for several pages, listing languages and classes. There must have been at least twenty languages, and dozens of class dates with openings over the next twelve months.

"Yon," Gritz said, slapping me on the back as he sometimes did, "You are the only nineteen-year-old in the Army wearing fake sergeant stripes who gets to come to Washington to pick what he wants. You still want Spanish?"

The woman said, "Take your time. You can take whatever is open."

I was feeling rather special, privileged, honored, and all that stuff. By choosing the language, I was also getting to choose the Group.

"Well, since this is Christmas and all, yes, I still want Spanish." I couldn't believe my luck. DLI was said to be the best language training available in the U.S.

The printout may as well have been a smorgasbord. Her finger searched down the list, suddenly stopped, and tapped the paper. She looked up and said, "The first Spanish opening starts in June." That was more than six months away, but a new class started every month.

"Is there a way to get into an earlier class?" I asked. It seemed strange, maybe even rude to have the smorgasbord spread out, then to ask for dessert. But this was no time to keep quiet.

"No," she said. "The only slot immediately open is German. It starts in January. Do you want that class?" That was only a month away, but that meant going to the 10th Group.

"No thank you. I'll wait for the Spanish slot."

But the prospect of sitting on my hands at Bragg for another six months settled like an anchor in my stomach. There was a whole world out there waiting for me to dive into, and I wanted to leave the shallow water and venture into the deep.

"Isn't there any other way to get in?" I asked.

Gritz chuckled, smiled at the woman, and gave me the customary pat on the back.

"No," she answered, "these classes are forecast out pretty far. You are very lucky to get a shot at German. Those slots are gobbled up fast. Someone's orders must have been canceled. It just came open."

"Oh, now," I smiled, "There must be *some* way to wiggle into the next Spanish class. Sergeant Gritz told me you know how to make this system work." Might as well go ahead and play the field.

"You are persistent, aren't you?" She returned my smile and playful tone. "Well, there might be a way, but it's chancy. You can go ahead and take the German slot, then when you report to DLI, ask to be reassigned to Spanish. It has worked before. But not always. It's your choice. I'm not advising either way." She looked me in the eyes.

"Okay. I'll try it." Here we go again. *Fortune favors the bold* and all those other silly one-liners that can get you into trouble.

"How did I know you would say that?" She smiled again and began fan-folding the printout. "You SF guys are so predictable."

Yeah, right.

I sent her flowers. (Gritz told me to.)

On the way back to Bragg, Gritz drove to his grandmother's house which was somewhere along the way, and soon we were in the living room talking. Sitting on the sofa, I looked out the window and spotted a big tree in her backyard. It had lots of good, solid branches. I said, "That looks like a good climbing tree." He and his grandmother burst into laughter, but I wasn't trying to be funny. I was serious. It was a good climbing tree, and I had climbed enough to know. Almost fell from one when my neighbor had gotten his *Playboy* in the mail and his wife had seen it.

Back at base, Gritz told the other TACs about the tree comment and it became a running joke. The older men wouldn't let it go. I was walking, minding my own business when a voice bellowed from a hundred meters away, "Hey *Yoooon*," (they also constantly poked fun at my name) "Is *that* a good climbing tree?" pointing to a pine tree.

"*Noooo*," I hollered, "too much *saaaaap*, not enough *braannnches!*" Who the hell climbs sticky pine trees?

I had worked so hard at being a junior TAC, and an acting sergeant, that before leaving on Christmas break, and then for the language institute, they threw a party and presented me with a little trophy. Captain Weaver awarded me an Army Achievement Medal and this summary sheet:

> . . . *Yon . . . distinguished himself by exceptionally meritorious achievement as a tactical advisor counselor (TAC) while assigned to Company C First Special Warfare Training Battalion (Airborne) United States Army John F. Kennedy Special Warfare Center . . . effectively served in a position reserved for mature senior enlisted men of comprehensive military backgrounds, and although he has been in the United States Army only a brief period he was able to assertively advise and counsel students of much higher grade and broader experiences . . . Yon's professionalism, determination and enthusiastic*

approach to all duties resulted in achievements which contributed significantly to the large student successful completion rate from the Special Forces Qualification Course. He consistently displayed all the qualities inherent in a truly professional soldier: attention to details, impressive management skills, tactful leadership traits and maturity. His intense dedication and loyalty to the successful completion of the mission reflects great credit upon himself, the First Special Warfare Training Battalion and the United States Army.

An Army Achievement Medal? What is it? What's it for? I wondered, thinking I had just been doing my job. It is important to issue letters of appreciation for a job well done, or maybe even a plaque, but the Army is constantly handing out trinkets (trinkets being those medals not earned for doing something risky such as making someone else bleed, or bleeding yourself) for simply doing your job in a secure environment.

I rolled out of bed every morning worried that I wouldn't measure up to their standards. I wondered what they would have thought had Steve Shaulis and I infiltrated Grenada. Before I left, Captain Weaver shook my hand saying that if I had any problems getting on an A-team after completing language school, to give him a call.

Steve had gotten orders months earlier for the same Spanish class that I wanted, and he was on Christmas leave in Ellicot City, Maryland, where we were to link-up after New Year's to drive to California.

I flew home for Christmas and joined my friend John Harrison, who was also on leave from the Army. At night we cruised the old high school hangouts as if we were salmon swimming back up the river. The tactic worked, and we met lots of our old friends, many who had not left Winter Haven. Others were home for college break.

I started hearing some of the rumors circulating about the events in Maryland, which was disheartening. Nobody knew what actually happened, so imaginative retellings created various stories, one of which was that I "was in uniform far away from base when a guy knocked the beret off" my head, so I "killed him." Somehow I escaped the murder charge "because the guy had started it." Moreover, the story continued, the "government made sure" I "got off."

Things had changed. They talked to one another as usual, but to them, I had morphed into a larger-than-life Green Beret killing-machine (complete with killer punches). The more I denied it, the more they believed it. But the effect of this was not altogether bad. The girls still liked me, some more than ever, and nobody seemed afraid, though there was an almost palpable distance, almost a moat between them and me. They talked about wild parties, while I thought about jumping out of airplanes at night, getting chased by the cops, or about how fast the world gets turned upside down. Suddenly we didn't have much in common. They talked about the same old stuff: cars, menial jobs, classes, teachers . . . blah, blah. . . . For me, that world was long, long ago, in a galaxy far, far away, and I saw that I'd never really been a part of it, even back in school. Now I truly felt like an outsider.

Richard White was an exception. One doesn't detonate bombs in an alligator-infested lake with just anybody. After New Year's, he planned to drive back to college in Pennsylvania, so I hitched a ride. He was to drop me off at Steve's place in Maryland.

After two days of driving, we made it to Maryland on a snowing January day. There, Steve and I loaded into his white Datsun pickup. Richard said goodbye and drove off to college, while Steve and I headed west on I-40 to California.

It was a long trip and we stopped in places like El Paso. *El* Paso. Actually, I'm not sure there is another place like *El* Paso. The Texans were friendly, but there were a lot fewer cowboys than I expected. We left Texas, and headed off through the desert, which, to our pleasant surprise, came in a variety of colors and styles, and found ourselves at the O.K. Corral. I couldn't get over how much desert the U.S. has. Arizona reminded me of the Road Runner and Wile E. Coyote, my all-time favorite cartoon. The best part was always when the Road Runner kicked it into high-gear and ran so fast that the desert road flew up in the air, then a smoke-trail chased him, and finally the smoke-trail caught on fire.

We made it to Monterey, California, where DLI was based, but they sent us both to San Francisco to another facility.

I hoped now, with Basic, AIT, Selection, Maryland, and all those hurdles behind me, that DLI would be a nice, relaxing, uneventful eight months of language training.

It was not.

DEFENSE LANGUAGE INSTITUTE
PRESIDIO OF SAN FRANCISCO, CALIFORNIA

THE ARMY HAD secretly created the Military Intelligence Service Language School in 1941. It was originally designed to train intelligence people to speak Japanese. For a condensed version of its history, in 1963, the Air Force and Navy consolidated their language programs with the Army's and that new school became the Defense Language Institute. The courses were intensive, expensive, and the slots were precious—very hard to get. As mentioned, this is said to be the finest language training in the country, and, in more recent years, NASA has sent astronauts to DLI before they worked in the Russian Mir space station. It was said that NASA pushed the astronauts through the program at an accelerated pace—believing that being astronauts meant they also had a natural gift for languages—and this was a mistake. Flop flop, fizz fizz, this takes time and hard work even for scientists and space shuttle commanders. This was not an easy course.

Many languages are taught at DLI, including Spanish, Chinese, Russian, and exotics, like Tagalog, which is spoken in the Philippines. A future SF teammate who went through the Polish and later the Tagalog course told me that there was a Tagalog word that meant, "to polish a floor with a coconut husk." The course could be very entertaining.

The school and living quarters of the students were inside an old hospital. Most of the students, unless they had achieved the rank of sergeant or higher, had to share living space with other students. A couple of days after reporting in, I was assigned a nice, private room.

That very night, an attractive young lass who was attending DLI knocked on my door and introduced herself. Most of the students there were from Military Intelligence (MI) with a mere sprinkling of SF, which made the SF soldiers more of a rarity. I was a little surprised to find the pretty girl standing, smiling, at my door, asking me if I wanted to walk with her to the store. *Wow!*

I didn't know what to say and only got out two words: "Uh, sure."

It was fun being rare.

As for language training, I was scheduled for German instead of Spanish, meaning that I was headed to the 10th instead of the 7th. Well, I had heard that Germany was a very nice country filled with women who were eager to meet me, but I still had other plans, and made my first move to swap classes by asking the sergeant major if I could change.

He said, "No," then looked down at my jungle boots and said: "You

Special Forces always come here out of uniform. Does this look like a god-damn jungle to you?!"

I thought, *Jeez, what a punk for a sergeant major.*

Actually, I *was* in uniform wearing jungle boots, *Special Forces* uniform, and jungle boots were much more comfortable than regular boots. "Oh well," I thought, "this is the famous DLI, and it looks like we have a ham-ster for a sergeant major."

Over time, Hamster-Major continued his gratuitous harassment of the SF soldiers and finally, I had seen the veins bulge in his neck one too many times. I did not care about his rank, and I was no man's punching bag. He was not my god. He was needlessly abusive as some power-nazis can be. He didn't talk, he barked.

In SF, the enlisted people were on a first name basis. I addressed people who had been on active duty for ten or twenty years by their first names, sometimes slept over at their houses, and some even became more like family to me than what they actually were, superior ranking soldiers. My first A-team called me "Mikey" which mutated to "Bam Bam."

Since I fought continuously to impart to the rest of the team, who typi-cally were considerably older, more appreciation for the beauty of physics, some team members called me the "Science Adviser," and joked that ours was probably the only A-team in Special Forces whose weapons man would just as soon study magnetism as mayhem. I often taught weapons and tac-tics classes, but occasionally, instead of preparing my lesson plan on mili-tary matters, I surprised them and gave classes on topics such as gravity. I dispelled the common idea that hot water freezes faster than cold (under most circumstances) by doing experiments in the team room.

My next A-team hung an ominous sounding title, "The Rock," over my head. I liked Mikey or Bam Bam or Science Advisor better; it was much easier to live up to those names than The Rock.

All that is to say that SF soldiers, the ones who thrive in an unstructured atmosphere, tend to be quasi-military. They see themselves as sort of in the Army, and sort of not, and they don't like hamsters chewing them out no matter what the hamster's rank. At the same time, he did outrank me accord-ing to the conventional military hierarchy. Only a dolt would come directly at him. That would not be good guerrilla warfare.

So, for several months, Steve and I pulled an endless stream of practical jokes on him. It was silly, but it still helped assuage a hostile attitude. And it was fun because the hamster would walk around angry while we laughed. *I beg your pardon sergeant major.* This is a jungle if you make it one.

Before beginning training, we were issued learning material ranging from a tape recorder with headphones and a box full of tapes, to more books than we could carry. If we graduated, meaning that we'd met the stringent academic standards without going insane, we got to keep everything but the tape recorder and headphones. So, as a prize, we would end up, if we graduated, with a little foreign language library.

Part of in-processing was the Security briefing. Around any military unit, Security is an important subject, but around Intelligence and Special Operations units, Security is extremely important. Soviet spooks and others busied themselves around the globe recruiting spies and gathering information, and those service members who attended DLI were prime targets for recruitment. A well-dressed FBI agent made us aware of some techniques used by spies to search for recruits. He pointed out that we merely had to drive by a Soviet consulate and look at the many antennae on the roof to see how busy they were.

The Soviets had two main intelligence agencies: The KGB and the GRU. These were roughly equivalent to our CIA and DIA (Defense Intelligence Agency). The KGB and our equivalent, the CIA, spread their intelligence nets and operations wide, targeting anything from economic and political intelligence to military intelligence. The GRU and our equivalent, the DIA, focused on military intelligence. Of course, every embassy and consulate comes complete with spies, and San Francisco had its share. Apparently, it was easy to tell who was KGB and who was GRU; when they played soccer on the weekends, they played on opposite teams.

It was assumed that our phones were tapped—on any military installation that is automatically presumed. Computer software would sift for key words like "weapons system" or "secret." A human interceptor, who likely had gone to their version of DLI, would listen to the particular recordings that were flagged by the software. This allowed eavesdroppers to sift through a much higher volume of conversations, searching for nuggets.

They also looked for people who were having personal problems, like loneliness or a broken heart, or money problems. In the case of loneliness, they could send "love." This method was called the honey trap. Eventually the "relationship" would be twisted around and the deceitful *amour* would be used as a cunning wedge, or perhaps as an ice pick, to pry out secrets. I thought this to be among the cruelest techniques, but then, what is fair in love and war?

If a soldier was married, the enemy might appeal to his or her susceptibility to promiscuity, if such existed, and they might provide an affair—making sure that all the lurid details were properly recorded with video and audio, of course. This taping was for the spouse, in case the target decided not to cooperate. A homosexual liaison could be particularly useful. I recall that later, while I was stationed in Germany, there was a soldier I heard about who met a girl in a bar. He went home with her. She stole his ID card which was then used to drive a car bomb onto an American base, where it exploded. Some days later, authorities found the murdered soldier's body. According to the story, the terrorists mailed his ID card to his mother. I cannot vouch for the details of that event, but the technique itself, in various forms, was widely used.

There were many other methods, the FBI agent explained, but the point was to beware of any signs of abnormality, and, if we saw them, to quietly and immediately pass them along to counter-intelligence.

The DLI courses began. I had not been allowed to switch languages, and soon was on the verge of flunking German, gambling that I would be reassigned to Spanish, when the Commander summoned me in his office. I thought, *Here is my chance. I'll convince him to send me to Spanish,* which is an easier language to learn than German. The Army already had me at DLI, so I hoped they would try to salvage their efforts by putting me in an easier program. I would get what I wanted. Made sense, right?

The Commander, who was a major, had thought of something else.

I was standing in his office in front of his desk when he started with "I've seen your type before." He paused and smiled. I smiled back. He stopped smiling. "You Special Forces guys think you can do anything you want."

Well, yeah, I thought, but kept quiet. He was right. That's one reason why people go to *Special* Forces; they like to do what they want. What's wrong with that? Just because you are in the Army doesn't mean you can't have it your way, at least some of the time.

He continued, "I looked at your DLAB scores and you should be having no problems in German. You could be in Korean." That was a scary possibility. I hoped he would leave it at that.

The DLAB, the Defense Language Aptitude Battery, is a crazy test with a made-up language administered to those who apply for DLI. Potential students have to score at different levels for different courses, and Spanish is one of the easiest. Korean is one of the hardest. German is just right. It's confusing enough to make one go bonkers, but not enough, by itself, to cause one to jump off what is alleged to be America's most scenic and popular suicide spot, the Golden Gate Bridge, which conveniently begins, or ends, right there at the Presidio.

The Major was a better leader than the sergeant major. He had me cornered, establishing the pecking order, making sure that I knew he was in control of this school, not me. But he was not demeaning. The officer continued, "If you flunk out of German, and you have no excuse if you do, I will *not* reassign you to Spanish. You will go back to your unit as a DLI failure."

Failure . . . that word sounded like a bomb.

He was serious as an earthquake. This was terrible news. I was so far behind that I didn't know if I could even catch up. He seemed like a serious man, and he was an Army officer probably twice my age. I no longer had my sergeant stripes from when I was a junior TAC. I had practically no voice, and was not in a position to negotiate. He looked me square in the eye, established solid, powerful eye contact, and spoke. "That's all I have. Dismissed," he said. I came to attention and saluted.

He saluted back.

I did an about face and started walking out the door, but before I got away, he said, "Oh, and one more thing, Yon." I stopped and turned around.

He smiled, "Nice try. I like to see soldiers with initiative. I would put you in Spanish, but Special Forces needs German speakers. That's why you're here. Put some of that energy into the books and you'll do fine."

"Yes sir," I said, and walked out, hat in hand.

The Great Oz had spoken, and I would do exactly as ordered—if possible—but things were not looking good for the home team. I was on the verge of flunking and was standing at the edge of that big cliff of insanity called *faiiillllllurrrreeee*. (That's what it sounds like when you fall off the Cliff of Failure.)

I buckled down and started studying like a man possessed. The last thing I wanted was to be standing in the Major's office again, a failure, and to then report to a Special Forces unit having wasted an expensive slot they had entrusted to me.

Some of us were put on academic probation, and soon a few of the MI people flunked out. I was still failing the quizzes, but was studying very hard, as if trying to pull up the nose of a crashing jet. Luckily, the teachers were helpful, giving advice on better study habits, and would spend time with me after class as needed. They were dedicated, similar to the TACs at Bragg, and when they knew you were giving your all, they helped.

I had paid practically no attention to my English classes in high school, and diagramming sentences felt like torture through tedium. So now, despite a high score on the DLAB test, which measures aptitude for learning, not knowledge of, a foreign language, I realized I didn't even know the language of learning a language. One of the first days, when the teacher asked me to "conjugate" a verb, I had to ask what "conjugate" meant. Sounded like a honeymoon.

And at times, DLI was like a honeymoon.

WONDER WOMAN

AS MENTIONED, THE school and living quarters of the language school were inside an abandoned hospital on the Presidio. I was downstairs, coming in the front doors when I spotted a girl, a woman rather, who was stretching after a run. She was very attractive and came complete with an athletic body. I had seen her around, and had been looking for any excuse to talk with her.

There she was. I thought: *This is it.* I moved in.

"Hey!" I said. "How far did you run?"

She looked up without expression and replied peacefully, "Only about ten miles; I didn't feel good."

Yeah, right. She likes me and is trying to impress me!

Her name was Brenda. From Punxsutawney, Pennsylvania, home of Phil, the groundhog that predicts the coming of springtime. Ironically, Groundhog Day stems from an old German superstition that if an animal casts a shadow on February 2, a holiday known as Candlemas, bad weather is on the way. If the allegedly clairvoyant rodent does not see its shadow, then there should be an early spring.

Regardless of what old Phil would have predicted, when I saw Brenda, springtime was in the air both literally and figuratively.

"I'll run with you sometime," I said, grinning, moving in like a lion.

"Okay," she said. "You are in Special Forces, right?" She smiled ever so slightly for a fraction of a second and brushed her hair behind her ear—*progress!*—I was about to melt.

"Yeah," I said.

She gave me a quick glance before going back to her stretching, "Well, you might be in a little better shape than me, but I'll run anytime you're ready."

Her tone sounded more self-assured than her words. Confidently cautious, a sign of someone who had slain a few beasts. An uncomfortable thought flittered through my head: "She might be some kind of Olympian sports goddess." Then I thought, "No, she's too pretty. She can't be *that* tough."

With all of my sports experience, and having seen people go through Basic Training twice, and Selection twice, I should have seen it coming.

For the run, we met on a beautiful Saturday morning. The air was fresh, the birds were singing, and I was moving in. I let her lead the way, figuring that she would tire out quickly and we could go get lunch.

She ran and ran all over the place. Five miles, six . . . eight . . . nine . . . .

She was pushing me hard and I was trying not to show it. She was like Wonder Woman, and I was wondering when the hell she was going to stop. It felt like I was going to die. She was stealing my thunder. She was stealing my energy points! I went from feeling like *Thunderman!* to Dumbo pulling a train up a mountain while trying to keep up with a cheetah.

After about eleven or twelve miles, she knew I'd had enough. I could have gone further, but not at a cheetah's pace. One can't hide pain from an athlete any more than flowers can hide from bees. Just when I thought it was over, she asked, "Hey, want to run over the bridge and back?" She meant the *Golden Gate* Bridge, and it would add about three more miles. It was very close to where we lived, and I wanted to go home!

A bad part of being in Special Forces is that when somebody gets you on the ropes, they want a knockout. They want that lion head hanging over the fireplace so that they can brag about it for the rest of their miserable lives. I have heard so many stories of people beating SF soldiers at something or other, that it has become a joke. But if Wonder Woman wanted to beat me, she would have to finish me, because I wasn't going to quit.

"Uh, sure," I gasped, and over the bridge we ran. She kept pushing. It was as impossible for me to keep up with her as it was for her to beat me arm wrestling. The run was a bad experience both in pain, and as a horrible ego-thrashing. By the time it was over, my thunder sounded like the crackle of static electricity on a transistor radio. Anyway, it was worth it; at least I got to know her.

Brenda was in Military Intelligence learning Korean. The Korean students kept pointing out that *Yon* is a Korean name, and I kept pointing out that I am American. She had joined the Army after running out of money and having been reduced to eating peanut butter to survive in college. She was no quitter, nor was she a mere survivor—she was attacking—and, despite being tough, she was feminine and sexy. She was the best kind of tough that a woman can be. Not like a man, but woman-tough. She didn't talk big or any of that insecure stuff. She just *was*. And she was very smart. In short, she drove me wild; I couldn't stop thinking about her. I became obsessed.

But I was intimidated because she was obviously more experienced, the consciousness of which made me clumsy. She was twenty-five, and I looked maybe sixteen. The problem was mainly of my own creation, but because of the five or six year age difference, and knowing that women her age don't usually go for younger men, my anxiety level was uncomfortably high.

I wanted her so badly. Any woman who could smoke me at PT, *and* be at the top of her Korean class, had the right stuff from Day One. Our personalities matched well. Now it was down to chemistry and romance. From my side, the chemistry was a done deal. But I was so much younger, and so clumsy that it made me sick. I realized that I didn't know exactly what to do, but awareness of ignorance doesn't provide sudden enlightenment.

She had an older, "more mature" boyfriend who was in MI studying Spanish. But I knew that she would have been better off with a younger, more sincere man like me—I would grow out of youth and still have my good heart—he would still be a jerk. And he wasn't more mature, he just *looked* older. I was smarter, faster, tougher, meaner when I had to be, and better-looking than him. What did he have—besides Brenda—that I didn't? I wanted to push him down the stairs, but that would blow it with Brenda for sure. After all, it would be hard to look a woman in the eyes and say, "But I pushed him down the stairs for *you*. And these flowers are for you, too."

Direct action would not be permissible under the current legal and social conditions. I would have to lure her away, and I set about the task, which must have amused her endlessly. I slipped notes under her door. Her punk boyfriend found one and got angry, but he never confronted me about it. Naturally I pointed out what a jerk he was for getting angry with her but not being man enough to come to me.

But let's face it, he looked like a man, while I looked like a boy who only needed to shave a couple of times a week. In the ring of romance, I really was a boy, and had no idea how to steal an older woman from an older man except, maybe, through friendly kidnapping. I could physically take her. Rent a car, gag her, and take her to a cabin over the weekend and convince her that I was the one. But that would be pushing it a little. If it worked, great, bingo, I'm a genius. If not, prison, and she would never talk to me again. But there was that sovereign military principle, *Audacity*.

Better sleep on that. Don't rush things that shouldn't be rushed. . . .

ORDNUNG IST ORDNUNG
(ORDER IS ORDER)

OUR TEACHERS WERE "serious Germans" or not-so-serious Austrians. In total there were about ten instructors, their minimum qualifications being a master's degree, while some had Ph.D's. Since they came from different parts of Germany and Austria, they spoke various dialects with different accents, though they taught High German, which is, for instance, the language spoken by their news reporters, just as our network reporters speak "without accent or dialect." It is the language common *to* the people, but not the common language *of* the people.

The instructors switched classes almost every hour so that we heard different accents—they retained some regional accent even when speaking High German—which forced us from the beginning to listen closely, and we acquired no distinctive regional accent during the course. German classes lasted six to seven hours daily, followed by several hours of homework; this went on five days a week for eight months.

The courses included listening, speaking, reading and writing. There was no chance to daydream; the classes blew by so fast that if you blinked, you missed a verb. By the time people started flunking out, there were fewer than ten students per class, and the teachers were constantly engaging us one on one.

Also, there was intensive cultural training. During the lessons we didn't learn to say things like, "Claudia has six apples," but "Claudia lives near the port in Hamburg in northern Germany." We sang German songs and listened to tapes of German radio, studied the nation's geography, customs, history, politics, and so on. Soccer is an enormously popular sport in Europe, so, for PT, we often played soccer with a coach who spoke only in German, and who tried to teach us the rules (which was easier than making us follow them).

Around the world, not only are our spoken languages different, but our manners and body languages are, too. Learning the language was just the start. These days I can, with a respectable level of accuracy, spot a German at a glance, and Germans can spot us just as easily. There are many indicators: they hold cigarettes differently, drive differently, eat differently, and often maintain a posture that is a giveaway of their nationality.

It's easy to offend people from other cultures if one is not careful. It is very rude to chew gum while talking with someone from countries such as Germany and Poland, and it is important to study their habits or risk being an "ugly American" when you think that you are being perfectly polite.

Yet there are a few things that seem to be the same in all cultures, religions, and economic strata. Though we have different body languages and expressions, our facial expressions show *Surprise, Fear, Sadness, Happiness, Anger*, and *Disgust* in the same ways.

Just remember "SF-SHAD."

Some scientists think this is a hardwired, universal human language. If you can interpret and demonstrate those basic facial expressions, you already know six of the most important "words" in the world.

Onomatopoeic words are those that mimic real sounds. For instance, bees *buzz*, bacon *sizzles*, and you *knock* on a door.

One might think that everybody around the world would, for instance, say *ouch!* the same way. I mean, if you pinch someone on the arm, *ouch!* is a reflexive exclamation, right? Wrong.

Since DLI, I have spent a great deal of time overseas, and have done extensive experimentation with *ouch!* Germans often say, *ouw ah!*; some Canadians say, *I oy!*, like chips a *hoy!* Some Russians say *Ouch!* like us. (Russians can be unpredictable and dangerous. Be careful trying this with Russians.) Mexicans and others in Central America sometimes say, *I ya!* Japanese make some kind of strange sound. It's really a lot of fun to pinch people from different countries and hear *tcha!* or whatever. But, unless you know them personally, it's better just to ask, or they will figure you for an ugly American. In Jersey they don't say anything; they punch you in the nose.

Once I was sitting around a dinner table with a Japanese, a Russian, a couple of Danes and people of several other nationalities and we started the "*Onomatanese* game." It was great fun and went on for more than an hour as we compared different *knock knocks* on the door. Germans go *klopf klopf.* And their dogs don't go *ruff ruff* they go *wow wow*. Their chickens go, *kluck kluck*. There are many interesting things to compare, like how they call a cat, or dog, or what sound they "hear" a zipper make. But one can't compare how phones ring, and sirens wail; they really *are* different, and, when in some countries, using the phones can seem like learning a new language.

It is extremely difficult to become truly fluent with a language, and to become bi-cultural. Some claim that spies can be trained to fit into another culture so well they are interchangeable with the natives. At best, that seems to be an over-optimistic claim, unless the spy has a similar background or learned the foreign language as a child so that he or she is without accent. *(Just pinch them!)* But, while short of becoming super-operatives from the movies, we could learn to communicate well, even fluently if we continued our studies and practiced. The Intelligence people had various reasons to learn languages, like voice interception, and prisoner interrogation. And no, Americans do not use torture, unless you include psychological tortures like isolation, which we also use on our ordinary prisoners.

Normally we learned about fifty new words each day, more on the weekends. But the words were only a small part of what we were studying, and the grammar was taxing. German was difficult for me, so I had to study three or four hours per night, though I was beginning to catch up and pass the quizzes and tests. Steve rarely if ever studied, and was at the top of his Spanish class. I was jealous. Sometimes at night my head was spinning with all this foreign language stuff, and, finally, I had studied so hard that it was ringing in my head! It was just ringing and ringing and ringing. I was studying too hard. I asked other people if their heads were ringing. No.

I thought, "Why am I learning *German?* There are no wars in Germany." During the past year or so the Army probably had invested enough in me to pay for four years of college tuition, and to give me a good start on a master's. Surely they wouldn't be cramming my head with all this expensive language training unless they thought it was important.

Sometimes it felt like my head was full; nothing else would fit until more room could be made. But I kept pushing, and by the seventh month of training—there was only one month to go—I was doing well in class. The Major had summoned me to his office and had offered exonerating congratulations for my comeback. I asked him if he had been serious about sending me back if I had failed German. He laughed and answered, "Yes."

Now I knew I would graduate unless something unexpected happened, but my head was *ringing!* I needed a break. Some classmates got the same idea, so we headed for Yosemite to unwind. Unfortunately, it would be a deadly trip, and it would have the opposite effect.

It was during that weekend, exactly one year since the disastrous night in Ocean City, that a newspaper ran a large story titled, "The Yon-Scott case 'You don't kill someone over a haircut'" by James Lilliefors.

WHEEL OF FORTUNE

ROY WAS FROM Brazil, which meant that he drove like a lunatic. There is no question that he was a skilled driver. Too skilled if you asked me, and I complained constantly that he was a road hazard. "Slow down Roy," I would say, "Use your blinker! You cut that guy off! Stop passing on double yellow lines! That light was *red* Roy. **Red, Red, Red!**"

A typical reply from Roy, dripping with sarcasm, was, "Stop acting like such an old woman. I thought you Special Forces guys had guts!" And he meant it.

"You Brazilians are crazy! Loco!" In German, "*Verrückt!*" for which a synonym might be "Brazilian driver."

"Americans don't know how to drive," he would lecture, "if you want to learn to drive you should spend some time in Rio. That's right. Rio baby! The women are beautiful, and they drive better than American men."

"Rio schmeo, macho-man, this is San Francisco!"

"Mike, if you don't like it, just be quiet. Enjoy the thrill. Just pretend that the windshield is a movie screen."

If you want a thrill, drive in Brazil.

Being such a great driver and all, Roy wouldn't buy insurance. He was sure that he could avoid the less skilled Americans. And I make no error in saying that he was *very* good, as are kids who play video games all day. The thing is, with video games, when you get killed, you just press the green button and start a new game. My favorite video game was "Asteroids." Every time my rocket ship crashed into a rock, I got three more ships for a quarter. Too bad it doesn't work that way in cars.

Besides feeling he was invincible behind the wheel of fortune, Roy had some pretty hard feelings about the insurance companies, whom he saw as Pac-Man bandits, swallowing your money and leaving nothing in its place. No argument there, but that wasn't the point. He had a Top Secret clearance and no insurance.

"Roy, if you have an accident and don't have insurance, I bet the Army will revoke your clearance."

"Never had a wreck, and I won't." He was so smug. Smart, but smug.

Roy was one of those people who could read an entire book in a single night, and he spoke Spanish and Portuguese fluently. His American English was without accent. He was exceptionally intelligent, had an easy time learning German, and he tried to make me feel better by saying things like, "After you speak two or three languages it gets much easier to learn another." Despite his driving habits, he was a good guy.

357

Roy, two other classmates from Military Intelligence, and I were headed to Yosemite for the weekend to go hiking. As we drove east, the sun set behind us, and hours later we found ourselves on a dark, desolate stretch of road, save for what appeared to be a bar or restaurant up ahead on the right. It was late and traffic was light. According to what would soon be reported in the newspaper, we were on Highway 108, about twenty miles west of Jamestown in western Tuolumne County.

Roy was driving his little Volkswagen, the old love-bug kind, down the four-lane road separated by a median. Our other two friends, Tom and Lori, were talking about something, but I was not tracking with them that night. I was in my own head, a couple of thousand miles away. It had been on this very night, the last Friday in July, that Steve and I were in the Surf-n-Suds in Ocean City. It was the same time of night—after eleven but before midnight—only now I was on the other side of the country, leaning my head against the car window, remembering. And trying to forget. The fight, the chase, the arrest on the beach, the jails, the charges, the pressure to try my case, and the waiting that seemed to last forever.

I had been in the Army for two years and one week. But the case had not been forgotten and "You don't kill someone over a haircut" was about to go to press. It was a large article backed by some investigation, complete with pictures. Life is full of surprises.

As Roy zipped us along in his VW to Yosemite, a four-wheel-drive vehicle without a top pulled onto the road ahead. A man was driving. He swerved a little. *Drunk?* Roy safely passed without incident. I looked back at the vehicle for some reason. I am fuzzy on the facts, but this is an approximation of what happened:

I watched for some seconds and the vehicle drove off the road onto the right shoulder. The man overcorrected to the left to get back on the road. He may have then swerved hard back to the right. Anyway, going at highway speed, the vehicle started skidding sideways. The tires grabbed the pavement, causing it to flip, side over side. Sparks went everywhere and it flew off the right shoulder, then rolled down a small embankment. I yelled at Roy to go back, but he was already hitting the brakes. It was a horrible crash and I felt a familiar fear. I have never gotten used to people screaming and moaning and bleeding all over the place, and by the time I was twenty, I had seen numerous accidents. I knew this one would be ugly, and feared it might be deadly.

Roy drove back and stopped, but it was hard to get the Volkswagen's headlights to shine on the wreckage. We were the only witnesses to the accident, and the only possible help. Roy parked the Volkswagen, and I jumped out to search for injured people. Down the embankment, the vehicle rested with the driver's side down, smoke pouring out. Adrenaline was surging through my veins.

There was no roof, just the roll bar. The driver was missing. He must have flown out. Maybe he was ripped in half in the bushes close by. I saw the silhouette of a woman. She was hanging from the seatbelt by one leg, arms limp and outstretched—like a football referee signaling a touchdown, only upside down across the driver's seat. She was unconscious.

I ran down the embankment and tried to pull her away before the vehicle caught fire. She was hanging upside down, which was bad even if there were no fire. My friends didn't come with me. I yelled at them to help. They stood silhouetted in the headlights.

A spinal injury was irrelevant if she burned or bled to death. I struggled, but couldn't get her seatbelt unbuckled. She somehow had only one leg in the seatbelt, the other had come out during the crash. With all the smoke and smells and my adrenaline pumping, I was sure that the vehicle was about to blow up. When it caught fire, I imagined, she would wake up; I would hear her screaming and burning to death, and that image would be seared into my memory for the rest of my life. I had to get her down and away.

I climbed up on the vehicle and slipped on blood or oil or something that was on my boots. I stood on top of the passenger side, her dangling body below me. Her right leg was torn and twisted. It was at my feet, wedged in the mangled frame against the seat. The seatbelt was still jammed. I tried with all my might to unsnap it. I pushed so hard on the button that it is a wonder my thumbs did not break. The buckle was jammed so tight that it might as well have been welded shut. I pulled out my pocketknife and cut her seatbelt. I was holding onto her ankle when I cut, because I thought she would fall on her head. But when I cut the belt, her leg was still tightly wedged in the frame. She didn't budge.

Then I saw that her leg was nearly pulled off her body; it was only hanging by a strand of muscle or other tissue. *Oh my God. I think she's dead.* My friends weren't helping. I screamed at them to come and grab her shoulders because I was going to pull her leg out of the frame. I was afraid that her leg was going to pop off in my hands; she would fall on her head, and I would just be holding her leg. *If her leg pops off, should I drop it or jump down with it?*

I pulled and twisted on her leg as hard as I could but it wouldn't come out. Smoke was rising behind me, but no fire. The driver staggered in from the darkness, came right up to the scene, and said, "She was driving." She was trapped in the passenger seat. I was still on top so I yelled at him to go sit down by the car and I would get to him.

My friends came closer to help.

Maybe another car shined its lights on her, but I recall that there was more light at this point. I saw her exposed muscle and fat; the skin on her leg was pulled away, flayed like a skinned rabbit. Her leg was almost completely ripped off at the hip. The light was hitting the meat on her leg, which was twitching and glistening. The wreckage smoked. I had to work fast. We could burn to death any second. She would scream and I would scream. *Is she dead?*

I pulled and pulled on her leg with incredible force, put my body into it like a weightlifter, but it would not budge. The angle was bad. My imagination was outrunning me. Her leg would come off in my hands and I would fly backwards and her leg would land on me. Maybe her blood would spurt out covering my face.

I pulled again, very hard; her leg finally popped free from the frame but stayed attached to her body. I was greatly relieved that she had not come apart. My friends were there below me, but at first seemed afraid to touch her. I have found this is typical behavior in these types of crisis, but not much help. Nevertheless, they moved in closer and overcame the fear they must have felt. They came right up to the wreck. I lowered her into their hands by her ankle. They pulled her into the light and prepared to do first-aid.

While I jumped off the wreck, I heard Roy say: "She's dead."

I came closer to look. The woman had suffered massive head wounds. Maybe it was the roll bar that knocked off the top of her head. No need for mouth to mouth for the benefit of the doubt. There was no question that she was dead.

The smell of death is sickening. It can be anything that you associate with the death. It is the smell that was there, whatever that was, but this time it was a sweet smell from some kind of plant. Occasionally I smell it somewhere and I remember that night.

By now, several cars had stopped, but nobody else came to help—something else I have seen many times. During almost every catastrophe that I have experienced, most witnesses did not help. They just talk, gawk, and get in the way.

The bleeding driver who had blamed the dead woman for the accident was gone. I asked the people standing in the darkness if they had seen him. *No.*

I yelled at the gaggle of onlookers to get out their flashlights and help us look for the man. He might die. They obeyed. I took a flashlight from someone and told the rest to get on line. We walked through the darkness, sweeping the area with flashlights for the man.

We found some guns, money, and a baby shoe. *Oh my God. Please don't let there be a baby.* There were still no police and no ambulance. No fire trucks. I ran up to the highway, because I had seen the vehicle flip several times. While Roy led the way as the people searched the area around the wreck, I thought the baby might have flown into the median.

As I moved up to cross the road, there was a jerry can in the headlights of an approaching semi-truck. The truck changed lanes and missed it. The can had fallen off the vehicle. It was sitting upright. Someone had literally picked it up and set it upright in the road. If it were filled with water, I thought, it might be useful for something. I opened it. It was full of gasoline. We could have been incinerated if that semi-truck had splattered the gas. *People were not thinking.*

The woman's hair and brains were on the road. I looked all through the median for the baby. It was not crying. I was shaking all over and didn't want to find it, or even to look. My experience with the woman had already shaken me badly, but the idea of a baby having been in the wreck made me feel numb all over. It *had* to be dead. I kept looking, looking and shaking.

Eventually police, firefighters, and ambulances started showing up. I felt like the Cavalry had arrived: action people who would know what to do. At times like that, police and firefighters seem like angels.

It turned out there was no baby, and the wreck never burned. It was probably not even in great danger of burning; the danger was generated by my fearful imagination, having seen so many movies and real explosions, and so much gore in my own life.

I don't recall making a police report. We drove on to Yosemite. The ride was quiet and we carried with us the smell of death. I tried to sleep under the Yosemite sky but sleep would not come. Someone's mother had died that night and I was feeling sick. Somewhere there must have been a baby that would never know its mother. I wished that I was numbed; it would have been easier. I don't know what bothered me more, the dead mother or the motherless baby.

MOVING ON . . .

ROY SAID THAT I panicked when I got up on the wreck. I have seen many people panic, and my reaction that night was not it. Panic generally means freezing, freaking, or running away—but never running forward into greater danger. I was afraid of burning to death, so was shouting commands. Of course, I became defensive and, in my anger, I told Roy that he'd frozen and refused to help, even though he had led part of the search.

But it was my anger talking and, more likely, Roy had seen that she was already dead, and wisely didn't risk his life trying to save a dead person. Being chauvinistic I had yelled at Lori to stay out of the way, and she did. Tom moved right in and helped when it was time to do so. Maybe they read the situation more clearly than I had. I know I would never have gotten up there had I realized she was dead.

I made some mistakes. I did not ever want to make them again. For one thing, I should have taken more time to try to examine her before diving in. I should have slowed down, tuned out the danger as much as possible, and just worked. But with my adrenaline going, I foolishly was shouting commands at a time when I should have been issuing instructions in a normal but firm tone. Fear breeds fear. Calm breeds calm. There is a time to shout, and a time merely to talk.

As time rolled by, there were, unfortunately, many opportunities to improve, and I got better.

PROFITEERS

THE WEEKEND OF the accident in California, on the other side of the country, the *Maryland Coast Dispatch* marked the anniversary of the fight with an article that came complete with four pictures.

The Yon-Scott case

'You don't kill someone over a haircut'

By James Lilliefors

First of two parts

> *"Tragedy throughout my life was*
> *more than I could bear.*
> *"But when I hit my knees to pray,*
> *He showed me that He cared.*
> *"He opened up my eyes and heart*
> *to this world of push and shove.*
> *"He took away my hatred and*
> *replaced it with His love."*
>
> -Song written by
> Charles William Scott in early 1983

Pasadena, Md. (Dispatch) -

Charles Scott's last call home was his annual "birthday call." It was made from a phone booth in Ocean City, one year ago this weekend.

"He was a rover," sighs [his mother]. She is sitting at the kitchen table in her narrow, one-story home here, chain smoking and sipping coffee.

"He couldn't stay in one place too long . . . But every year on his birthday he'd call me. Collect."

This time, the phone call was not a pleasant one. Scott— whom his family called "Buzz"—argued with his sister Dawnetta, and hung up on her.

That afternoon, at the downtown Ocean City restaurant where he worked, Scott was "crazed" according to a co-worker.

"He was throwing dishes around in the kitchen," his

363

supervisor said. "He'd had an argument with someone and was very upset . . . out of control. I told him to leave at about 3 o'clock. I planned to fire him the next morning."

The second call that day from Ocean City was placed by Scott's younger brother James, at the police station. He said only a few words and hung up. When he called back, he asked his mother if she was sitting down.

"What's happened to Buzz?" [She] said.

In the year since that day, [She] has tried to make sense out of the bizarre death of her son, who collapsed after being punched four times by a 19-year-old Green Beret. And out of the fact that charges against the soldier were later dropped and the case closed.

"You just wonder," she says. "Buzz was like me. Totally. That's why I can't see this happening. Fighting? No way. He wasn't a fighter.

"I put him in wrestling when he was a young kid. He went twice, then came in and said, 'I can't go back any more. That instructor hurt me.'

"He would tease people, then say, 'Hey, my big brother's coming out' . . . He was not rough. He just wasn't that kind of kid."

When Charles Scott died in Ocean City last summer, at 23, he had been there for only a month. [She] remembers the two brothers leaving her house in June with knapsacks on their backs. Neither had been to Ocean City before.

"I'm the one that told them to go there." [She] says. "He wanted to hitchhike to Florida and take [his younger brother] with him. I said go to Ocean City first. I didn't want [his brother] that far away from home . . . Where else can boys go to pick up a little spending money?"

It was the final leg of a restless five years of travel for Scott that had taken him to California, Washington, Texas and Pennsylvania.

"He wanted to see as much of the country as he could," [She] says. He was a dreamer . . . but I think he was very disillusioned, too."

[She] raised Scott from the time he was five, after being divorced from his father, and says of her five children, he was the one most like her. Scott grew up largely in the poor, industrial town of Washington, Pa. During his high school years, the family lived in a trailer park near Baltimore.

"Buzz was a C student just like me," [she] says. "He liked school . . . but he got into an argument with one of the teachers. The teacher said, 'You don't like school, why don't you just get out?' That's what happened."

After quitting, he took a job with Howard Johnson's. He quit that to work at a "rug place." Then he joined the Army Reserves.

"He took a number of jobs but I don't think he ever found what it was he wanted to do . . . He had bad luck. If he hadn't had bad luck, he wouldn't have had any luck at all."

[She] laughs heartily for a moment, then looks back at her coffee cup.

The woman Scott worked for in Ocean City describes him as a good worker but a difficult person.

"He did his job, but was real hard to get along with. The waitresses didn't want to go into the kitchen with him.

"The whole eight hours I was there, he'd tell me what I should be doing. He wanted to be a bartender or something. He didn't want to be a cook all his life.

"He wasn't sure what he wanted to do but he would have done anything, I think, to move up."

That Friday, Scott, a tall, medium-built man with a red tatoo [sic] on one arm, argued with his sister about their younger brother.

"I told him [Scott] to quit picking on him." Dawnetta, 27, says. "Those two fought a lot . . . and I was agitating him. He was upset. I wasn't."

She describes the argument, though, as "typical" ("All of us get along, but all of us fight like cats and dogs. Buzz and I really understood each other").

The phone call upset Scott. His coworkers at the restaurant say they had never seen him so riled up before. When his supervisor told him to leave the restaurant, she decided it would be his last day.

"I was afraid of Chuck and looking for any reason to fire him," she says, "I was going to fire him the next day, but he died. I was kind of disappointed to hear that . . . I was mad for about three days that I hadn't been able to fire him."

Scott spent the night of his 23rd birthday at the Surf 'n Suds bar on the Boardwalk downtown.

Normally he was not a heavy drinker ("He'd drink Cokes all day," his supervisor says) and didn't spend a lot of time in bars. But on July 29, he was upset and had a number of beers at the Surf 'n Suds.

According to reports, he was picking on two soldiers— Michael Yon and Stephen [sic] Shalus [sic]—because of their short, military hair styles. Each time the soldiers passed by him, Scott would initiate a verbal altercation, which began to center on Yon.

Yon, a stocky 5¹/₂-foot native of Winter Haven, Fla., had earlier that day become a Green Beret. A commanding officer at Fort Bragg described him as "a leader, one of the best soldiers in Special Forces training."

Over a period of about two hours that night, the two were separated several times by the bar's doorman, and asked to stay on opposite sides of the room. At one point, their differences appeared settled, and Yon bought Scott a drink.

But not long afterward, Yon struck Scott with four blows in rapid succession to the right side of his face. Scott, who had not thrown a punch, fell. (When [his mother] saw the body later, she says "he didn't look human.")

The doorman at the Surf 'n Suds hurried across the room and tried to detain Yon. But the Green Beret broke away and ran out across the Boardwalk to the beach. Scott was carried outside, where he died in the grass behind the bar.

Almost two hours later, Yon was arrested and charged with second-degree murder and assault with intent to commit murder.

Three days later, the charges were reduced to involuntary manslaughter. And in December, following a grand jury recommendation, the manslaughter charge was dropped.

The decision to drop charges "has left a bad taste in the mouth of this whole department," a spokesman for the Ocean City Police Department said recently. It also has been disappointing to [the mother], and especially Dawnetta Scott, who says, "I'm going to fight this. You don't kill someone over a haircut."

A month ago, Dawnetta gave birth to her second child and named him Charles. The infant looks remarkably like baby pictures of Scott.

[The mother] says she is disappointed that she wasn't kept abreast of the proceedings, "I asked the state's attorney to be included in any decisions, but I wasn't. I didn't even hear about the charges being dropped until several weeks after it happened."

She says she had a lawyer investigate the possibility of filing a lawsuit. But, "the funny part of it was he couldn't even get an autopsy report or anything. I thought he might be able to find out a little more."

The first full report of the event she received, [she] says, came this summer, when she was contacted by the *Maryland Coast Dispatch*.

"This thing surprised me because he seemed like he was just starting to get his life in order when he left here."

He had even, she says, written two religious songs in recent months. The songs became eulogies; they were sung at Scott's funeral in Pennsylvania last August.

(The second part of this series will examine the military's reaction to the case, and the process through which charges against Yon were dropped.)

Some journalists sell people's lives and reputations like used cars, and this one was simply looking to pick a fight with a twenty-year-old soldier who had no access to the press, when there was no longer any issue to fight over. This particular journalist was not a mindless scribbler, but a very ambitious man, digging for something to haul himself into the limelight. Today, he is also the author of the novel *Bananaville*, which was brought to market by one of the most prestigious publishers in the United States, St. Martin's Press in New York. According to the book-jacket, the story is about "a well-meaning journalist long since looking for his 'Big Story'. . . ."

Bananaville contains the following dialogue between the protagonist (an investigative reporter) and his boss on pages 88-89:

"'I want you to give me investigative stories.'" Says the boss. "'Stuff they can't get anywhere else. I want you to climb right back on this Reed story, go after it from every angle you can think of.'" His slow, southern accent seemed to have disappeared. "'Give me a story a day, if you can. Make it hard-hitting, even a little sensationalistic. I want the town talking.'"

On page 91 the journalist's frustration is described:

"Sometimes the Big Story seemed perpetually beyond his reach. . . ."

The novel is about a reporter searching for answers to a murder in a fictional town called Bananaville, which presumably is in Florida, though the writer is vague. The book's victim is killed, ironically, on the beach after an assailant cracks him on the head with a flashlight and gets away.

According to the book jacket: "James Lilliefors has written for the *Washington Post, US magazine, Runners World*, and elsewhere. He's currently a staff writer at the *Naples Daily News*, in Florida, and contributes frequently to other publications. Author of travelogue Highway 50 . . . " It goes on to say that he is working on another book.

Unfortunately, unscrupulous column-fillers give the real journalists, who are among the most important guardians of freedom, a bad rap. In this instance, by writing "You don't kill someone over a haircut," Lilliefors showed himself not to be a journalist and guardian, but a writer looking for tantalizing tales with sensationalistic appeals, seeking to fill blank pages, to induce Joe Reader to spend his hard-earned quarters, and then to spend them again. The greater the circulation, the more the advertising department can charge for space. Journalism is a business, after all. Controversy sells.

The writer was digging into an appropriately closed case, and making it appear that justice might not have been served. Likely, the majority of people who read the article sided with me anyway, based on earlier, more accurate stories, the court's decision, and the police department's opinion of me—which I've learned was favorable—but the title was strongly slanted: 'You don't kill someone over a haircut.'

In the body of the story, Lilliefors implies judicial impropriety and leaves important questions unanswered. For example, this quotation makes a nasty implication:

The decision to drop charges "has left a bad taste in the

> mouth of this whole department," a spokesman for the
> Ocean City Police Department said recently.

From police statements already cited, it is obvious that this was not true. Given the trajectory of the story, it would seem that Lilliefors either misquoted the police, took the statement out of context or, perhaps, found himself a single voice in the department whom he misrepresented as the department's spokesman.

Similarly, he glossed over other important facts such as witnesses' accounts of Scott's badgering me (instead of my simply passing by him off and on throughout the night, as if by chance, as the article suggests) and the availability of autopsy records which clearly show that Scott did look "human" despite the sensational comment that Lilliefors chose to print. He avoids mentioning that I turned myself in, went quietly, and was fully cooperative (except for exercising my constitutional rights) in police custody. Also, it is evident that Lilliefors has taken the time to thoroughly interview Scott's family, yet he has apparently made no effort to interview the other persons primarily involved, Steve Shaulis or me, or to quote the important eyewitness accounts. But how can the readers know this?

Had the article appeared at the time of the incident, it certainly would have been exposed as inaccurate and biased by more thorough journalists working from an understanding of the facts and not, as this one apparently would like us to think, from a feeling of sympathy for a mother who understandably feels pain and outrage about the death, albeit accidentally caused, of her son.

The article says of the mother: "The first full report of the event she received . . . came this summer, when she was contacted by the *Maryland Coast Dispatch.*"

It causes one to wonder what "full report of the event she received," since the *Maryland Coast Dispatch* and Mr. Lilliefors were not reporting the news; they were making it by kicking the hive. A grieving mother and sister cannot be faulted for wishing to know what happened to their son and brother, or for feeling robbed of a loved one when they suspect that a misdeed occurred. But newsmen should not reopen old wounds by pretending to give the "first full report," and spurring painful emotions to evoke highly subjective opinions about a legal case. How can the newspaper give the "first full report" when it either does not know what happened, as its inaccurate presentation indicates, or is deliberately stooping to distortion to incite the anger of a grieving family?

Lilliefors sheds light on the real issue on page 211 of his book *Bananaville*, in a dialogue between two newsmen:

"One of our problems, you see, is this business we're in. No longer are we—as a country, I mean, now, as a people—much interested in the language of the spirit, other than in its most temporal, superficial manifestations. No, we're far more interested now in the news of the day, aren't we? And that's the business we *perpetuate* [my emphasis] . . . As soon as what we do is digested, it is not news anymore, it's discarded, as unnecessary as an empty soda pop can. That's what we do here all week: We produce soda pop. And I suppose it's time we ought to fess up to it."

In "You don't kill someone over a haircut" Mr. Lilliefors wrote, "Over a period of about two hours that night, the two were separated several times by the bar's doorman, and asked to stay on opposite sides of the room."

This is an outright falsification. It was obvious from the witnesses' testimony that I had been *asking* for help. Nobody *separated* us. Saying that the doorman separated us conjures up visions of a referee stepping between two willing fighters, and telling them to go to their corners. It spins the story as if the Green Beret actively helped escalate the hostility.

He wrote that Scott did not throw a punch. Wrong. Rather, Scott did not land a punch. Saying he did not throw one is like saying that he shot, but missed, so his attack was not real. Fighting is not a game; that is why the military calls it "hand to hand combat." In this article Lilliefors overlooked the police statement showing that Steve tried to help the man with first aid, and numerous statements by witnesses, which could have precluded the controversy, are conspicuously absent. There were other inaccuracies and distortions in the article, but they are not worth itemizing. Lilliefors was trying to stir up people, much as I once stirred up my third grade class by yelling **"let's have a riot"**—without considering the consequences of my actions.

Perhaps Lilliefors wanted me to become incensed by the article so that I would tell my side. Luckily for me, I was more saddened than provoked by his words. Had I allowed the older and more experienced journalist to provoke me, he could have written another article, and perhaps spun that story, and really set the hive abuzz. It's a formula straight from *Bananaville:* "Give me a story a day, if you can. Make it hard-hitting, even a little sensationalistic. I want the town talking."

The reporter almost had his "Big Story" that seemed "perpetually beyond his reach" as I will explain later. But first let's talk about lawsuits.

Around this time I was told that I was in a strong position to win a civil suit against the Surf-n-Suds, and that in this lawsuit, it was likely the defendants would settle for any reasonable offer. This type of complaint is well established in the courts: a suit based upon the fact that the bouncers did not do their jobs, a failure resulting in avoidable injuries. But I had escaped with my skin, and wanted to put it all behind me. I didn't want to become embroiled in any lawsuits after all this time. Yet Lilliefors was not allowing me to let go.

He presented his article as if it were fact. His irresponsible presentation could have caused me problems with the military. As a citizen, I was also in a position to sue Mr. Lilliefors for dragging me into public view in a false light. However, I did not go looking for an attorney to sue Mr. Lilliefors, either. I took my lumps and kept going.

The irony is that his could have been a great story if he'd simply told the truth and fairly represented the facts on both sides of the issue. In that case, had he contacted me, I may have granted him interviews to tell my side, and he could have heard about the very frightening hours of evasion, the jail with the police outside the window, and the "snitch." He could have written about Daniel Long, the lawyer with a sense of justice stronger than his desire for political advantage. He could have written about Special Forces Selection and all the extra training I completed while charges were pending, and how the Army not only didn't toss me in the brig, but actually made me a "sergeant." *That* is a story.

Since few knew that I was completely exonerated, an accurate article could have explained why that had come about. Instead, people were likely under the impression that I simply wasn't convicted for a crime I had, in some eyes, committed. In cases where the accused goes free, there will be rumors that the police "just didn't have enough evidence to convict," implying, as the slang expression so pointedly has it: someone "got away with murder."

Indeed, for years, whenever I met someone, my first thought was: *Do they know about what happened in Maryland? How long before they find out?* Experience showed that when I made new friends, it was just a matter of time. When people did find out, experience also showed, there was about a 90% chance (to put a number on it) that they would hear a more imaginative than factual version of the story. I should qualify that; around Army circles, soldiers, unlike the civilians, generally got a fairly accurate account.

How could I quell such rumors? It's not something that I could casually bring up like: "Hey, ah, gee, did you hear what happened in Ocean City? If not, well, you will, so I would like to set the record straight." It is a difficult subject to discuss, but if I didn't discuss it, it was left up to the imagination. It is important to defend your reputation—your reputation is worth fighting for—but the very act of defending yourself makes it look like you are hiding something, and it can make you feel dirty even when you know you are clean.

As the years unfolded, the events could have provided another "Big Story," but Lilliefors didn't get it. The Big Story eluded him. I have tried to contact Mr. Lilliefors. I have even considered that maybe it would change my mind about some things to hear his side of the story on the article. But he doesn't return my calls. Perhaps in the future, we will meet for coffee under better circumstances.

THE LONG WEEKEND

WHILE THE LILLIEFORS story was being distributed to the good citizens of Maryland on the East Coast, my friends and I finished our weekend in Yosemite and headed back to the West Coast. The weekend was not as enjoyable or relaxing as we had hoped. The smells of the accident lingered still in Roy's car, and we took the same route back to San Francisco.

The Army awards medals for the type of action in which we were involved, but we never told the Army what happened. Personally, I didn't even want to think about it, much less talk about it. A medal would only be a reminder of something I hoped to forget.

During the course of writing this book, I contacted the Modesto Library to see if the accident had made the papers. A librarian was kind enough to search the microfiche for me. One announcement said the woman was thrown from the vehicle, and that her head was pinned beneath the roll bar. Not entirely accurate, but close enough. It said that she was twenty-six years old, and the mother of two sons and a daughter.

It also said that the driver was twenty-four years old, and was found at 6:50 A.M. the next day when a citizen called the authorities to report that he was asking for help. The California Highway Patrol said that it would recommend felony hit and run charges, and possibly manslaughter when he was released from the hospital.

THE PRESIDIO

A *PRESIDIO* IS a fortification, basically a defensive position, and there, my eight months of unrelenting language study came to a close. I had been far behind when the Major put me on academic probation, but had managed to pull away, back from the brink of failure. By the end, I had learned my lessons and was ready to fly away from the Presidio to a real Special Forces team.

The professors gathered around and poked good-natured fun at the way I passed part of the final exam. We were given a surprise subject and were required to talk about it for an entire minute without pause into a tape-recorder. It was harder than it may seem; talking for an entire minute in *English* without interruption is hard for me. When they said "without pause," I took it to mean literally *without* pause. So I rattled on hardly taking a breath.

Translated from German back to English it went something like:

OhnoIhavetotalkforanentireminutewithoutstoppingwhichisv erydifficulttodobecauseI'llneedtobreatheatsomepoint.OKthe subjectisGermancitiesandGermanpeopleandIhavetotalkfora nentireminute.BerlinseemslikeanastyplacewithallthoseRussi ansaroundbutI'llbetthereareralotofGermangirlstherewhoare waitingformetorescuethemfromtyranny.That'smyjobandIpla ntobedamngoodatit........Istheminuteupyet?.....OKthenther eisHamburginthenorthandtheteachernevermentionsHambu rgwithoutmentioningtheredlightdistrict.What'supwiththat? Hemusthavemoremoneythanlooks. OH, my God. Please don'tfailmeforsayingthat.Iwasonlyjoking.Isthisminutenotupy et?Youmustbejoking,thisisthelongestminutethatIhaveeverh adwhileIwastakingatest. Beep.

Time's up. *Whew!*

I had achieved the basic level of fluency in German required to graduate, and more. I didn't graduate at the top, but was close, which wasn't hard because there were so few students. We'd lost three or four, so fewer than ten remained. Even if I graduated last, I would still be near the top! It was difficult for me, but I tried hard. A couple of students had already taken German in high school or college and they helped me a lot. But the teachers said that I had the best *accent*, which made me feel good, since I had worked so hard on it. Later, Germans sometimes commented that my accent and grammar were proper and refined. But, then again, Germans are as a whole polite people, and whenever you struggle with their language, they usually chip in with a smile to help. As for DLI, it was the best academic training that I received anytime or anywhere. It was an awesome school, and I highly recommend it.

Somehow I graduated with the "Book Award," which I wondered if they just made up to make me feel better because I had to study more than the rest. Turns out it was real, and for "outstanding academic achievement." The red, hardbound, 428-page book I received was in German, and still sits on the shelf.

The title: ***Die unendliche Geschichte***
The Never Ending Story

As for kidnapping Brenda, there was that other military principle that sometimes balances audacity: *common sense*. Kidnapping would not be acceptable in this day and age, though had I lived a few hundred years ago, I probably would have gone for it. And she kept dating that jerk. I had tried to cover up my disappointment by running wild. That first week after arrival, I realized that Green Beret = Girls. Lots and lots of girls. *Girl*-illas were everywhere. Being a minor celebrity, it was easy to meet them when they introduced themselves. Often, while diligently studying at night, that knock-knock came on the door. *Who is that knocking? Sounds like a new knock.* Some girl would be standing there smiling. I was amazed, but wasn't complaining about it. At least my ego was assuaged. But ego was just the tip of it. I never expected in my wildest dreams that women would come knocking on my door, and it made me crazy that the one that I really wanted had a jerk boyfriend—and that she thought I was too young.

Her course in Korean was much more difficult than mine in German, so she would remain at the DLI for several months after I left. Orders came assigning me to the 10th Special Forces Group at Fort Devens, Massachusetts. As a result, Brenda and I never had a big romance except in my head. In my dreams we lived out in the country and had lots of babies. In my dreams I was not intimidated that she was older—and I could outrun her. I wanted her to know that she was safe and protected. I wanted her to know that *I can* . . . because she is a woman worth fighting for, and even worth kidnapping.

We wrote each other for maybe a year after DLI. Later, we were stationed at the same base for a time, but I was away a lot and hardly saw her.

Eventually she married that same boyfriend. I was happy for her but regretted that we never had a romantic relationship, that I never got my chance. Sometimes the lioness gets away. But the lion never quits.

ROAD-TRIP!

ANOTHER SF MAN who went through Spanish got orders for the 7th at Fort Bragg. I planned to go to Florida for leave after DLI, but my friend mentioned that he was going to Calgary, Canada, to visit his family before heading to Bragg. I asked to tag along because I'd never been to Canada. Off we went.

I was amazed at the trees as we drove through northern California. I always suspected it, but this certified it for me—I'm a nature-lover, a child of the forests and the clean air. Those big trees and virgin stands of forest seemed like something out of my wildest imaginings. I felt like I could just walk off into the forest and live with all the plants and animals.

We made it through parts of British Columbia and found the Canadians were friendly people, but often when I said, "I'm an American" they reminded me that people from the U.S. are not the only Americans. Canadians are Americans, as are Mexicans and others. Of course, I retorted that it just doesn't sing to say: "I'm a United Statesian." The Canadians were a lot of fun, except for a Mounty who stopped us, thinking we might be AWOL.

Finally, we made it to Calgary, finished our visit, and then one afternoon as we were sitting in a gas station about to head south, I found myself examining the map. I held the atlas on my lap and saw a tiny speck far to the north called Yellowknife. *Yellowknife*, Northwest Territories.

North, north and more north

Yellowknife is all alone. From Calgary, it is about a thousand mile drive north, most of which was not paved. That meant a drive of about two thousand miles just to get back to Calgary.

Saying Yellowknife is isolated is like saying the Arctic has some ice; Yellowknife is so far removed from the rest of the world that I just had to go there. Now. It was literally at the end of the road. My friend finished pumping the gas and got back in the truck. I said, "Hey, let's go to Yellowknife." He checked the atlas for directions, said "Okay," and without further consideration we headed north instead of south.

Much farther up the road, he was asleep while I drove the four-wheel drive pickup, going a little too fast on the forever-gravel road, I lost control and started sliding sideways. I almost wrecked the truck, but somehow managed to straighten out without spinning around or slipping off the road. He woke up due to the noise and sudden direction changes that bumped him around and asked, "What's up?"

"Nothing, just a little turbulence; we passed through it." Scared the hell out of me. I might have been a Green Beret, DLI graduate, and all those things, but I had never owned a car, and it seemed like every time I drove one there was a near disaster. Once, as I test drove a Toyota Supra (that I couldn't afford, I just wanted to drive it) in San Francisco, about five minutes into the drive the salesman had nervously asked me if I had a valid driver's license. "Of course," I said, "I can drive big Army trucks."

During the trip up to Yellowknife, we saw a black bear with two cubs, and later another adult black bear. Then some moose. The place was very wild. (Word to the wise. If you ever drive to Yellowknife, *never* pass a gas station without filling up.)

We drove all through the night, and had watched the Northern Lights ahead in the sky. They were mesmerizing. We just kept on pushing until we had spent about twenty-four hours in the truck.

We made it to Yellowknife, got gas and arrived at a local diner just in time for breakfast. The place was filled with smoke; the customers appeared to be local men, drinking coffee, and talking about whatever men in Yellowknife talk about. And they looked rugged. They took note as we walked in, but they were cordial and polite. It looked like the kind of place where a man could get himself into trouble really fast if he broke the rules, whatever they were.

You could buy ammo for a high-powered rifle, and a loaf of bread at any little store, perhaps even on the same aisle. You could buy a steel trap, a lantern, and a sleeping bag on the next aisle, along with a dozen eggs and a gallon of milk. I liked Yellowknife and its joke that deer piss will do for beer. We talked with some of the locals at the diner and asked directions for a good place to camp. When they realized we were American soldiers on leave they warmed up—being a soldier is respectable work—and we found them to be very helpful. After breakfast, we said our good-byes and one old timer told us to pay attention and be careful; we were in wild country. We thanked him for the advice, he just nodded his head, and we drove out of Yellowknife, continuing into the wilderness until the road ended.

At night, the Northern Lights were awesome. They were without a doubt the most spectacular show I have ever experienced—bar none—including rocket-launches, gigantic explosions, nearby lightning strikes, erupting volcanoes, out-of-body experiences and being abducted by aliens—*nothing* compares to the Northern Lights. They were stunningly bright and colorful, like a rainbow on growth hormones.

They come in many forms, but for an idea of how they looked on that trip, imagine a giant rainbow ten times brighter than any you have ever seen, stretching from horizon to horizon. Now imagine that on one end of that rainbow there is a fan so powerful that it can smash a hurricane. That hurricane-smashing fan is blowing on the rainbow, causing it to wave in the wind. The giant rainbow is waving like a flag from horizon to horizon—all night long, from sunset to sunrise. Incredibly spectacular.

A crystal-clear lake was only yards away from where we camped. We were deep in a beautiful wilderness so far from civilization that radio reception was in doubt. It was quiet and crisp and at night the Northern Lights flittered off the lake in a dancing show indescribably brilliant and colorful, waving in the heavens, tranquil and powerful, but silent. Not a sound. At times like that I could think of only one thing: *romance*. At that moment I knew that when I met the woman that I had been looking for, I would take her to Yellowknife to see the show, then we could go on our honeymoon somewhere on an island in the South Pacific, or wherever she wanted. My honeymoon would be in her arms.

We stayed a few days in Yellowknife then headed back south to some Canadian city. From there, I caught a flight back to Florida, where I bought my first vehicle. A Toyota Landcruiser. Four-wheel-drive.

I wrecked it within a week.

IN THE BEGINNING

ONE BRIGHT DAY in twelfth grade drama class, I donned a gorilla suit for some reason, probably as an assignment. I was a natural gorilla and thought that I could walk just like one. A girl I liked was in another class, so I decided to liberate her from her tormentors.

Surely she was daydreaming that I would storm in and rescue her as her Prince Charming. Wearing the suit, I "gorilla walked" out of my class while ignoring—or at least not heeding—the calls of my teacher. I was on a mission, and gorillas know instinctively that Missions Come First.

Down the hall I went, grunting gorilla sounds all the way, and smacking lockers with my fists. I barged into her class and approached her as gently as an untamed beast can manage, grunting and scratching my hairy chest. I tilted my gorilla head back and forth admiring her, and scooped her up. Through the eyeholes I saw her smiling, and I was becoming very excited as she put her arms around my black, hairy neck! Her teacher said nothing, and my teacher had not even bothered to follow me. Maybe she knew that I would come back when I got hungry.

The girl knew it was me, and it was working. She was laughing, obviously flattered that someone had taken the time and risk to single out and kidnap her—in a friendly sort of way—instead of one of the other thousand girls at school. Unfortunately, when I started to carry her out the door, I accidentally smashed her head on the frame. *Crack!*

"Ouch!" she yelled, grabbing her head.

Oh no! The backfire from hell!

The Law of Unintended Consequences was in full force that day.

The head-bumping sound and the pain in her voice sent a chill through my body.

I put her down, stopped acting like a gorilla and asked, "Are you okay?" She grimaced and rubbed the place on her head that would soon be a knot.

"Yes," she said, glaring through my eyeholes. Pain has a way of stealing the humor—and romance.

My shoulders drooped, my head tilted down shamefully of its own sorry weight.

I needed to get the heck out of there, and Richard was always up for adventure.

Road Triiip! We piled camping gear into the back of his old black pickup truck, and headed north on I-75 through Georgia up to Tennessee, then zipped over to North Carolina for the week of Spring Break.

We stopped at a little mountain store in backwoods North Carolina to get something to slake our thirst. Richard grabbed a strange bottle labeled simply "Cheerwine," which was supposed to be a soft drink. He popped off the top with a key, guzzled some down and said, "Wow! Try this!" as he handed over the bottle.

"What? *Cheerwine?* Sounds like some kind of joke." The corny bottle said:

BOTTLING GOOD CHEER SINCE 1917

"SMILE"
CHEERWINE
IT'S FULL OF GOOD CHEER

"I don't want that," I said, and refused the bottle.

"Just try it," he prodded. "You can't judge a drink by its bottle. This stuff is awesome." I had never known Richard to cry wolf, so that time I took the bottle and pulled a swig.

"Hey. That is good." I guzzled down the rest of the cheery cherry-flavored carbonated soda as he reached in the cooler for two more. We headed to the counter, paid, returned the empty bottle, and walked out the door on our way to the river.

From there, we hooked up with a guide from the Nantahala Outdoor Center, and whitewater-rafted down the Ocoee river in Tennessee.

Having survived the Ocoee, we set off for bigger game on the South Carolina/Georgia border: The Chattooga river, where *Deliverance* was filmed. The Chattooga is one of the most difficult and dangerous in the Southeast.

On the eve of the trip, we overnighted in Clayton, Georgia. It was raining, and the rivers were rising.

Rapids are classified by their difficulty.

Class 1 = Easy: Small waves, clear passages.

Class 2 = Medium: Clear passages, irregular waves.

Our trip down the Chattooga would begin here, on the following class levels, on Section IV of the river.

Class 3 = Difficult: Numerous waves, rocks, eddies and narrow passages.

Class 4 = **Very Difficult:** Powerful waves, numerous rocks, difficult passages, precise maneuvering required.

Class 5 = **Extremely Difficult:** Long and violent rapids in quick succession, violent currents, steep gradients.

Class 6 = Unrunnable: Not attempted by commercial outfitters. (Experts run these at risk of death.)

We'd each had our eighteenth birthdays within the month, and signed the legal waivers specifically warning that this could be a fatal trip. It felt good to be eighteen, lawfully permitted to sign up for a death ride on our own authority.

Before the trip, the guide had recited one of those safety briefings that makes you wonder how anybody survives the ordeal or would pay good money for such lunacy. But, having heard so many warnings before, we found it hard to know what to take seriously, and what to take in stride.

Our guide briefed: *This river is so old that dinosaurs used to splash in it. It carries a gazillion cubic feet of water per second. That's equivalent to 432,000 showerheads all running at once. Water has no conscience. It doesn't care about us, so we have to look out for each other. Yes, people get hurt and killed every year on whitewater, but we can minimize the risk by following some simple precautions.*

Today the water level is up, so the river is especially challenging. Some of the hazards are hypothermia, foot entrapment, hydraulics, and strainers.

Then he explained what all that meant. A foot entrapment occurs when your foot gets caught in the rocks: the water simply knocks you down and drowns you.

What he didn't explain were some of the interesting things the river guides know about drowning victims. For instance, when the victim disappears underwater and his helmet and lifejacket surface, the guides know that the victim has drowned and is limp, with his head facing downstream. If two shoes float to the surface, the victim has *not* fallen to a foot entrapment. The river sometimes strips the clothes off the victim, and it can take many hours for rescuers to free the body. During the rescue there are sometimes "secondary victims." For instance, when a person sees a family member die, the person will often go into shock, or suffer a heart attack. Another type of secondary victim is "the rescuer" who is often a father. When a father sees his child wash from the boat, he might dive in immediately—making two people to rescue.

During the rescue, it is important to watch the watchers. After such trauma, the guide sometimes decides that guiding is no longer a fun and dashing job, and he quits.

He continued,

Other hazards include your paddles. People have lost teeth because rafters didn't keep their hands on the T-grips. It is a very bloody mess, and I would rather not have teeth floating around in the bottom of my boat. And *this is **my** boat. This is a dictatorship not a democracy. If you do what we are about to practice, and what I say without fail, we will have a memorable trip, and everybody should get to go home. If not, well—*[he pauses for effect]—*it's not too late to back out. We will refund your money. Are there any questions?*

In all, six customers were going in our boat at a cost of about forty bucks a pop. Besides the guide and us, the crew of castaways included a quiet twenty-something lovebird mating pair from Atlanta, and "The Couple." The Couple consisted of a big, muscular man who sported an attractive, compliant brunette like an accessory. They had arrived in a fancy red sports car and were of unknown origin.

During the practice part of the briefing, the guide told everyone to don helmets. Big Man responded by holding out his helmet, looking down at the guide and saying, "I don't need one of these things."

The guide ignored the comment. Big Man was trying to take charge of the boat. It was uncomfortable for everyone, and he was reinforcing that negative stereotype about muscles and brains—or the absence thereof—with a talent that only practice could have perfected. The lovebirds from Atlanta turned away and snapped on their armor, while Richard and I did the same, wondering what would come next.

The guide was half of Big Man's size, but looked up and said "If you want to ride in my boat, put your helmet on, and grab your paddle. Remember what I said about the T-grip."

Silence.

The brunette looked at her muscle man and asked in what must have been her sweetest voice, "Honey, *please*, for me? It's the rules."

He glanced at the guide, then back at his love kitten who smiled some secret smile that obviously meant something special, and he said, "Okay, I'll wear it for you" with a little grin.

That settled, the guide had us practice various procedures until he deemed we were ready. If he yelled, *"Highside!"* we were to jump on the side of the raft that was facing downstream, and into the obstacle, to push the high tube down. This was to prevent capsizing if we smashed into an obstacle in dangerous water. If we were not fast enough, or it didn't work, we would all dump into the rapids. This was before the advent of self-bailing boats, so the guide explained that we would have to manually bail with buckets each time the boat got flooded.

After the briefing and practice, we lugged the boat to the water. It was raining. The air and water were cold, probably fifty degrees or less. The trip would take us down five and a half miles of river, then we would have to paddle two miles across a lake. Our time on the water would be about five hours. Five *cold* hours.

I stepped into the water with my plastic river shoes, and, when the water touched my ankles and soaked through the grey wool socks, a shiver quaked through my body. Richard smiled in his normal show-no-stress way and announced his presence to the river with, "It's *Show Time.*" He may as well have been an English biplane pilot from WWI, tossing the silk scarf back over his shoulder, stepping into the cockpit to hunt the Red Baron.

Within a minute or so, we were all in the boat. The guide started us off in the calm water practicing procedures and paddling. Big Man wasted no time unbuckling his life jacket. The guide said, "Buckle that jacket."

Big Man snarled, "What? For this? You said this river is supposed to be hard and dangerous. This is a kiddie ride."

The lovebirds sat quietly and looked out the boat. Richard smirked. By now I had cinched my jacket as tightly as it would go without cutting off my breath. The brunette intervened, but her tone now had an edge, "Honey, please, just buckle your jacket. It's the rules." No secret smile this time.

The guide chuckled, and with a gentle voice simply said, "You hear that roaring up ahead? That's not the airport. Buckle your jacket, or I will put you on shore." Big Man mumbled something under his breath and snapped up his jacket. Soon we were into several rapids, bouncing around like a pinball, water splashing everywhere—like riding a baby bull, but with the daddy bull still up ahead.

The guide warned that the most dangerous part of our journey was known as The Five Falls. This treacherous run has five rapids ranging from Class 3 to 5 over a distance of less than 500 yards. According to other sources, when the water is high, *all* the rapids in The Five Falls are strong Class 4's, if not 5's.

The water level was high. People sometimes die in Class 2, which is somewhat akin to dying in a swimming pool in a stiff breeze, but we had just negotiated numerous Class 3-4s, and realized just how serious this was. The argumentative man was no longer a nuisance, but the brunette sounded like she'd hit the jackpot after every rapid, and seemed to be having the time of her life.

As we approached The Five Falls, all six customers were still in the boat. The guide sat in the rear. Nobody was laughing. Nobody was talking. All anticipated the jaws ahead. The woman suddenly burst out, "Honey, this was a *great* idea!" She smiled and her face looked like that of a little girl opening Christmas presents. "I can't believe I didn't want to do this! Next, I want to try kayaking." She bubbled with enthusiasm, but her muscle man didn't answer. He only looked at the bottom of the middle of the boat, where he had jumped during the action on one of the last rapids.

As we moved forward and down on our watery escalator, the deep roar growing louder and louder foretold what lay ahead. The guide said, "Relax everyone." We all stopped paddling, "Turn around for a minute and listen to me." He was wearing his game face. "We are entering The Five Falls. Stay alert. You will not have time to think or ask questions. Do what you are told. Things are about to get very exciting. Do what you practiced without hesitation, and everything will go fine. Don't fall out," he said, "Lock in. Nobody ever died *inside* the boat. Remember, keep your hands on your T-grips. That is very important."

Then he yelled, "Alright! Heads up! This is the best part of the trip!"

The water was *kkold*, and it was still raining, so the threat of hypothermia was real and high. My body was shaking with a mixture of cold and anticipation, my feet were completely numb, and my fingers were painfully stiff. It had been snowing the day before in Tennessee; it was the second time in my life that I had seen snow, and the cold weather had moved east with us.

The Couple kicked into gear again. The man sat behind me, and was coming to grips with his character. He sniveled, "My feet are cold; I think I'm getting frostbite."

The woman answered in exasperation with a raft-guide expression: "It's not cold enough to get frostbite. Pull those panties off your head."

Wow! So much for the tame kitty following her man!

As we descended into The Five Falls, the river was rumbling like a jet, but it was probably more powerful than any airliner. There was no use talking in normal tones. The thundering water drowned out practically all but its own voice, though we could hear the guide when he yelled commands, and, as we blasted down the rapids, suddenly he was yelling, *"Highside! Highside!"* He grabbed a passenger who wasn't moving fast enough by the jacket and threw him to the opposite side of the raft.

I was up front on the right, and dove highside, just as our boat slammed violently against a rock on the left, and became pinned. Paddles flew dangerously around the boat as people braced for the emergency. We were in danger of capsizing and dumping all six passengers and the guide. There were still violent rapids ahead. Passengers screamed from inside the boat, but the river was so loud that the words coming through to me were garbled.

The adrenaline was pumping. This was not a controlled ride; in fact the water was so powerful that it was pushing the right tube down below the surface. As the freezing cold water slammed into us, the raft bucked like a bull and a wave swept through with irresistible force, washing Richard from the boat.

Richard's paddle was gone, and he desperately grabbed for the raft, but the current was simply overwhelming. He was about to shoot down the rapids like a helpless leaf.

As he shot by the front of the boat in a blur, I lunged over and grabbed his lifejacket by the shoulder, which nearly jerked me out. The guide was yelling something, but the thundering whitewater muffled his words. The river was smashing us against the rock, while I was fighting to pull Richard back inside. A losing battle. Though holding on with all my strength, I was still not pulling Richard into the boat, but I was pulling the boat the rest of the way over. Richard's body was like a water anchor, causing the left side to ride up the rock, forcing the right tube down. It was going to dump the lot of us.

I could hold onto my friend and dump the boat, or let go. He would take his chances with the rapids, alone. The others were simply fighting to stay inside. The boat rode higher and was about to flip. Richard was not going to make it. I had to make a choice. Now.

Goodbye my friend.

I released him into the roaring water.

He was gone in an instant, swallowed by the froth.

Suddenly I felt unspeakably vile, the lowest form of traitor. *What have I done?*

I pulled back into the boat, and within a few seconds it somehow got unpinned. The bull was free, and we shot every way but straight—*where's Richard?*—down the rapids, slammed against some boulders and bounced off as people clocked each other with paddles and screamed.

The boat was swamped and there were more rapids ahead, but no Richard, as we entered a short stretch of calmer water. The guide was in control of himself, which settled down the customers. He'd regained control of the passengers, but not the boat. He could not steer because it was completely swamped, and therefore weighted down with water, riding low, like an overloaded freighter. There was only one bucket for bailing, and it was floating in the middle next to muscleman, attached by a cord. The guide pointed to him and commanded, "You! Bail!"

There was another rapid ahead, and the water had to go before we got there. Muscleman hesitated as if he didn't hear the command. He made no move for the bucket. The woman from the lovebird couple lunged over and grabbed the bucket and began bailing like some kind of pumping machine. She was moving so fast she resembled a cartoon character, breathing heavily, scooping full buckets of water, and slinging them back to the river in wide arches. Soon she emptied the boat enough that we were no longer riding low in the river, and the guide said, "Good job. Let it rest." And he began giving steering commands.

Richard seemed long forgotten by the crew, but the guide was scanning the water for a brightly colored helmet.

Where is he? Trapped under a rock?

Is he behind us, in front, or underwater?

We didn't have to wait long.

There he is! Up ahead, waving his arms!

The guide started us paddling toward Richard. The guy formerly known as Big Man had managed to hunker down in the middle of the boat during most of the whitewater, and didn't help with anything. The brunette commanded sharply, "Get up and paddle! You're not going to fall out."

We scooped up a soggy, shivering Richard, who looked like a marshmallow floating on calm water. The brunette and I grabbed him under the armpits, and hauled him into the boat. He was shaking, and barking a few angry words in my general direction. Richard was raised better than me; he didn't cuss, but he made his point just as forcefully. *Why did you let me go!*

He piled into the bottom of the boat, on his back by the cold feet of the crew, and let out a war cry, ***"Yeee Haaaa!"*** We found his paddle, and he resumed his position.

When it was over, we had to paddle almost two miles across Lake Tugaloo, and Richard was fuming, though, I think, he secretly liked the ride. But I knew there would be no end of it. He kept saying over and over: "You let me go. You let your *friend* go down the river. You let me go."

It would not have been so bad if a cowardly person was spouting off opinions about emergency situations. Unfortunately, Richard was anything but cowardly. True friends look out for each other come hell or high water.

But hey man, you're still alive! And how many people can claim the honor of having crashed down some of The Five Falls without a boat?

We paddled two long miles across the lake, giving me plenty of time to contemplate my sins. *I can't believe I let him go. But—I had to! What was I supposed to do? Dump the whole boat?*

Meanwhile, the woman was high on adrenaline and excitedly asked the guide if she could make another trip, but her docile male friend re-entered the scene, whimpering about being tired. The woman grimaced. Before the trip, when they had arrived in the fancy red car, she seemed proud to be at his side, but her Prince Charming was not the brave warrior she must have imagined, and now she must have thought he was just 225 pounds of imitation man, like the unidentifiable concoction in the grocery store is "crabmeat."

"I'm finished rafting," he said.

She fired again, "Then you can just sit in the car with the heater on."

Wow! Another pretty boy bites the dust. Always a sight.

The poor river guide would probably hope to never see a crew like ours again, and the lovebirds returned to Atlanta with a story to tell. And it's true: Life *does* move pretty fast. If you don't stop and look around once in a while, you could miss it. But how could they explain to their friends living in the shadows of those skyscrapers what it was like to roar down The Five Falls—free as a mountain bird to take your chances, to live?

That night Richard and I camped in the woods near another river. We set up the tent, but didn't stake it down. As we did camp duties, heating chicken noodle soup, opening the saltines, and drinking Cheerwine, a big gust of wind swooped in like a hawk, grabbed the tent as if plucking a mouse from a field, and dropped it into the river. It was floating downstream, upright. Without words, we jumped into the water and hauled it out, then staked it down.

By this time, we had sanctioned Cheerwine as our official soft drink. I never had anything like it. It was like a supercharged cherry cola, and at the end of the trip, we bought a couple of cases to haul back home. You never know what you will find in those mountains.

On the way back, we stopped to camp alone by Orange Grove Sink in northern Florida, near Live Oak. The "sink" is a spring out in the woods. The forest was lush in that area and smelled like forever-life, as if it had always been there. The water in the spring was magically clear, and plunged down about seventy feet to where the mouth of the cave disappeared into the darkness of the earth, and the clear water became black; there was no light. From there began a gigantic underwater cave system, one of the largest in the United States. Divers have explored more than five and a half miles of passageway that can be accessed through this entrance. If you scuba down there, you will find a sign warning of your likely death. A diver had better know exactly what scuba and spelunking risks he or she is taking before venturing inside, for this cave is said to have swallowed many souls.

The surface of the water marked the mouth of the watery cave. Above that, there was a big rope swing suspended from a tree branch. Our bomb-making days were over and we were both environmentally sound thinkers, but. . . . Despite our being environmentally conscious, and my tree hugging tendencies, we then did something, in pursuit of adventure, that we knew was environmentally indefensible: We poured white gas on the water and set it ablaze.

It was night and the flames illuminated and flickered off the surrounding trees and forest. On the rope swing, we swung into the night, screaming like Tarzan, *AH EEE AHH EEE AHHH!!!* but when those flames were suddenly beneath us there was a strong temptation to grip tighter and hang on. On the first go 'round, I swung back over land, having felt the heat— Richard jeered, *let go!*—on the second swing, I plunged through the flames—*splash*—into the dark, cool water. And, beneath the surface, through the clearness, I watched the flickering, glowing flames burning overhead in the air. I held my breath and looked up—*k-splash!*—Richard plunged in.

The fire on the water rolled back as we approached, and, luckily, did not burn us. We jumped over and over and over until the gas had consumed itself, drew its last breath, flickered and faded out. Again, there was darkness.

DE OPPRESSO LIBER:
TO FREE THE OPPRESSED

BILLY HAD MOVED out several years back, when I was about fifteen, and was taken to live with a doctor and his family. When he first moved in, the doctor's wife started fattening Billy up, telling him that he had not been eating enough, so his life suddenly became fuller. After Billy graduated from high school, a lawyer from our church who had become a judge helped him get a scholarship at a Nazarene college in Tennessee. Billy was long gone, leaving Susan and me to co-exist with "Dad."

Susan and I moved in with our grandparents when she was a sophomore, I a senior. It was several days before "Dad" realized we were gone. Susan had pulled back into herself, and found solace in animals, but she was not one to be permanently deterred by our current state of poverty. She was a fighter, and poverty was a challenge like any other. It was merely something to be reckoned with. During her tenth grade year, she managed to buy a horse named Misty, which she stabled at our grandparents' place. Richard was visiting and we were out back with Misty when we got the idea of riding the mare to school and talking only "Indian."

We prepared for glorious battle with our straight-laced, humorless school principal, a mean and autocratic man. The showdown would be public. We would ride Misty to school, and reclaim it for the students.

After Richard's Bill Gurley election nearly three years earlier, and whatever else he had perpetrated—admittedly, it was a lot—Richard was one of the principal's least favorite students, though, in reality, neither Richard nor I were troublemakers; for the most part we followed the rules. (The ones we deemed "relevant," anyway.)

But there stood a formidable obstacle between us and our plan for student liberation: Susan.

She wouldn't let us ride Misty to school because she was afraid that we would hurt or lose her horse. She had gone to great lengths to get Misty, not to mention the natural emotional attachment she had for the animal. Susan's sole purpose in life seemed to revolve around working to make money to feed and care for Misty.

When Richard and I explained our idea to her, her answer was straightforward enough.

"Yeah, right!" She laughed. Not a promising start in negotiations.

I tried reasoning, *"C'mon Susan!* You know that Richard and I would never do anything rash." I was blowing the deal.

Richard quieted me before I could damage our cause fatally, and interjected, "Never mind that. But how can we lose an entire horse?"

She laughed a little, crossing her left arm over her middle, and covering her mouth with her right hand, but at least she was listening to Richard.

I stepped back in the dust to let Richard argue our case. He was an excellent chess player, and a persuasive speaker. Susan and Richard negotiated while Misty munched and crunched hay from my hand. I patted her neck and *shoooed* away some flies. Her tail flicked, her tongue licked, her teeth chomped, her hooves stomped, her skin reflexively quivered away the flies as she looked at me with those big horse eyes. Several times I started to talk, but Richard held up his hand; I kept quiet, lest I come out with some silly rhyme.

Richard had more say with my sister than I did. Susan *knew* that I was crazy, but there must have been some reasonable doubt about Richard. Luckily she didn't know him as I did, and that was our only hope, that she would see him as the grounded one, not as the lake bomber, or someone screaming louder than Tarzan and plunging through fire. That would have wrecked the deal, but somehow Richard convinced Susan that he, at least, was truly rational, and that Misty was in good hands.

We would wear rabbit skins. We prepared a "parchment" by cutting up a brown grocery bag and burning its edges. We folded and unfolded the declaration-to-be many times to make it look old and worn, then attached sticks and made it into a scroll. Our writing was all in pictures, like hieroglyphs, and we decided what to say. I would be the Indian Chief on the horse who didn't speak English, and Richard would "translate" from the ground.

We considered the consequences of our actions and figured that the worst that could happen was expulsion, but that seemed unlikely. After all, we were not fist fighting or bringing a gun to school, just making a little protest and having fun doing it. Moreover, we had never heard of a rule against riding a horse to school. Most likely we would only be punished with "the rod"—actually, the paddle—or, as they put it, "corrected by corporal punishment."

On the Monday morning that we were to go I felt sick, so I phoned Richard and announced that I wanted to cancel; it was a three-mile ride to school. Maybe my mind had made my body sick because I knew that this was a bad idea. It would be a shame to get expelled only months from graduation. Richard's reply: "It's *show* **time!**"

Show time. I remembered lots of other "show times." Dozens. What would happen today? Riding the horse to school could backfire in some way that we had not imagined. When it came time to actually *execute* a risky plan, like asking a girl for a date, it always looked different. The edges were sharper, the slopes more slippery and steeper, the fall was farther, the rocks at the bottom were more jagged and this was where we separate men from boys.

"I don't know, Richard," I said meekly.

"Okay, I understand," he replied over the phone. And I knew he did.

I walked back to bed, crawled under the clean sheets on the comfy mattress and commenced tossing and turning. We were separating men from boys, and I was in bed where it was safe.

But it's stupid to stick to a stupid plan. Why risk getting expelled so close to graduation?

One time, when Richard and I went to a movie, the show turned out to be as boring as watching docile milk cows eat grass, and we were wasting our time sitting there. Richard whispered over to me under the beam of the projector on the silver screen, "Do you like this?" he asked.

"No, it's lame."

"We've wasted our money; let's not waste our time," Richard said, and he stood up and walked out with me trailing behind.

Often, people will eat a bad meal at a restaurant just because they bought it, or sit through a boring movie just because they paid, or stick to a losing relationship because of the effort that they have already invested. The money or effort is already gone. Spent. Richard had grasped as a teenager what many middle-aged people are missing: *Future investment should be based on future results. Forget the past and what is already spent. It is irrelevant.* Cut your losses.

We had sewn together the rabbit skins, made a spear, gathered feathers, and acquired both the horse and a place to keep it near the school when we were done. Prep work had taken a week, but still, we shouldn't execute a silly plan no matter how much was invested.

But still . . . I wasn't *that* sick. I just didn't feel well enough for the confrontation that was bound to ensue, or for getting expelled and not graduating. I had joined the Army months earlier under the Delayed Entry Program, and if I didn't graduate, I couldn't go to Basic.

I lay in bed a few minutes more, staring at the ceiling, then tossing around, then staring at the ceiling again. It was still dark outside. This was a good plan. I knew it. Felt it. A little risky, but good.

Something inside would not let me sell out. My feet took me to the phone, my fingers dialed Richard, my mouth said, "The show must go on." Richard snickered over the line, "I wondered how long it would be before you called back. I've been getting ready."

I roused Susan from her bed in the next room. She wanted to saddle Misty herself. I donned my rabbit skins and war paint. Granddad had already gone to work. Granny was in her bedroom with the light on. I walked out the back door into the morning darkness and fog, crossed the yard through dew covered grass that wet my sneakers, passed the gate, and was at the stable.

In the darkness overhead, there beamed a giant cross that was attached to a 500-foot-tall radio antenna. At night when the cross was lighted, it could be seen (and still can be) in all directions for miles around. Sometimes when I gave school friends instructions on how to get to my house, I would say: *just go to the cross!* It became something of a joke, but the antenna was like a lightning magnet, and when it got struck, the house shook. During sunny days, the cross served as a perch for hawks who either had no interest in symbolism, or no sense of irony whatsoever.

Misty was saddled, the bit was in her mouth and her tongue flickered out against the shadows of the house lights. Susan adjusted the straps and said her good-byes to Misty as I hoisted myself into the saddle.

"Thanks Susan," I said, holding the reins.

"You're welcome," she answered apprehensively, "*Please* be careful with Misty."

"Don't worry, your horse is in good hands," I said looking down from Misty, "See you at school." I loosened the reins and the horse started walking. To battle.

The clock was ticking, the plan being executed. As the sun rose, people saw me in war paint and feathers riding Misty. Some of my friends passed in cars, blew their horns and waved. They knew something was up.

I was afraid the horn blowing or traffic might spook Misty, but we just trudged along. She was golden brown, and was working up a horse sweat, smelling good the way horses do, and I patted her neck. As Misty cut a swath through the still damp grass, dogs barked from fenced yards and from porches. Some were alarmed, some protective of their homes—still others seemed to want to join us.

People drove by in their horse-less carriages. Horns blew. Misty trudged. I kept my back straight and proud as befit an Indian chief and great warrior. We passed by a lake, the sun was rising, fish were breaking the glass of the water's surface; birds were on the move, and squirrels chased each other through the trees as the sun pushed higher. The symphony of life played on.

As we passed an orange tree, I picked a juicy orange and peeled it. Breakfast in the saddle. Winter Haven was a great place to grow up, and the area has one of the highest populations of bald eagles in the country. Though they were still rare, I was hoping to see one soaring overhead, watching me moving forward. It would have been an encouraging omen, but evidently the eagles had other obligations that morning.

A policeman passed in his cruiser. I waved and smiled as if this were all normal. He waved back and kept going. Misty's hooves *klopp klopped* across the streets, but mostly we stuck to back ways and grass wherever possible.

Yellow school buses rumbled by filled with younger kids, and they screamed and waved out the windows. After all, how often does one see a blonde-headed Indian warrior riding a horse downtown? Most days one sits obediently on the bus, in the stiff green seat, wondering how many marbles one might win or lose before the first bell rings, or whether that mean math teacher would snicker while springing another pop quiz.

Richard met me close to the school in his little black truck. We planned our arrival to coincide with the arrival of throngs of students gathering before the morning bell. Richard was on foot, bare-legged and bare-chested in his sneakers and rabbit skins. As he walked, I rode Misty, carrying an ornate spear that Richard had brought in his truck.

There must have been a hundred or more students watching our approach. They stopped their morning pre-class discussion by the gymnasium, and humming like a hive, turned to Richard, Misty and me.

Utter silence settled over the crowd.

I can only try to imagine what must have simultaneously gone through their minds: *What are those two lunatics doing this time?*

Silence.

We were almost surrounded by students in a U-shaped formation, and we walked into the U.

Still Silence . . .

Mouths agape . . .

We waited . . .

Finally, I pulled in a deep breath, and yelled something in "guttural-Indian," which was just sounds that I was making up, and Richard translated it into "broken English." He spoke with a faked, heavy accent and poor English grammar.

Richard began with authority: "Chief say his greeting and hope all is well with your tribe. Chief say he hope your spears find many deer and buffalo. Chief say you have many beautiful squaws worth **many** rabbit skins but first we talk of important matters."

I looked down at a girl who was smiling.

The crowd erupted in laughter.

We were just getting warmed up when the bell rang for class, but they stayed put, and the crowd quickly swelled.

I talked only Indian.

Richard translated like Tonto: "This land is **sacred** burial ground," he paused; "You must **tear** down school and **leave!**"

The crowd burst out in sudden and deafening laughter, and continued to grow.

The principal heard the commotion and charged onto the scene. With all the excitement and the students not going to class, he marched up to Richard, Misty and me, and yelled directly at me in a voice choked with anger, **"Get down off that horse!"**

He was already losing his cool before having taken in the situation. His mistake.

Richard had been in the arena before. He had nerves of steel and refused to flinch or show undue emotion before the angry principal. The fifteen-year-old man-child who engineered Bill Gurley's election was now eighteen, and not easily disturbed.

The sounds of many new students and teachers swelling the already sizable crowd were heard over the silence. Muffled voices asked, "What's going on?" but nobody could answer. People jostled for better positions to see and hear, and there was the collective excitement of the crowd. The herd. The *wonderful* momentum! They were behind us, and we were leading them to freedom.

The principal is not our God! See him standing before us! *Powerless!*

This is where the principal goes berserk.

He screamed, **"Get down off that horse!"** but I would not budge. He shouldn't give orders to a Great Indian Chief, a leader, a warrior, as if he were yelling at his dog to get down from the couch. I looked down at him with consummate dignity and flipped my hand.

"Shooo," the gesture spoke the words.

The students' response was deafening laughter, as though the home team had scored a touchdown in the final moments of the Homecoming game. Only, instead of cheering, they were laughing. The principal knew that he was being mocked. He was completely red-faced and visibly experiencing the elevated blood pressure of someone straining to lift a weight too heavy for him.

It was going much better than we had hoped, but we were having an unexpected problem as Misty began chomping some flowers. I was trying to stop her without spoiling the moment.

I looked down and spoke to the principal, one Chief to another, loudly for all to hear, gesturing dramatically with my left hand. *"Landnom!"* I paused. *"Jestem pravda lono-maka-ihe."*

"Don't talk like that!" screamed the principal.

Richard translated, "Chief say no need for anger. Need only move school. Okay to talk about squaws later."

"Richard White!" The principal screamed, **"You have finally pushed me too far! Get to my office!"** Then he looked up at me, **"And I will not say again to get down off that horse!"**

Richard merely straightened his back and stood silently, the crowd again erupted in laughter.

I looked down at the principal and patted Misty's neck, *"Semiz kalunus-lunos baboy kopek!"*

Richard translated my words: "Chief say, horse not like when man scream in ear."

The crowd was going crazy!

The principal just stood there. Straight as a Georgia pine. Shocked that we were ignoring him.

I sat up straight and proud in the saddle, and pointed to the scroll that Richard held. *"Spottdrossellied es iyi huylu. Meg sem tudott mukkanni."*

The principal seemed ready to banish us to Iceland, or Greenland, or wherever that place is with all the ice. Richard translated and explained about the sacred land, unfurled the scroll, and pointed to the pictures. For an instant, as if unconsciously, the principal actually stepped forward and started to examine the scroll until he realized what he had done.

Deafening laughter.

The pretty girl was still there, laughing, and she smiled at me.

Richard held up his hand to quiet the crowd, waited for silence, then attacked. He told the principal: "You are Great Chief. You must remove this school from sacred burial ground or we return with many warriors. There will be great battle. Many will die."

As we completed each utterance, the students' reaction was so sudden and loud that I was afraid Misty would spook. Richard looked up and I saw that he was thinking the same thing.

But we would not go out with a whimper. We kept our dignity as liberators of the oppressed student body. Richard nodded to me. I nodded back, and accidentally glanced at the girl for about five seconds.

Richard began walking to the principal's office, who screamed up at me one last time **"Get down off that horse! Get rid of it!"** and **"Get to my office!"**

I stayed anchored in the saddle and uttered one last unholy goulash of sounds: *"Sat chit ananda!"* as he stomped away.

We had stowed some clothes in our lockers so that we could go to class, gambling that we would not be expelled or suspended. The plan was to leave Misty at a friend's place on a nearby lake so she would have water, so I set off on my short journey.

The pretty girl dashed from the crowd and asked if she could ride with me. *Hot diggitty dog!* I reached down my arm and pulled her up behind me. We rode to the lake. This wasn't such a bad idea, after all!

I took my time getting back. Meanwhile, the principal was calling

Richard's dad, a well-known local orthodontist, and pillar-of-the-community type. But Dr. White was really cool and he knew how to raise kids.

When I talked with Dr. White while writing this book, he said that he had laughed when the fuming principal called him. We weren't out robbing houses or mugging people or selling drugs, but we were not lemmings, either.

The principal told Dr. White that he thought we were on drugs, and were undermining his authority over the student body.

When I walked into the office, he screamed **"Sit Down!"** at me, and proceeded to call my grandmother. He promptly offended her by insisting she come down to get the horse. At least he didn't tell Granny his theory that we were strung out on dope. Granny was a little upset about the horse part, but she knew Richard, and after the principal had been so rude to her—and after accusing us of everything but high treason and improper lane changing—she took our side!

"Why, goodness," she said to me with a little smile, "he *was* a mean man" and she chuckled as I asked her to remember how she saw it that day.

We didn't bother to defend ourselves against the accusation of being high on drugs; Dr. White knew better and got a good laugh from the charge, especially when we explained the details. He would later say, "Boy, I wish I could have seen that." Too bad there were no pictures.

I guess there was no law against riding a horse to school. Not much happened; we were not suspended, expelled, or executed, but got a few licks with the big, wooden paddle. I think it had a skull and crossbones on it, but that's probably just my imagination.

When it came around to our high school graduation ceremonies, the principal called us in his office and announced that we would not graduate if we caused any disturbance. Richard was called in frequently, whereas I was deemed more of a "happened to be there" kind of person. The man was clueless.

We hadn't actually planned to do anything to disrupt the ceremony, but the principal's threats nearly inspired us to show him who was boss. We already knew that we were in charge of ourselves, if not the school. And if we wanted to do something, the principal would have an extremely hard time stopping us. Free will is a wonderful, mystical thing to have.

During our final weeks at high school, Richard and I had not signed each other's yearbooks. After all of our adventures, we simply could not think of anything appropriate to say.

We thought about it for a month or so, and our deadline for the yearbook entries was graduation day.

During the waning days at Winter Haven High School, we often talked about what adventures lay before us. Would one of us become president? Start a war? *Stop* a war?

Whatever the case, we decided that if life is nothing more than a long running drama, we would play our parts so that, when we reached the final curtain, we would never look back and say, "I *should* have. . . ."

And on graduation day, he wrote only a few words:

> Mike,
> You are the craziest person I know. Please don't blow me up. Ha ha. Good luck. Keep in touch.
> Richard

We shook hands, and went our separate ways. Doubtless we both were wondering if we would keep in touch.

EPILOGUE

I AM SITTING in the Cataloochee Valley deep in the North Carolina mountains at a special place, a place where I had so much happiness as a young child. I am alone, wearing an old pair of blue jeans, no shirt or shoes, and I feel the rough bark of a tree pressing into my back. I am sitting on a cold rock and there is the smell of rain while my feet dangle in the soothing mountain water. I could have used this water on that desert mountain in Nevada where we began this journey with talk of casinos, luck, and other such matters.

Now I hear the clear mountain creek, rushing water over smoothed stones, as the wind pushes gently through the trees. A squirrel is watching me nearby—none of the squirrels up here answer to the name Chipper, but they sure act like Chipper, that little squirrel we brought home after it had fallen from a tree. *Rescuers!* A hornet has been buzzing by my head and is back again. This place is hornet-central. Now the yellow and black bug is sitting next to me eating a little piece of meat that fell from my sandwich.

One day I will write a letter to my children, just in case I die while they are still young. In that letter I will explain many things to them individually, and I will tell them how much I love them. If I had a letter like that from my mother it would be my second-most prized possession. I do have my memories and pictures of us together, which are my most precious blessings. The many great memories she left with me, what she taught me, and the love that we shared during those seven brief years.

My grandparents came here every year for more than fifty years. When my mother was born she came here every year for twenty-eight, and now, I come too.

Today, I live close enough to venture here each weekend, but I don't. The ground is sacred to me, so I only journey here when I feel its pull. I dream that my own children will splash in this water.

The weathered tree behind me feels reassuring against the skin of my back, and my feet have settled against a stone under the cold water. This is the spot. In my mind's eye, I see a skinny, white-headed little five-year-old boy splashing around in the water with his mother only slightly more than arm's reach from where I sit. It is a joyful time and they are having a pretty serious water fight.

She is crouched in the stream at his level so that it will be fair. His mother says, *"Hey, let's see who can hold their breath the longest!"* The boy lights up, eyes wide-open, big smiles as they each dip their heads below the water. She is holding her boy's hand so she can feel his grip tighten. She knows that when his limit is reached, her boy will unconsciously tighten his grip on her fingers.

She feels his hand grip harder. She holds out another few moments and—just before he pops up, having reached his limit—she pops up. When his face leaves the water his mother is already there, gasping for breath—he gets a big kiss. It was worth it! Her little white-haired boy thinks he pushed himself to his limit and he won, or at least he thinks he won—and in reality he did.

The boy feels sure of himself and wants another kiss from his mother so he says, *"C'mon Mommy let's do it again."* Big smiles, their hands meet underwater; they each take big breaths. But this time they only put their mouths and noses under. Their eyes are still above the rippling surface, locked in excitement. She feels his grip tighten; she puts a pained look on her face, her eyes squinting, but she holds out. She sees that her boy is fighting; she sees the pain sweep across his face. He pops up and blows the air from his little chest and sucks in a mouthful of mountain air. She pops up and does the same. She says, *"You almost had me! One more second and you would have won."* Big smiles. She says excitedly, *"Time for the tie-breaker."*

Big smiles. Deep breaths, their hands meet underwater. . . .

Mothers are the greatest teachers. Irreplaceable.

Again in my mind's eye I can see the same boy a little older, sitting where I am now sitting, a few feet from where he splashed with his mother. He is thinking. His grandfather scrambles down the steep bank using a branch to lower himself and says, *"Let's catch some crawdads."* He teaches the boy how to catch crawdads using his toes for bait. At this moment I see my feet under the water at the same spot, luring a new generation of crawdads. Grandparents are irreplaceable.

I feel the forest wrapped around me like a warm blanket. I am a part of this place and it is part of me. We are one. My grandfather was right: *God made the world for me and me for the world.* I hope that he doesn't expect me to go to a wooden church—I'm here. The squirrel is gone and the hornet has flown away.

Yes, if I could speak to my mother for just one minute I would tell her a lifetime. First I would apologize for that day she drove away when I was angry with the bullies. That final kiss and hug that I refused haunted me through the years.

Maybe I was born to tell her story, the story of all great mothers, and to say this: *The most important people on Earth are not soldiers, scientists, or lawyers. They are our mothers who whisper their sweet breath in our faces when we are small, and our fathers who protect us and our mothers.*

If my mother could hear my words, I would tell her that I miss her. I would hold her and tell her that everything turned out fine, and that if I could tell her the whole story, she would be proud of me. I know that she would be proud of me. I would say how hard I tried. How I kept the faith. If I could tell her only one thing, I would thank her for the life that she gave me, and tell her that our seven years were the most important, and the best of my life. I would tell her that she was a great mother.

She never really died. A mother lives on in her children. She is the angel who has been watching over me. I am sitting here among the old trees by this clear mountain stream and it smells like eternity.